talking adolescence

D1611831

Howard Giles
General Editor

Vol. 3

PETER LANG
New York • Washington, D.C./Baltimore • Bern
Frankfurt am Main • Berlin • Brussels • Vienna • Oxford

talking adolescence

perspectives on communication in the teenage years

EDITED BY

Angie Williams &
Crispin Thurlow

PETER LANG
New York • Washington, D.C./Baltimore • Bern
Frankfurt am Main • Berlin • Brussels • Vienna • Oxford

Library of Congress Cataloging-in-Publication Data

Talking adolescence: perspectives on communication in the teenage years /
edited by Angie Williams and Crispin Thurlow.
p. cm. — (Language as social action; v. 3)
Includes bibliographical references and index.
1. Adolescence. 2. Interpersonal communication in adolescence.
3. Teenagers and adults. I. Williams, Angie.
II. Thurlow, Crispin. III. Series.
HQ796.T345 305.235—dc22 2005015695
ISBN 978-0-8204-7097-9
ISSN 1529-2436

Bibliographic information published by **Die Deutsche Bibliothek**.
Die Deutsche Bibliothek lists this publication in the "Deutsche
Nationalbibliografie"; detailed bibliographic data are available
on the Internet at http://dnb.ddb.de/.

Cover design by Lisa Barfield

The paper in this book meets the guidelines for permanence and durability
of the Committee on Production Guidelines for Book Longevity
of the Council of Library Resources.

Contents

Preface   vii

1   Deconstructing adolescent communication   1
CRISPIN THURLOW

Part I Adult constructions of young people's communication

2   Youth in the media: Adult stereotypes of young people   23
JOHANNA WYN

3   Adults' perceptions of communication with young people   35
PETER GARRETT AND ANGIE WILLIAMS

4   From apprehension to awareness: Toward more critical understandings of young people's communication experiences   53
CRISPIN THURLOW AND ALICE MARWICK

5   Hearing their voices: Young people, citizenship and online news   73
CYNTHIA CARTER AND STUART ALLAN

Part II Young people's communication in peer contexts

6   Stylistic practice and the adolescent social order   93
PENELOPE ECKERT

7   Slang and swearing as markers of   111
    inclusion and exclusion in adolescence
    VIVIAN DE KLERK

8   The language of love: Romantic   129
    relationships in adolescence
    LAUREN BERGER, DANA MCMAKIN AND WYNDOL FURMAN

9   Ticket to a Queer planet? Communication   147
    issues affecting young lesbian and gay people
    SARAH O'FLYNN

10 'Talkin', doin' and bein' with friends': Leisure   163
    and communication in adolescence
    LEO HENDRY AND MARION KLOEP

11 Wired whizzes or techno-slaves? Young people   185
    and their emergent communication technologies
    SUSAN MCKAY, CRISPIN THURLOW
    AND HEATHER TOOMEY ZIMMERMAN

Part III Young people in communication with adults

12 Communication with parents and other family   207
    members: The implications of family process
    for young people's well-being
    PATRICIA NOLLER

13 Young people's communication with   229
    adults in the institutional order
    JOHN DRURY

14 In the classroom: Instructional communication   245
    with young people
    JOSEPH CHESEBRO

15 Communication and 'risky' behavior in   265
    adolescence
    SUSAN MCKAY

    List of contributors   283
    Index   289

Preface

The initial inspiration for this book was Angie's appointment in 2001 by the executive committee of the International Association of Language and Social Psychology (IALSP) to head a task force into social psychological aspects of language and communication in adolescence. Having recently joined the faculty at Cardiff University, Crispin not only became a contributing member of the task force but also supported Angie in bringing the work of the task force to completion. The remit of this task force was fourfold: to prepare a selective review of the literatures on adolescence, with particular attention to language and communication; to identify relevant questions with respect to social psychology; to present a critical evaluation of current knowledge; and, finally, to offer recommendations for future research. By July 2002, the task force's findings were ready for presentation, first by Angie during a symposium on adolescence at the 8th International Conference for Language and Social Psychology in Hong Kong, and then by Crispin in a special session of the 52nd annual convention of the International Communication Association in Seoul. Following open discussion at both of these conferences, a revised overview of the final report was published in 2003 as a colloquy in the *Journal of Language and Social Psychology* (Volume 22: Issue 1).

Once the the work of the task force had been completed, we immediately started thinking about working towards a more substantial account of communication in adolescence. As original members of the task force, John Drury, Susan McKay, Penelope Eckert and Patricia Noller agreed to rework their reports into chapters. With this excellent start, we then turned our attention to identifying experts in the field who would complement the work already done by opening up the disciplinary focus of the original task force, extending its international scope, and including a range of new contexts and issues. To this end, we were delighted eventually to find ourselves working with such an outstanding group of well-known researchers on adolescence, but also having the opportunity to work collaboratively with newer scholars. We are immensely grateful to all the contributors for agreeing to work with us on this project and for bearing with us during 2004, which unexpectedly turned out to be an especially challenging year for both of us.

We would then like to start by thanking Howard Giles, series editor, for initially encouraging us to put this volume together; as president of IALSP (2000–2002), it was also his initial vision which helped make the original task force a reality. We are also extremely grateful to Damon Zucca, our editor at Peter Lang, for his patient support. We are grateful too for the work of Bernadette Shade and our unknown Peter Lang proof-reader. For helping to prepare the final manuscript we thank Nancy Van Leuven and especially Hazel Lin, Crispin's graduate research assistants at the University of Washington. Thank you also to Crispin's colleague, Kristi De Vadder, for her last-minute, creative input on the cover design. Crispin would also like to acknowledge the College of Arts and Sciences at the University of Washington for a Junior Faculty Development Award (Autumn 2004), which helped to create some of the time he needed for writing and editing.

AW and CT
June 2005

1

Deconstructing adolescent communication

Crispin Thurlow

You're an adult when they want you to be, you're a child when they want you to be.[1]

Adolescence is first and foremost an economic and institutional construction, invariably marked less by chronological age and biological stage as it is by the conditions and realities established by formal education, the law and employment in the marketplace. Beyond that, adolescence is pretty much whatever adults say it is! In fact, it seems that young people are often the last people to conceive of themselves as adolescents. Caught impossibly between adult mythologies of 'childhood innocence' and 'adult sophistication,' young people's innocence is typically dismissed as naïveté and their sophistication construed as cunning. Not surprisingly, most young people (like the one in the quote above) are seldom able to get it right—which is to say, they find themselves in a double bind of being always too young and too old. And this is a uniquely uncomfortable dilemma which is merely exacerbated by the relentless demands of the post-industrial marketplace. In his searing critique of the corporatization and exploitation of young people, Henry Giroux (2000:4) concludes that there is therefore only one appropriate way to approach the study of adolescence: confronting what he calls the 'politics of culture.'

The politics of culture provide the conceptual space in which [youth] is constructed, experienced, and struggled over. Culture is the primary terrain in which adults exercise power over [young people] both ideologically and institutionally. Only by questioning specific cultural formations and contexts in which youth is organized, learned and lived can educators [and scholars] understand and challenge the ways in which cultural practices establish power relations that shape [young people's] experiences.

Although it is still very common to hear reference to phrases like youth culture, many contemporary scholars like Giroux (see others below) now reject the tendency to present young people as uniformly oppositional and monolithic in terms of their social norms and cultural values. From this more critical perspective, it is acknowledged that adolescent 'development' and 'trajectories' can only ever be described as patterned generalizations; that for every young person whose life is marked by the proverbial sex, drugs and rock and roll, there are countless others whose lives do not feature unwanted pregnancies, substance misuses and criminal activities. Of course, this is not to say that lay discourse or all academic discourse necessarily follow suit. The persistence of the 'storm and stress' stereotype of the teenage years is still a very powerful regime of truth (*cf* Foucault, 1980) in depicting and accounting for adolescence—as Angie Williams and her colleague have found in their research (see Williams & Garrett, 2002). A striking example of the dominance of this mythology and the complicity of science is found in a brochure titled *Surviving Adolescence*, produced and widely distributed by the Royal College of Psychiatrists in Britain; the opening paragraph of the brochure confidently asserts that

> the teenage years can be an emotional assault course for all concerned. Parents and their teenage children can seem always to be at each other's throats. We call this stormy time adolescence.[2]

One important part of the process of reconceptualizing adolescence has been a concern to describe and understand something of the multidimensional nature and lived experience of adolescent social interaction and peer relations, what Ball (1981:118) refers to as their 'systems of relevance.' Within developmental psychology, for example, there has always been a fairly consistent preoccupation among researchers to align the study of adolescence with the traditional landmarks of biological and cognitive development, and, especially, so-called 'identity formation.' However, as research continues to find even these markers of adolescence to be contextually relative and variable (Adams *et al.*, 1996; Goosens & Phinney, 1996), the relation has, in effect, been reversed so that more social and cultural approaches to adolescence are increasingly becoming the norm (e.g., Ball, 1981; Eckert, 1989; Eder, 1998; Miles, 2000; Wyn & White, 1997). Together with a move away from an undue focus on deviance and pathology, the value of researching young people's 'normal' social orientations and everyday interactions is also seen as more and more worthy of discussion.

On this basis, young people's social interaction and peer relations are not surprisingly one of the key areas of interest in the study of adolescence. Arguably, this is nowadays more important than ever given what Roy Baumeister and Mark Muraven (1996:407) see as the 'newly difficult nature of adolescence.' Lynne Chisholm and Klaus Hurrelmann (1995:130) too suggest that, as a hallmark of late-twentieth century adolescence, 'socialization contexts have become more differentiated and, in the process, peer group relations have accreted [yet] more significance.' It is commonly acknowledged by scholars that young people today face a number of major macrostructural changes which are reshaping their lives in terms of rapid social, occupational and social change (Mortimer & Larson, 2002). It is also obvious that their peer orientations and the organization of sociality will continue to be central to the ways young people manage and make sense of these changes. Young people certainly value their peer relations highly (Youniss & Smollar, 1985) and social relationships are a crucial factor in their well-being (see, for example, Hendry & Reid, 2000). What is of particular relevance to the current volume is that all of these interpersonal needs are necessarily achieved in communication—whether as a channel or a context for social interaction (*cf* Brown *et al.*, 1994; Thurlow, 2001a). Communication is also one of the key resources by which young people may also be better able to shape and, to some extent, control their position in the face of societal change (Youniss & Ruth, 2002). We return to this point in a moment.

A word about *adolescence*

Before we move on, it would be remiss of us not to at least acknowledge the politics of labeling by saying something about the problematic inherent in the very term 'adolescence.' We have, like John Coleman (1974) long before us, decided to make no substantial attempt in this volume to define adolescence or to justify its existence. As Coleman says, adolescence 'can be defined in various ways depending on one's perspective, and social, economic or political notions do not always accord with a psychological viewpoint' (p. ix). In some respects, the term 'teenager' often proves to be a more useful label simply because it is a less ambiguous, age-based description (i.e., thir*teen* to nine*teen*). By contrast, 'adolescent' opens up the whole debate about when this still culturally determined period begins and ends. Certainly, the two most common boundary markers of adolescence are themselves of little real use. First, because the onset of puberty (typically indicated by menarche and spermarche) is understood to be substantially earlier than it was some 100 years ago (Wyn & White, 1997), even so-called biological hard-wiring is unable to offer an absolute starting/cut-off point. Second, as Chisholm and Hurrelmann (1995) and other writers have shown, socioeconomic indicators such as the termination of education and the start of employment also no longer guarantee the same clarity they once did, with young people increasingly delaying both either by force or by choice. In fact, it is partly for this very reason that Jeffrey Arnett (2000) proposes the conceptual and sociological merits of what he describes as 'emerging adulthood' (between 18 and 25). By the same token, underpinning Johanna Wyn and Rob White's (1997) well-known book *Rethinking Youth* is a concern to rethink both the labels and the period of the lifespan they describe.[3]

We have already noted above the extent to which adolescence is constructed and mythologized, and, as scholars of language and communication, we are ourselves very conscious of the potential for distinctive but vague labels like 'adolescent' or 'adolescence' to overcategorize people and, in this case, to exaggerate social distances between young people and other people. In terms of social identity theory, we know that this is often all that is needed for adults to construe and experience their communication with young people as a form of intergroup or even intercultural communication [see Garrett & Williams—chapter 3—for more on this point]. Although it is by no means a perfect solution, we ourselves tend, for the most part, to use the term 'young people' in order to eschew chronological specificity and cultural connotations of 'adolescent' as something inferior or undesirable (see below); we also value the lifespan perspective inherent in their still being regarded as people, however young.

Notwithstanding this, and following the lead of so much research on this period of the lifespan, we take 'adolescence' to index an experientially and discursively recognized period of the lifespan which stretches anywhere from the age of eleven to twenty-one or twenty-two. However, like Burman (1994), we are also concerned not to assume, or to depend too heavily on, the naturalized, prescribed compartmentalization of the lifespan—so long the hallmark of mainstream developmental psychology. As we understand it, development is a lifespan affair, and many of the concerns and issues discussed in the chapters that follow are, neither quantitatively nor qualitatively speaking, necessarily any less germane to adult life.

This perspective has important implications for many of the topics dear to the hearts of conventional adolescent researchers—most notably, identity. For most social theorists and critical scholars, it is now received wisdom that identity (cultural, social or otherwise) is an intensely dynamic, *lifelong* project (*cf* Giddens, 1991; Hall, 1996). In spite of the volley of postmodernist (i.e., feminist, postcolonial, Queer) critiques, however, this is an idea to which developmental psychology appears exceptionally resistant in its fixation with normative trajectories and stages (Côté, 1996).[4] Developmental psychologists and other practitioners (see Royal College of Psychiatrists, p.2 above) often seem very reluctant to discuss identity as a dynamic process, that we all work with multiple identit*ies*, that the cultural-structural landscape itself is simply changing, that context plays a role in all domains of adolescent experience, and, finally, that identity is not the particular 'task' of adolescence.[5] Nevertheless, it also true to say that traditional models of adolescent identity resting on notions of crisis and developmental stages (e.g., those of Erik Erikson or James Marcia) are coming under critique; the linearity and unitariness of their conceptualizations of identity can no longer account for the variability, multifariousness and fluidity that identification entails.

In these terms, the dominant paradigm of adolescent identity formation is clearly problematic on at least two fronts: its apparent essentialism on the one hand, and its undue ascription to adolescence. What, one might wonder, of the enormous identity challenges inherent in the complexity of long-term relationships; the responsibility and revelations of parenthood; the chronic servitude of work; the unexpected ravages of serious illness; and the challenges and discoveries of old age? All these lifespan factors unpredictably and variously release a barrage of demands on one's self-esteem and sense of self. The storms and stresses continue unabated! To suggest otherwise is not only to reject the critiques of contemporary writing, but to deny the full experience of life. That we, as adults, learn to feel it in silence—or rather to feel it silenced—is another matter. We simply learn to be 'grown up' about our uncertainty and confusion in the struggle to tell a meaningful, coherent story about ourselves. It is for this very reason that, in debunking the notion of an exclusively adolescent 'identity crisis,' James Côté (1996:167) argues that, far from being a matter of 'formation' or 'achievement,' identity entails diffusion and dissipation. As such, the communicative process of identification never ceases; it is certainly not unique to young people, nor is it their sole preoccupation.

Communication in adolescence

This book most obviously concerns itself with the role of communication in structuring and facilitating the lives of young people. In his presidential speech at the International Communication Association's annual conference in 1999, Howard Giles spoke of an inherent ageism in communication research and, among other things, exhorted communication scholars to 'work toward understanding the injustices allied to all phases of the life span [and] to rebel against these' (Giles, 1999:170). Although speaking of the other end of the lifespan, Giles' comments might just as easily refer to the relative neglect of communication issues in adolescence and childhood. Too often, it seems, there are important perspectives not attended to outside of mainstream adult communication—which is to say between age eighteen and retirement! What is more, this academic silence or hiatus to which Giles refers merely exacerbates the communicative disenfranchisement of adolescents. On this basis, there are at least three important ways in which academic research and writing concerning communication in adolescence might promote itself. Given what we just said, perhaps the most obvious of these is the understandable impulse to want to redress an existing gap in the literature on lifespan communication and ('developmental') social psychology. To our mind this is a legitimate goal in and of itself.

A second, perhaps more substantial, reason for looking at adolescent communication, however, lies in the more transactional or instrumental value of communication as an obvious identificational and relational resource. In the process of exploring and sustaining their relationships with parents, siblings, peers, and so on, young people must necessarily learn to understand others' feelings, others' goals, social rules, and others' minds (Dunn, 1988). They must also learn to understand and judge the complex role of power in everyday communication (*cf* Ng & Bradac, 1993). Arguably, much of this learning relies on their being adept and self-aware communicators. As we suggested above, there is nowadays also increasing importance attached to finding more effective ways of empowering young people with the communication capital *and* the critical understanding they need to face even more complex social challenges and to access diminishing economic resources (Thurlow, 2003). Now more than ever before, young people must also negotiate and make sense of an intensely semioticized world as post-industrial economies are premised increasingly on symbolism, imagery and 'design-intensity' (Lash & Urry, 1994: 193). As John Gumperz and Jenny Cook-Gumperz (1982:4) note, for quite some time this has also been a world of immense cultural diversity and rapid change:

> The role of [communication] has...been radically altered in our society. The ability to manage or adapt to diverse communicative situations has become essential and the ability to interact with people with whom one has no personal acquaintance is crucial to acquiring even a small measure of personal and social control. We have to talk in order to establish our rights and entitlements.

For all these reasons, Norman Fairclough (e.g., 1999) and others stress the importance of critical, needs-based approaches in enabling people to respond to the heightened communication demands of late modernity. Certainly, however well-meaning, cookbook approaches to teaching adults and young people about communication (e.g., the PBS *Frontline* program, next paragraph) and the current preoccupation in education policy for communication as a 'key skill' (Cameron, 2000) not only are theoretically and politically reactionary, but may be simply inadequate to the expressed needs of young people [see Thurlow & Marwick—chapter 4, this volume—for more on this point]. Arguably, for many young people, an important aspect of the diversity of communicative situations to which Gumperz and Cook-Gumperz refer lies in the experience of living in an increasingly globalized, interconnected world (*cf* Pennycook, 2003). The importance of communication to young people as a more operational resource is perhaps even greater also for those young people living in larger and more economically deprived (urban) environments.

A third reason for research in this area goes beyond technical empowerment and toward a sense of advocacy—specifically, the more politicized desire to challenge some of the received stereotypes of young people and their communication practices. Described by Mike Males (1996) as the 'scapegoat generation,' young people (and especially young men and boys) are too often defined as inadequate communicators or language users and it is not infrequently that one hears the exaggerated folk-linguistic complaint, 'I just can't understand what teenagers are saying these days—it's like a different language!' As suggested above, communication between young people and adults is thus all too frequently construed in both public and academic discourse as *intergroup* communication. Research merely confirms this common tendency of adults to problematize adolescent communication (Drury & Dennison, 1999; Williams & Garrett, 2002). Again, we find dramatic examples of this at every turn. In 2002, for example, a US Public Broadcast Service *Frontline* documentary called *Inside the Teenage Brain* had as one of its central topics the problem (sic) of 'teen-adult' communication, and, among other things, scientific research was cited to explain communication breakdowns as a function of neurological differences.[6] It seems hard to imagine that for any other major social group defined, say, by race, age or sex, would it nowadays be acceptable to seek explanations for interpersonal and interactional differences on the basis of biology or anatomy. In many ways, therefore, young people may be rightly viewed as a social group routinely misunderstood and even mistreated by adults. Just as Deborah Cameron (1998) describes the experience of women, young people are a group whose communication capital (Thurlow, 2001b after Bourdieu, 1991) is always greatly devalued or denied. Indeed, media representations like the *Frontline* program are one good example of just how prevalent this attitude is.

'Teen talk': Getting a bad press

> The excesses of the young provide a little of the excitement otherwise lacking. The outcome is a growing shallowness. ... An adolescent culture is one that

lives on the surface, unencumbered by memory, light on knowledge and devoid of wisdom. (Jacques, *Guardian Newspaper*, 2004)

At one point in their extensive overview of the literature on adolescence, Coleman and Hendry (1999:80) note that, in the face of evidence to the contrary,
there continues to be little explanation for the persistence in public discourse of
the idea of a generation gap. One possible explanation, they propose, is the constant stereotyping of teenagers in the media. Certainly, few people in Britain can
have missed the cinema debut of *Kevin*, the parodic embodiment of popular beliefs about adolescence by the television comic Harry Enfield.[7] Meanwhile, in
his allegorical critique of contemporary British society and what he calls the
'Western condition,' journalist Martin Jacques (quote above) epitomizes the
more negative way in which youth is commonly portrayed in the mainstream
media. In fact, this common representation of adolescence as an attack on
adulthood is something which Johanna Wyn [see chapter 2, this volume] discusses in more detail; suffice it to say, however, that this discourse runs completely contrary to Giroux's (ibid.) assessment of the contemporary 'assault on
youth,' prompting someone like Males (1999) to declare the last decade of the
twentieth century as the 'most anti-youth period in American history.' It is the
same old 'storm and stress' image of adolescence which feeds this characterization and the representation of young people more widely in the media (Porteous
& Colston, 1980). And central to this mythology of adolescence is the noncommunicative or communicatively inept young person.

There are several academic literatures that point to the prejudicial impact of
cultural constructions of adolescence. As already suggested, writers in the fields
of critical linguistics and feminist sociolinguistics have demonstrated clearly how
the way in which members of political minorities are spoken about can be instrumental in their prejudicial and unequal treatment (e.g., Cameron, 1998; van
Dijk, 1992). Elsewhere, and with specific attention to adolescence, an increasing
number of writers in sociology, psychology and cultural studies have addressed
the extent to which adolescence is widely portrayed in unrealistically uniform,
largely negative, and ultimately unidimensional ways. As Christine Griffin
(1993:25) describes it, '"youth" is/are continually being represented as different,
Other, strange, exotic and transitory—by and for adults.'[8] Indeed, the academic
treatment (in all senses of the word) of young people has also been very influential in further feeding the media with its own already robust images of adolescence. And so it is that a sharp contrast is drawn between the 'somewhat mun-
dane lives and attitudes of the majority of contemporary young people in actual-
ity and the range of considerably heightened images of youth that is to be found
in much of the popular and professional social theorizing of recent years'
(Davis, 1990: 2). It is for this very reason that John Davis goes on to propose
that it is the gap between image and reality itself which is ultimately in need of

explanation and remedy. If so, this again demands the attention of communication scholars who are ideally placed to investigate the role of language, visual semiosis and mediatized representation in constituting social realities.

In much the same way that cultural critics have sought to do with other minoritized social groups, the intention must be to show that the ways young people are treated in cultural representation is part and parcel of how, in the words of Richard Dyer (1993:1), 'they are treated in life, that poverty, harassment, self-hate and discrimination...are shored up and instituted by representation.' Although lay discourse is often slow to change, and even though adults can remain very resistant to scholarly evidence which explicitly contradicts popular framings of young people (see Gilliam & Bales, 2001), these are surely important steps within academia.

Deconstructing adolescent communication

Given this bad press, and to reiterate our point from above, there is, we think, certainly a sense in which one might reasonably approach the study of communication in adolescence with the same kind of ideological sensibility and political advocacy as those writers in sociolinguistics who have been concerned with the communicative disenfranchisement and alienation of their own target groups. In some respects at least, young people too are a political minority (*cf* van Heeswyk, 1997) and an important part of the 'myth of adolescence' (Hockey & James, 1993) is their apparent ignorance (i.e., lack of skill and/or awareness) of ('good') communication.

And so, in putting this book together, we cannot help but be provoked by the deconstructive agenda set out by Erica Burman (1994), herself inspired by the critical stance of Gayatri Spivak (1990: 103), who writes:

> In one way or another academics are in the business of ideological production [and] our institutional responsibility is of course to offer a responsible critique of the structure of production of the knowledge...

In this regard, those of us contributing to this volume are concerned in different ways to speak on behalf of a group whose voice is often silenced or at least consistently devalued. Having said this, we cannot help but recognize the imperfection of our attempt to take on the role of advocate. As Deborah Cameron and her colleagues (1992) note, advocacy—speaking as experts *for* others—as a scholarly goal is fraught with problems; ideally, they argue, scholars should look instead to *empower* people by doing research *with* them and arising from their own agendas and needs. Of course, for practical economic and institutional reasons this is often not possible when it comes to young people. As editors, Angie and I also openly acknowledge, for example, that our collection here is largely Anglophone in its demographic coverage even though we have papers from Britain, Australia, South Africa and the United States of America. (One exception is Kloep & Hendry in chapter 10 of this volume, who cite their research with young Swedish people.) We cannot—nor do we claim to—therefore speak of all young people; others are able to do this with much greater authority (e.g., Brown *et al.*, 2002).

Notwithstanding these constraints and limitations, what we as editors hope to achieve in our own research and by putting together a volume such as this is to critique (or deconstruct) both the pervasive stereotype of the communicatively ignorant or incompetent teenager, and, thereby, the overly homogenizing and pathologizing notions of adolescence *per se*. We do not presume to *know* what it means to be a young person growing up nowadays and no young people have actually asked us to speak on their behalf; however, we do know that many young people do not recognize themselves in the way adults so often characterize them (Falchikov, 1986; 1989) and that they are often frustrated by these tired misrepresentations (Home Office, 2000). Instead of dismissing the stereotypical 'teenage' complaint 'you just don't understand' as mere folly and fodder for adult othering, perhaps it is time that adult researchers at least start paying more attention to the ways in which communication is organized and experienced during the teenage years. As Giroux (2000) recommends, criticizing misrepresentations of young people in adult discourse and adult-controlled institutions is an end in itself; in doing so, we go some way at least toward combating the on-going 'attack on youth' which continues to gate-keep and structure their lives in very material, disadvantageous ways.

The structure and content of this volume

In putting this book together, we start from the understanding that all communication is about social relationships and, therefore, a matter of identification. Regardless of where one is in the lifespan, human interactions are necessarily mediated by our concerns for identity and relationship. By the same token, people's identities and relationships are constituted primarily through communication, which is to say linguistic, nonverbal, visual or other meaning-making practices. It is for this reason that we have deliberately avoided trying to divide up our volume into some of the usual categories or tropes of adolescent research. For example, to present young people's identity processes as being somehow separate from other aspects of their lives seems to us theoretically and phenomenologically nonsensical. Therefore there is no section here on 'identity in adolescence.' Instead, we have chosen to group chapters into three broadly de-fined parts: (1) adult constructions of young people's communication; (2) young people's communication in peer contexts; and (3) young people in communica-tion with adults.

Part I: Adult constructions of young people's communication

In the first part, we start with four chapters whose authors are in different ways concerned to challenge the framing of young people's communication by adults. As we suggested above, young people are in many ways a communicatively dis-enfranchised political minority—partly because their ways of speaking are often regarded as having low cultural capital or prestige, and partly because they themselves seldom have control over the very mechanisms of representation which perpetuate dominant stereotypes about adolescence—most obviously in the media, which is precisely where we start.

In chapter 2, Johanna Wyn examines the competing discourses which shape media images and representations of young people. At a broad level, she identifies the tension between a narrative preoccupation with 'youth as (violent) threat' in the context of *generational* change, and 'youth as hope for the future' in the context of *socioeconomic* change. In either case, it seems young people are po-sitioned unfavorably and, in the words of Henri Giroux (1998: 23), as projec-tions of 'the desires, fantasies and interests of the adult world.' Where, in the case of the first discourse, young people are typically portrayed as a threat to adult security and the traditional order, the second discourse promotes a roman-ticized but equally narrow view of young people.

Given the media context outlined by Wyn in chapter 2, from an intergroup communication perspective, Peter Garrett and Angie Williams (chapter 3) pre-sent a review of intergenerational and lifespan communication research, includ-ing their own, which time and again demonstrates the negativity of adult per-ceptions of young people's communication practices. But their work also shows that evaluations of age outgroups change across the lifespan as people claim and relinquish membership of such groups. As Garrett and Williams point out, an ingroup-outgroup perspective is not confined to interaction between strangers and acquaintances but can manifest itself in close relationships too—such as within the family.

In chapter 4, Crispin Thurlow and Alice Marwick turn their attention to another institutional context in which adults may be seen to prejudge—or mis-judge even—the communication of young people. In this case it is academics who inadvertently devalue young people's needs and experiences as everyday communicators, by seeking to evaluate them against competence-based models of communication. Using the example of communication apprehension, Thurlow and Marwick note how, among other things, dominant scholarly and popular discourses promote a normative ideology of 'talk as good communication' as well as a decontextualized, pathologizing framework for understanding young people's communication.

In the last chapter in Part I, Cynthia Carter and Stuart Allan return to look at the role of media in shaping the lives of young people. In this case, however, they focus on the value of media education in helping young people to find a political voice. In doing so, they also offer a powerful critique of past and current institutional discourses about citizenship, literacy and democracy. As Carter and Allan note, these plans are often ideologically problematic and misconceived in making grave assumptions about the political and instructional communication needs of young people. They then demonstrate the positive impact young people can have when given interactive opportunities to express their own opinions.

Part II: Young people's communication in peer contexts

In Part II, we have grouped together those chapters which focus primarily on the practices and experiences of young people in communication with each other in the context of so-called peer culture. For most young people peer relations constitute the primary communities of practice by which they construct and reproduce their place in the world. For this reason especially, we are pleased to start this part of the book with a contribution by Penelope Eckert, whose ethnographic work in this area is so well known.

In chapter 6, Eckert focuses on language and the stylistic practices of young people and their peer groups, specifically—'language is a resource for constructing social meaning.' Style, according to Eckert, creates ingroups as well as outgroups. It defines and marks one group as distinct from another, and although group labels are important, this goes far beyond group labels. Speech style therefore constructs identity as much as do clothes, makeup, jewelery and so forth. As she points out, styles are created when linguistic resources are appropriated and recommissioned to make something new and unique. Stylistic elements in themselves do not signal category but indicate a set of stances, beliefs, attitudes, and values—a lifestyle—that in turn indicates the category or group membership.

Building on this theme and continuing the focus on language, Vivian de Klerk discusses slang and swearing in chapter 7. Again, here we see the use of language as a primary resource for the indexing of ingroups and outgroups. In her discussion, de Klerk makes a useful distinction between slang and swearing.

As a versatile way of maintaining group boundaries, slang is ever changing, innovative, and often used by adolescents to create distance from adults and other outgroups; it is also flexible enough that it can be changed to maintain distance if outgroups acquire and use the code (and therein attempt to reduce distance). Swearing, on the other hand, is more enduring and stable but might be used to create distance through its shock potential. De Klerk also provides a useful discussion of the way that slang can be used as a means of coercion (for example, in maintaining mainstream gender distinctions).

In chapter 8, Lauren Berger, Dana McMakin and Wyndol Furman outline what they call a *behavioral systems* approach in order to identify some of the primary communicative aspects in establishing and maintaining romantic relationships during adolescence. Focusing mainly on the experiences of young people who identify as heterosexual, Berger and her colleagues explore how patterns of affiliation, sexual behavior, attachment and caregiving frame young people's initial experiences of love and desire. Although research shows that they negotiate status and conflict in many of the same ways as adults, there are also some important differences which reflect the particular social and institutional challenges faced by young people.

While Berger and her colleagues acknowledge the heterosexual bias of their chapter, Sarah O'Flynn's chapter (9) serves to present another important side of the 'love story.' Based on her experiences as both a community volunteer and a scholar, O'Flynn examines the impact of institutional 'silence' in the lives of young lesbian, gay and bisexual people, noting how they remain one of the most underrepresented groups in the research literature. Communication is a central feature of these young people's lives in two particular ways: on the one hand, they are obliged to verbalize and constitute their sexual identity in language; on the other hand, much of their lives is marked by an *absence* of communication in the face of cultural and political sanction.

In chapter 10, Leo Hendry and Marion Kloep open up the focus on peer relations to consider the culture of leisure which serves as both a context and a channel for relational and interpersonal communication (*cf* Brown *et al.*, 1994). Framed conceptually by their own Lifespan Model of Developmental Challenge, and with reference to the firsthand accounts of their own young research participants, Hendry and Kloep organize their discussion neatly around three interactional patterns or 'styles': communication as leisure, leisure for communication, and leisure as communication. It is in this way that Hendry and Kloep are able to show the vital role that leisure plays as a context for development and identity work in the formation and maintenance of relationships, building ingroup membership and so forth.

In the final chapter of Part II, Susan McKay, Crispin Thurlow and Heather Toomey Zimmerman examine the ways in which 'new' media offer the potential for some young people to counteract their long-standing disempowerment by, and misrepresentation in, older media like print and broadcast news. As such, the chapter by McKay and her coauthors usefully extends the issues raised by Carter and Allan in chapter 5. In debunking the popular myth of the 'net generation', McKay, Thurlow and Toomey Zimmerman note how communication technologies are ever evolving, but so too are the ways young people shape technology to satisfy their need for information, entertainment and socialization.

Part III: Young people in communication with adults

Although young people are themselves powerful in creating and regulating their own social meanings, it is invariably adults who dictate the institutional structures and ideological frameworks for so much of adolescent life. In this third part of the book we therefore include a series of chapters which attend more directly to young people's communication with adults in several key contexts of interaction.

In chapter 12 Pat Noller comprehensively reviews a rich academic literature concerned with a variety of risk factors such as stress that negatively influence outcomes for young people, as well as protective factors such as positive communication that may buffer the effects of psychosocial stressors. Grouping these factors in terms of family stress factors, protective factors and risk factors, Noller explores the impact of each on young people's psychological adjustment and 'problem' behaviors.

Picking up on our general concern for the misrepresentation of young people's communication, in chapter 13 John Drury shows nicely how adults in authority typically view adolescent communication as unskilled and/or unmotivated compared to that of adults. There are significant consequences here of an inherent power imbalance in these relationships. Importantly, however, Drury explains how young people are aware of such imbalances and their communication strategies may represent various ways of coping with such situations. For example, Drury considers various ways in which young people may creatively attempt to redress the imbalance.

Focusing attention on yet another adolescent-adult communication context, Chesebro in chapter 14 draws on instructional communication research, so far conducted mostly in US colleges, to illustrate the possible similarities and differences in young people's learning environments. Reviewing research on teacher skills such as nonverbal immediacy, content relevance, teacher clarity as well as out-of-class communication, Chesebro looks to provide direction for future research along these lines, pointing to theories that may help to summarize and promote further understanding in this area.

In drawing the volume to a close, in chapter 15 Susan McKay discusses 'health' as a context for young people's communication. Echoing the various adult-adolescent contexts elsewhere in Part II, McKay starts by noting how young people are often construed as problematic or 'at risk,' and how such discourses frame adolescent interaction with adults. Although McKay refers specifically to health contexts, these are common practices of adult communities interacting with young people. In this case, adolescent risk is typically viewed in terms of a variety of social problems, from teenage pregnancy to smoking, drug abuse and other sensation-seeking risky behavior. McKay considers the various social contexts (such as peer and family relationships) that may influence young people's connection with health and health providers. Nevertheless, the message here is clear: young people are construed as 'at risk' and, in some cases, this simply establishes itself as a self-fulfilling prophesy.

Summing up before moving on

As we have suggested elsewhere (Thurlow, 2005), there is a need always to examine, to bring under academic scrutiny, and to problematize the hegemonic benefactors of 'adolescence'—especially those adults (professional and academic, among others) who control a society's mechanisms of representation. Writers like Burman and Griffin remind us that we need always to be wary of merely perpetuating the very category we mean to deconstruct, in the way that the sociolinguistic analysis of gender has, until recently at least, tended to do (e.g., compare the 'two-cultures' and 'performativity' approaches to gender identity; see Cameron, 1997). More often than not, we (as adults) explain, interpret and frame (or simply dismiss) young people's behavior and language as *adolescent*. For this reason at least, it is important that we begin to establish what young people think about themselves (*cf* Williams *et al.*, 1997) and their own communication (*cf* Thurlow, 2001b). We also need to start talking (and publishing) about young people in terms other than their youth; like adults, age is one of any number of identities they may orient to (e.g., ethnicity, class, nationality, institution, physical ability, sexuality, gender). While we cannot be sure that we (as editors and contributors) have ourselves been wholly successful in this regard, a theme which does occur across most of this collection is the authors' concern to challenge many popular assumptions about adolescence. Indeed, a number of the authors are also specifically concerned to confront institutional and academic complicity in misrepresenting or disadvantaging young people.

Notwithstanding this, perhaps the greatest strength of our volume, we believe, is that it covers such a wide range of scholarly backgrounds, theoretical perspectives and methodological styles while focusing on young people's communication experiences and practices. Although there are authors who identify themselves as scholars of language and communication (e.g., de Klerk, McKay, Eckert, Garrett, Chesebro, and ourselves), there are others from social and clinical psychology (e.g., Drury, Noller, Kloep, Hendry, Berger and her colleagues), media and cultural studies (e.g., Wyn, Marwick, Carter, Allan), and education (e.g., O'Flynn, Toomey Zimmerman). We think it is especially important given the topic (i.e., communication) and the domain of social life (i.e., adolescence) that we can offer a more interdisciplinary volume in which contributors are able to draw on their own diverse research in reviewing existing work in each area and pointing to directions for future study. As editors, we are pleased to be able to offer to the growing literature on intergenerational and lifespan communication (see for example Williams & Nussbaum, 2001) this first substantive contribution focused on adolescence.

Notes

1. This comment was made by one of the young male prisoners interviewed by Anita Wilson (2003: 175).
2. This leaflet is also available (24 January 2005) online at <www.rcpsych.ac.uk/info/help/adol>.
3. In a very informative discussion with Johanna Wyn on the issue of naming practices, she and I discussed our reservations also with the pejorative tone of 'youth' in some contexts which, additionally, often implies young men and boys. One is, we concluded, obliged always to select the lesser of several evils.
4. Of course there are exceptions such as more lifespan-oriented scholars like Richard Lerner (e.g., 2002) or Laurence Steinberg (e.g., Steinberg & Morris, 2001).
5. In addition to a chapter on 'communicating with adolescents,' psychiatrist George Orvin's (1995) book *Understanding the Adolescent*, for example, has principle sections titled *Who Are Adolescents?* and *Problems in Adolescence*; chapters in these sections include 'normality and adolescence,' 'adolescents' evolving personal identity,' and 'adolescents' evolving sexual identity.'
6. This program is accompanied by an elaborate website available (25 January 2005) at <http://www.pbs.org/wgbh/pages/frontline/shows/teenbrain>. The full program can be viewed in segments by streaming media; we recommend the segment titled *You Just Don't Understand*. Elsewhere on the site, under the heading *Do your teens seem like aliens?*, the producers make available 'resources for parents and teenagers to help improve mutual understanding and communication.'

7. For more on *Kevin*, see the BBC's own webpage at <http://www.bbc.co.uk/comedy/guide/articles/h/harryenfieldandc_66601360.shtml>.
8. In the USA, one pop-cultural litmus of social attitudes towards adolescence is the widely syndicated cartoon strip *Zits* by Jerry Scott and Jim Borgman (see www.kingfeatures.com/features/comics/zits/). Setting the tone for many of these apparently harmless portrayals, *Zits* invites readers to 'enter the life of Jeremy Duncan, a 15-year-old aspiring rock musician, riddled with angst, boredom and parents who don't understand anything. Let him show you the wonderfully lousy world of being a 15-year-old. [Also] meet Jeremy's parents … watch as they continue to try to figure out the mysterious science of parenting a teenager....'
9. Shortly before completing this introduction, I was fortunate to be asked to review the 2003 volume edited by Jannis Androutsopoulos and Alexandra Georgakopoulou (see Thurlow, 2005). While some of the thoughts expressed in the book review are repeated here, I mention it only because I recommend their volume as an excellent complement to our edited collection here. In taking a more micro-level, uniformly qualitative angle, Androutsopoulos and Georgakopoulou present a series of sociolinguistic studies in diverse domains of adolescent life.

References

Adams, G. R., Montemayor, R. & Gullotta, T. P. (eds). (1996). *Psychosocial Development During Adolescence*. Thousand Oaks, CA: Sage.

Arnett, J. J. (2000). Emerging adulthood: A theory of development from the late teens through the twenties. *American Psychologist*, 55(5), 469–480.

Ball, S. J. (1981). *Beachside Comprehensive: A Case-study of Secondary Schooling*. Cambridge: Cambridge University Press.

Baumeister, R. F. & Muraven, M. (1996). Identity as adaptation to social, cultural, and historical context. *Journal of Adolescence*, 19, 405–416.

Baxter, L. A. & Goldsmith, D. (1990). Cultural terms for communication events among some American high school adolescents. *Western Journal of Speech Communication*, 54, 377–394.

Bourdieu, P. (1991 [1999]). Language and symbolic power. In A. Jaworski & N. Coupland (eds), *The Discourse Reader* (pp. 502–513). London: Routledge.

Brown, B. B., Mory, M. S. & Kinney, D. (1994). Casting adolescent crowds in a relational perspective: Caricature, channel, and context. In R. Montemayor, G. Adams & T. Gullotta (eds), *Personal Relationships During Adolescence* (pp. 123–167). Thousand Oaks, CA: Sage.

Brown, B. B., Larson, R. & Saraswathi, T. S. (2002). *The World's Youth: Adolescence in Eight Regions of the Globe*. New York: Cambridge University Press.

Burman, E. (1994). *Deconstructing Developmental Psychology*. London: Routledge.

Cameron, D. (1997). Performing gender identity: Young men's talk and the construction of heterosexual masculinity. In S. Johnson & U. Meinhof (eds), *Language and Masculinity* (pp. 47–64). Oxford: Blackwell.

Cameron, D. (1998). Introduction: Why is language a feminist issue? In D. Cameron (ed.), *The Feminist Critique of Language: A Reader (2nd ed.)* (pp. 1–21). London: Routledge.

Cameron, D. (2000). *Good to Talk? Living and Working in a Communication Culture.* London: Sage.

Cameron, D., Frazer, E., Harvey, P., Rampton, B. & Richardson, K. (1992 [1999]). Power/knowledge: The politics of social science. In A. Jaworski & N. Coupland (eds), *The Discourse Reader* (pp. 141–157). London: Routledge.

Chisholm, L. & Hurrelmann, K. (1995). Adolescence in modern Europe. Pluralized transition patterns and their implications for personal and social risks. *Journal of Adolescence*, 18, 129–158.

Coleman, J. C. (1974). *Relationships in Adolescence.* London: Routledge and Kegan Paul.

Coleman, J. C. & Hendry, L. B. (1999). *The Nature of Adolescence.* London: Routledge.

Côté, J. E. (1996). Identity: A multidimensional approach. In G. R. Adams, R. Montemayor & T. P. Gullotta (eds), *Psychosocial Development During Adolescence* (pp. 130–180). Thousand Oaks, CA: Sage.

Davis, J. (1990). *Youth and the Condition of Britain: Images of Adolescent Conflict.* London: Athlone.

Drury, J. & Dennison, C. (1999). Individual responsibility versus social category problems: Benefit officers' perceptions of communication with young people. *Journal of Youth Studies*, 2(2), 171–192.

Dunn, J. (1988). *The Beginnings of Social Understanding.* Oxford: Blackwell.

Dyer, R. (1993). *The Matter of Images: Essays on Representations.* London: Routledge.

Eckert, P. (1989). *Jocks and Burnouts: Social Categories and Identity in the High School.* New York: Teachers College Press.

Eder, D. (1998). Developing adolescent peer culture through collaborative narration. In S.M. Hoyle & C.T. Adger (eds), *Kids Talk: Strategic Language Use in Later Childhood* (pp. 82–94). New York: Oxford University Press.

Fairclough, N. (1999). Global capitalism and critical awareness of language. *Language Awareness*, 8(2), 71–83.

Falchikov, N. (1986). Images of adolescence: An investigation into the accuracy of the image of adolescence constructed by British newspapers. *Journal of Adolescence*, 9, 167–180.

Falchikov, N. (1989). Adolescent images of adolescence. *Journal of Adolescence*, 12, 139–154.

Foucault, M. (1980). *Power/Knowledge.* New York: Pantheon.

Giddens, A. (1991). *Modernity and Self-identity: Self and Society in the Late Modern Age.* Cambridge: Polity Press.

Giles, H. (1999). Managing dilemmas in the 'silent revolution': A call to arms! [1999 ICA presidential address]. *Journal of Communication*, 49(4), 170–182.

Gilliam, F. D. & Bales, S. N. (2001). *Strategic Framing Analysis: Reframing America's Youth.* Center for Communications and Community. Available (26 May 2005) online at <http://repositories.cdlib.org/ccc/children/005>.

Giroux, H. A. (1998). Teenage sexuality, body politics and the pedagogy of display. In J. S. Epstein (ed.), *Youth Culture: Identity In A Postmodern World* (pp. 24–55). Oxford: Blackwell.

Giroux, H. A. (2000). *Stealing Innocence: Youth, Corporate Power, and the Politics of Culture.* New York: St. Martin's Press.

Goosens, L. & Phinney, J. S. (1996). Identity, context, and development. *Journal of Adolescence*, 19, 491–496.

Griffin, C. (1993). *Representations of Youth: The Study of Youth and Adolescence in Britain and America.* Cambridge: Polity.

Gumperz, J. & Cook-Gumperz, J. (1982). Introduction: Language and the communication of social identity. In J. Gumperz (ed.), *Language and Social Identity* (pp. 1–21). Cambridge: Cambridge University Press.

Hall, S. (1996). Introduction: Who needs identity? In S. Hall & P. du Gay (eds), *Questions of Cultural Identity* (pp. 1-17). London: Sage.

Hendry, L. B. & Reid, M. (2000). Social relationships and health: The meaning of social 'connectedness' and how it relates to health concerns for rural Scottish adolescents. *Journal of Adolescence*, 23, 705–719.

Hockey, J. & James, A. (1993). *Growing Up and Growing Old: Ageing and Dependency in the Life Course.* London: Sage.

Home Office, UK Government. (2000) *Listen Up: A Dialogue with Young People.* Available (15 April 2005) online at < http://www.homeoffice.gov.uk/docs/listen.html>.

Jacques, M. (2004, December). We're all teenagers now: Age and wisdom have been cast out by our infantalised society as the whims of youth are served. *Guardian Newspaper*, December 4. Also available (25/05/05) online at: <http://www.guardian.co.uk/comment/ story/0,3604,1366267,00.html>.

Lash, S. & Urry, J. (1994). *Economies of Signs and Spaces.* London: Sage.

Lerner, R. M. (2002). *Concepts and Theories of Human Development.* Hillsdale, NJ: Lawrence Erlbaum.

Males, M. A. (1996). *The Scapegoat Generation: America's War on Adolescents.* Monroe, ME: Common Courage Press.

Males, M. A. (1999). *Framing Youth: Ten Myths About the Next Generation.* Monroe, ME: Common Courage Press.

Miles, S. (2000). *Youth Lifestyles in a Changing World.* Buckingham: Open University Press.

Mortimer, J. T. & Larson, R. W. (2002). Macrostructural trends and the reshaping of adolescence. In J. T. Mortimer & R. W. Larson (eds), *The Changing Adolescent Experience: Societal Trends and the Transition to Adulthood* (pp. 1–17). Cambridge: Cambridge University Press.

Ng, S. H. & Bradac, J. J. (1993). *Power in Language: Verbal Communication and Social Influence.* Newbury Park, CA: Sage.

Orvin, G. H. (1995). *Understanding the Adolescent.* Washington, DC: American Psychiatric Press.

Pennycook, A. (2003). Global Englishes, Rip Slyme and performativity. *Journal of Sociolinguistics*, 7(4), 513–533.

Porteous, M. A. & Colston, N. J. (1980). How adolescents are reported in the British press. *Journal of Adolescence*, 3, 197–207.

Spivak, G. C. (1990). Practical politics of the open end. In S. Harsym (ed.), *The Post-Colonial Critic: Interviews, Strategies, Dialogues* (pp. 95–112). London: Routledge.

Steinberg, L. & Morris, A. S. (2001). Adolescent development. In S. T. Fiske, D. L. Schachter & C. Zahn-Waxler (eds), *Annual Review of Psychology*, 52, 83–110.

Thurlow, C. (2001a). The usual suspects? A comparative investigation of crowds and social-type labeling among young British teenagers. *Journal of Youth Studies*, 4(3), 319–334.

Thurlow, C. (2001b). Talkin' 'bout my communication: Communication awareness in early adolescence. *Language Awareness*, 10 (2&3), 213 –231.

Thurlow, C. (2003). Teenagers *in* communication, teenagers *on* communication. *Journal of Language & Social Psychology*, 22(1), 50–57.

Thurlow, C. (2005). Book review: 'Discourse constructions of youth identities' [eds J. K. Androutsopoulos & A. Georgakopoulou]. *Journal of Sociolinguistics*, 9(2).

van Dijk, T. A. (1992). Discourse and the denial of racism. *Discourse and Society*, 3(1), 87–118.

van Heeswyk, P. (1997). *Analysing Adolescence*. London: Sheldon Press.

Williams, A. & Garrett, P. (2002) Communication evaluations across the lifespan: From adolescent storm and stress to elder aches and pains. *Journal of Language and Social Psychology*, 21, 101–126.

Williams, A. & Nussbaum, J. (2001). *Intergenerational Communication Across the Life Span*. Mahwah, NJ: Lawrence Erlbaum.

Williams, A., Coupland, J., Folwell, A. & Sparks, L. (1997). Talking about Generation X: Defining them as they define themselves. *Journal of Language and Social Psychology*, 16, 251–277.

Wilson, A. (2003). 'Nike trainers, my one true love—without you I am nothing': Youth, identity and the language of trainers for young men in prison. In J. K. Androutsopoulos & A. Georgakopoulou (eds), *Discourse Constructions of Youth Identities* (pp. 173–196). Amsterdam: John Benjamins.

Wyn, J. & White, R. (1997). *Rethinking Youth*. London: Sage.

Youniss, J. & Smollar, J. (1985). *Adolescent Relations with Mothers, Fathers and Friends*. Chicago: University of Chicago Press.

Youniss, J. & Ruth, A. (2002). Approaching policy for adolescent development in the 21st century. In J. T. Mortimer & R. W. Larson (eds), *The Changing Adolescent Experience: Societal Trends and the Transition to Adulthood* (pp. 250–271). Cambridge: Cambridge University Press.

Part I

Adult constructions of young people's communication

2

Youth in the media: Adult stereotypes of young people

Johanna Wyn

This chapter explores media images and representations of young people and discusses the ways in which the media draws on and reinforces particular conceptions or stereotypes of youth. It draws on research conducted in the United States, Australia, New Zealand and the United Kingdom which analyzes how mainstream print media and television portray young people. The research reveals a long tradition of media misrepresentations of young people, who are portrayed in a negative light. In particular, 'moral panics' (Cohen, 1987) about young people's sexuality, drugs and violence surface regularly. Media also reinforce the use of stereotypes to categorize an entire generation. For example, through the category 'Gen Y,'[1] media characterize an entire generation as 'different' from previous generations, and at the same time as being at risk of having 'failed' transitions to adulthood.

Media stereotypes of young people are not unwaveringly negative, however. Stereotypes of Gen Y also send positive messages about young people. They are portrayed as foreshadowing the lifestyles and priorities of future generations: entrepreneurial 'wiz kids' in the fashion business; savvy users of new information technologies; and citizens of the future. This stereotype emphasizes youth entrepreneurship and an ease and facility with new technologies that is often lacking in the older generation [see McKay *et al.*, chapter 11, this volume]. Narratives focusing on the self-assurance, technological know-how, business sense and lifestyle decisions of these young people convey the message that they are demonstrating how to live life in the twenty-first Century.

This chapter discusses these media stereotypes, drawing on the observation that the media have portrayed young people both as a potential threat to the stability of society and as a symbol of hope for the future of society. This distinction provides a framework within which to analyze the way in which the media contribute to understandings of the relationship of adolescence to society. It also provides a framework for discussing adult perceptions of young people.

In the following section, I provide a brief discussion of the conceptualization of 'youth' in different media representations, setting the scene for a discussion of the ways in which researchers have analyzed these representations and stereotypes.

Characterizing young people and media representations

Media representations of young people can be seen as an expression of two key, interrelated elements that are involved in understanding their lives: generational change and social change. The adolescence research literature emphasizes the need for these elements to be seen in relationship to each other (Wyn & White, 1997; White & Wyn, 2004). In particular, researchers of young people point out the weaknesses of a concept of generational change that does not take into account the ways in which each generation is shaped by the times (Cohen, 1997; Dwyer & Wyn, 2001). Because many of the features of media representations of young people can be understood in relation to these elements, I expand briefly on these ideas here.

Youth and generation

A focus on young people from the perspective of generational change tends to emphasize the essential nature of adolescence as a period of life, regardless of historical period or culture. A focus on 'youth and generation,' in isolation from an understanding of social conditions under which young people are growing up, inevitably focuses on young people as a threat to the established order. Elsewhere, I have discussed this as a 'categorical approach' to young people (Wyn & White, 1997). Indeed, Cohen highlights this approach as one commonly shared by politicians, policy makers and professionals (including, I would argue, media professionals), involving the following assumptions about adolescence:

1. adolescence is a unitary category, with certain psychological characteristics and social needs common to the age group;
2. adolescence is an especially formative stage of development where attitudes and values become anchored to ideologies and remain fixed in this mould in later life;
3. the transition from childhood dependence to adult autonomy normally involves a rebellious phase, which is itself part of a cultural tradition transmitted from one generation to the next;
4. young people in modern societies experience difficulty in making successful transitions and require professional help, advice and support to do so.… are the interrelated elements of generational change and social change (1997: 182).

This approach emphasizes the separateness of young people from adults, ignoring the many ways in which they share much with older people, including their culture, their geographic location, their class background and, often, their gender identity. The approach also focuses on adolescence as a difficult and possibly dangerous time, for both individual young people and for society as a whole, and emphasizes the need for the guidance and at times intervention of older people and professionals. From this perspective, the perceived danger to young people is that they will not complete the 'developmental process' to achieve 'normal' adulthood properly, whereas the perceived danger to society is that social conventions from the previous generation may not be successfully transferred to the next generation. If young people do not grow up to reproduce the patterns of life and the values of the previous generation, then they appear to represent a threat to the traditional order.

The tendency for the media to take this view of adolescence was brought to light in the early 1970s by Stanley Cohen (see 1987), who described how the media representations of young people in the 1960s portrayed them as 'folk devils,' creating what he called a 'moral panic' about youth as threat. Focusing on the 'mods and rockers' at a seaside town in Britain, Cohen showed how media images fostered a perceived threat of violence and unrest through young people's collective leisure activities and their cultivation of new styles of dress and music. The media representations in turn heightened the perception that there was a need for special control measures and vigilance by the general public and the authorities (Bennett, 2000). Cohen's description of the creation of moral panics about young people in the United Kingdom in the 1950s is echoed by Males' discussion of the ways in which young people were 'framed' by the US media in the 1990s. Males (1999) identifies ten media 'myths' that combine to portray young people in the United States. as threats to law and order and to the values that underpin US American life because of their failure to make the transition to adulthood appropriately.[2]

Youth and social change

A focus on social change is a less common, but nonetheless recurring, theme in media representations of young people. From this perspective, young people tend to be represented in a more positive light in the media, because of their capacity to engage with new realities and conditions. Rather than presenting young people as a challenge to the established order, this perspective tends to highlight the ways in which they represent and embody the future of any society. Underlying print media stories of young people who are smart, autonomous workers in the new (urban) economies, volunteer workers for causes they believe in and socially integrated within both local and virtual communities is the expression of some hope for the future and recognition that change is not necessarily negative. The view of the role young people play in the new urban economies today is similar to the media acknowledgment of the symbolic role of young people in a previous era, in a very different economy. For example, at the turn of the previous century, when Australia's economy was dominated by primary production, young rural people symbolized the future of the emerging economy based on natural resources, as this extract from a leading newspaper illustrates:

> Boys and girls who live outside of our cities we salute you—(In you) is found the best of home, country, kindred, sunshine and love—every instinct that the heart most deeply enshrines (*Bulletin*, 13 March 1922, quoted in Bessant, 1993: 82).

Although characterizations of so-called Generations X and Y in the media today are far more ambivalent than those in the above quote, both recognize that young people are also young workers and citizens who are shaping the future. In another newspaper article, the following claim is made:

> They are more diverse than boomers and more cheerful than their older siblings, X-gen's angst-ridden 'lost generation'. Under 30s are overwhelmingly optimistic. It is an ebullience that seems bullet-proof (Ellingsen, 2000: 4).

In a feature article on the lives of Generations X and Y, Ellingsen describes the elements that distinguish them from the previous generation, acknowledging that the very concept of characterizing a generation is flawed. He points out that both Gen X and Gen Y are seen as posing a new marketing challenge, because their priorities and goals differ from those of the previous generation.

These new generations are seen as being cynical about the materialism of their parents' generation, interested in plotting their own course and in taking responsibility for themselves. Yet, despite attempts by the print mass media to characterize this generation, Ellingsen found that young people simply did not recognize themselves in mass media representations (Ellingsen, 2000).

Analyzing media stereotypes of young people

Moral panics about the priorities and lifestyles of young people that surface in the media are often backed up by contemporary research. The sense that all young people are at risk of 'faulty' transitions to adulthood is a common theme, occasionally supported by evidence of their failure to marry, to buy homes, to remain in stable jobs and generally to 'settle down.' Researchers use terms such as 'arrested adulthood,' 'extended youth,' 'post adolescence,' 'stranded generation' and 'generation on hold' to describe young people (Wyn, 2004a; Wyn, 2004b). These terms merely exaggerate the notion that young people often face problematic transitions to adulthood.

In contrast to this approach, the Life-Patterns study of young Australians, which has tracked the trajectories and life experiences of 2000 young people from the time they left secondary school in 1991 to 1994, provides evidence in support of the view that young people are shaping a 'new adulthood' (Dwyer & Wyn, 2001). Rather than being victims of failed transitions to adulthood, young people are shaping for themselves new priorities, in response to changing social and economic realities which include the fragmentation of social life, the disintegration of traditional structures and the increased pressure on individuals to take responsibility for their own lives. Post-1970 generations place a strong emphasis on personal autonomy and on the ability to be mobile and flexible. If generational change is located in the context of social change, therefore, the new approaches to life that are evident in the life patterns of successive generations are seen as adaptive responses to the only world they know.

Stereotypes of young people as a threat, as 'at risk' or as having 'failed transitions' often derive from the perspective of an older generation who expect that young people will grow into the adulthood that was available to them. As Cohen points out, 'it is all too easy to read social changes through the particular ideas and experiences which were strategic in forming the historical generation to which we belong' (Cohen, 1997: 180).

Social researchers drawing on the insights of Mannheim (1952) have pointed out that each generation of young people come to be the bearers of a kind of special generational consciousness. From this point of view, the different sensibilities and life patterns that are forged by new generations are necessarily also a product of changes in the economic, political and social forces in their own society. These broader changes, such as new communications technologies and changes in the nature of workplaces, are also shaped by young people [see McKay *et al.*—chapter 11, this volume]. For example, the trend toward part-time, contract and short-term employment in Australia has by and large been embraced by young people. Within one generation, the notion of 'career' as a permanent, full-time job has been replaced by a more individualized concept of career as a 'state of mind' which is not necessarily related to paid employment (Dwyer *et al.*, 2003).

When media representations engage with the broader, contextual elements of young people's lives, it is possible to go beyond the simplistic narratives of young people as a universal 'threat,' to present narratives that do offer a more positive or realistic view of young people, but that may also signal new dangers and risks.

Young people and the media discourse of threat

The literature on media stereotypes of young people overwhelmingly takes the view that the representations of young people are negative, limited or biased. Writers make different assumptions about the reasons for this and their effects, and about the type of media that is most significant. For example, the work of Heintz-Knowles (2000), which is often cited in writing on this topic, is based on the content analysis of a narrow slice of media: prime-time television entertainment programming in the United States. Heintz-Knowles also cites a range of other studies that provide evidence for the salience of prime-time entertainment programming. This evidence reveals that television is both a reflection of the 'values and ideals of American society' and an influence on the views and attitudes of Americans. For example, the 'cultivation hypothesis' proposed by mass communication scholar Gerbner and his colleagues argues that heavy viewers of television cultivate perceptions about the 'real world' based on the stereotypes they see on television (Gerbner *et al*, 1994). The 'cultivation hypothesis' has been described by Jefferes (1997) as an accumulated effect that comes with long-term, heavy television viewing.

Importantly, however, Heintz-Knowles does not surmise about the effects of television viewing for the population of the United States that would not come into the category of 'long-term, heavy' viewers. The effect of stereotypical portrayals of young U.S. people on non-US viewers in Australia, the United Kingdom or other countries where US American television shows are regularly screened is even less researched. However, the findings by Heintz-Knowles do raise important questions about the kind of 'cultural story' that television offers

(Heintz-Knowles, 2000: 2). She found that 'TV youth' are not an accurate reflection of the demographics of US young people. Instead, 'TV youth' are
slightly more likely to be female and are overwhelmingly white' (p. 6). Young
people are not necessarily presented on these programs in a negative light. For
example, it was common for young people to be portrayed as capable of solving
problems without adult help, or as creating problems that adults must fix. Ado-
lescence-oriented issues most frequently discussed in the media are parent-teen
relationships, romantic relationships, doing well in school and social pres-
sure/popularity. On this basis, Heintz-Knowles argues that popular television
reflects adults' views of adolescence and assumptions about young people that
are common in US culture. Perhaps her most significant finding is that young
people are most commonly portrayed as having few connections with parents
or wider family. In fact, she points out that in many of the programs that she
analyzed, the family situations of the main characters were unknown and apparently irrelevant. In contrast to the adultlike autonomy and problem-solving skills
of 'TV youth,' Heintz-Knowles points out that young people are also portrayed
as set apart from adults, and are characterized as immature through terms such
as 'kids' or 'girls' (2000: 22) [see also Noller—chapter 12, this volume].

The media message that young people do not need connections to families
or to the larger community is also noted by Nichols and Good (2004). In response to a collection of US media representations of young people since 1998,
these writers have taken issue with the way in which media perpetrate a 'careless
indifference' toward young people. Nichols and Good draw the conclusion that
entertainment and news media provide 'a negatively skewed perspective on
youth and children' (p. 8) and argue that media stereotypes of young people
therefore contribute to a dangerous lack of knowledge about them which may
be contributing to a 'laissez-faire approach to youth socialization' (p. xi). What
concerns Nichols and Good is that young people should receive more attention
of a positive nature from adults, including guidance and help.

Returning to the theme of television, Aubrun and Grady (2000) find that
television has a number of negative consequences for people's thinking about
young people. They argue that television reduces people's thinking to stereotyped scripts about adolescence, and, echoing the concerns of Nichols and
Good, these writers find that television encourages viewers to feel distanced
from young people, taking a 'spectator view' of their lives. They also conclude
that television emphasizes a social distance between young people and other
people (Aubrun & Grady, 2000: 11).

Already mentioned earlier, an even more negative assessment of media
stereotypes of young people is that offered by Males (1999), who documents the
'systematic maligning' of young people by the media by identifying a number of
media myths that are constantly recirculated about young people, summed up as
the myth that 'today's youth are America's worst generation ever' (p. 1). Males

argues that young people are in fact scapegoats for a society in which disparities between rich and poor are becoming greater and in which 'adults over the age of 30—*white* adults … consistently display the largest increases in serious (felony) violent, property and drug-related crime rates' (p. 5).

This theme is picked up in analyses of representations of young people in the media across many societies and in different periods of time. For example, Smith *et al.* (2002) describe how young Maori people in contemporary New Zealand are inevitably portrayed in the popular media as failing to make a normative transition to adulthood, as lawbreakers and as drugtakers. Her research highlights the ways in which media discourses of young people are often radicalized, and how particular ethnic groups are identified as 'other.' Other writers too have pointed out how the general threat posed by young people is often overlaid with racist overtones through the denationalization of occasional violent incidents involving young men from particular ethnic groups. For example, vivid descriptions of young people's activities have included graphic illustrations of the use of machetes and hint at interethnic gang warfare on the streets, in the schools and in nightclubs (White & Wyn, 2004). Writing about Australia in the 1960s, Johnson (1993) demonstrates how the discourse of 'youth as threat to the established order' was taken up in the Australian media. She draws on 1960s media reports to show how 'youth' was typically portrayed as a time of potentially dangerous experimentation with new fashions and styles (or 'wacky teen fashions'). Johnson also shows how this discourse was drawn on to create a role for professionals who could measure youth development and treat those who were outside the norm (*cf* Burman, 1994).

Young people and the media discourse of hope

Although the characteristics of Gen Y have often been portrayed by the media as being at risk of failed transitions to adulthood, some media representations acknowledge that the capacity to be flexible and cope with uncertainty may be very positive in today's society. As I have already indicated, a discourse of hope is apparent in media representations of young people in which the focus shifts from that of generational change to that of social change. From this perspective, it can be seen that media constructs young people and, in particular, young women, as 'a social space in which to talk about the characteristics of people in modernity, to worry about the possibilities of …social changes' (Lesko, 2001: 5). For these terms, representations of girlhood, it is argued, function as a space for social concerns about social change. As Harris (2004) also points out, modern times are characterized by dislocation, flux, and globalization, and demand citizens who are flexible and self-realizing, and who have the capacity for self-regulation. Media (especially advertising) play an important role in reflecting this focus on adolescence as integral to the successful transition to a new social order. In her book *Future Girl*, Harris argues that young women have become integral to the social and economic futures of Western societies, providing evidence that 'a mainstream image of young women who are successful and flexible has been constructed through this process' (p. 151). In making her case, Harris examines the lives of young women in a 'global perspective' with respect to school, work, power and sexuality.

Whereas the story lines of prime-time television entertainment programming may continue to represent young people as simply a generation apart, in cinema new story lines about cultural transition can be seen to emerge. Examples of this can be seen in the success of films set in the early 2000s, such as *Bend It Like Beckham* and *Whale Rider*. The lead characters in both films are young women whose strength and personal vision are shown to pave a way forward from seemingly impossible situations. *Bend It Like Beckham*, set in the United Kingdom, and *Whale Rider*, set in New Zealand, both also feature contemporary struggles over race and gender, played out in the lives of individual young women. In *Bend It Like Beckham*, for example, the lead character is a soccer-playing girl from a traditional Indian family that has migrated to the United Kingdom. The film describes how she overcomes the constraints of tradition to fulfill her dream of playing soccer. Meanwhile, in *Whale Rider*, the lead character challenges the traditions of exclusive male leadership within her tribe to show how an indigenous community can maintain its relevance and cultural pride in an increasingly globalized society. In both of these films, young women unambiguously represent hope for a new social order.

While acknowledging the positive elements of these new story lines, Harris nonetheless comes to the gloomy conclusion that young people themselves still have very little say in the ways in which they are represented in policies, in research and especially in the media. Even though media may place young women centrally within the discourse about 'how to prevail today, utilizing the motifs of can-do and at-risk,' she argues that these discourses deny young women real participation or capacity to articulate 'positions of greater complexity and dissent' (2004: 185–186).

Conclusion: Caught between competing discourses

The representation of young people in the mass media in all its different forms is complex. In this chapter I have examined two enduring themes that characterize media representations of young people: generational change and social change. The dominant stereotype of 'youth as threat' focuses on generational change and reinforces messages about young people as potentially violent law-breakers and as the victims of faulty developmental transition processes. Importantly, researchers have analyzed the ways in which this kind of publicity creates moral panics about new generations of young people, and justifies the intervention of professionals. Other researchers draw on media images to argue that young people are typically 'set apart' in these representations, despite the fact that they often need adult guidance and support.

Representations of adolescence as 'hope for the future' tend to frame young people within a broader context of social, political and economic change. From this point of view, young people inevitably foreshadow new ways of being adult. Their views, priorities and life patterns are not simply a phase that they will grow out of, but are potentially new ways of living and being. But, even though positive story lines about young people may emerge from this perspective, many researchers conclude that these representations overwhelmingly frame adolescence within narrow boundaries that have more to do with the construction of identities within late capitalism than with the real lives and needs of young people.

Ultimately, both of the themes informing adult stereotypes of young people in the media derive more from 'the desires, fantasies and interests of the adult world' (Giroux, 1998: 23) than they do from young people's own perceptions and experiences of the world. The stereotyping of young people and their communication in the traditional media reflect a society in which young people's access to public communication and public space is controlled and limited. Yet, young people have a lot to contribute to our understandings of social change and the future shape of work, education and life.

Notes

1. Definitions of when membership of Gen Y starts and ends, and how this relates to Gen X vary. Broadly, Gen Y is the seen to encompass people born between 1979 and 1995 and Gen X those born between 1963 and 1978 (*cf* Williams *et al*, 1997).
2. The myths about young (US) people which Males identifies are that they are the worst generation ever; are violent thugs; need more policing; are druggie wastoids; are drunken killers; are camel clones; are ruining the country; are reckless, suicidal, and 'at risk'; are not oppressed; and are in 'moral meltdown'. The final myth about adolescence is that the media tell the truth about young people.

References

Aubron, A. & Grady, J. (2000). *Aliens in the Living Room: How TV Shapes Our Understanding of 'Teens'*. Washington, DC: The Frameworks Institute.

Bennett, A. (2000). *Popular Music and Youth Culture*. London: MacMillan.

Bessant, J. (1993). A patchwork: The life-worlds and 'cultures' of young Australians 1900–1950. In R. White (ed.), *Youth Subcultures: Theory, History and the Australian Experience*. Hobart: National Clearinghouse for Youth Studies.

Burman, E. (1994). *Deconstructing Developmental Psychology*. London: Routledge.

Cohen, P. (1997). *Rethinking the Youth Question, Education, Labour and Cultural Studies*. London: MacMillan.

Cohen, S. (1987). *Folk Devils and Moral Panics: The Creation of the Mods and Rockers*, 3rd Edition. Oxford: Basil Blackwell.

Dwyer, P., Smith, G., Tyler, D. & Wyn, J. (2003). *Life-Patterns, Career Outcomes and Adult Choices*. Melbourne: Australian Youth Research Centre.

Dwyer, P. & Wyn, J. (2001). *Youth, Education and Risk: Facing the Future*. London: Routledge/Falmer.

Ellingsen, P. (2000). Don't call us a generation. *Melbourne Age*, Extra, May 6, 2000. 1, 4 & 5.

Gerber, G., Gross, L., Morgan, M. & Signorielli, N. (1994). Growing up with television: The cultivation perspective. In J. Bryant and D. Zillmann (eds), *Media Effects: Advances in Theory and Research* (pp. 17–42). Hillsdale, NJ: Erlbaum.

Giroux, H. (1998). Teenage sexuality, body politics and the pedagogy of display. In J. Epstein (ed.), *Youth Culture: Identity in a Postmodern World*. Malden, U.K.:Blackwell.

Harris, A. (2004). *Future Girl: Young Women in the Twenty-first Century*. New York: Routledge.

Heintz-Knowles, K. E. (2000). *Images of Youth: A Content Analysis of Adolescents in Prime-Time Entertainment Programming*. Washington, DC: The Frameworks Institute.

Jefferes, L. (1997). *Mass Media Effects*. Prospect Heights, IL: Waveland Press, Inc.

Johnson, L. (1993). *The Modern Girl: Girlhood and Growing Up*. Sydney: Allen and Unwin.

Lesko, N. (2001). *Act Your Age! A Cultural Construction of Adolescence*. New York: Routledge-Falmer.

Males, M. (1999). *Framing Youth: Ten Myths about the Next Generation*. Maine: Common Courage Press.

Mannheim, K. (1952). *Essays in the Sociology of Knowledge*. London: Routledge & Kegan Paul.

Nichols, S. L. & Good, T. L. (2004). *America's Teenagers: Myths and Realities*. New Jersey: Erlbaum.

Smith, T. L., Smith, G. H., Boler, M., Kempton, M., Ormond, A., Chueh, H. & Waetford, R. (2002). Do you guys hate Aucklanders too? Youth: Voicing differences from the rural heartland. *Journal of Rural Studies*, 18, 179–178.

White, R. & Wyn, J. (2004). *Youth and Society: Exploring the Social Dynamics of Youth Experience*. Oxford: Oxford University Press.

Williams, A., Coupland, J., Folwell, A. & Sparks, L. (1997). Talking about Generation X: Defining them as they define themselves. *Journal of Language and Social Psychology*, 16, 251–277.

Wyn, J. (2004a). Becoming adult in the 2000s. *Family Matters*, 68, 6–12.

Wyn, J.(2004b). What is happening to 'Adolescence'? Growing up in changing Times. In J. A. Vadeboncoeur, & L. P. Stevens (eds), *Re/Constructing the 'Adolescent': Sign, Symbol and Body*. New York: Peter Lang.

Wyn, J. & White, R. (1997). *Rethinking Youth*. London: Sage.

3

Adults' perceptions of communication with young people

Peter Garrett and Angie Williams

We start this chapter by reviewing the main theoretical approaches that have been employed in intergenerational research, namely, intergroup theory and communication accommodation theory (CAT), and some of the complexities pertaining to the consideration of age groups as social categories. We then show how these approaches have been applied to the study of communication between generations up to now, arguing that research into communication with young people has received relatively little attention compared to that with the elderly. We then review the research that our colleagues have conducted, which we hope offers some insights into communication between young people and older adults outside the family, including notions of 'good communication.' We then look at work focusing on communication within families, this time with reference to the theoretical perspective of Communication Boundary Management (Petronio, 1991) [see Noller—chapter 12, this volume]. Finally, we draw out some general conclusions.

Intergenerational communication as intergroup communication

Intergroup theories have been usefully applied to communication across a range of social groups, particularly categories of race and ethnicity (see Giles & Coupland, 1991). A central tenet of one such theory, social identity theory

(SIT), is that an individual's self-concept comprises two parts: personal and social identity. Whereas the former includes personal characteristics, individual preferences, and idiosyncrasies, the latter relates to our membership in social groups. These social groups emerge from the psychological process of social categorization (Taylor, 1981). Tajfel and Turner (1979) claim that we make comparisons between our own group's position in society and the positions of other groups, and in so doing, we strive to distinguish our own group in a positive light. In various ways, stereotypes play a central role in providing the content of social categories. In their review of stereotypes and social groups, Hewstone and Giles (1986) point to three essential aspects of this process. Firstly, other individuals are categorized, usually on the basis of identifiable characteristics such as ethnicity, speech style, or sex. Secondly, a set of traits, emotions, etc. are associated with members of the category, who are in turn taken to be similar to each other but different from other groups on these qualities. Thirdly, these qualities are then associated with any member of that category. Tajfel (1981) sees stereotypes as playing, on the one hand, a 'social explanatory' function, to maintain group ideologies that provide justifications and explanations for intergroup relations (especially reactions to and behavior toward members of outgroups), and, on the other, a function of creating, strengthening and preserving positively valued differentiations between the ingroup and various outgroups. Specific traits are selected as stereotypical, and judgments of these hold salience when they are pertinent to a specific intergroup context.

Even though intergroup theory has encountered some critique (e.g., Billig, 1985), there is considerable evidence of a tendency to seek positive distinctiveness for one's ingroup, even to those one has been assigned to arbitrarily (Tajfel *et al.*, 1971). And there is also evidence that we derive some level of self-esteem from the assignment of positive features to the ingroup and the exclusion of the outgroup from these features (Branscombe & Wann, 1994; Finchilescu, 1986; Sachdev & Bourhis, 1987, for debate on this aspect).

Our starting point, then, has to be whether *agegroups* constitute 'groups' in the social identity sense of the term. We maintain that they do. To draw upon Giddens (1991:146), the notion of a cohort—for example, 'the generation of the 1950s,' 'the generation of the 1960s'—is important for making sense of the different experiences of different age collectivities across various historical periods. Cohorts may be united by shared experiences, especially if they have lived through major historical events. It has been suggested by Mannheim (1952) that such experiences can transform an age cohort into a generation, even if they do not affect every individual in the same way. Developmental factors also impact on generational identity, of course. In early adulthood, for example, people typically develop a stronger sense of self and move toward autonomy apart from parents, while still being dependent on family support and social networks (Baltes & Silverberg, 1994).

Examples of empirical evidence for considering age groups as 'groups' include the pervasiveness of broad age categorization labels: for example, 'young,' 'middle-aged,' and 'old' (Coupland & Coupland, 1990; Giles, 1999), along with more sophisticated distinctions in certain areas, such as 'infant,' 'toddler,' and 'adolescent.' And, looking at the negotiation of generational identities through talk, and demonstrating how intergroup categories can surface strategically in discourse, Williams *et al.* (1997) have shown respondents from so-called Generation X interacting with popularized accounts of their generation, collectively defending themselves against negative stereotyping of their group, claiming a uniqueness for their group based on sociohistorical distinctiveness, and also making negative outgroup comparisons to build positive ingroup distinctiveness. Interestingly, too, the authors conclude that they 'have shown how participants exhibit a clear-sighted grasp that intergroup (in these cases, intergenerational) comparisons are an inevitable and recycling aspect of social life in history.'

Where do age groups begin and end in terms of actual ages, and, in particular for our purposes here, where does adolescence begin and end? A number of studies have asked respondents what ages they associate with labels such as 'adolescence,' 'young adulthood,' 'middle age,' and 'old age.' For example, studies suggest that young American respondents place 'young adulthood' from the midteens to about 30, with 'middle age' from 30 to 50, and 'old' adulthood starting at 50 (Harwood *et al.*, 1994). Giles *et al.* (2002) found respondents from Canada, New Zealand, Australia and the United States of America (average 20 years) seeing 'young adulthood' extending from 17 to 28 years of age. In our own research, we have found that adolescence is usually deemed to extend between 12 and 17 years of age, and 'young adulthood' between 18 and 26 years. This separation of adolescence from young adulthood in the late teens is a notion taken up by Arnett (2000), who maintains that the 18–25 age period should be more appropriately labeled 'emerging adulthood,' because people of this age can be regarded as distinct from adolescents in at least three significant ways. They tend to have more variable living arrangements, they tend to define themselves as no longer being adolescents, while not yet having the responsibilities and independence of adults, and they are still exploring their identities in terms of romance, work and worldview.

In any event, we see, inevitably, some variation in people's perceptions of where age categories begin and end, perhaps reflecting cultural differences in some cases but also, evidently, relating to the respondents' own age. For example, Williams and Garrett (2002) found 20–29 year olds defining 'middle age' from 37 to 54, whereas the 40–49 year olds moved the lower boundary up to 40 or 41 and the upper boundary to 57. Seemingly, the 40–49 year olds were raising the lower boundaries to exclude themselves for longer. This also suggests the applicability of intergroup theory and SIT: people are likely to avoid self-categorization in terms of negatively perceived groups (Tajfel & Turner, 1986). Indeed, in comparison with some other categories, such as sex, age might be seen as a distinctive category in intergroup communication, in that social psychological factors of social identification can make age group membership more of an issue of communicative negotiation at times.

Communication accommodation theory

A large proportion of intergenerational research has used communication accommodation theory (CAT) as its main analytical approach. Drawing upon social identity and intergroup theory, CAT seeks to explain the processes by which individuals adjust their communication to each other, both as individuals and as social group members (Giles *et al.*, 1991). In our communication, we move closer to interlocutors through a process of accommodation (or 'convergence'). For example, we may adjust our topic, the pace and timing of the conversation, or our lexical and grammatical choices. Conversely, we may distance ourselves through a process of nonaccommodation (or 'divergence') in order to signal distance from our conversational partner. For example, we may not attend carefully to what she or he says because we wish to pursue our own agenda or to indicate a lack of common ground. Generally, we prefer our conversational partners to be accommodative rather than nonaccommodative. In addition, CAT claims that we try to adjust to where we *believe* our partner is communicatively and psychologically. Inaccurate beliefs are likely to lead to over- or under-accommodation. Overaccommodation (overadjustment) could lead us, for example, to address a very capable elderly person as if they were a baby (see also Garrett, 1992, on 'hyperaccommodation' in foreign language settings). An example of underaccommodation (insufficient adjustment) is an expert on computers using overly technical language with people who are not very familiar with that field and its jargon (see also Platt & Weber, 1984). Communication behavior can often be guided more by characteristics of group and social identities than by individual characteristics and identities (Tajfel, 1978). Hence group stereotypes may have more impact on communication than the personal qualities of individual interlocutors (Coupland *et al.*, 1988).

To a great extent, intergenerational communication to date has focused on evaluations made by college students (in their late teens or early twenties) about communication with elderly people (65 and over), usually outside the respondents' own families. One example of how Intergenerational Research and Communication Accommodation Theory perspectives have been applied to this area is that Williams and Giles (1996) found that their college students in the United States found communication with nonfamilial 65–75 year olds more satisfying (and with age less salient) when they felt the elders were more accommodative to the younger person's needs (e.g., were attentive, gave compliments), and when mutual understanding was achieved, with positive emotions being expressed on both sides. Communication was judged dissatisfying when elders were seen as unaccommodative (e.g., inattentive) and complaining (e.g., about their health, or making accusations about others). Similar judgments have been reported in New Zealand, Australia and Canada (Giles *et al.*, 2002).

This overwhelmingly negative view of communication with the elderly has been tempered by at least some signs of positivity. Hummert *et al.* (2004) found adults having multiple positive and negative stereotypes of the elderly. An illustration of this can be found in Williams and Giles (1996), where younger respondents described older conversational partners in satisfying encounters as being 'like a typical grandparent.' And indeed nonaccommodative behavior from the elderly is not always judged negatively (Williams, 1996).

To sum up, then, CAT and intergroup theory have taken center stage in much intergenerational work so far. And the main focus, which has largely been on young people's views of conversation with the elderly, has yielded important insights. Overall, older adults outside the family are a marked communication group in young people's reports, in both satisfying (within certain limits) and dissatisfying outcomes. And in terms of the evaluative factors emerging from these studies, the judgments tend to focus around the degree (positive or negative) of accommodation (e.g., were attentive, gave welcome advice) and nonaccommodation (e.g., complained about life, talked down to me), and the degree of respect and obligation (e.g., felt obliged to be polite, avoided certain topics).

We have argued elsewhere (e.g., Williams & Garrett, 2002) for the importance of extending intergenerational research across the lifespan, on the grounds that people of different ages may view communication interactions differently according to their cohort group or their point in the lifespan. Intergenerational communication, both familial and non-familial, is likely to change considerably, in both its nature and its functions, as peer reference groups, social networks, roles and responsibilities change and develop. And if there are two developmental phases of life in particular that are often seen as socially problematic, the other one of these is adolescence. Compared to the work on communication with the elderly, intergenerational communication scholars have given little attention to the stereotypes associated with adolescence and intergenerational communication with teenagers. Yet there is research evidence that adults do stereotype the young.

Adolescence: Communication and identity

Identity development is a major issue for adolescence, and scholars working in this area recognize the role of both autonomy from family of origin (Noom *et al.*, 1999) and attachment for psychosocial adjustment (e.g., Baltes & Silverberg, 1994). Autonomy is generally seen as the 'ability to regulate one's own behavior.' Attachment is 'the quality of the relationship with significant others.' Baltes and Silverberg (1994) state that 'the developmental task of adolescence seems to be a complicated one that calls for a negotiated balance between an emerging sense of self as a competent individual on the one hand, and transformed, but continued, feeling of connection with significant others on the other' (p. 57).

There are three types of adolescent autonomy, according to Beyers and Goossens (1999). *Emotional autonomy* occurs when teenagers are not emotionally dependent on parents, and when they see their parents more as individuals than as parents. *Behavioral autonomy* occurs when teenagers are able to make independent decisions about all types of behavior. *Attitudinal autonomy* occurs as teenagers begin to develop and express a set of independent opinions outside the realm of parental influence. It is thought that young people who are in the middle of autonomous transitions find it most stressful, and that those who gain various types of autonomy too hastily are most at risk. It is also thought, in contrast, that increased autonomy in late adolescence is associated with positive adjustment.

In tandem with developing more autonomy from parents, teenagers have to forge rewarding and supportive relationships with peers. As adults' overseeing of peer relationships decreases, teenagers have to negotiate their peer terrain to a large extent on their own, at a time, during their midteens, when they are experiencing rapid change and development in terms of physical changes and self-concept (Baker, 1992). According to Brown *et al.* (1994), an important component of this process is the exploration of 'crowds.' Interest in or allegiance to a crowd, and the awareness of social distance among crowds, help these young people to decide which peers to seek relationships with and which to ignore or shun. One explicit aspect of this process is the allocation of evaluative names to groups and their members, such as 'druggies,' 'normals,' and 'brainies' (see Eckert, 1989; Thurlow, 2001a). Attitudes research by Garrett *et al.* (2003) similarly shows how mid-teenagers in Wales evaluatively label each other across their dialect communities, from rural 'sheepshaggers' and 'shitshovellers' to urban 'townies,' for example.

Stereotypes and ageism toward young people

In a study by Ng *et al.* (1991), respondents were asked to formulate questions to put to people across various ages (16 to 91) who had apparently been involved in a car accident, the cause of which was left ambiguous (see also Franklyn-Stokes *et al.,* 1988). For the older people, respondents rated items on health, physical condition, and mental alertness as being appropriate, whereas for the younger ones, items about alcohol consumption and speeding were deemed most appropriate. Although the study focused on stereotypes and expectations of older people, it is striking how it echoes stereotypical representations of the young as reckless, irresponsible, more likely to abuse alcohol etc. (Williams & Giles, 1996).

Studies in the United States also reveal common stereotypical representations of adolescence as a period of storm and stress (Arnett, 1999). Buchanan *et al.*'s (1990) survey of parents and teachers showed the majority seeing adolescence as a difficult time for teenagers (as well as for their parents and teachers). A subsequent study by Buchanan and Holmbeck (1998) also revealed that college students and parents of teenagers believed that, in comparison with secondary school children, young people were more likely to have socio-behavioral problems connected with risk-taking, rebelliousness, recklessness, and impulsiveness, and emotional problems such as anxiety, insecurity and depression. Whether they really are more likely to have such problems, of course, is another issue.

Young people are certainly sensitive to such perceptions about them (Falchikov, 1989). Williams and Giles (1996), for example, found them reporting that the stereotypical communication toward them reflected assumptions that they are reckless, feckless and irresponsible. They felt that older people patronized them, disapprovingly referring to them as 'party animals,' for example, or 'overparenting' them. Media representations can be perceived to reinforce such negative views, as Williams *et al.* (1997) found in their study of Generation X [see also Wyn—chapter 2, this volume].

The research referred to so far in this section has concerned young people in what one might refer to as late adolescence (18–20). But there is reason to believe that younger teenagers are victims of even more problematic stigmatization in intergenerational communication. Drury *et al.* (1998) found in their study of about four thousand 12–20 year olds in the United Kingdom that 13–19 year-olds reported more negative than positive communication experiences with non-family adults. But their study also indicated developmental trends: 12–15 year olds reported significantly more negative and less positive communication than the 16–20 year olds. This difference extended beyond communication with non-family adults to include that with friends as well (Catan *et al.*, 1996). This suggestion that young teenagers might be seen as a distinct communicative group is perhaps strengthened when considered against the backdrop of 'progressive identity formation' (Waterman, 1982), the role of peer groups, peer pressure and conformity in early adolescence (Bixenstine *et al.*, 1976; Newman & Newman, 1988), and, as we referred to in the previous section, the role of language and communication in such processes.

Other research (Catan *et al.*, 1996; Drury *et al.*, 1998) has found that formal adult-defined contexts are particularly problematic, with real and perceived power differentials that are seemingly strongly linked with communication problems. Young people reported most communication difficulty with adults in professional or official roles.

Evaluations across the lifespan

In our own work (see Williams & Garrett, 2002), we surveyed evaluations from 495 UK community adults aged 20 to 59 years old on their communication experiences with three age groups of non-familial targets: their age-peers, elders (65–85 years old) and young teenagers (13–16 years old). In the data analysis, the respondents were divided into four age cohorts: 20–29, 30–39, 40–49, and 50–59. Self-report data was also collected on frequency of contact.

In terms of the respondents' perceptions of their own communicative behavior, the evaluative dimensions found in this study were familiar from earlier research into the elderly: communication adjustments (e.g., 'spoke slower')— which closely matches the 'patronising speech' of Ryan *et al.* (1995)— respect/obligation, discomfort, and topic accommodation. However, when respondents were asked about communication behavior toward them by peers, elders and young teenagers, they responded not only in terms of accommodation and nonaccommodation but also in terms of two dimensions new to intergenerational research: noncommunication (e.g., 'gave short answers,' 'were uncommunicative') and of self-promotion (e.g., 'tried to impress,' 'were cheeky,' 'were overconfident'). It seems then that the well-established judgmental dimensions from earlier (and elders-focused) intergenerational research need complementing in order to develop a framework that might encompass the whole lifespan.

Taking all the age cohorts together, we found that, in terms of perceptions of others' communication behavior, although elders were seen to be more nonaccommodative than teenagers or peers, young teenagers stood out from the other age groups insofar as they were seen to be less accommodative, more noncommunicative and more self-promotional. So the new dimensions of non-communication and self-promotion certainly seem to have emerged through the incorporation of teenagers into the research design. In terms of how they saw their own communication behavior, respondents reported that they felt more discomfort in communication with teenagers than with peers or elders, but that they were also less likely to adjust their topics of conversation or their communication style in interactions with young teenagers compared to with elders. They were also less likely to feel respect/obligation with teenagers than with elders.

Although there were few cohort distinctions in the evaluations of communication with young teenagers, these were nevertheless of some interest. The 20–29 year olds reported the least respect/obligation to teenagers compared to the 40–49 and 50–59 year olds. Even so, they reported more likelihood of making communication adjustments to the young teenagers than did the other age cohorts. Perhaps the most interesting cohort in this regard, however, and one that has been overlooked in previous intergenerational research, was the 30–39 year olds. This cohort stood out from the others in a variety of ways. In relation to young teenagers, they saw them as more nonaccommodative than did the other respondent cohorts (a judgmental dimension otherwise associated more with elder targets). They also saw them as more noncommunicative than did the other respondents. Interestingly, too, they saw them as more accommodative than the other respondents. This age group certainly merits further research. It may be that their particular lifestage starts to give them some distance from their own teenage years, with those at the older end of the cohort perhaps parenting or anticipating their own first teenage offspring (and having more engagement with friends of these young people). The newness of such contact may give it more intensity and engagement, even if in terms of frequency of (at least nonfamilial) contact, this cohort does not differ from the others. Or it may be something in this cohort's sociohistorical background that explains the profile. More work is certainly needed here.

It is worth noting that, whereas in earlier intergenerational research focusing on college students and elders, there was some indication that frequency of contact had an impact on evaluations (mitigating the impact of social stereotypes), we found no such signs in our study; self-reported frequency of contact was not linked to any differences in evaluations. Future work may need to focus more on the nature and quality of contact, as well as frequency. For example, the college student respondents in the United States may be more 'campus-bound,' with only exceptional rather than day-to-day contact with elders, compared with the various cohorts of judges in our study.

Developing further this research, (see Williams *et al.*, 2004), we also sought evaluations from 208 respondents aged 18–25 years on the same scales as the study above. However, in this second study, respondents were asked to evaluate their communication experiences with their age peers and with young teenagers (13–16 years old). Affective questions were also included; respondents were asked to assess their own feelings during their communication. And five questions were added to evaluate the respondents' intergroup awareness during interactions with young people. They were asked questions about their awareness of age differences in such conversations, and whether they felt like or acted like a typical older person.

The results of this study confirmed the nine dimensions found in the earlier study: accommodation, nonaccommodation, noncommunication, self-promotion, discomfort, communication adjustments, respect/obligation, and topic accommodation. Affective items factored into 'support/nurturing' (kind, helpful, supportive, generous), 'negativity' (angry, bored, frustrated, emotionally negative), 'satisfaction' (satisfied, happy, emotionally positive, relaxed, interested), and 'tension' (guarded, defensive, anxious, anxious to leave). In their evaluations, these young adults differentiated their communication experiences in much the same way as in the previous study: young teenagers were seen to be less accommodative, more nonaccommodative, and more noncommunicative than same-age peers. And the respondents reported more discomfort, more communication adjustment, and more topic accommodation with young teenagers. On the affective items, three out of the four factors differentiated the age groups. The young adults reported more tension and negativity, and less satisfaction, in their communication with young teenagers. In addition, the high scores on all the intergroup awareness items led the authors to conclude that the respondents perceived their communication encounters in intergroup terms.

'Good' communication

There is often a tendency for adults to view young people as being unskilled communicators. Drury and Dennison (1999), for example, found benefits officers in the United Kingdom making negative generalizations about their communication experiences with young people, and the view is echoed in data collected from police officers (Drury & Dennison, 2000). Teachers, too, may view encounters with teenagers as problematic (Williams & Cockram 2002). Indeed, in the context of writings on late-modernity and the fragmentation of individual identities (Giddens, 1991), it is claimed that there is a contemporary lack of clarity on how to enact various social roles (salesperson, consumer, colleague etc.) and how to produce and make sense of new ways of speaking and writing for successful professionals. Designing new 'competences' is increasingly seen as essential for contemporary life, and this has contributed to various codifications of communication skills (Cameron, 2000; Thurlow, 2001b). Communication lessons are now a common feature in educational institutions in the United Kingdom. But whereas contemporary theories of interpersonal communication have focused on the importance of shared and negotiated meanings, courses on 'good' communication skills tend to take a behavioral approach, grounded in the assumption that communication can be broken down into component parts which can then be taught [see Thurlow & Marwick—chapter 4, this volume].

Within the limitations of our data, we explored the notion of 'good communication' from the perspective of our young adult respondents. On the basis of regression analyses with 'satisfaction' as the dependent measure, we found that there was a great deal of similarity overall in the way that 'good' (henceforth, satisfying) communication was perceived to operate with young adult peers and young teenagers. Accommodation and self-promotion by the other party were seen as core properties of satisfying communication for both groups. To this were added affective factors: the respondents' own feelings of supportiveness, and low levels of tension. Such affective issues are absent in the behavioral model employed in the training contexts referred to above. Interestingly, too, nonaccommodation and noncommunication from others were not found to have any bearing on satisfying communication. Given that these are well-established factors in intergenerational communication, these are interesting findings, and suggest that properties associated with satisfying communication may vary across the lifespan. Given the considerable contemporary institutional emphasis on 'good' communication referred to above, it seems important to pursue this area further.

Communication within the family

As with intergenerational communication outside the family, research into that occurring within the family has, again, tended to focus on the upper end of the age spectrum and interactions with young college students. Investigations into communication with grandparents (e.g., Harwood & Lin, 2000; Harwood, 2000) have certainly established that intergroup interaction can occur in the context of family relationships, but there is a need to employ the approach across more of the lifespan. There has been more work done on young people in the field of interpersonal communication, however. The development and application of Petronio's (1991) Communication Boundary Management perspective has provided a particularly fruitful approach to the understanding of communication between parents and children at the interpersonal level, as children seek more autonomy [see Noller—chapter 12, this volume].

The basis of this perspective is that, so as to maintain privacy within the family, it is necessary for family members to recognize ownership of space, possessions and information. Although such attempts to define and maintain privacy rights are largely beneficial, conflict may arise when one person's boundaries compromise another member's definition of privacy. Individuals tend to tighten up control of boundaries if they feel vulnerable, and allow more access to them at times when they feel more secure. For example, parents may feel they have ownership rights to their children's bedroom space or insist that the room should be tidy, but children may define it as their own and insist it is up to them to decide if they want it tidy or not. Privacy invasion can be claimed to occur when parents do not fully grant their children's independence. Petronio's (1994) data is taken from older (mean age 19) rather than younger teenage respondents, but the categories of privacy invasion reported by these teenagers are likely to include at least some of those experienced by younger teenagers, since the gradual granting of privacy control by parents is a critical factor for teenagers generally for their ability to experience a sense of independence from the family and explore their own identity. The most common categories of privacy invasion found in her study were entering a bedroom without knocking, listening to telephone conversations, asking personal questions, and opening mail, with the teenagers' most common responses being locking bedroom doors, using signs such as 'keep out,' making phone calls from outside the home, and hiding personal belongings.

Petronio divided the parental tactics into 'subversive invasion' (e.g., opening mail) and 'direct invasion' (e.g., asking personal questions). The teenagers' responses were divided into 'evasive tactics' (e.g., making phone calls from outside the home) and 'confrontational tactics' (e.g., asking their parents to stop). The evasive responses are more proactive in nature, in response to interventions that are known or can be anticipated, whereas the latter are a form of retroactive restoration. She found that, while both evasive and confrontational tactics were available to teenagers when privacy invasion was direct in nature, they were more limited to confrontational responses when privacy invasion was subversive, since they were less able to predict when these would happen and had to rely on discovery.

With both evasive and confrontational responses aimed at protecting their boundaries, teenagers saw trust and relational quality with their parents declining. In the case of confrontational responses, they also reported an increased openness, but Petronio suggests that this kind of openness is more adversarial than an openness involving candor, and she questions whether such openness really outweighs the reduction in trust and quality. The ability of parents to give their children more space to explore their own values and ideas aids progression into adulthood. Yet teenagers' desire for a degree of separation and autonomy is pursued in conjunction with a need for continued connection with parents. Parental privacy invasion may jeopardize those dual needs. At the same time, parents may feel that confrontation by their children shows positive development in terms of learning to cope with difficult situations, and nevertheless feel that invasions are bound up with notions of good parenting.

More recently, Golish and Caughlin (2002) have extended this analytic perspective to stepfamilies. Their focus is on one particular response by teenagers and young adults: topic avoidance. This tactic is found to be a solution to problems of self-protection (e.g., wanting to avoid embarrassment), relationship protection (e.g., anger, or anything that might deteriorate the relationship), and wishing to avoid conflict. In this way, they may create more impermeable boundaries with some adults and much looser ones with others. The authors argue that the decisions that children in stepfamilies have to make about topic avoidance are likely to be quite different from those of children in other families. Their respondents reported most avoidance with stepparents, somewhat less with fathers, and least with mothers.

From an intergroup perspective, it would be illuminating to add to this insightful work within the family to explore under what circumstances the protection of interpersonal boundaries takes on intergroup significance, and what the purposes and consequences are in such instances. In the case of the elderly, for example, there are some excellent examples of how family relationships can swing between two opposing poles on an intergroup-interpersonal dialectic (Tajfel & Turner, 1986). Elderly family members may be highly individuated at some moments, whereas at others, they may be seen as typical elders. In the discourse data of Coupland and Coupland (2000: 224), a daughter present at a medical consultation between her mother and a doctor moves from an interpersonal stance of 'she's not sure whether she's got angina or no this is what …' to an intergroup one of 'I think when you get to her age you get a bit confused actually.' So in the context of communication involving young people, it will be revealing to study points where communication partners are seen in intergroup terms such as 'typical parent,' 'typical teenager,' 'typical stepparent' etc. In a recent study in the United Kingdom by Anderson, Tunaley and Walker (2000), a mother said of her teenage son, 'So far it's very good …. I'm still holding my breath a bit because you are waiting for it to happen. You can't get through life and there not be any major problems, especially when you get to the sixteen to eighteen bit.' Such assumptions may have wide-ranging implications.

Conclusion

Intergenerational research within the family has benefited from research gathering data about groups stretching more broadly across the lifespan. The work on communication with teenagers has led to a more inclusive factorial matrix of evaluative dimensions. The identification of such additional dimensions is important for uncovering a more detailed evaluative lifeline across the lifespan. There are now clear indications of how attitudes to both the elderly and to teenagers vary across different age groups. And we have seen in our own work specifically how, in particular, the 30–39 year old age group stands out in both these regards. We have also established empirically a marked communicative subdivision between young teenagers and young adults, reflecting Arnett's (2000) claims about 'emerging adulthood.'

In addition, the inclusion of affective judgments alongside behavioral ones has enabled us to explore notions of 'good communication.' This approach is certainly in marked contrast to the behavioral skills approach to fostering 'good communication' based on formulaic training through a checklist of competencies. Arguably, some of the miscommunication that stems from such communication skills approaches (see Cameron, 2000, for example) results from a lack of awareness of their affective deficiencies. The importance of this issue increases in particular with the growing contemporary emphasis on professional communication between service sector employees and clients. Cameron herself stresses that, with such a narrow view of 'good communication,' communication training is not only dumbing down competent speakers, but also leading to oppressive practices [also see chapter 4, this volume].

Finally, we have argued that although there has been some movement toward a broader lifespan focus in intergenerational research outside the family, there is still a relatively narrow focus in familial contexts. In particular, it would be revealing to see whether, how, under what circumstances and to what ends teenagers use age to claim independence or dependence. Similarly, it would be useful to examine the way in which age stereotypes are used within family interactions, for example, where they are used in interactions concerning parental decisions about teenagers, or where they are used by teenagers in relation to their attributions of validity to parental advice or demands. A corollary of such work would be the investigation of self-stereotyping within the family, and actions attributed to one's own age-typical behaviour. For example, teenagers may feel that they are *expected* to act in a rebellious fashion, just as elders telling stories about family history might be conceived as role or age-related self-stereotyping. The family is undoubtedly an inherently dynamic site for intergenerational communication.

References

Anderson, M., Tunaley, J. & Walker, J. (2000). *Relatively Speaking: Communication in families*. London: BT Future Talk.

Arnett, J. (1999). Adolescent storm and stress, reconsidered. *American Psychologist*, 54, 317–326.

Arnett, J. (2000). Emerging adulthood: A theory of development from the late teens through the twenties. *American Psychologist*, 55, 469–480.

Baker, C. (1992). *Attitudes and Language*. Clevedon: Multilingual Matters.

Baltes, M. & Silverberg, S. (1994). The dynamics between dependency and autonomy. In D. Featherman, R. Lerner & M. Perlmutter (eds), *Lifespan Development and Behaviour* (pp. 41–90). Hillsdale, NJ: Lawrence Erlbaum.

Beyers, W. & Goossens, L. (1999). Emotional autonomy, psychosocial adjustment and parenting: Interactions, moderating and mediating effects. *Journal of Adolescence*, 22, 753–769.

Billig, M. (1985). Prejudice, categorisation and particularisation. *European Journal of Social Psychology*, 15, 79–103.

Bixenstine, V., DeCorte, M. & Bixenstine, R. (1976). Conformity to peer sponsored misconduct at four grade levels. *Developmental Psychology*, 12, 226–236.

Brown, B. B., Mory, M. & Kinney, D. (1994). Casting adolescent crowds in a relational perspective: Caricature, channel, and context. In R. Montemayor, G. Adams, & T. Gullotta (eds), *Personal Relationships during Adolescence* (pp. 123–160). Thousand Oaks, CA: Sage.

Branscombe, N. & Wann, D. (1994). Collective self-esteem consequences of outgroup derogation when a valued social identity is on trial. *European Journal of Social Psychology*, 24, 641–657.

Buchanan, C., Eccles, J., Flanagan, C., Midgely, C., Feldlaufer, H. & Harold, R. (1990). Parents' and teachers' beliefs about adolescents: Effects of sex and experience. *Journal of Youth and Adolescence*, 19, 363–394.

Buchanan, C. & Holmbeck, G. (1998). Measuring beliefs about adolescent personality and behaviour. *Journal of Youth and Adolescence*, 27, 609–629.

Cameron, D. (2000). *Good to Talk? Living and working in a communication culture*. London: Sage.

Catan, L., Dennison, C. & Coleman, J. (1996). *Getting Through: Effective communication in the teenage years*. London: BT Forum.

Coupland, N., Coupland, J., Giles, H. & Henwood, K. (1988). Accommodating the elderly: Invoking and extending a theory. *Language in Society*, 17, 1–41.

Coupland, N. & Coupland, J. (1990). Language and later life: The diachrony and decrement predicament. In H. Giles & P. Robinson (eds), *The Handbook of Language and Social Psychology* (pp. 451-468). Chichester: Wiley.

Coupland, N. & Coupland, J. (2000). Relational frames and pronominal reference: The discourse of geriatric medical triads. In S. Sarangi & M. Coulthard (eds), *Discourse and Social Life* (pp. 207–229). London: Pearson.

Drury, J., Catan, L., Dennison, C. & Brody, R. (1998). Exploring teenagers' accounts of bad communication: A new basis for intervention. *Journal of Adolescence*, 21, 177–196.

Drury, J. & Dennison, C. (1999). Individual responsibility versus social category problems: Benefit officers' perceptions of communication with young people. *Journal of Youth Studies*, 2, 171–192.

Drury, J. & Dennison, C. (2000). Representations of teenagers among police officers: Some implications for their communication with young people. *Youth and Policy*, 66, 62–87.

Eckert, P. (1989). *Jocks and Burnouts: Social Categories and Identity in the High School.* New York: New York Teachers College Press.

Falchikov, N. (1989). Adolescent images of adolescence. *Journal of Adolescence*, 12, 139–154.

Finchilescu, G. (1986). Effect of incompatibility between internal and external group membership criteria on intergroup behaviour. *European Journal of Sociology*, 16, 83–87.

Franklyn-Stokes, A., Harriman, J., Giles, H. & Coupland, N. (1988). Information seeking across the lifespan. *Journal of Social Psychology*, 128, 419–421.

Garrett, P. (1992). Accommodation and hyperaccommodation in foreign language learners: contrasting responses to French and Spanish English speakers by native and non-native recipients. *Language and Communication*, 12, 295–315.

Garrett, P., Coupland, N. & Williams, A. (2003). *Investigating Language Attitudes: Social meanings of dialect, ethnicity and performance.* Cardiff: University of Wales Press.

Giddens, A. (1991). *Modernity and Self-Identity: Self and society in the late modern age.* Cambridge: Cambridge University Press.

Giles, H. (1999). Managing dilemmas in the 'silent revolution': A call to arms! *Journal of Communication*, 49, 170–182.

Giles, H. & Coupland, N. (1991). *Language: Contexts and consequences.* Milton Keynes: Open University Press.

Giles, H., Coupland, J. & Coupland, N. (eds). (1991). *Contexts of Accommodation: Developments in Applied Sociolinguistics.* Cambridge: Cambridge University Press.

Giles, H., McCann, R., Ota, H. & Noels, K. (2002). Challenging intergenerational stereotypes across Eastern and Western cultures. In M. S. Kaplan, N. Z. Henkin & A. T. Kusano (eds), *Linking Lifetimes: A global view of intergenerational exchange* (pp.13–28). Honolulu, HI: University Press of America.

Golish, T. & Caughlin, J. (2002). 'I'd rather not talk about it.': Adolescents' and young adults' use of topic avoidance in stepfamilies. *Journal of Applied Communication Research*, 30, 78–106.

Harwood, J. (2000). Communicative predictors of solidarity in the grandparent-grandchild relationship. *Journal of Social and Personal Relationships*, 17, 743–766.

Harwood, J., Giles, H., Clément, R., Pierson, H. & Fox, S. (1994). Vitality of age groups across cultures. *Journal of Multilingual and Multicultural Development*, 15, 311–318.

Harwood, J. & Lin, M-C. (2000). Affiliation, pride, exchange, and distance: grandparents' accounts of relationships with their college-age grandchildren. *Journal of Communication*, 50, 31–47.

Hewstone, M. & Giles, H. (1986). Social groups and social stereotypes in intergroup communication: A review and model of intergroup communication breakdown. In W. Gudykunst (ed.), *Intergroup Communication* (pp. 10–26). London: Edward Arnold.

Hummert, M-L., Gartska, T. R., Ryan, E. B. & Bonnesen, J. L. (2004). The role of age stereotypes in interpersonal communication. In J. Nussbaum & J. Coupland (eds), *Handbook of Communication and Aging Research* (pp. 91–114). Mahwah, NJ: Lawrence Erlbaum.

Mannheim, K. (1952). *Essays in the Sociology of Knowledge*. Oxford: Oxford University Press.

Newman, P. & Newman, B. (1988). Early adolescence and its conflict: Group identity vs. alienation. *Adolescence*, 11, 261–274.

Ng, S-H., Moody, J. & Giles, H. (1991). Information-seeking triggered by age. *International Journal of Aging and Human Development*, 33, 269–277.

Noom, M., Dekovic, M. & Meeus, W. (1999). Autonomy, attachment, and psychosocial adjustment during adolescence: A double-edged sword? *Journal of Adolescence*, 22, 771–783.

Petronio, S. (1991). Communication boundary management: A theoretical model of managing disclosure of private information between marital couples. *Communication Theory*, 1, 311–335.

Petronio, S. (1994). Privacy binds in family interactions: The case of parental privacy invasion. In W. Cupach & B. Spitzberg (eds), *The Dark Side of Interpersonal Communication* (pp. 241–257). Hillsdale, NJ: Lawrence Erlbaum.

Platt, J. & Weber, H. (1984). Speech convergence miscarried: An investigation into inappropriate accommodation strategies. *International Journal of the Sociology of Language*, 46, 131–146.

Ryan, E. B., Hummert, M. L. & Boich, L. H. (1995). Communication predicaments of aging: Patronising behaviour toward older adults. *Journal of Language and Social Psychology*, 14, 144–166.

Sachdev, I. & Bourhis, R. (1987). Status differentials and intergroup behaviour: Does minimal intergroup discrimination make social identity more positive? *European Journal of Sociology*, 17, 277–293.

Tajfel, H. (ed.). (1978). *Differentiation between Social Groups*. London: Academic Press.

Tajfel, H. (1981). Social stereotypes and social groups. In J. Turner and H. Giles (eds), *Intergroup Behaviour* (pp. 144–165). Oxford: Blackwell.

Tajfel, H., Billig, M., Bundy, R. & Flament, C. (1971). Social categorisation and intergroup behaviour. *European Journal of Sociology*, 1, 149–178.

Tajfel, H. & Turner, J. (1979). An integrative theory of intergroup conflict. In W. Austin and S. Worchel (eds), *The Social Psychology of Intergroup Relations* (pp. 33–53). Monterey, CA: Brooks/Cole.

Tajfel, H. & Turner, J. (1986). The social identity theory of intergroup behaviour. In S. Worschel & W. Austin (eds), *The Social Psychology of Intergroup Relations* (pp. 7–24). Chicago: Nelson Hall.

Taylor, S. (1981). A categorisation approach to stereotyping. In D. Hamilton (ed.), *Cognitive Processes in Stereotyping and Intergroup Behaviour* (pp. 83–114). Hillsdale, NJ: Lawrence Erlbaum.

Thurlow, C. (2001a). The usual suspects? A comparative investigation of crowds and social-type labelling among young British teenagers. *Journal of Youth Studies,* 4, 319–34.

Thurlow, C. (2001b). Talkin' 'bout my communication: Communication awareness in early adolescence. *Language Awareness,* 10 (2&3), 213–231.

Waterman, A. (1982). Identity development from adolescence to adulthood: An extension of theory and a review of research. *Developmental Psychology,* 18, 341–358.

Williams, A. (1996). Young people's evaluations of intergenerational versus peer underaccommodation: Sometimes older is better? *Journal of Language and SocialPsychology,* 15, 291–311.

Williams, A. & Cockram, M. (2002). *Authority versus affiliation: Dialectics of teachers' communication with adolescent pupils.* Paper presented at the 8th International Conference on Language and Social Psychology (ICLASP8), Hong Kong, July 2002.

Williams, A., Coupland, J., Folwell, A. & Sparks, L. (1997). Talking about Generation X: Defining them as they define themselves. *Journal of Language and Social Psychology,* 16, 251–277.

Williams, A. & Garrett, P. (2002). Communication evaluations across the lifespan: From adolescent storm and stress to elder aches and pains. *Journal of Language and Social Psychology,* 21, 101–126.

Williams, A., Garrett, P. & Tennant, R. (2004). Seeing the difference, feeling the difference: Emergent adults' perceptions of communication and 'good' communication with peers and adolescents. In S. Ng, C. Candlin & C. Chiu (eds), *Language Matters: Communication, Culture, and Identity* (pp. 111–136). Hong Kong: City University of Hong Kong Press.

Williams, A. & Giles, H. (1996). Intergenerational conversations: Young adults' retrospective accounts. *Human Communication Research,* 23, 220–250.

4

From apprehension to awareness: Toward more critical understandings of young people's communication experiences

Crispin Thurlow and Alice Marwick

In a world of aggressive consumerism and the corporatization of public life, it is perhaps not surprising that young people find themselves increasingly positioned by market forces (*cf* Fairclough, 1993; Giroux, 2003). This manifests most obviously in the large-scale changes in (Western) job markets, delaying many young people's entry into working life and extending their dependence on the parental home (Chisholm & Hurrelmann, 1995; Mortimer & Larson, 2002). Of course, commerce knows only too well that young people—affluent or not—are nowadays also profitable customers for lifestyle advertising; as a result they are constantly branded and targeted by marketers selling everything from chewing gum to sport utility vehicles. There are, however, also more subtle ways in which young people find themselves having to respond to changing economic and other institutional circumstances. Take, for example, the following two statements made by one of the largest telecommunications companies in Europe:

> Innumerable studies have shown that being able to express yourself clearly and understand with equal clarity what other people are saying to you is a fundamental enabling skill of life. A proficiency at interpersonal communication is strongly linked to educational achievement, positive social behavior, physical and mental well-being, and ultimately employability.

> When people stop communicating… things go wrong. When people commu-
> nicate well, good things happen. Better interpersonal communication is the
> key enabling skill for a better life in the 21st Century. BT is best placed as the
> leading communications company in the UK to help people improve their
> communication skills.[1]

As social theorists have noted, the commodification of so much of social life
has inevitably also come to include language and communication (e.g., Fairclough, 1996; 1999; Lash & Urry, 1994). Indeed, the evaluation of, and demand
for, communication as a tangible *skill* has become a key educational and work-
place reality. One rarely sees a job advertisement these days which does not at
some point demand 'good communication skills.' No doubt driven by the demands of the marketplace, educational policy-makers—at least those in the
countries of North America and Western Europe—are themselves increasingly
concerned with *training* (as opposed to educating) young people in the ways of
'good' or 'effective' or at least marketable communication. Elsewhere, this contemporary preoccupation with communication manifests itself in the way that
communication is so commonly presented as a kind of societal, interpersonal
and, in the case of psychotherapy, psychic panacea (Cameron, 2000; also Philipsen *et al.*, 1999).

As in the dramatic quotations above, the boundary between communication as a supposedly key educational skill and as a major life resource is being
blurred all the time—and usually with little or no empirical evidence for linking
the two (the 'innumerable studies' referenced by BT remain conspicuously unspecified). In serving these various ends, communication is typically simplified
as a quantifiable commodity, construed in terms of measurable outcomes and as
a transferable 'skill' or technical ability. (Hence BT's blurring of human communication and mass communications.) It is in this way too that the communication practices and abilities of young people often come to be evaluated as deficient and in need of fixing—usually in the form of skills training or therapy.
Seldom are young people invited to think critically about the nature of communication, nor is there an attempt to evaluate their communication in the context
of their own lives—other than in the most material (or economic) and scholastic terms. As such, their communication is disciplined in educational contexts in
much the same way it is in media discourse where an adult mythology of the
communication-ignorant or inept teenager is still dominant (Falchikov, 1989; *cf*
also Williams & Garrett, 2002).

For scholars of communication, this itself should be a matter of some concern, because of what it says about lay (mis)understandings of human communication and meaning-making practices. For scholars of adolescence, it should
also be a concern because they too have been responsible at times for misrepresenting young people and for feeding the media with many of its most troubling

ideas (Burman, 1994; Davis, 1990). Indeed, scholars ought always to reflect on their complicity in constructing the 'myth of adolescence' (Hockey & James, 1993) and in ways which may not be in the best interests of the very group they mean to help. On this basis, we would like to examine one case-study example of how, with the best of intentions, communication scholarship has itself problematically approached young people's communication—which is to say, in a way which may ultimately and unwittingly devalue young people's needs and practices as everyday communicators. Specifically, we consider the field of Communication Apprehension. To be clear, we do not mean to question the professional or personal integrity with which scholarship in this area has been developed. We recognize also that the institutional demands of classroom- or college-based praxis are not always compatible with the poetics of academic theorizing. Nonetheless, just as scholars need always to be informed by the realities of application, theoretical critique is essential for any area of scholarly activity—especially those which look to influence educational policy and practice, and thereby shape the opportunities of young people.

Communication apprehension: A case in point

> About one of every five persons—20 percent of all college students—is communication apprehensive. (Pearson & Nelson, 1999: 24)

The term *communication apprehension* (from hereon CA) was introduced in 1970 by McCroskey, who first described it as 'the fear or anxiety associated with either real or anticipated communication with another person or persons' (see McCroskey, 1970; 1984: 13). Since then, it has become a well-established topic of scholarly concern, especially in the United States. Papers on CA are published regularly in major journals such as *Communication Education*, and others are presented every year at the conventions of both the International and the National Communication Associations (ICA and NCA); in fact the NCA now has a specialized division on Communication Apprehension and Avoidance. Not surprisingly, CA is also a topic usually covered in mainstream introductory textbooks (e.g., Pearson & Nelson above; also Beebe *et al.*, 2004; Gamble & Gamble, 2001). Although not intended solely for use with young people, the notion of CA has been applied consistently to young people in educational settings, often with older, college-age teenagers (e.g., Chesebro *et al.*, 1992; McCroskey *et al.*, 1989; Proctor *et al.*, 1994; Rosenfeld *et al.*, 1995), but also with younger high schoolers (e.g., MacIntyre *et al.*, 2003). What we offer here is a brief overview of the basic tenets of CA as it is usually presented by scholars whose work orients directly or indirectly to the field.

McCroskey, Richmond, and their associates undertook most of the early, defining work on CA, usually conceptualizing it as a specifically cognitive trait related to communicators' feelings of nervousness, fear and worry when contemplating the act of *oral* communication in particular (McCroskey, 1982; McCroskey, 1984; Richmond & McCroskey, 1998).[2] In hypothesizing CA as cognitive, a distinction is also drawn between *shyness* or *reticence* as a behavioral manifestation (e.g., remaining quiet during a conversation), and *willingness to communicate* (WTC) as a personality-based predisposition or motivation for 'actively' communicating.[3] Although not clearly explained, a relation of causality between CA and 'ineffective' communication is implied throughout much of the academic, educational and psychological literature on the subject (see, for example, Horwitz, 2002; also McCroskey, 1984: 37). (We return to this point shortly.) Scholars have also looked to establish a connection between CA and academic success, measured in terms of attendance, student-teacher interaction, scholastic achievement and grades (e.g., Watson & Monroe, 1990).

In looking to situate CA conceptually and experientially, Richmond and McCroskey (1998: 35–37) identify eight categories of shy people, or what they call 'low verbalizers.' For example, in their first category, 'skill deficient' people are those with 'poor communication skills' who may tend to avoid communication situations as a result. The second and third categories cover socially and culturally introverted people, which takes into account how different cultures may construct communication differently; as such, measuring a person's shyness by Western standards may overlook cross-cultural differences. The fourth category of shy people described by Richmond and McCroskey comprises the 'socially alienated,' those people who do not conform to social norms, and the fifth category is made up of ethnically or culturally diverse people who, like cultural introverts, may come from a cultural tradition that does not adhere to majority norms for speaking. Finally, it is in the seventh category that Richmond and McCroskey identify those who suffer (sic) from communication apprehension as the 'fear of communicating.' CA is thus held to be both a type of shyness and one of its primary causes.

Across the CA literature there is a noticeable lack of definitional clarity between the range of disparate terms used, which leads to a fair amount of theoretical ambiguity. Terms like *shyness, reticence, audience anxiety*, and *willingness to communicate* often appear to be discussed and conceptualized differently. For example, by no means a precise term itself, there are two well-known scales to assess *shyness* (see Crozier, 2001); however, neither one appears to correlate—or to have been correlated—with CA. By the same token, while some researchers use McCroskey's delineation of CA as 'trait' and shyness as its behavioral manifestation or dimension, others use the notion of CA interchangeably with, for example, shyness (e.g., Manning & Ray, 1993) and reticence (e.g., Kelly *et al.*,

2001). It is this lack of precision which makes it especially difficult to determine what conceptual consensus exists in the field as a whole and what exactly is being examined. Indeed, Leary (1983), who himself uses McCroskey's distinction between cognitive traits (CA, 'audience anxiety') and behavior (shyness, reticence), does raise the concern that the literature runs the risk of becoming meaningless if researchers are not able to use their terms precisely. For example, the added notion of willingness to communicate is described by MacIntyre *et al.* (2003) as a personality-based orientation toward communication and the extent to which someone is predisposed to communication. Although they ally this to CA, by their own definition WTC is more a question of motivation rather than a cognitive trait. Without definitional clarity, however, it becomes extremely difficult to compare empirical studies of CA or to draw conclusions about the applied validity of the notion.

Conceptually, the link between CA and shyness is generally thought to be that of social anxiety. According to Ayers (1997), for example, CA arises from a person's conflict about being perceived negatively, combined with a self-perceived lack of competence and motivation to avoid this negative perception. Speaking about shyness, Crozier (2001) discusses this social anxiety model in depth, noting that shy individuals must likewise possess both the desire to make a certain type of impression—although not necessarily a positive one—and the inability to do so. In either case, it is anxiety about impression management that is generally presented as the (primary) cause for apprehension and/or its behavioral aspect, shyness. Although CA is also frequently linked to shy or reticent behavior, the relationship is *not* consistently presented as causal throughout the literature; for this reason it does not necessarily follow that a person with high CA will necessarily behave in a shy manner. In fact, allowing for the distinction drawn between CA as a *cognitive* capacity and shyness as behavioral, it is quite possible for people who are apprehensive about communicating still to communicate 'effectively,' just as people who do not, need not necessarily be communication apprehensive. Kuhlemeier *et al.* (2002) arguably deal with best this confusion by conceptualizing CA as a 'continuum' that can be experienced differently by the same person, depending on the situation, audience and type of communication activity. For the most part, however, the trait-state ambiguity of CA is either left unaccounted for in the literature or assumed to be a *fixed* trait (see McCroskey, 1984: 16) which predominates.

Even if one accepts the standard conceptualization of CA as a trait and not a behavior (e.g., McCroskey & Richmond, 1982), the relation between the two still remains uncertain. For example, a person may score very high on a test that measures CA, but still be an 'effective' communicator. It is also quite possible for a young person to avoid communicating for reasons other than anxiety or fear. Certainly, the lack of a causal relationship—or at least an explanation of one—between these two dimensions/elements makes it difficult to evaluate attempts to remedy or 'treat' CA. Indeed, Allen and Bourhis (1996) point out that typical treatments of communication apprehension—those which focus on reducing anxiety—have not been proven to affect the development of communication skills (*cf* McCroskey, 1984: 16 & 37). What is more, if, as is sometimes the case (e.g., Kuhlemeier *et al.* 2002), CA is then reconceived as a continuum in which people experience apprehension differently depending on the situation, then assessment and intervention are even more difficult to evaluate because one's degree of CA, and the behavior one exhibits as a result, are open to endless, state-specific variations. Finally, Crozier (2001) rightly points out that it is often other people's *perceptions* of shyness that have the most negative effects for shy people, who are often characterized—or stereotyped—as aloof, rude or of deliberately making no effort to interact. In this case, therefore, it would be the manifest behavior of shyness, and not any putative internal trait (i.e., CA), which has the negative impact. Interventions—assessment and treatment—at the level of the individual fail to address co-constituted social judgments of shyness.

In spite of the lack of definitional clarity, and as a means of establishing its prevalence and significance as a problem worthy of study and intervention, it is frequently mentioned in the CA literature that 20 percent of the population, or one in five people, 'suffers' from communication apprehension (see, for example, Horwitz, 2002; Richmond & McCroskey, 1998; McCroskey, L. *et al.*, 2002). However, it is never made clear how this figure is derived.[4] Horwitz (2002), for example, cites two studies for the prevalence of CA; the first references an 'Epidemiological Catchment Area survey' of 13,000 Americans, which reported that 20 percent of the population reported a specific fear of embarrassment while speaking, writing, or eating in public' (p. 11). As we have understood it from our own readings of the CA literature, 'fear of embarrassment' is not equivalent to CA, nor would 'eating in public' usually be considered a mode of communication. (Which is not to say that it might not constitute meaningful behavior.) The other study cited by Horwitz found that, of 500 participants in one US city, 21 percent 'indicated avoidance of public activities because of embarrassment' (ibid.). Whether this embarrassment was due to CA, social phobia, social anxiety or something quite different is not discussed. Ultimately, if one accepts that CA is conceptualized as a specific type of social anxiety which manifests itself in a wide range of contextually variable communication choices, it does seem difficult to imagine how one might ever validate broad claims to prevalence and therefore consequence. Through the mystification of their specific origins in public speaking, and by their reliance on the quantification of social interaction, CA's methodological biases also generate a number of important cultural and ideological preconceptions.

Recontextualizing communication in adolescence

> Experience shows that communication skills can be taught ... all children benefit from learning skills which will make them better friends, better employees, better life-partners and better human beings.[5]

Validity and definitional issues aside, our main concerns with CA are to be located at a more theoretical and, to some extent, political level. Specifically, we are troubled by the instrumental, goal-directed notion of communication at the heart of CA—both as a field and as a construct. As such, CA seems to remain largely unaware of its own cultural and ideological stance. Of course, these issues are by no means unique to the field of CA, which, in effect, serves only as a vehicle for expressing our wider concerns about communication in adolescence. As we have suggested from the start, and as writers like Cameron (2000) and we ourselves (see Thurlow, 2001; 2003) have argued elsewhere, the problems underlying approaches such as CA are those which also characterize the dominant paradigms of conventional ('social scientific') communication theory and application more generally. They are also indicative, or even constitutive, of common themes in popular discourse—as exemplified by the BT statements quoted above and at the start of this section.

Perhaps one of the most striking aspects of the literature on CA is how the notion of 'communication' is itself handled. While CA is at times discussed in the context of written and sung communication, for the most part the literature clearly privileges *oral* communication—whether in the form of group discussions, informal conversations or public speeches. Having said which, in one definition, Richmond and McCroskey (1998:1), for example, do present human communication as 'the process by which a person (or persons) stimulates meaning in the mind of another person (or persons) through the use of verbal and/or nonverbal messages.' In spite of this somewhat more inclusive, multichannel conceptualization, CA is nonetheless most commonly premised on a more conventional notion of communication competence as spoken and transactional—most notably in the very particular context of speech-making and other forms of public address. The instrumentality and specificity of CA invariably relegates, if not ignores, nonverbal communicative forms (e.g., listening and silence) and everyday relational or phatic functions (*cf* Coupland, 2000; Jaworski, 1993). In this vein, the field of CA puts a great deal of emphasis on communication 'skills' and attaining 'appropriate' or 'effective' communication; these terms, however, often remain unspecified and unqualified. Certainly, they usually remain unproblematized (Fairclough, 1992).

Arising from this first concern about CA's inherent prioritization of talk is the extent to which it thereby devalues taciturnity/quietude more generally. For us, this speaks more of a cultural bias than it does of the realities of everyday communication. Although researchers in the field recognize that quality does not necessarily equal quantity—and vice versa—the underlying assumption in CA is always that loquacity is tantamount to *good* communication, which echoes widely held cultural beliefs (Cameron, 2000; Philipsen *et al.*, 1999). For the specific situational demands of public speech-making, this may make some sense; however, CA typically assumes far greater applicability. The inherent value judgment in CA is exemplified in the following extract, which on the surface seems uncontroversial, but for the fact that no attempt is made to challenge the prejudice which it highlights:

> ...the student who seldom interacts with peers, seldom asks questions in class, seldom goes to social functions, and rarely responds to the teacher's questions might be perceived negatively by peers as slow, unreliable, noncaring, or perhaps even as a troublemaker. (Richmond & McCroskey, 1998: 28)

In evaluating young people without question against models of communication such as the one proposed by CA, a hegemonic bias is thereby reinforced which promotes normative control rather than encourages diversity—even within any Western 'standard' (see above). As Jaworski & Sachdev (2004) have noted, this failure to challenge the institutional and societal construction of shyness as always negative—rather than a matter of personal preference or communicative choice—can have a potentially very problematic gate-keeping effect on young people's futures when teachers are encouraged to value the expressive/talkative over the reserved/quiet.

There is clearly a tendency among CA writers—as with so many communication scholars—to render communication overly problematic and individual (*cf* Coupland *et al.*, 1991), and to pathologize the nonnormative—in this case, the apprehensive or quiet. Shyness/apprehension is also typically conceived in behavioral terms as non-communication—specifically, absence of talk—which itself presupposes an 'off-on' model of communication and excludes the possibility that taciturnity (silence) can itself be communicative—and powerfully so (Jaworski, 1993).[6] Moreover, shyness is throughout, either implicitly or explicitly, equated with a lack of communication skill. Skillful communication is held to be verbal, oral, and active; reticence, on the other hand, is linked to a lack of success in 'social, work, and school relationships' (Richmond & McCroskey, 1998: 25). This is a way of thinking about human interaction which is premised on a largely quantified and commodified notion of communication. There is little space here for a more socially-constructed communication, by which judgments of 'good,' 'effective,' 'shy' and even 'skillful' would be understood as co-

constructed social realities rooted in institutional ideologies and relations of power.

Cameron (2000) provides a valuable critique of the ubiquity and dominance of the instrumentalist communication paradigm in educational settings—for which CA openly promotes itself. This fashion for measurable and 'transferable' outcomes forms part of a much broader shift in education away from the teaching of content (i.e., what you *know*) to skills training (i.e., what you can *do*), and itself has been brought upon in part by the shift to a service-oriented economy in which communication skills are increasingly valued. For Fairclough (1996), this has resulted in what he calls the 'technologization of communication.' As such, certain acceptable communication skills also become a form of symbolic capital (*cf* Bourdieu, 1991) by which the ability to speak (and write) in a particular way becomes more valuable than what it is you say and the reasons why you say it. This new (often hidden) agenda is, however, hierarchical, socially differentiated and informed by the interests of class and commerce. As Cameron (2000: 130) notes, education in particular plays a large role in 'distributing the cultural and linguistic capital that communication skills represent, and it does so in ways that reflect and reproduce social differences' or inequalities. Although we do not mean unfairly to single it out as being either all bad or especially bad, the notion of CA is one way in which certain communication choices (*speaking* actively, articulately and frequently) come to be privileged as 'good,' and other communication choices (listening, reticence, quietness) become uniformally ranked as 'bad'—or at least troublesome. For us, it is certainly no coincidence that 'at-risk' students from lower socioeconomic backgrounds show higher levels of CA than do more privileged, 'gifted' students (Chesebro *et al.*, 1992; Rosenfeld *et al.*, 1995).

As we suggested at the beginning, a central part of popular and institutional discourses on communication these days is the belief that communication is a 'natural' panacea for a multiplicity of social ills. Talking, it is widely believed, will make everything all right: from family breakdown, to romantic conflict, to international disputes. This is a mythology which not only belies the realities of human communication itself, but also conceals important structural factors and inequalities. So, when CA scholars like Chesebro *et al.* (1992: 345) write that 'effective oral communication is likely to play a critical role in reversing the outcome predicted for at-risk students,' the structural reasons why some children are more 'at risk' than others is very unfortunately written out of the discussion. Nor is it acknowledged that 'gifted' children tend to be of a different socioeconomic class than 'at-risk' students—something which presumably cannot sensibly be attributed (soley, if at all) to their poor communication skills.[7] The implication that a variety of problems are caused by 'poor' communication—or any neatly identifiable apprehension—and thus can be solved by improving one's communication 'skills' too readily assumes, then, that each speaker should communicate in the same way. And yet 'ways of speaking' (indeed, the choice not to speak at all) are an important part of people's self-presentation and identity construction. It is hard not to wonder whether training young people to communicate in a preconceived, acceptable way is not simply a means by which to discipline them into an institutional order rather than to truly empower them.

Although CA generally downplays or disregards contextual and institutional factors that may encourage some people to be apprehensive, or, alternatively, to decide strategically to refrain from communicating verbally, Crozier (2001) in fact notes that many students labeled shy or reticent do not remain so when in situations with friends and family. For example, Asendorpf and Meier (1993 in Crozier) found that there was no difference between shy and sociable children in out-of-school contexts. Thus it appears that the institutional setting of a classroom is the trigger for many 'apprehensive' behaviors, which could have alternate causes such as social situations, conflict with an instructor, boredom or daydreaming (Crozier, 2001). The overreliance on individual cognitive 'structures' of CA as a 'cause' of shy behavior ignores such contextual factors. Instead of thinking in terms of a person's 'being afraid to talk,' and thereby laying blame with the individual, CA scholars might do better to consider how people may be made to feel intimidated, devalued or undermined by cultural norms and institutional expectations.

A disregard for contextual factors has even more practical ramifications for an approach like that of CA. Speaking of shyness, Crozier (2001), for example, points out that being tested in an institutional setting by a stranger inherently increases nervousness and anxiety. (This is in much the same way that people's blood pressure typically rises when measured in a doctor's surgery.) However, in using a self-report instrument (e.g., the PRCA-24—see Note 2) to assess CA, a person is required to identify and report correctly his or her cognitive state at a particular time; as such another series of assumptions are made which are not unproblematic. This type of *mentalist* approach to investigating the subtleties of human communication and other social behavior has long since been critiqued as unreliable (see, for example, Potter & Wetherell, 1987; Harré & Stearns, 1995). Report-based measures for investigating complex, situated social behavior presupposes accessible, coherent internal states (e.g., feelings, motivations, attitudes and personality traits) divorced from the institutional and interactional context in which they are first experienced and then reported. Mental constructs such as memory, belief, and apprehension are, by necessity, also discursively realized. By the same reasoning, young people's apprehension in communication is surely situated in/by personal, interpersonal and educational social practice, and, as such, may have no 'inner referent' (Potter & Wetherell, 1987: 179) to begin with. It is important at least that communication scholars especially start addressing some of these epistemological issues—and most certainly before any serious attempt is made to promote a *genetic* explanation for communication behaviors (see Beatty & McCroskey, 2001).

Of course it is not really possible to hold scholars totally responsible for the ways in which lay people or other nonexperts take up or appropriate their ideas. Nevertheless, the fact remains that, in a Foucauldian framework of power/knowledge, scholarly research both generates and legitimates ideas beyond academia (*cf* Burman, 1994; Davis, 1990). For example, Horwitz's (2002) book *Communication Apprehension: Origins and Management* is a striking example of how the instrumentalist, individualizing approach of CA has been taken up in a clinical setting and, arguably, (mis)applied more widely. Presenting itself as a guide for speech-language pathologists to the treatment of CA patients (sic), Horwitz's book hinges on the incorrect assumption (see Allen & Bourhis, 1996) that the treatment of CA necessarily results in behavioral change—and, by extension, major life changes. On this basis, the 'real-life' case studies that appear throughout Horwitz's book all follow much the same trajectory: a person with 'poor' communication skills suffers from a series of problems (e.g., low self-esteem, lack of success at work), is identified or self-identifies as communication apprehensive, is treated through a series of therapeutic visits, is cured, and has a better life as a result (e.g., finds a new job, takes an exciting trip, becomes successful). As such, this book exemplifies the sway of popular misconceptions about communication, as well as highlights the need for scholars to examine their own complicity in promoting these misconceptions, however inadvertently.

Reconceiving young people's communication

What we would like to do in the last part of this chapter is to point very briefly to an alternative way of approaching communication in adolescence—both theoretically and in practice. For the most part, these ideas are based on the framework of *communication awareness* which, in responding to some of the issues outlined at the start of our chapter, proposes the value of approaching communication from the perspective of young people themselves (see Thurlow, 2001). Importantly, this framework is rooted in key epistemological precedents established by earlier research in the areas of communication ethnography (e.g., Katriel & Philipsen, 1981), language awareness (e.g., Hawkins, 1984) and folk linguistics (e.g., Preston, 1993).[8]

One major rationale for researching communication in adolescence these days is to find more suitable and sensitive ways of 'empowering' young people with the kind of 'communication capital' (Thurlow, 2003 after Bourdieu, 1991) they need in order to face increasingly complex social and economic challenges and to respond more successfully to the heightened semioticization of contemporary life (see also Lash & Urry, 1994). This should, however, only ever be done by means of what Fairclough (1992: 16) calls a critical needs-based approach, which he explains thus:

> Links should constantly be made between work on the development of [communication] awareness and the [communication] practices of the learner. This practice must be 'purposeful'. That is, it must be tied to the learner's *real wishes and needs* to communicate with specific people. (emphasis ours)

In this sense, approaches to assessing and developing young people's communication should be first and foremost rooted in their existing capabilities and understandings, such that they are also encouraged to think of their own (and others') communication practices with reference to everyday, firsthand experiences, as well as to relational and institutional contexts of power and inequality. In the tradition of communication ethnographers, the best place to start therefore is by asking young people what they already know about communication (*cf* Katriel & Philipsen, 1981).

Adults are always problematizing young people's communication (see, for example, Drury & Dennison, 1999; Williams & Garrett, 2002) and yet few studies explicitly examine communication from the perspective of young people themselves. This is all the more surprising given how much is also written about the state of young people's communication in the media. Within the field of language and communication research, Baxter and Goldsmith (1990: 383) have attested to 'the rich communicative resources with which [teenagers] frame their everyday accounts to others of their own and others' communicative practices.' Other isolated examples of research in which young people have been asked to reflect directly on communication include de Klerk's (1997; see also chapter 7, this volume) work on young people's use of expletives and Garrett and his colleagues' study of young people's language attitudes (e.g., Garrett *et al.*, 2004; see also chapter 3, this volume). In addition, there are also examples from other fields, such as psychology, in which researchers have examined communication in a way which prioritizes young people's firsthand accounts (e.g., Hortaçsu, 1989; Noller & Bagi, 1985; Rosenthal & Peart, 1996).

In addition to this handful of studies, some of the only other research we know of which focuses explicitly on young people's existing understandings of communication is that done by researchers working for the Trust for the Study of Adolescence in England (e.g., Drury *et al.*, 1998, 1999; see also chapter 13 here). What this work has in common with the more recent findings of our own (e.g., Thurlow, 2001; in prep), is that it shows how, contrary to adult stereotypes, young people often understand communication in complex ways and certainly in ways which are more contextually sensitive than mainstream communication scholarship sometimes presents it.

> Young people may not be in communication with adults or in ways which adults would like them to be, but this does not mean that they have no sense of communication or that they necessarily have an awareness different from adults. (Thurlow, 2001: 220)

Establishing what young people already know about, and understand by, communication addresses an otherwise noticeable hiatus in the academic literature which writers have for some time suggested was worth addressing (e.g., Spitzberg & Cupach, 1984). This research also complements existing social and life-span research in other fields. Patterns of interaction and so-called youth culture are changing all the time, so research which reports afresh on any aspect of the lives of young people helps to sustain the validity and currency of both academic and applied understanding. Young people's own ideas also offer a potential starting point not only for further research, theorization and intervention, but also for classroom discussion and intervention. In these terms, and in an attempt to move away from unduly pathologizing competence-based models of communication, it is also important that young people not be evaluated willy-nilly against preconceived standards of what is (is not) 'appropriate' or acceptable in only certain very specific settings (Fairclough, 1992). In other words, they should not simply be taught *how* to communicate (properly), but also be taught *about* communication, and about how some forms of communication come to be valued and codified as correct (or proper) and others do not. Otherwise, argues Cameron (2000: 132), we run the risk of merely *styling* young people rather than skilling or empowering them.

Acknowledgement

We are particularly grateful to Matt McGarrity for his very careful peer review of this chapter and for bringing our attention at the last minute to Jo Sprague's reassuring critique of the dominant social scientific approach to communication education research (e.g., Sprague, 1993).

Notes

1. The first of these two statements comes from a BT 'social investment and corporate responsibility' program titled *Communication Skills for Life*—see

<www.bteducation.bt.com/education/for_you/making_the_case.cfm> (accessed 10 January 2005). Based on an earlier BT program, the second statement was made as part of a 1998 consultation with the UK government's Select Committee on Culture, Media and Sport—see <http://www.publications.parliament.uk/pa/cm199798/cmselect/cmcumeds/818/8070919.htm> (accessed 10 Jan 2005). See also Note 5 below.

2. McCroskey and his colleagues have developed a series of self-report questionnaires for assessing CA and related aspects; the PRCA-24 scale is the standard measure for CA itself. Items on this scale include the following (out of a possible 24):

    - *Engaging in a group discussion with new people makes me tense & nervous.*
    - *I am afraid to express myself at meetings.*
    - *Ordinarily I am very calm and relaxed in conversations.*
    - *Certain parts of my body feel very tense and rigid while I am giving a speech.*

    Other scales developed by McCroskey and his colleagues include WAT (writing apprehension), TOSA (singing apprehension) and PRICA (intercultural apprehension). A situational measure of CA is the SCAM scale. (More information is available at <www.jamescmccroskey.com>.) A short example of the type of scales used is FOP (fear of physician—see Richmond *et al.*, 1998):

    Please indicate how well each statement describes how you feel when communicating with your physician employing the following scale:

    1 = not at all; 2 = somewhat; 3 = moderately so; 4 = very much so
    _____ *1. When communicating with my physician, I feel tense.*
    _____ *2. When communicating with my physician, I feel calm.*
    _____ *3. When communicating with my physician, I feel jittery.*
    _____ *4. When communicating with my physician, I feel nervous.*
    _____ *5. When communicating with my physician, I feel relaxed.*

3. Willingness to communicate (WTC) is defined as 'a person's general attitude towards talking with others' (Richmond & McCroskey, 1998:38).
4. From our own investigations, it seems that the widely cited figure in the CA literature is extrapolated from a variety of surveys that span more than 30 years and include some 60,000 participants. Although this is an impressive research population, the individual studies differ both in methodology and in what was measured; although some look at CA, and some at social anxiety, others consider the effectiveness of systematic desensitization as the usual 'treatment' for CA.
5. This comment by Phillips (1998—quoted by Cameron, 2000: 125) is from a research project funded by another of BT's program (see Note 1 above) *FutureTalk: A Life Support System for the 21ˢᵗ Century.*

6. Studies looking to link CA and scholastic achievement have had mixed success (see, for example, Ericson & Gardener, 1992; Dobos, 1996). Along similar lines, Jaworski and Sachdev (2004) note that there is no research evidence for a correlation between amount of speaking in class and academic achievement.

7. In a cursory review of a major English-language dictionary and thesaurus, we noticed how the semantic field indexed by 'shyness' does reveal a certain cultural ambivalence similar to other communicative behaviors such as small talk (see Coupland, 2000) and silence (see Jaworski, 1993). In addition to an apparent vagueness between the *incommunicative* (i.e., not able) and *uncommunicative* (i.e., not willing or inclined), and an ambiguity between *taciturnity* and *reticence*, we identified a contradictory valence running across the range of synonyms for 'shy' with more negatively connoted terms (e.g., curt, sullen, monosyllabic, evasive, antisocial, inarticulate), more 'neutral' terms (e.g., secretive, cautious, guarded, reserved, laconic, unsociable) and more positively connoted terms (e.g., concise, succinct, self-contained, mum). It is unclear why CA writing eschews these common terms or avoids theorizing their semantico-lexical boundaries in relation to CA.

8. As part of more recent research, Thurlow is also looking to extend his interest in awareness to include young people's sense of themselves as communicators (e.g., Thurlow, in prep).

9. This chapter is based on research funded in part by the UK's *Nuffield Foundation* in the form of a grant awarded to Crispin Thurlow (No. SGS/00692, 2002–2004).

References

Allen, M. & Bourhis, J. (1996). The relationship of communication apprehension to communication behavior: A meta-analysis. *Communication Quarterly*, 44(2), 214–227.

Asendorpf, J. B. & Meier, G. H. (1993). Personality effects on children's speech in everyday life: Sociability-mediated exposure and shyness-mediated reactivity to social situations. *Journal of Personality and Social Psychology*, 64, 1072–1083.

Ayers, J. (1997). *A Component Theory of Communication Apprehension*. Ruston, WA: Communication Ventures.

Baxter, L. A. & Goldsmith, D. (1990). Cultural terms for communication events among some American high school adolescents. *Western Journal of Speech Communication*, 54, 377–394.

Beatty, M. J. & McCroskey, J. C. (2001). *The Biology of Communication: A Communibio Logical Perspective*. Cresskill, NJ: Hampton Press.

Beebe, S. A., Beebe, S. J. & Ivy, D. K. (2004). *Communication: Principles for a Lifetime*. Boston: Allyn-Bacon.

Bourdieu, P. (1991/1999). Language and symbolic power. In A. Jaworski & N. Coupland (eds), *The Discourse Reader* (pp. 502–13). London: Routledge.

Burman, E. (1994). *Deconstructing Developmental Psychology*. London: Routledge.

Cameron, D. (2000). *Good to Talk? Living and Working in a Communication Culture*. London: Sage.

Chesebro, J. W., McCroskey, J. C., Atwater, D. F., Bahrenfuss, R. M., Cawelti, G., Gaudino, J. L. & Hodges, H. (1992). Communication apprehension and self-perceived communication competence in at-risk students. *Communication Education* 41, 345–360.

Chisholm, L. & Hurrelmann, K. (1995). Adolescence in modern Europe. Pluralized transition patterns and their implications for personal and social risks. *Journal of Adolescence*, 18, 129–158.

Coupland, J. (ed.). (2000). *Small Talk*. London: Longman.

Coupland, N., Wiemann, J. M. & Giles, H. (1991). Talk as 'problem' and communication as 'miscommunication': An integrative analysis. In N. Coupland, H. Giles & J. M. Wiemann (eds), *'Miscommunication' and Problematic Talk* (pp. 1–17). Newbury Park, CA: Sage.

Crozier, W. R. (2001). *Understanding Shyness: Psychological Perspectives*. Basingstoke: Palgrave.

Davis, J. (1990). *Youth and the Condition of Britain: Images of Adolescent Conflict*. London: Athlone.

de Klerk, V. (1997). The role of expletives in the construction of masculinity. In S. Johnson & U. H. Meinhof (eds), *Language and Masculinity* (pp. 144–158). Oxford: Blackwell.

Dobos, J. (1996). Collaborative learning: effects of student expectations and communication apprehension on student motivation. *Communication Education*, 45, 293–312.

Drury, J. & Dennison, C. (1999). Individual responsibility versus social category problems: Benefit officers' perceptions of communication with young people. *Journal of Youth Studies*, 2 (2), 171–192.

Drury, J., Catan, L., Dennison, C. & Brody, R. (1998). Exploring teenagers' accounts of bad communication: A new basis for intervention. *Journal of Adolescence*, 21, 177–196.

Ericson, P. M. & Gardener, J. W. (1992). Two longitudinal studies of communication apprehension and its effects on college students' success. *Communication Quarterly*, 40(2), 127–137.

Fairclough, N. (1992). The appropriacy of appropriateness. In N. Fairclough (ed.), *Critical Discourse Awareness* (pp. 20–50). London: Longman.

Fairclough, N. (1993). Critical discourse analysis and the marketization of public discourse: The universities. *Discourse & Society*, 4, 133–168.

Fairclough, N. (1996). Technologization of discourse. In C. R. Caldas-Coulthard & M. Coulthard (eds), *Texts and Practices: Readings in Critical Discourse Analysis* (pp. 71–83). London: Routledge.

Fairclough, N. (1999). Global capitalism and critical awareness of language. *Language Awareness*, 8 (2), 71–83.

Falchikov, N. (1989). Adolescent images of adolescence. *Journal of Adolescence*, 12, 139–154.

Gamble, T. K & Gamble, M. (2001). *Communication Works*. New York: McGraw-Hill.

Garrett, P., Coupland, N. & Williams, A. (2004). Adolescents' lexical repertoires of peer evaluation: 'Boring prats' and 'English snobs'. In A. Jaworski, N. Coupland & D. Galasinski (eds), *Metalanguage: Social and Ideological Perspectives* (pp. 193–226). Berlin: Mouton de Gruyter.

Giroux, H. (2003). Betraying the intellectual tradition: Public intellectuals and the crisis of youth. *Language and Intercultural Communication*, 3 (3), 172–186.

Harré, R. & Stearns, P. (eds). (1995). *Discursive Psychology in Practice*. London: Sage.

Hawkins, E. (1984). *Awareness of Language: An Introduction*. Cambridge: Cambridge University Press.

Hockey, J. & James, A. (1993). *Growing Up and Growing Old: Ageing and Dependency in the Life Course*. London: Sage.

Hortaçsu, N. (1989). Targets of communication during adolescence. *Journal of Adolescence*, 12, 253–263.

Horwitz, B. (2002). *Communication Apprehension: Origins and Management*. Albany, NY: Singular / Thomson Learning.

Jaworski, A. (1993). *The Power of Silence: Social and Pragmatic Perspectives*. London: Sage.

Jaworski, A. & Sachdev, I. (2004). Teachers' beliefs about students' talk and silence: Constructing academic success and failure through metapragmatic comments. In A. Jaworski, N. Coupland & D. Galasinski (eds), *Metalanguage: Social and Ideological Perspectives* (pp. 227–244). Berlin: Mouton de Gruyter.

Katriel, T. & Philipsen, G. (1981). 'What we need is communication': 'Communication' as a cultural term in some American speech. *Communication Monographs*, 48, 301–17.

Kelly, L., Duran, R. L. & Zolten, J. J. (2001). The effect of reticence on college students' use of electronic mail to communicate with faculty. *Communication Education*, 50, 170–176.

Kuhlemeier, H., van den Bergh, H. & Rijlaarsdam, G. (2002). The dimensionality of speaking and writing: A multilevel factor analysis of situational, task and school effects. *British Journal of Educational Psychology*, 72 (4), 467–482.

Lash, S. & Urry, J. (1994). *Economies of Signs and Spaces*. London: Sage.

Leary, M. (1983). The conceptual distinctions are important: Another look at communication apprehension and related constructs. *Human Communication Research*, 10 (2), 305–312.

MacIntyre, P. D., Baker, S. C., Clement, R. & Donovan, L. A. (2003). Sex and age effects on willingness to communicate, anxiety, perceived competence, and L2 motivation among junior high school French immersion students. *Language Learning*, 53 (1), 137–65.

Manning, P. & Ray, G. (1993). Shyness, self-confidence, and social interaction. *Social Psychology Quarterly*, 56 (3), 178–192.

McCroskey, J. C. (1970). Measures of communication-bound anxiety. *Speech Monographs*, 31, 79–84.

McCroskey, J. C. (1982). Oral communication apprehension: A reconceptualization. In M. Burgoon (ed.), *Communication Yearbook 6* (pp. 136–170). Beverly Hills, CA: Sage.

McCroskey, J. C. (1984). The communication apprehension perspective. In J. A. Daly and J. C. McCroskey (eds), *Avoiding Communication: Shyness, Reticence, and Communication Apprehension* (pp. 13–38). Beverly Hills: Sage.

McCroskey, J. C., Booth-Butterfield, S. & Payne, S. K. (1989). The impact of communication apprehension on college student retention and success. *Communication Quarterly*, 37, 100–107.

McCroskey, J. C. & Richmond, V. P. (1982). Communication apprehension and shyness: Conceptual and operational distinctions. *Central States Speech Journal*, 33, 458–468.

McCroskey, L. L., Richmond, V. P. & McCroskey, J. C. (2002). The scholarship of teaching and learning: Contributions from the discipline of communication. *Communication Education*, 51(4), 383–391.

Mortimer, J. T. & Larson, R. W. (eds). (2002). *The Changing Adolescent Experience: Societal Trends and the Transition to Adulthood*. New York: Cambridge University Press.

Noller, P. & Bagi, S. (1985). Parent-adolescent communication. *Journal of Adolescence*, 8, 125–144.

Pearson, J. C. & Nelson, P. E. (1999). *An Introduction to Human Communication: Understanding and Sharing*. New York: McGraw-Hill.

Philipsen, G., Horkley, N. & Huhman, M. (1999). *What do people mean when they say 'communication'*. Paper presented at the 49th Annual ICA Conference, San Francisco, CA.

Phillips, A. (1998). *Communication: A Key Skill for Education*. London: The BT Forum Education Consultation Report.

Potter, J. & Wetherell, M. (1987). *Discourse and Social Psychology: Beyond Attitudes and Behaviour*. London: Sage.

Preston, D. R. (1993). The uses of folk linguistics. *International Journal of Applied Linguistics*, 3 (2), 181–259.

Proctor, R. F., Douglas, A. T., Garera-Izquierdo, T. & Wartman, S. L. (1994). Approach, avoidance, and apprehension: Talking with high-CA students about getting help. *Communication Education*, 43 (4), 312–321.

Richmond, V. P. & McCroskey, J. C. (1998). *Communication Apprehension, Avoidance, and Effectiveness*. Boston: Allyn and Bacon.

Richmond, V. P., Smith, R. S., Heisel, A. M. & McCroskey, J. C. (1998). The impact of communication apprehension and fear of talking with a physician and perceived medical outcomes. *Communication Research Reports*, 15, 344–353.

Rosenfeld, L. B., Grant, C. H. & McCroskey, J. C. (1995). Communication apprehension and self-perceived communication competence of academically gifted students. *Communication Education*, 44 (1), 79–86.

Rosenthal, D. & Peart, R. (1996). The rules of the game: Teenagers communicating about sex. *Journal of Adolescence*, 19, 321–332.

Spitzberg, B. H. & Cupach, W. R. (eds). (1984). *Interpersonal communication competence*. London: Sage.

Sprague, J. (1993). Retrieving the research agenda for communication education: Asking the pedagogical questions that are "embarrassments to theory". *Communication Education*, 42, 106–122.

Thurlow, C. (2001). Talkin' 'bout my communication: Communication awareness in early adolescence. *Language Awareness*, 10 (2&3), 213–231.

Thurlow, C. (2003). Teenagers in communication, teenagers on communication. *Journal of Language and Social Psychology*, 22 (1), 50–57.

Thurlow, C. (in prep). A study of young people's self-awareness in communication: Directions for critical understanding.

Watson, A. K. & Monroe, E. E. (1990). Academic achievement: A study of relationships of IQ, communication apprehension, and teacher perception. *Communication Reports*, 3, 28–36.

Williams, A. & Garrett, P. (2002). Communication evaluations across the lifespan: From adolescent storm and stress to elder aches and pains. *Journal of Language and Social Psychology*, 21, 101–126.

5

Hearing their voices: Young people, citizenship and online news

Cynthia Carter and Stuart Allan

Precisely what counts as 'citizenship' is being openly contested in Western, democratic societies today (Crick, 2000; Furlong and Cartmel, 1997; Jones, 2003; Roche, 1999; Stevenson, 2003). For quite some time now, public participation in elections (both local and national) has been regarded as a cause of concern, particularly with respect to the involvement of young people. In the United States, for example, some 40 percent of the electorate did not vote in the 2004 election. Of those who did vote, fewer than one in ten were aged 18 to 24 (about the same proportion of the electorate as in 2000, when 29 percent of 18–24 year olds voted for president). 'Young people don't vote in large numbers,' Courtney Hickson, 22, editor in chief of the University of Connecticut's student newspaper, *Daily Campus*, stated prior to the election, 'because they are largely ignored by politicians' (cited in Glover, 2004). In the United Kingdom, the 2001 general election witnessed the lowest voter turnout since 1918. Out of all those eligible to vote, only 59 percent marked their ballot paper. Worse still, in the 18–24 year old age group, only 39 percent cast a vote.

This type of election data suggests that a worrying percentage of young people are failing to exercise their democratic rights as citizens. This appears to be so despite the determined efforts of many educators to engage them in the world of politics. In the case of the US, where school curricula are developed and delivered at the state level, civics education has long been taught as a central subject in high schools. In the 1960s, 'civics education' was usually comprised of separate courses on civics, democracy and government, alongside a separate one on US history. Since the early 1970s, however, perceptions that teenagers have become increasingly apathetic about politics have grown, which in turn has affected how civics education is delivered. Today, most states have condensed it into a single course on American government, retaining United States history as a separate course. Citizenship skills are generally perceived to be a part of civics education, comprising the 'knowledge, skills and dispositions' that teenagers need in order to participate effectively in politics (Education Commission of the States, 2003). Party leaders, alarmed by the prospect of losing 'the youth vote' come election time, have been renewing their efforts to find ways to reach out to young people disillusioned with contemporary politics.[2]

Turning to the United Kingdom, there have been similar concerns about teenagers' apparent lack of interest in party politics. To this end, the national Department for Education and Skills (DfES) launched the National Curriculum (a standardized educational program across the UK) citizenship education scheme in the autumn of 2002, which pupils study during 'Key Stage 3' of their secondary school education (between the ages of 11–14) and 'Key Stage 4' (14–19).[3] Topics include government, elections and voting, as well as human rights, cultural diversity, war, crime and animal rights, among others (Department for Education and Skills, 2003). The DfES 'Citizenship' site offers information for teachers, pupils and parents about citizenship study, outlining what the DfES believes to be the main issues, and how best to define what citizenship means. Firstly, it is said to be about 'social and moral responsibility,' where the emphasis is on building pupils' 'self confidence and socially and morally responsible behavior both in and beyond the classroom.' Secondly, citizenship entails 'community involvement.' That is, young people are encouraged to become involved in the activities of local people. A 'good citizen' is described as one who is 'politically literate,' that is, knowledgeable about democratic political structures. Young people are encouraged to learn about 'the institutions, problems and practices of our democracy and how to make themselves *effective* in the life of the nation, locally, regionally and nationally through skills and values as well as knowledge—a concept wider than political knowledge alone.'[4]

Nongovernmental organizations have also contributed to the development of citizenship education for teenagers in the UK. For example, the Institute for Citizenship (IC) recently produced a series of 'citizenship education resources' for teachers and students.[5] The thinking behind the development of these lessons is that more needs to be done to ensure that future citizens feel more connected to the state and civil society than is currently the case. There is no clear definition of citizenship in IC materials, however. In the case of the website, though, it is stated that citizenship is about teenagers 'having their say, being involved, making things happen [and] taking part in decisions.'[6] In other words, what is being assumed here is that young people's opinions are important and ought to figure prominently in developing future definitions of what constitutes citizenship in the United Kingdom. One of the IC's key citizenship projects is 'Democracy through Citizenship,' funded for three years by a UK charitable trust, the Joseph Rowntree Foundation. This project consists of a National Curriculum Key Stage 3 unit called 'Introduction to Citizenship.' In this unit, young people learn about the concepts of community and individual rights and responsibilities, where community is defined primarily as a local concept (home, school, town/city).

In considering these and related initiatives, it quickly becomes apparent that ongoing attempts to encourage the active participation of young people in public life are encountering serious difficulties. One researcher after the next in this area is expressing their concern about the problems associated with changing the lived culture of citizenship. Teenagers, many of them fear, are becoming increasingly disengaged from a political process which they believe largely ignores them and their interests. Political detachment, as Buckingham (2000) argues, can be interpreted as a response to young people's 'positive exclusion from that domain—in effect, as a response to disenfranchisement' (2000: 218). Communication research has done little to address this sense of disenfranchisement among young people, because it has tended to focus almost exclusively on 'adult' communication. This relative neglect of issues related to communication in adolescence has been accompanied by a widely held view that adolescence is a problematic period in the lifespan. According to Thurlow and Williams [see chapter 1, this volume], this situation has resulted in exacerbating the communicative disenfranchisement of teenagers. Here, then, it is important to note the growing number of researchers who recognize the importance of examining afresh the role of media education for young people in this context.

It is with this challenge in mind that our chapter focuses, in the first instance, on media education in the United Kingdom. Several pertinent issues, not least that of 'media literacy,' are identified for analysis in the course of making the case for a critical media pedagogy that emphasizes the development of forms of media critique that politically empower young people. Such critiques, we shall argue, need to acknowledge the importance of their lived experiences of everyday media cultures while, at the same time, encouraging them to continuously question their own assumptions in a self-reflexive manner. Next, and in order to contribute to new directions for research inquiry along these lines, attention turns to examine postings made by young people to the British Broadcasting Corporation's (BBC) *Newsround* (news for children and young people) website. Of particular interest, it will be shown, is the extent to which these postings highlight their awareness of world events and a willingness to engage in political debate as citizens in the making.

Media education

The origins of media education in Britain, it has been often pointed out, are traceable at least as far back as to the publication of F. R. Leavis and Denys Thompson's book *Culture and Environment* in 1933. Their savage indictment of what they perceived to be the media's degenerative influences, particularly where the corruption of the morality of young people was concerned, pinpointed a host of fears about the cultural decline of society. According to Leavis and Thompson:

> Those who in school are offered (perhaps) the beginnings of education in taste are exposed, out of school, to the competing exploitation of the cheapest emotional responses; films, newspapers, publicity in all its forms, commercially-catered fiction—all offer satisfaction at the lowest level, and inculcate the choosing of the most immediate pleasures, got with the least effort .
> (Leavis & Thompson, 1933: 3)

As they proceed to make clear, responsibility for instilling in teenagers the means to uphold 'civilizing values' would have to be borne by teachers of English literary criticism. Young people needed to be equipped with the means to distinguish between 'authentic' and 'inauthentic' culture as a matter of 'taste,' Leavis and Thompson argued, if the 'human spirit' was to be sustained. Once again, in their words:

> ...if one is to believe in education at all one must believe that something worth doing can be done. And if one is to believe in anything one must believe in education. The moral for the educator is to be more ambitious: the training of literary taste must be supplemented by something more... [W]e are committed to more consciousness; that way, if any, lies salvation. We cannot, as we might in a healthy state of culture, leave the citizen to be formed unconsciously by his [sic] environment; if anything like a worthy idea of satisfactory living is to be saved, he must be trained to discriminate and to resist.
> (Leavis & Thompson, 1933: 4–5)

The need to engage with media forms and practices in the classroom was therefore an exigent priority, they insisted, not least because the future of 'a world of depressed and cynical aimlessness' stood in the balance. The teaching of media criticism, if not quite respectable in their eyes, was nevertheless becoming increasingly inevitable. Once a student is provided with an awareness of adequate 'standards,' Leavis and Thompson maintained, 'the offerings of the mass media will appear cut down to size.'

One can only speculate, of course, about what Leavis and Thompson might have had to say about media studies as it is taught in secondary schools today, but there is no denying that the kinds of arguments they made then still echo in contemporary debates about media pedagogy. If the participants in current debates tend to be less inclined to use a language of 'taste' and 'discrimination' to express their convictions, many of them nevertheless continue to sound the alarm over what they perceive to be the damaging effects of media representations on teenagers. The rationale for media education, as a result, is often couched in the terms of 'media literacy.' A media-literate student, at least in this rather elitist formulation of the phrase, is one who has been sensitized to the ways in which various media institutions seek to 'distort' or 'falsify' reality in order to advance their (usually commercial) interests. As such, she or he will be sufficiently equipped to defend themselves against these harmful influences, and thereby be better able to uphold higher values of decency and a strong sense of moral purpose. Underlying this notion of media literacy, then, is the assumption that media education needs to operate at the level of inoculation. That is to say, students must be partly exposed to the debilitating 'effects' of media influence in the classroom so as to ultimately enhance their immunity from manipulation. In this way, teachers fulfil their role of ensuring the 'improvement' of the student's personal sense of refinement and her or his capacity for cultivated judgment.

It goes without saying, of course, that prefigured in any conception of how best to teach students how to analyze the media is an array of presuppositions about how students actually learn, and what they want and need to learn about. The type of 'Leavisite' or discriminatory approach briefly sketched above takes for granted the belief that students are willing and able to be instilled with the desire to resist the enticements of media texts and imagery. In other words, it assumes that students can learn to share their teacher's 'finer sensibilities,' and that once so qualified will feel compelled to elevate themselves from the realm of 'low' or 'popular' culture into that of 'high' culture or the 'fine arts.' No doubt there are contexts in which such an approach might be deemed relevant—the teaching of aesthetics in art history, for example, may be one—but there is little chance that this will prove to be the case in the media studies classroom. Far from regarding the media as pernicious purveyors of 'cheap thrills' or 'feeble-minded distractions,' today's media studies student is much more likely to consider different genres of media content as sources of intense self-identification and pleasure. Moreover, many such students are interested in learning how to make their own media texts, quite possibly with the hope of eventually finding employment in one of the media industries.

Regrettably it is the case that very little research has been conducted to date concerning precisely what it is that students are hoping to learn about the media in media studies programs. One such investigation, however, is a British Film Institute (BFI) Education Research Report by A.J.B. Barratt (1998), titled *Media Studies: What Students Think?* This report presents a range of findings drawn from a questionnaire distributed to approximately forty thousand 16 to 19 year-old media students via a free supplement in the popular magazine *Sight and Sound* in 1996. Some 4,125 questionnaires were returned (a sample of about 10 percent) from secondary school students on different programs. According to Barratt's (1998: 1) findings:

> Nearly three-quarters of the sample said they chose their course because they thought it might help them to get a career in the media. Over two-thirds said it was because they have an interest in TV and films, and they found the course relevant. Just over half said it was because of the practical component offered by certain courses. Only 4 per cent said it was because they thought Media Studies was an easy option. ...54 percent of the sample intend to do a Media Studies degree at university on completion of their course. 51 per cent would like to go into a career in the media.

This kind of evidence, while needing to be treated with caution given the limitations of the questionnaire, nevertheless produces an interesting insight into why media studies is one of the fastest-growing subjects for young people in this age range. Specifically, in attempting to discern the main reason for this popularity, Barratt's investigation suggests to him that it appears to be attributable to the perception among these students that media studies is highly relevant to their personal lives and experiences. And here, in our view at least, he makes a crucial point:

> Rather than dismiss this as evidence of its low cultural and educative value, as some do, it is possible to see this as a positive bonus in the classroom. What better pedagogical starting point is there than dealing with issues close to students' hearts, and which can draw upon and enlighten their everyday experiences? (Barratt, 1998: 16)

Few media teachers, it seems fair to say, are likely to deny that an appreciation of the importance of the 'everyday' for young people can inform critical pedagogical approaches to teaching and learning to advantage. The question remains, of course, as to how best to realize this objective in practice.

Bearing this question in mind, we would suggest that it is necessary to reconsider what 'media literacy' might mean for students learning to negotiate the processes of social inclusion and exclusion endemic to the 'knowledge society' around them. Kellner (2002), for example, argues that we need to develop 'multiple literacies' so as to better respond to the globalizing demands for a more informed, participatory and active citizenry in political, economic and cultural terms. Literacy, in this conception, 'comprises gaining competencies in effectively using socially constructed forms of communication and representation' (2002: 92). More specifically, media literacy 'helps people to use media intelligently, to discriminate and evaluate media content, to dissect media forms critically, and to investigate media effects and uses' (2002: 93). In the new multimedia environment, Kellner maintains, this type of literacy has never been more important, especially with regard to the development of skills to create 'good citizens' motivated to play an active role in social life. He points out that the same technologies of communication capable of turning 'spectators into cultural zombies' may, at the same time, be used to invigorate democratic debate and participation. The problem, of course, is how to bring about the latter on the terrain of the former. That is, how to take the texts of popular culture enjoyed by students seriously, recognizing and respecting their ideas, values and competencies, without 'romanticiz[ing] student views that may be superficial, mistaken, uninformed and full of various problematical biases' (2002: 94). One way forward, Kellner suggests, is to adapt new computer technologies to education so as to facilitate the development of new literacies [compare with McKay *et al.*— chapter 11, this volume].

In seeking to expand upon familiar conceptions of literacy, Kellner draws attention to emergent forms of what he terms 'computer literacy.' Important here, he argues, is the need to push this concept beyond its usual meaning, namely, as the technical ability to use computer programs and hardware. A broader definition, it follows, would attend to information and multimedia literacy as well. That is to say, Kellner's extended conception of computer literacy would include learning how to use computers, locate information via search engines, operate e-mail and list servers, and construct websites. Computer and information literacies, he writes, involve 'learning where information is found, how to access it, and how to organize, interpret and evaluate it' (2002: 95). At the same time, they also entail 'learning how to read hypertexts, to traverse the ever-changing fields of cyberculture, and to participate in a digital and interactive multimedia culture that encompasses work, education, politics, culture and everyday life' (2002: 95; see also Hassan, 2004; Lievrouw & Livingstone, 2002). Clearly at stake here, then, is the teaching of more than just technical forms of knowledge and skills. By stretching the notion of literacy to include new strategies of reading, writing, researching and communicating abilities appropriate to a larger computer culture, Kellner is helping to discern the conceptual space necessary to engage with an array of different, yet interrelated, types of media interaction among young people.

News on the web

Evidently, then, news discourses—online or otherwise—can be read against the grain, so to speak, so as to discern what journalists are implicitly telling young people about their role as citizens in a democracy. Seemingly 'commonsensical' choices routinely made in the language of news reporting, in particular, are likely to invite normative responses which may, in turn, have profound implications for the communicative enfranchisement of young people in our public culture.

Accordingly, our attention now turns to consider the news website provided for young people by the BBC. Operating in conjunction with its television counterpart, the *Newsround* website offers an important forum for its users to actively participate in dialogue and debate about news events, but also with respect to how and why these events are being reported in the way that they are for young audiences. Our examination of *Newsround* discussion boards highlights a number of points of engagement in young people's negotiation of news discourse. Needless to say, of course, we make no claim as to the quantitative representativeness of their comments. Rather, we cite extracts from discussions that illustrate a sense of participants' knowledge about world events and those which demonstrate a reflexive stance on the importance of young peoples' opinions as citizens in the making.[8]

Briefly, by way of background context, it is worth pointing out that *Newsround* launched its website (http://news.bbc.co.uk/cbbcnews/default.stm) in 2001. It offers considerable scope for young people to engage with a wider array of issues in the news, and is one of the few truly interactive sites for news available. Indeed, by and large, it covers a much broader range of issues than its television counterpart. Interestingly, for our purposes here, it may be noted that on its interactive message boards, where users comment upon stories as they feature in the news, young people often complain about how their views are often discounted as childish or completely ignored by adults. This is a criticism that is consistently voiced as a source of great frustration by many chat contributors, and understandably so. In our view, there are significant insights generated by young people in their online chat that could inform efforts to engage young people in politics (see also Jones, 2003; Livingstone, 2002). Such chat yields a rich source of information about teenagers' interests, experiences and knowledges. Chat also highlights the importance of equipping all young people with the tools of critical media analysis (Buckingham, 2000; Carter, 2004; Tidhar & Lemish, 2003). These tools are crucially important, as the discussion above would suggest, since they provide young people with the means to become much more politically enabled, engaged and active adult citizens.

Presently we turn our attention to an array of online messages posted by young people responding to two recent traumatic news events—the war in Iraq in 2003 and the Madrid train bombings in 2004—on the *Newsround* website.[9] Comments about these events, as might be expected, offer valuable evidence of users' knowledge of world events, their willingness to engage with differing points of view, and their perceptions of both similarities and differences with respect to how the adult news media tend to report such events. More specifically, we examine the message board 'What's in the News' that can be found online on *Newsround*,where many young people voice their opinions of these as well as a wide range of other political issues currently in the news. We also consider young people's posted email comments made in relation to specific news reports.

At the time of writing, the war in Iraq had been officially over for more than one year. However, the everyday reality of life in Iraq has been that attacks on Iraqi citizens and coalition soldiers have continued with little relief, even after Saddam Hussein's capture in December 2003, an event some political commentators had suggested at the time effectively marked the formal end of the conflict. As Zainab, 15, notes in response to *Newsround*'s online story on this event:

> Yep, we were so pleased to hear about the capture. My uncle was one of Saddam's victims. He was murdered and my parents came here. I hope there will be a fair trial, no punishment will justify what this man did to thousands of people. Somehow... I still don't trust the American government—like someone mentioned, he was propped up by them and given loads of weapons to use against his people. Saddam didn't just turn up this year, he was killing Iraqis for 20 yrs. That's what annoys me most. I don't know about execution... maybe he should do 5 years community service at the sewage works first—see how it feels. (posted 19 December 2003)

Young people discussing Iraq on the 'What's in the News' message board appear to use it as one of a number of strategies for understanding what is going on (many mention routinely reading and watching adults' and children's news and having discussions about news events with parents and friends), as well as how they see young people's place in the world, and how the news is shaping their thoughts on citizenship (Buckingham, 2000; Jones, 2003; Livingstone, 2002). Although these young people expect to have their views taken seriously by other users, of course, some of them point out that adults seem largely uninterested in what they have to say about the political significance of the war.

Other users, in sharp contrast, give voice to their view that adults are too inclined to want to protect them from certain news events, effectively withholding information which they believe might be too traumatic. For some users this is reasonable; for others, understandably enough, it is considered patronizing. In the words of 15-year-old Becca:

> If people would listen to children properly as if what we had to say was important (which it is) they would see the easiest way to sort things out. We, as children, see things simpler, without thinking about pride, shame or politics. War is something adults do for pride and politics, they can't admit they are wrong. (posted 25 March 2003; emphasis in original)

Although various young people admit in their online discussions that they were sometimes frightened about the war, what seems to upset some of them the most is a sense that adults appear to think that young people's views are ill-informed and of little value. On 'What's in the News,' young people repeatedly state that they want to be accepted as citizens who possess legitimate points of view and rights. After all, today's young people will have to live with the consequences of the actions of decisions taken today by adults, yet they rarely have the chance to influence these decisions. This point was made most clearly by 10-year-old Cara-Leigh, in response to a *Newsround* online story:

> I am very scared about the war with Iraq, because President Bush and Tony Blair are not giving our selves, 'children' a chance to speak about it, because it may change our lives. (posted 25 March 2003)

In early March 2003, thousands of schoolchildren (mainly teenagers) across the United Kingdom walked out of school to join antiwar marches. Five hundred or so made their way to the prime minister's residence at 10 Downing Street and held a sit-in at the gates to the street, blocking it. *Newsround* posted the story 'Did you march against the war?' which asked young people whether they participated in an antiwar protest. Ally, 16, was very pleased that the march she went on included many young people who were there with family or friends. As she remarked:

> I went down to London for the march against the war in Iraq. I think the amount of *children* who did really shows what the adults of tomorrow will be like. Better. (posted 25 March 2003; emphasis in the original)

In Ally's view, young people's willingness to become informed about the war in Iraq and to join peace marches where their presence and voices would count for something echoes what many others said on *Newsround* online. Although of course some young people supported the war, many did not, and they were not afraid to say that war did not solve anything regardless of the situation (even though all agreed that Saddam Hussein was an 'evil dictator'). A prevailing view, it seems, is that young people already know and appreciate the fact that war almost always does far more to damage people than to help them in most circumstances.

The antiwar protests held around the United Kingdom were well organized and included a strong representation of young people, in part, because they used the internet and mobile phone texting to make other young people aware of the issues and to tell them where to go to participate. Young people's contributions to demonstrations was the topic of many conversations on 'What's in the News' for months after these events. The majority of those who contributed to these discussions, in our reading, believed that the demonstrations offered fellow young people a potentially valuable opportunity to have their views widely heard. There was a high interest among participants in this discussion in finding out who attended demonstrations and their views about young people's contributions—real and potential—to their overall political effectiveness.

Noreen, 16, who lives in Pakistan, responded enthusiastically to the question posed by the journalist who wrote the *Newsround* story 'Did you march against war?'[10] Said Noreen:

> I didn't march because it can get very violent here, but if I could I would have. They should listen to what we have to say. Bush has no excuse to kill millions of innocent people to get Saddam out of the way and even if there was a war what good will come out of it? Bush should see what the rest of the world has to say. Not the leader, PM or presidents, but what the public has to say. Let us all say NO to war. (posted 23 March 2003)

What is discernible in Noreen's response to *Newsround*'s story on antiwar demonstrations, in our reading at least, is her apparent anger, but also her recourse to an online environment to express a viewpoint which could not be safely articulated (in her judgment) otherwise. Evident, too, is her belief that world opinion matters and that it should be taken into account by political leaders. It would be interesting to know whether, in formulating her position, a sense of global citizenship underpins her thinking. In any case, however, *Newsround* is clearly being used as a public forum for young people like Noreen to actively participate in public dialogue and debate in relative safety.

Next we move forward in time to March 11, 2004, when several bombs went off on train lines in Madrid during the Spanish election campaign. As news of the crisis broke, young people on *Newsround*'s 'What's in the News' message board started discussing what had happened, whether al-Qaeda or ETA were to blame, and how the attacks might be linked to the war in Iraq and Spain's support for that war. The following exchange is broadly typical of some of the ways in which young people considered this attack.

```
AGE OF TERRORISM
thereisnospoon - 14th post - 11 Mar 2004 20:16
We are entering a new age. The age of terrorism. But all that it means
is more people are having a say in the way our world is run. I'm not
saying I agree with what they're doing, coz I don't. But isn't it
strange that we live in a 'democratic' country, but as soon as somebody
puts across an idea that 'the machine' doesn't agree with they are la-
belled terrorist. Their views are just as valid as any body else's. Peo-
ple only see them as being wrong because it's different. If we lived in
a world where there were explosions everywhere then we wouldn't think
this was strange or horrible. And aren't we heading that way? I turn on
the telly, open a paper and I see that more United States soldiers are
being killed, more bombs are going off. But it doesn't affect me that
much any more. Soon, unless the government learn to listen to every one
we will be immune to death, because there will be more suicide, car,
train bombs. I don't think any of this is right, but it's the way, in my
mind, we're heading.
Zebrox

DROP BUSH NOT BOMBS ▸Reply
    ⌐ 🗎re: AGE OF TERRORISM
harmony - 1440th post - 12 Mar 2004 17:46
Exactly, people have to start listening to the so-called terrorists.
They do what they do for a reason, it's to get noticed so their beliefs
are recognised. It's sad that we live in an age when people have to lose
lives just so others can have a voice. Maybe the west needs to open its
ears and begin to listen before people resort to drastic measures. ▸Re-
ply
        ⌐ 🗎re: AGE OF TERRORISM
    snicker_doodle - 676th post - 12 Mar 2004 22:56
    Either your parents have put this into your head or your brain has been
    washed! O.K. lets go with the terrorist! We can all grab a gun and start
    killing ourselves! Weeee this is fun! See it doesn't work that way; you
    have to fight (yeah you may be killed, but at least it's for a better
    world) or in your case follow some corrupt leader and be killed. If we
    were to follow the 'terrorist way' there would more killings. ▸Reply
            ⌐ 🗎re: AGE OF TERRORISM
        harmony - 1444th post - 13 Mar 2004 15:32
        I'm not saying we go the terrorist ways. I'm saying we should listen to
        them before it gets to them resorting to violence. Follow some corrupt
        leader? Excuse me? And no my parents allow me to think for myself, and I
        don't do brainwashing. I read and I look at what isn't there rather than
        what is. ▸Reply
```

The exchange between thereisnospoon (signed Zebrox), harmony and snicker_doodle provides another illustrative instance of how some teenagers (a judgment about relative age being made on the basis of these and related posts) are struggling to deconstruct official discourses of 'terrorism.' Apparent in their comments, in our reading, is a refusal to uphold the normative binarism of 'us' (morally superior) versus 'them' (those who resort to violence to communicate their views), at least in the familiar sense. References to 'having a say,' 'put[ting] an idea across,' 'voice,' and the like are similarly significant, in our view, possibly suggestive of a larger commitment to cultural—and, crucially, generational—diversity so as to ensure that a plurality of viewpoints find adequate expression. The consequences of governments (and, by extension, the news media) failing to 'learn to listen' are being framed, at least implicitly, as engendering a rationale for violent responses.

Future citizens

Today's young people are coming to political awareness in a world transformed by ongoing crises of war and conflict. Such events—ranging from September 11, 2001, to the US-led invasion of Afghanistan and Iraq and the aftermath—have prompted many of the young people contributing to *Newsround*'s website to make a greater effort to be informed by following the news. On the first anniversary of the September 11 attacks, for example, the following two young people had this to say in response to *Newsround*'s query: 'How has 11 September changed the world?':

> It really made me realize how bad life is for some people and it's made me pay more attention to what's going on in the world. It was really, really terrible! (Susan, 13; posted 13 September 2002)

> It's made me watch the news more and aware of what's happening in the world. (Frankie, 13; posted 13 September 2002)

In contrast with some critics who argue that young people typically find such events too traumatic or frightening (thereby inviting censure on the part of parents), these voices demand to know what is going on. Noteworthy, as well, is the implied sense of responsibility they feel, namely to remain alert about unfolding events. Attempts to withhold information from them, it follows, risk encouraging the sense that they are being patronized by adults.

Illustrative of this latter point are comments made by Gemma, 14, who posted her 'Press Pack Report' (effectively an opinion piece) stating:

> It really annoys me when something controversial happens in the news, adults say 'it may have a bad impression on children'.
> Insulting!
> This may be the case with very little children, but when they say children, they mean everyone ranging from toddlers to 18-year-olds.
> They do not seem to understand that people my age have some mind of their own and that by saying that something may have a bad impression on us is insulting our intelligence. (posted 29 May 2003)

In a similar vein, 13-year-old Joe made the following contribution in response to a *Newsround* online story asking young people if they were frightened by some news stories:

> I think news is sometimes scary, but I think we need to be told. If stories got left out to save us from being scared then it would be very patronising and we

would not know that there is anything bad in the world, and we couldn't be as careful as we should be. (Joe, 13; posted 18 October 2002)

Contrary views were also expressed, of course, yet these examples are broadly indicative of the typical sorts of statements made. Indeed, it is our sense in reading through the postings that there is sufficient evidence in this material to render problematic certain familiar assertions about causative links between traumatic news events and the 'emotional damage' they may inflict upon younger viewers.

Similarly relevant here is the view of Carla Thompson, associated with Parents and Children Together (PACT) in the United Kingdom, who maintains that parents need to talk to their sons and daughters about news stories that frighten them. Attempting to shield young people from the truth, she believes, may actually make them more anxious and upset when traumatic events occur. In her view, television news programs are a particularly good resource, one that parents can use to respond to their children's' concerns and fears. Commenting on these issues less than one week after the war in Iraq began in March 2003, Thompson (quoted in Davies, 2003: 47) stated:

> Teenagers will be discussing the war at school and having assemblies about the subject, which is helpful. Programs such as *Newsround* can also help. …The worst thing any parent can do is try and keep their children away from the news or pretend war isn't happening, as they will find out. It's far better to discuss things and let them share their worries with you.

In the aftermath of the rail bombings in Madrid in March 2004, *Guardian* journalist Jerome Monahan (2004) commented in a similar vein. 'The United Kingdom is currently a stated target of international terrorists,' he wrote. Consequently, and given that young people will be following events in the news, it is important to seize the opportunity in the classroom to ask questions about such events and to talk about their concerns. The key question, however, is this: 'How is it possible to make sense of such terrible events,' he asks, 'in a way that does not fuel [their] prejudices or fan their undoubted anxieties?'

In light of this chapter's discussion, it is all too apparent that this question is as easy to pose as it is difficult to resolve. In our view, such circumstances demand that educators provide all young people with the conceptual tools required to engage in critical media analyses of their own [see Thurlow & Marwick—chapter 4, this volume]. At the same time, news organizations have never been more obliged to make the necessary investment to provide their younger audiences with the informational resources they deserve. In societies that purport to be democratic, young people must be made to feel actively connected to the events taking place around them, and empowered to make their voices heard. Abstract discourses of citizenship are of little value. Not only must young people be encouraged to play their part in public decisions, but their opinions also have to be seen to count. The challenge, then, is to find ways to enrich a culture of citizenship that will help to sustain them throughout their political lives.

In an increasingly information-saturated world, part of what it means to become a citizen necessarily entails an engagement with the ways in which the news media help define the most pressing issues of the day. Effective school curricula, it follows, should therefore seek to provide young people with the means and wherewithal to interrogate the guiding assumptions informing the media forms and practices they encounter in their daily lives. 'Rather than ignoring or seeking to invalidate their everyday social experiences,' as Buckingham (2000) contends, 'educators must enable students to build connections between the personal and the political, and hence prepare them for a participatory form of citizenship which can function across a whole range of social domains.' And yet, he adds, 'in the context of increasing educational conservatism, the difficulty of developing and sustaining a curriculum that is relevant to the lives of [future citizens] is likely to become increasingly intense' (2000: 223). It is with some degree of optimism, therefore, that we have pointed to the potential of online resources such as *Newsround*'s website to revitalize young people's news and, equally importantly, to re-engage its audiences in the world around them. Here we promptly acknowledge the obvious, though—namely, that much work remains to be done.

Notes

1. We are pleased to acknowledge that some of the ideas developed in this paper have benefited from our collaborative field research on children and news with colleagues Dr Máire Messenger Davies (University of Ulster) and Dr Karin Wahl-Jorgensen (Cardiff University). For further information abut this ongoing research project, see <http://www.cf.ac.uk/jomec/research/firsted.html>.
2. There has been a particular interest in how best to cultivate citizenship skills in adolescents so as to ensure the future health of democratic politics. For example, in 2002, the United States Department of State announced a new presidential initiative entitled *We the People*, designed to support the teaching of United States history and civic education. It was developed, in part, to tackle the poor civics and history exam results produced by the National Assessment of Education Progress (NAEP).
3. There are four stages in the delivery of the UK's national curriculum. The purpose of these stages is to assess the intellectual progress of students from earliest primary education to the end of secondary school at age 18. For further details see <www.qca.org.uk/14-19>.

4. The notion of effectiveness here assumes that by obtaining these knowledge and skills, young people are enfranchised as citizens, and thus enabled to make positive and active contributions to the greater good of the society in which they live. Similar initiatives have been undertaken in other countries. For example, between 1997–2004, the Australian government provided almost $32 million to fund its *Discovering Democracy* program to support civics and citizenship education in schools. Likewise, since 2002, South African children from years R–9 have been taught citizenship through the subject *Life Orientation*.

5. The Institute for Citizenship is an independent charitable trust established in 1992 by United Kingdom member of parliament Bernard Weatherill (see http://www.citizen.org.uk/ducation.html).

6. See <http://www.citizen.org.uk/Democracy/democracy.html> for more information.

7. Elsewhere in Barratt's (1998: 1) study he cites pertinent statistics (albeit without identifying their source) to support this claim: 'In 1990, 664 students took the Media Studies and Film Studies A level examinations; in 1997, 11,737 candidates sat these examinations. What is more, the rate of increase is accelerating: there was a 30 percent increase in numbers between 1996 and 1997, compared with a 20 percent increase in the previous year. There were a further 2,930 students enrolled for the Advanced GNVQ in Media Communication and Production in September 1996.' These increases, he observes, 'represent student choice to some extent, but they also reflect what schools and colleges are offering' (see also O'Sullivan, 1997).

8. *Newsround* went to air on April 4, 1972, anchored by journalist John Craven using a similar set and presentational style to adult news programs of the time. By 1975, the program was regularly attracting an audience of 5.5 million young people. Shortly after Craven left the program in 1989, substantial changes were made in the programme's format to make it more 'entertaining' for the younger viewer. Over the course of the 1990s, *Newsround* went through nine presenters, almost all of whom were young adult television presenters rather than journalists at the beginning of their career. Today it is the only news program of its kind in the UK, and certainly the most watched amongst young people (see Atwal *et al.*, 2003). Given that its target audience is 8–14 year olds, it is not surprising that each edition of the 10-minute weekday newscast tends to be composed of news stories related to their interests. *Newsround* reporters cover usually five main news items from the field, with stories about interesting facts, celebrities, sports, animals and nature being particularly prominent.

9. All of the quotations from young people used in this paper are publicly available on the CBBC *Newsround* website <http://news.bbc.co.uk/cbbcnews/default.stm>. Young people are identified either by first name only or by their own choice of pseudonym. Needless to say, it is our assumption that the posting content is sincere, but its actual status—including authorship—is impossible to verify on the internet.

10. Responses to this question are posted at the bottom of the news story, although discussion on this issue has been raised periodically since then on the *What's in the News?* message board.
11. PACT is a registered Christian charity based in England, whose main activities include child adoption and fostering, social housing projects, play schemes for children, and family social care education for NGOs and others in the voluntary sector. Many of the families with whom they work are homeless. It is also a pressure group seeking to influence governmental family policy in its areas of operation.

References

Atwal, K., Millwood-Hargrave, A. and Sancho, J. (2003). *What Children Watch: An Analysis of Children's Programme Provision between 1997–2001, and Children's Views.* London: Broadcasting Standards Commission and the Independent Television Commission.

Barratt, A.J.B. (1998). *Media Studies: What Students Think.* London: BFI Information and Education.

Buckingham, D. (2000). *The Making of Citizens: Young People, News and Politics.* London: Routledge.

Carter, C. (2004). Scary news: Children's responses to news of war. *Mediactive*, 3, 67–85.

Crick, B. (2000). *Essays on Citizenship.* London: Continuum.

Department for Education and Skills (DfES). (2003). Available (07/04/04) online at: <www.dfes.gov.uk/citizenship/>.

Davies, A. (2003). Family life: But what shall we tell the children?: War can be as disturbing for children as for adults, if not more so. *Birmingham Post*, 22 March.

Furlong, A. & Cartmel, F. (1997). *'Politics and Participation,' Young People and Social Change: Individualization and Risk in Late Modernity.* Buckingham and Philadelphia: Open University Press.

Glover, M. (2004). Kerry hopes to get young voters to the polls. *Associated Press*, 17 April. Available (19 April 2004) online at: <http://story.news.yahoo.com/news?tmpl=story&cid=694&ncid=2043&e=15&u=/ap/20040417/ap_on_el_pr/kerry_students>.

Hassan, R. (2004). *Media, Politics and the Network Society.* Maidenhead and New York: Open University Press.

Institute for Citizenship. (2003). Available (17 October 2003) online at: <www.citizen.org.uk/ducation.html>.

Jones, J. (2003). *'Wired, Disenfranchised but not Necessarily Out of Touch: Youth Attitudes Towards Mediated Democracy.'* Working Paper, University of Wales, Aberystwyth, March.

Kellner, D. (2002). New media and new literacies: Reconstructing education for the new millennium. In L.A. Lievrouw & S. Livingstone (eds), *Handbook of New Media* (pp. 90–104). London: Sage.

Leavis, F. R. & Thompson, D. (1933). *Culture and Environment*. London: Chatto and Windus.

Lievrouw, L. A. & Livingstone, S. (eds). (2002). *Handbook of New Media*. London: Sage.

Livingstone, S. (2002). *Young People and New Media*. London: Sage.

Monahan, J. (2004). Tackling terror. *Education Guardian*, 23 March.

O'Sullivan, T. (1997). What lies between mechatronics and medicine? The critical mass of media studies. *Media Education Journal*, 22, 17–24.

Roche, J. (1999). Children: Rights, participation and citizenship. *Childhood*, 6(4), 475–93.

Stevenson, N. (2004). *Cultural Citizenship*. Maidenhead and New York: Open University Press.

Tidhar, C. E. & Lemish, D. (2003). The making of television: Young viewers' developing perceptions. *Journal of Broadcasting & Electronic Media*, 47(3), 375–393.

Part II

Young people's communication in peer contexts

6

Stylistic practice and the adolescent social order

Penelope Eckert

Adolescents have a special place in American ideology, as a delegitimized age group. They are generally considered sloppy, frivolous and irresponsible, and this stereotype is projected onto their supposed ways of speaking in such a way that the latter are viewed as unfolding naturally from the former. Gal and Irvine (1995) argue that this process, which they call *iconization*, is a fundamental ideological process in the creation of social distinctions. Both adolescents and their language are commonly viewed as sloppy, rebellious and irresponsible. The recent coining of the term *Mallspeak* to refer to English containing such features as the use of *like* as a quotative and discourse marker reifies the connection between what the coiners see as lax speech and lax leisure habits. This usage is commonly cited as evidence of adolescent sloppiness, vagueness, and unwillingness to commit. A 2003 website (www.laotao.org/mallspeak.html) had this to say about adolescents and their 'Mallspeak':

> There was a time when young people went to the lake or a city park for the fun of it. For over a generation now the young slouch around the halls of the malls. There in the malls they practice their mallspeak…

> The inability of today's students to complete a spoken sentence, without a few 'you knows' and 'like, man' is more than a language problem. It is a language disease that could destroy the English language as we know it today. Good, well-spoken English is slowly disappearing.

It may be an empirical issue whether any of the popular characterizations of adolescent language are valid. But what is more interesting is their sheer existence. Adolescence unfolds under a powerful adult gaze—a gaze that emphasizes and naturalizes the differences between the two age groups.

The life stage of adolescence is a product of industrial society. It was created by the development of universal institutionalized secondary education, which moved responsibility for vocational preparation into the public sector. As a result, young people have been isolated from adult society as they move toward adulthood, excluded from the workforce, and confined to age-homogeneous institutions. Adolescence as we know it, and as we study it, is a response to the constraints (and opportunities) that these conditions place on the age group. Expected to spend long hours in institutions of secondary education, crowded into a small space with hundreds or thousands of age mates, they must find meaning in their institutionally dominated lives. And virtually isolated from the adult sphere, excluded from adult activities, they are unable to make a mark in the world of adults. What is commonly referred to as *youth culture* is a self-made social order in which adolescents can make a mark. It is the product of kids' work to make sense of themselves in an odd situation—to construct identities as they move from a place in the family to a place in the wider social world, but without real access to that wider world. With adolescence set aside as a separate stage in the life course, an adolescent social order emerges, giving a kind of concreteness and permanent status to what would otherwise be a transition. It is important to recognize that youth culture is separate from the adult social order because of adult-dominated institutional arrangements and expectations, and not because of some 'natural' inclination of adolescents to stick to themselves (see also Thurlow, 2001).

If adolescents are put in a problematic situation, they do not occupy it passively but respond with considerable creativity. The stylistic efflorescence that one sees among youth is evidence of their need and ability to make meaning, and in the process of making meaning, they serve as major agents of change—both social and linguistic. Adolescents lead all other age groups in linguistic change—not just the kinds of lexical innovation that they're best known for, but 'regular' change as well (Chambers, 1995). At the same time, by virtue of their transitional place in the life course, adolescents are in a particularly strong position to respond to change in the conditions of life, and in so doing bring about lasting social change. The perspective in the following pages is that adolescent social and linguistic practices, far from reflecting pathology, reflect creativity in adapting to a situation that might be called pathological. My focus will be on stylistic practice as the linguistic locus of adolescent creativity, and as a major resource in the production and maintenance of the adolescent social order.

Peer groups, crowds, communities of practice

In childhood, it is primarily adults who set norms and attend to children's behavior. As an age cohort moves into adolescence, it develops the means to organize its own social control, appropriating power and control from adults such as teachers and parents, setting itself up in distinction from both children and adults. The viability of this emerging social order depends on its structural integrity, and on its adaptation to the situation in which the age group finds itself.

The adolescent social order is structured around, and structures, salient social distinctions, manifesting these distinctions in the formation of groups and categories. The following discussion will focus on peer groups of various kinds as *communities of practice*. This construct is particularly useful in the examination of the relation between social groups and language use because it focuses us on the co-construction of the individual, the group, and linguistic practice. Defined by Lave and Wenger (1991; Wenger, 2000), the community of practice is an aggregation of people who come together on a regular basis as they engage in some enterprise (cheerleading, being friends, being religious, doing family activities, doing or selling drugs, avoiding school). In the course of this engagement, they develop practices, or ways of doing things—including ways of speaking—and these practices come to structure forms of participation within the group and relations to the social world around them. The construct *community of practice* focuses us on language not as a system, but as a practice, and ties it directly to the activities and identities of individuals as they constitute groups.

All individuals participate in a variety of communities of practice as they move from home to school to work and as they engage in a range of activities. Some of these will be more defining for the individual than others, and not all participants in a given community will be equally engaged. The communities of practice referred to as adolescent peer groups are important to all their participants, although not equally—for instance, some may be more engaged with their families, some with other peer groups. And participants in any community of practice bring to it their other affiliations—their knowledge, their experience, their identities—and these play a role in their participation and identity within the community.

Adolescent peer groups are primary loci for jointly viewing the social world and assessing one's place in it—participants situate themselves as a group with respect to the social world around them, and with respect to other specific communities of practice. In this way, the community of practice is the nexus between the individual and the wider social world, making individual and group identity work inseparable. It stands to reason, then, that the very oppositions that distinguish a given community of practice from others will function within the community as well. If a group distinguishes itself with respect to others along the lines of, for example, toughness or race or intelligence, there will be differentiation within the group along the same lines. This kind of nesting of oppositions, or recursiveness (Gal & Irvine, 1995), is an important mechanism in the co-construction of the individual, the group, and the wider social order.

The school institution provides the overarching environment for the emergence of the adolescent social order, figuring centrally in the norms that affect them all whether they are in school or have dropped out. Societal norms expect adolescents to both attend, and to be active in, school. These expectations set up a fundamental and salient distinction between those who do and who do not attend school. And within the school, they (recursively) set up a fundamental and salient distinction between those who do and who do not embrace the institution. This institutional orientation interacts intimately with class, race, ethnicity, gender and other social hierarchies both because social differences can be amplified within the confined conditions of the school itself, and because these hierarchies often relate directly to opportunities within schooling and in the life that schooling is preparing them for. Cooperative participation in school presupposes submission to adult authority, acceptance of age segregation, and acceptance of middle class institutional norms. All three of these are terms of disagreement and differentiation among the adolescent population in almost any school, and all three of them can coincide with differences that divide the adult population as well—such as class, race, gender and ethnicity. Each of these, therefore, is co-constructed with, hence inseparable from, adolescence. There is nothing homogeneous about adolescence or adolescents, and there is nothing homogeneous about members' age and their relation to the life stage. Indeed, although much literature about adolescence focuses on similarities, and on conformity, adolescent life is about diversity.

White middle class life tends to align with normative institutions, particularly the schools, and white middle class adolescents tend to come to secondary school prepared to mold their social lives to the institution. Social groups that emerge within the school tend to be age-homogeneous (Eckert, 1989), both because schools overtly encourage such patterns of association and because schools also structure contact along age. Working class life, on the other hand, tends to be more neighborhood-based (see, e.g., Bott, 1957), yielding more age-heterogeneous groups and making school more an interruption than a complement to youths' social life. Gangs are the extreme in neighborhood-based groups, and they are also the extreme in age-heterogeneity inasmuch as they tend to be directly plugged into the activities and networks of gang-oriented adults. This means that school-based and neighborhood-based youth are inserted quite differently into the life course and orient quite differently to the adolescent life stage. Immigrant groups often engage their children in ethnically-based networks that complicate their relation to school as well. And to the extent that neighborhoods are ethnically segregated, neighborhood orientation will also be an ethnic orientation. All this is to say that the age and school components of adolescence are complicated by significant differences in age and school orientation, which in turn are related to other major social hierarchies. And all of these figure quite saliently in peer categories and groups, and in the linguistic practice that helps constitute them.

The following discussion will focus on the use of linguistic resources from the perspective of the creation and maintenance of groups and categories, and with a focus on the creation and maintenance of distinctiveness. Language participates in a variety of ways in this endeavor. On the one hand, it is the vehicle for the explicit negotiation of norms and distinctions. On the other hand, it provides the means to perform one's place among those norms and distinctions. I will discuss two general kinds of linguistic practice—the labeling and verbal play that calls distinctions into being, and the explicitly stylistic use of the grammar and lexicon that performs these distinctions.

Calling distinctions into being

Engaged in a fierce negotiation of social values and differences, adolescents are continually making new distinctions and evaluations of behavior, in the course of which they coin new terms for social evaluation and social types. The intensity of adolescent life gives rise to a good deal of innovation in evaluative terms (*cool*) and intensifiers (*hella, totally*), but more notably, it gives rise to a myriad of terms that label social categories or groups, and commonly assign local value to what are global categories. For example, secondary schools commonly have social categories based on opposing school orientations (Willis, 1977; Eckert, 1989). While this opposition is quite universal because of the role of schooling in the life stage, it has local manifestations. Those who base their social lives in the school institution may be called *jocks* (Eckert, 1989), *rednecks* (Habick, 1991) or *ear 'oles* (Willis, 1977), depending on the place; those who reject the school as the locus of their social lives may be called *burnouts* in Detroit, *grits* in Baltimore or *lads* in the United Kingdom. Emerging as they do with reference to the institution of schooling, these categories will reflect the local nature of schooling. Thurlow (2001) has found that category labels appear to be less widespread in British secondary schools than is reported for US schools. I have argued elsewhere (Eckert, 1989) that the relative intensity of social categorization in US schools may well be related to the fact that the US educational system emphasizes the secondary school as a total institution (Goffman, 1961), striving to dominate most aspects of its students' lives. With the passage of time and social change, while the categories are continuous, their names may change along with a shift in emphasis in defining a category. Thus, for example, the shift from *greasers* in the 1970s to *burnouts* in the 1980s in Detroit corresponds to a shift in salience from car culture to drug use. The coining of new terms, therefore, is part of social change—it does not simply reflect change, but is part of what brings about shifts in salience (Wong, in press).

The actual deployment of these labels is a crucial part of social practice. Labeling is an important means of producing and maintaining social distinctions, as the coining of a term for a social type creates a category, and allows the category to enter into everyday discourse. Labels do not emerge abstractly, but arise in use, and in relation to specific people in real situations (Bucholtz, 2001; Eckert & McConnell-Ginet, 1995). It is in speech activities such as making observations and judgments about people, pointing people out to others, describing absent people, that speakers endow labels with meaning and in the process create categorizations. In this way, the day-to-day use and reuse of labels brings about the continual ebb and flow of meaning and social change. The use of these labels can also exert social control. In every school, a proliferation of labels maps out the local social terrain, the margins of respectability, and the terms of evaluation (Labov, 1992).

While labels for social types are a means for negotiating the affordances for social identity, the term *slang* more commonly refers to the coining of items in other areas of the lexicon. And the motivation most often cited is secrecy—for example, being able to talk about illegitimate activities in public without fear of discovery. Another motivation often cited is rarification—inasmuch as appropriate slang usage signals membership, the constant renewal of the lexicon serves a gate-keeping function and allows people to signal local knowledge and membership.

Lexical innovation of other kinds can also underline salient social issues. In her study of the slang used in the favelas of Rio De Janeiro, Roth-Gordon (2002) found that speakers associated their slang with the poverty, racial status and disaffection of the favela, and with the illegal activity and relation to the police that emerges from that status. Roth-Gordon emphasizes the status of slang as an ideological construct, and shows that slang is a heightened symbol of the favela throughout all segments of Rio society. This slang is sufficiently different from standard usage that it can be used in a way that renders it incomprehensible to nonspeakers, and the extent of this difference reflects the extent of the social difference that generates it. Similarly, the extreme innovative practice of the Parisian suburbs, Verlan, involves operations on French words—beginning with syllable reversals—that require considerable practice and skill and that render Verlan incomprehensible to the outsider. This 'slang' variety is the product of a predominantly North African and poor adolescent population, and is associated with disenfranchisement and alienation from normative institutions.

Slang is a term commonly used to refer to lexical innovation by delegitimized groups such as criminals, gang members and poor minority groups, implying a qualitative difference from other kinds of lexical innovation. Every community of practice coins new lexical items as its members develop new ways of doing things, and new ways of talking about what they are doing that suit their joint purposes. The fate of these innovations depends in part on the status of the innovators. Depending on the community and the endeavor, lexical innovations might be called 'technical terminology,' 'jargon,' or 'slang.' From the viewpoint of function within a community, there is no difference between the status of the terms *dot-commer* and *homie*, both of which name a salient social category. Homies will be around at least as long as dot-commers, and the term will be as well. Yet the former is generally not considered to be slang while the latter is.

Narrative is an important means for constructing norms and group identity, and for building cohesion as well. As such it may be particularly meaningful. Having a narrative to tell and having the right to tell it is an indication of social status and in the case of preadolescents (because the ability to tell good narratives comes fairly late in childhood or preadolescence) it is an indication of maturity and social competence. Narration also foregrounds the activities of the group and emphasizes the group as a community of practice, and the right to tell one's narratives (Shuman, 1986) is a clear indication of one's status in the group, and the acceptance of the events in that narrative as important to the group. (Of course, it is difficult to separate the ability from the right to tell a narrative—since narration requires practice.) Narrative events, therefore, simultaneously construct group cohesion and status difference. Moore's analysis of a girls' continual attempts to tell her own narrative (Moore, 2002; 2003) is a good example of this, and emphasizes that the entire nature of the community of practice is being co-constructed with that one person's status.

Collaborative narration is a common strategy for making the narrative group property, and for putting events into group memory and perhaps group lore. Eder (1988), in her study of adolescent girls' collaborative narration, views such narration as building cohesion. Her definition, however, limits collaborative talk to instances in which one participant's utterance ratifies the previous utterance in some way. However, collaboration does not always imply consensus. Collaborative narratives can involve a good deal of contestation about the story itself. As one person begins the story, another participant in the event being narrated may offer additional information, or may challenge the other teller's rendering of events in some way. Even this kind of co-narration can build solidarity and cohesion, as the interaction between or among narrators emphasizes the sharing of the events in question, and the contestation can emphasize the entering of the narrative into group history.

Although it is commonly claimed that females are more prone to collaborative narration, and collaborative talk in general (Coates, 1996; Tannen, 1990), it appears that this conclusion is based more on norms than on evidence, and that these norms can also bias an investigator's interpretation of the evidence. Cameron (1997), for example, shows how a group of US male undergraduates show tremendous collaboration in a gossip session in which they completely trash one of their peers. This dominant discourse that women and girls are more cooperative and egalitarian, whereas men and boys are more competitive and hierarchical, also prevents investigators from considering alternatives. For example, whether males and females are hierarchical or egalitarian in different situations and in different ways.

Although the use of labels can function by either presupposing (e.g., 'John and his nerd friends') or explicitly imposing (e.g., 'what a nerd') categorization, face-threatening acts such as insults are a quite explicit invoker of norms. Ritual insults have been documented among adolescents, particularly males (Dundes, 1972; Labov, 1972b), as demonstrations and competitions of verbal skill and humor. The insults are highly constrained, specifically in order to limit the potential for real offense. Although the recipient of an insult is expected to assume that the insulter believes that the content of the insult is untrue, the insulter is expected to avoid content that could be potentially true. It is specifically this trust and this restraint that binds the group, allowing the insults to emphasize solidarity through the mutual acknowledgment in the face of potentially face-threatening acts that this is 'just play' (Bateson, 1972). Meanwhile, real insults may flow within and between groups. Eder and her colleagues (Eder *et al.*, 1995) have documented the flow of public insults among groups in the cafeteria of a junior high school—insults that put norms and norm violations on the public table. Although norms tend to be discussed overtly in small and more intimate groups (Eckert, 1990b), their public airing both makes explicit the differing norms of different groups and serves as competition among groups to set norms for the rest of the cohort. While most of the literature on insults has focused on boys, Eder and her colleagues found junior high school girls as well as boys engaging in public insulting, and Goodwin (2002) has shown striking examples of girls engaging in overt face-to-face insults. The perception that females are in some way gentler and more cooperative than males permeates both popular and academic literature on gender, but appears to reflect norms more closely than does actual behavior. A more recent trend in the US—a media focus on 'mean girls'—is flipping the stereotype, arguing that girls can be as mean or meaner than boys. In some cases (Fields, 2002), authors argue that this is a result of feminism, as if girls' meanness were a new phenomenon. Although white middle class gender norms may convince some girls to take a less confrontational style (but note that Goodwinm, 2002, focuses on white middle class girls), these norms are fairly specific to the white middle class, and they do not exclude other forms of exclusionary practice. Compliments are the flip side of insults, and an equally powerful form of social control. In my own fieldwork in elementary schools, I saw preadolescent white middle class girls beginning to engage in constant complimenting as they moved toward adolescence. This behavior, both when it was sarcastic and when it was sincere, served overwhelmingly to set and exercise norms (particularly of appearance) and to exercise control not simply on the receiver of the compliment but on the onlookers.

Stylistic practice

Stylistic practice is a process of *bricolage* (Hebdige, 1984), in which stylistic agents (in this case speakers) appropriate and recombine resources already existing out in the environment to construct something new. As speakers look out on the social landscape, they come to associate particular styles with particular kinds of people. And inasmuch as styles may differ in fairly small ways, they may select elements of styles that appear to be making the salient difference, and incorporate these elements into their preexisting repertoire. Whereas, such things as race, ethnicity, class and gender play a central role in the structuring of the social landscape, stylistic elements rarely index these categories directly; rather, they index attitudes, stances, and activities that are in turn associated with the categories (Ochs, 1991).

Linguistic style is just one of a range of semiotic systems that serve this purpose—from bodily hexis (Bourdieu, 1977b) and clothing and other kinds of body adornment to eating habits and territory (Eckert, 1989). Mendoza-Denton's (1995; 1996) study of Mexican American girls in Northern California shows how gang girls use a wide range of semiotic means, from language choice and variation to makeup and dress to lay claim to gang identity and practice. Specific features of this style (e.g., the span of black eyeliner) are iconic of toughness, simultaneously signaling ethnic identity to non-Latinos, claiming access to the male prerogative of toughness, and setting themselves off from tamer girls.

The significance of being female or being Chicana, for example, is tied up with a variety of local and nonlocal issues—first of all, they interact among themselves so that, for example, race is rarely experienced or displayed independently of class and gender. At the same time, these may be associated with stances such as toughness or intellectual superiority. A single linguistic feature, therefore, may be deployed in multiple styles, and combined with others to create a style rich in social meaning.

Language offers up a range of resources in the realms of voice quality and prosody, segmental phonology, morphology, syntax, lexicon and so on up to the level of discourse, speech acts, activities and events. Indeed, discourse practices discussed above can function stylistically, as frequent engagement in ritual or serious insults can define an interactive style; and the use of labels can signal access to the labels and their use. To the extent that category labels signal distinctions that are particularly locally based, the use of social category labels (like the use of other local terms such as landmark nicknames) can mark the speaker as a member. Brenneis (1977), in a study of the use of category names in a college fraternity, found that the regular use of terms like *weenie* was most intense among the entering classes. As they got older, fraternity members gradually gave up this use. The use of taboo labels may signal a speaker's affiliation with a group stance with respect to the target group—whether in opposition to that target group or as a member of the target group that is reclaiming the term.

Since school is basic to adolescence, the most obvious starting point in discussing the relation between language and adolescence is in the connection between standard language and education. The school is a prime locus of the standard language market (Bourdieu & Boltanski, 1975; Bourdieu, 1977a), and participation in the school involves an internalization of standard norms. Vernaculars, by virtue of the contrast, are associated both with lack of, or opposition to, education and with the local as opposed to the institutional. Whereas standard language emphasizes global homogeneity and conservatism, vernaculars emphasize local differentiation and innovation.

The opposition between standard and vernacular figures prominently in the opposition between institutionally and locally oriented groups. At the same time, the elaboration of vernaculars facilitates the creation and maintenance of distinctiveness among neighborhood-oriented groups. My work with Detroit-area white adolescents (Eckert, 1989; 2000) shows a robust correlation between the use of standard versus vernacular variables and participation in the school-based categories of jocks and burnouts discussed earlier. The opposition between standard features and white urban vernacular features serves—along with many aspects of material style—to maintain the opposition between those who base their social lives in the school (the jocks) and those who base their social lives in the neighborhood and more generally the urban continuum (the burnouts). Burnouts lead jocks in the use of a variety of phonological features associated with the urban area, as well as negative concord. Furthermore, these features serve as signs of urban engagement among those who affiliate with neither the jocks nor the burnouts (called *in-betweens* in the school). And finally, they also distinguish quite dramatically between the more extreme burnout girls (referred to by many as *burned-out burnouts*) and the rest (*regular burnouts*) (see Eckert, 1996). It is worth noting that girls' linguistic behavior defines both the standard and the vernacular extremes of the entire cohort, whereas boys' linguistic output lies in between. This is one of many indications that females do not range at the conservative end of the linguistic spectrum as is often claimed, but may intensify certain social and linguistic distinctions (Eckert, 1990a; Eckert & McConnell-Ginet, 2003). This pattern appears to be more common among adolescents than among adults.

The distinction between the regular and burned-out burnouts is an example of the recursiveness discussed by Gal and Irvine (1995), in which the opposition between salient categories is nested within the categories as well, hence increasingly the distinction's salience. This pattern shows up in Laks' (1983) study of adolescents hanging out in a youth center in the working class Paris suburb of Villejuif. Laks found an overarching opposition in the local adolescent population between *street kids* and *center kids* (i.e., kids who affiliated with the adult-run, education-oriented institution). As the center kids placed themselves in relation to other groups according to this opposition, they played out the same opposition among themselves, structuring the group itself with respect to individual members' closeness to street culture and center culture. These distinctions surfaced in the boys' use of several phonological and morphological variables associated with street culture.

Labov's (1972a) study of an African American adolescent peer group in Harlem shows a similar dynamic manifesting itself in syntactic patterns. As in the Laks case, this peer group hung out at a community center but had something of a gang orientation. The opposition between institution and neighborhood orientation locates this peer group within the local social landscape, and also figures in the relations among its members. Those who were more family and school oriented were on the margins of the network cluster defined by this peer group and showed marked linguistic differences from the more street-oriented members. Not only did they use less of the salient African American feature zero copula (e.g., *he bad*), but they also showed different syntactic constraints on their use of the copula.

Some communities of practice may be more saliently gendered than others. Among the most striking examples are US college fraternities and sororities, which are private nationally based residential and/or eating clubs that serve as socializing and networking transitions to the undergraduate world. In a sociolinguistic and ethnographic study of one fraternity, Kiesling (1997) shows how verbal interaction within the hierarchical structure of the fraternity constructs, among other things, white middle class male power and authority. Masculinity is, of course, inseparable from other primary categories—it does not take just one form. Connell (1995) argues that there are multiple masculinities, and elaborates a distinction between *technical* (or upper middle class) masculinity and *physical* (or working class) masculinity. Among other things, the former is based on structural, institutional power whereas the latter is based on physical power. In secondary school, where students have relatively little access to structural power, boys tend to emphasize physical power. The fraternity represents a transition to the possibility of greater structural power, and Kiesling argues that the two kinds of masculinity interact in the fraternity. Focusing on the reduction of *–ing* (i.e., *walkin'*), Kiesling finds that individuals who make extreme use of the reduced (more vernacular) variant use it strategically to index working-class cultural models and confrontational stances.

Although the gender status quo may be reproduced in sororities and fraternities, there are plenty of cases in which groups call on language to challenge gender norms. Bucholtz gives an account of a group of girls in Northern California (Bucholtz, 1996) who lay claim on *nerd* status—a status normally reserved for males. Although nerds in schools have been generally stigmatized, their increased power and visibility in the high-tech industry, and the increasing visibility of technological expertise in school itself, feeds back into an increasingly self-proclaimed status in high school. These girls, in appropriating an aggressively intellectual and independent style, are making a claim about their ability not only to be smart but, like boys, to 'make the rules': to be independently smart, beyond the control of teachers. In the aid of this claim, they construct a style of speech that includes specialized names, lexicon, and phonological variables. The latter is particularly interesting, as it involves most saliently the release of word-final voiceless stops. Characteristic of British dialects, this constitutes hyperarticulation in American English and, no doubt by association both with reading style and with British speech, it carries a connotation of intelligence and articulateness.

Benor (2002) documents the use of final stop release in an Orthodox Jewish community, and within that community the association of this linguistic feature with Talmudic study. As they move toward adolescence, the boys in this community begin to engage intensely in Talmudic study, a practice that is locally associated with masculinity. Benor found that as they move toward adolescence, boys come to use more of this feature than do girls. In addition, the feature shows up in verbal strategy as boys use it particularly to signal an authoritative stance. Thus a feature that signals Jewish, and particularly Orthodox Jewish, identity is also used in male adolescent groups within the community to signal the kind of stance that is salient to peer status.

If hyperarticulation is incorporated into a style to lend a particular kind of standard legitimacy, the situated appropriation of stigmatized dialect features allows 'mainstream' kids to lay temporary claim to aspects of disaffected youth images. White Anglo kids use features of Latino and African American features to signal coolness, toughness or attitude. And although these acts of identity may indicate admiration, the admiration is for a specific set of attributes, and as such, as argued by people such as Bucholtz (1999), Cutler (1999) and Hill (1993), preserves the racial hierarchy.

According to Méla (1997), the extent and the ways in which Verlan transforms French gives it an insolent and threatening quality. Both Méla and Roth-Gordon emphasize that slang usage that originates in, and represents, disaffected groups of adolescents, is also picked up by more middle class youth to establish their connection to youth culture. With limited access to native speakers of these slangs, middle class kids use a fairly tame version. But also, their orientation to the communities where the slangs originate is limited to a desire to adopt some of their autonomy—to set themselves off from the older generation, but not to set themselves off from the middle class. Citing the example of a middle class girl teasing her father because his slang is out of date, Roth-Gordon points out that although the middle class of each generation takes up slang usage during adolescence, they expect to move away from it—to become out of date—in adulthood. Originating in the tough poor favelas, urban slang represents youthful autonomy, but it is also linked to crime, race and poverty. In their selective use of favela slang, middle class kids assert that they are the upcoming generation, but signal restraint. And their ability to dispassionately appropriate favela youth resources constitutes, in their view and their parent's, legitimate adolescence, and an anticipation of legitimate adulthood. In other words, they construct their age group as aligned with their parents' class position. The native speaker, the favela resident, on the other hand, expects to use slang, and to change with slang, for a lifetime. The use of slang by the white middle class, thus, is very much part of the construction of privilege whereas its use by the kids in the favela is very much part of the construction of disenfranchisement.

It is particularly apparent with immigrant groups that adolescents are society's transition teams, reinterpreting the world, resolving the old with the new, substrate with superstrate, culture with culture, local with transnational. Méla (1997) emphasizes the role of Verlan in forging an 'interstitial' identity among the young North African adolescent population in France. Tetrault (2000) describes the multilingual punning of French adolescents of North African descent as they play *hachek*, a competitive word duel. Played by two participants, hachek involves rhyming play between Arabic and French, allowing them to play with cultural meaning as they construct a new cultural space, or as Tetrault puts it, 'creating cultural crossroads from which to speak.' Mendoza-Denton's examination (1997) of the raising of [I] and the fortition of [θ] in the speech of Latino adolescents shows the importation of Spanish phonology into English, transforming English into a language that can construct Latino identities. Particularly, the heightened use of this particular phonological feature in a highlighted discourse use of *and everything*, which calls upon the listener to orient to salient shared information, relates it directly to the US life of these adolescents.

Rampton (1995), in his study of crossing among immigrant youth in the United Kingdom, argues for the use of other languages as a means of expressing affiliation across ethnic lines. Roberts (2000), in her study of the history of the creolization of Hawaiian English Pidgin, found that in the early days of immigration into Hawaii, kids whose native languages were Hawaiian, Chinese, Japanese and Portuguese tended to learn enough of each other's languages to be able to play together. But as the number of multilingual but Hawaiian-born kids increased, Pidgin became a common language and symbolic of a new kind of locally based social order. Roberts argues that it was within adolescent peer groups, and specifically as a vehicle of common identity separate both from adults and from the dominant white Anglo population of Hawaii, that the pidgin became elaborated and developed into a creole.

Kids in immigrant communities are mediating cultures, and they can do it not simply because they are a transitional generation, but precisely because of their life stage. As youth, they are expected to mess with meaning. By virtue of their location in time and social and cultural space, they have special knowledge, and in working with this knowledge—in making new meanings—they are constructing authenticity of a new kind. They are not just resolving ethnicity, gender, class and race for today, but constructing permanent meanings that they will carry into adulthood, to be worked on by the next generation.

Conclusions

This brief exploration of research on stylistic practice in adolescent peer groups has been intended above all to present a view of language as a resource for the construction of social meaning in adolescent life. A key role of language in the creation and maintenance of peer groups is in creating and supporting differentiation. This is done both in conversation and through the construction of linguistic style—a way of deploying linguistic resources that sets the community off from others, and that is designed to represent the community's character. Speech style joins with other aspects of style (e.g., dress and other adornment, substance use, musical taste, territory, activities, movement), all of which are continually changing. The acceleration of change in the adolescent life stage can be attributed to the centrality of personal and social change, engaged as young people are in constructing a viable social order and in placing themselves in it during a time of age transition and within the context of wider social change.

Although this activity may be accelerated in adolescence, it is no different from stylistic practice among adults.

As a life stage, adolescence is generally compared with adulthood, rather than with the life stage that precedes it. As a result, comparisons tend to be negative, and adolescents tend to be viewed in terms of the development that they have not yet accomplished rather than what they have accomplished. Rather than seeing the adolescent social order as a poor version of the adult one, it would be productive to see it as the tremendous leap that it is from the arrangements of childhood. At the same time, we need to be extremely cautious in attributing behavior thought of as typically adolescent to biological, cognitive, social or emotional development. Although there are indeed significant developmental changes taking place during this life stage, the actual effects of those changes can be molded by the situations that provide the environment for development. The traditional focus on adolescence and adolescents—indeed on adolescent language—as problematic generally does not take into consideration that the situation that society has provided for adolescents is itself highly problematic.

If I were to make recommendations for future study of the language of adolescents, I would take the risk of appearing contradictory, and argue that adolescents could benefit from more research on middle-aged adult speech than research on adolescent speech. And particularly, I would like to see research on adults that takes the perspective that so much research on adolescent language takes. Most particularly, examination of identity construction, social groups, and peer pressure would help to demystify the notion of adolescent language, and to put these phenomena into a more central perspective for all age groups.

References

Bateson, G. (1972). *Steps to an Ecology of Mind*. New York: Ballantine.

Benor, S. (2002). *Sounding learned: The gendered use of /t/ in Orthodox Jewish English*. Penn working papers in linguistics: Selected papers from NWAV 2000.

Bott, E. (1957). *Family and Social Network*. London: Tavistock.

Bourdieu, P. (1977a). The economics of linguistic exchanges. *Social Science Information, 16*, 645–68.

Bourdieu, P. (1977b). *Outline of a Theory of Practice*. Cambridge: Cambridge University Press.

Bourdieu, P. & Boltanski, L. (1975). Le fétichisme de la langue. *Actes de la Recherche en Sciences Sociales*, 2–32.

Brenneis, D. (1977). 'Turkey,' 'wienie,' 'animal,' 'stud': Intragroup variation in folk speech. *Western Folklore, 36*, 238–46.

Bucholtz, M. (1996). Geek the girl: Language, femininity and female nerds. In N. Warner *et al.* (eds), *Gender and Belief Systems* (pp. 119–131). Berkeley: Berkeley Women and Language Group.

Bucholtz, M. (1999). You da man: Narrating the racial other in the production of white masculinity. *Journal of Sociolinguistics*, 3, 443–460.

Bucholtz, M. (2001). *Word up: Social meanings of slang in California youth culture.* Language and culture symposium 8. culture.org/colloquia/symposia/bucholtz-mary/.

Cameron, D. (1997). Performing gender identity: Young men's talk and the construction of heterosexual masculinity. In S. Johnson and U. Meinhof (eds), *Language and Masculinity* (pp. 47–64). Oxford: Blackwell.

Chambers, J. K. (1995). *Sociolinguistic Theory.* Oxford: Blackwell.

Coates, J. (1996). *Women Talk: Conversation Between Women and Friends.* Oxford: Blackwell.

Connell, R. (1995). *Masculinities.* Berkeley: University of California Press.

Cutler, C. A. (1999). Yorkville crossing; White teens, hip hop and African American English. *Journal of Sociolinguistics*, 3, 428–41.

Dundes, A. (1972). Turkish boy's duelling rhymes. In J. Gumperz & D. Hymes (eds), *Directions in Sociolinguistics.* New York: Holt, Rinehart and Winston.

Eckert, P. (1989). *Jocks and Burnouts: Social Categories and Identity in the High School.* New York: Teachers College Press.

Eckert, P. (1990a). The whole woman: Sex and gender differences in variation. *Language Variation and Change*, 1, 245–267.

Eckert, P. (1990b). Cooperative competition in adolescent girl talk. *Discourse Processes*, 13, 92–122.

Eckert, P. (1996). (ay) goes to the city: Exploring the expressive use of variation. In J. Baugh, C. Feagin, G. Guy & D. Schiffrin (eds), *Towards a Social Science of Language: Festschrift for William Labov* (pp. 47–68). Philadelphia and Amsterdam: John Benjamins.

Eckert, P. (2000). *Linguistic Variation as Social Practice.* Oxford: Blackwell.

Eckert, P. & McConnell-Ginet, S. (1995). Constructing meaning, constructing selves: Snapshots of language, gender and class from Belten High. In M. Bucholtz & K. Hall (eds) *Gender Articulated: Language and the Culturally Constructed Self* (pp. 469–507). London: Routledge.

Eckert, P. & McConnell-Ginet, S. (2003). *Language and Gender.* Cambridge: Cambridge University Press.

Eder, D. (1988). Building cohesion through collaborative narration. *Social Psychology Quarterly*, 51, 225–235.

Eder, D., Evans, C. C. & Parker, S. (1995). *School Talk: Gender and Adolescent Culture.* New Brunswick: Rutgers University Press.

Fields, S. (2002). *Mean Girls in the Mean Streets of Middle School.* The Washington Times.

Gal, S. & Irvine, J. T. (1995). The boundaries of languages and disciplines: How ideologies construct difference. *Social Research*, 62, 967–1001.

Goffman, E. (1961). *Asylums: Essays on the Social Situation of Mental Patients and Other Inmates.* New York: Anchor.

Goodwin, M. H. (2002). Exclusion in girls' peer groups: Ethnographic analysis of languages practices on the playground. *Human Development*, 45, 392–415.

Habick, T. (1991). Burnouts versus rednecks: Effects of group membership on the phonemic system. In P. Eckert, (ed.) *New Ways of Analyzing Sound Change* (pp. 185–212). San Diego: Academic Press.

Hebdige, D. (1984). *Subculture: The Meaning of Style.* New York: Methuen.

Hill, J. H. (1993). Hasta la vista, baby: Anglo Spanish in the American Southwest. *Critique of Anthropology,* 13, 145–176.

Kiesling, S. F. (1997). Power and the language of men. In S. Johnson and U. Meinhof (eds), *Language and Masculinity* (pp. 65–85). Oxford: Blackwell.

Labov, T. (1992). Social and language boundaries among adolescents. *American Speech,* 67, 339–366.

Labov, W. (1972a). The linguistic consequences of being a lame. In W. Labov (ed.) *Language in the Inner City* (pp. 255–297). Philadelphia: University of Pennsylvania Press.

Labov, W. (1972b). Rules for ritual insults. In W. Labov (ed.) *Language in the Inner City* (pp. 297–353). Philadelphia: University of Pennsylvania Press.

Laks, B. (1983). Langage et pratiques sociales: Étude sociollinguistique d'un groupe d'adolescents. *Actes de la Recherche en Sciences Sociales,* 46, 73–79.

Lave, J. & Wenger, E. (1991). *Situated Learning: Legitimate Peripheral Participation.* Cambridge: Cambridge University Press.

Méla, V. (1997). Verlan 2000. *Langue Française,* 114, 16–34.

Mendoza-Denton, N. (1995). Language attitudes and gang affiliation among California Latina girls. In M. Bucholtz, A.C. Liang, L. A. Sutton & C. Hines (eds) *Cultural Performances* (pp. 478–486). Berkeley: Berkeley Women and Language Group.

Mendoza-Denton, N. (1996). Muy macha: Gender and ideology in gang girls' discourse about makeup. *Ethnos,* 61, 47–63.

Mendoza-Denton, N. (1997). *Chicana/Mexicana identity and linguistic variation: An ethnographic and sociolinguistic study of gang affiliation in an urban high school.* Unpublished PhD dissertation, Stanford University.

Moore, E. (2002). *'You tell all the stories': The narrative construction of dominance in the interaction of adolescent girls.* Paper presented at IGALA2 (Conference of the International Gender and Language Association). Lancaster University.

Moore, E. (2003). *Learning style and identity: A sociolinguistic analysis of a Bolton high school, Linguistics.* Unpublished PhD thesis, University of Manchester.

Ochs, E. (1991). Indexing gender. In A. Duranti & C. Goodwin (eds) *Rethinking Context* (pp. 335–358). Cambridge: Cambridge University Press.

Rampton, B. (1995). *Crossing: Language and Ethnicity Among Adolescents.* London and New York: Longman.

Roberts, S. J. (2000). Nativization and the genesis of Hawaiian Creole. In J. H. McWhorter (ed.) *Language Change and Language Contact in Pidgins and Creoles.* Amsterdam: Benjamins.

Roth-Gordon, J. (2002). *Slang and the Struggle over Meaning: Race, Language, and Power in Brazil.* Unpublished PhD dissertation, Stanford University.

Shuman, A. (1986). *Storytelling Rights.* Cambridge: Cambridge University Press.

Tannen, D. (1990). *You Just Don't Understand: Women and Men in Conversation.* New York: William Morrow.

Tetrault, C. (2000). *Adolescents' multilingual punning and identity play in a French cité*. Paper presented at the Annual Meeting of the American Anthropological Society. San Francisco.

Thurlow, C. (2001). The usual suspects? A comparative investigation of crowds and social-type labelling among young British teenagers. *Journal of Youth Studies, 4,* 319–334.

Wenger, E. (2000). *Communities of Practice*. New York: Cambridge University Press.

Willis, P. (1977). *Learning to Labour*. London: Routledge and Kegan Paul.

Wong, A. (in press). The re-appropriation of Tongzhi. *Language in Society*.

7

Slang and swearing as markers of inclusion and exclusion in adolescence

Vivian de Klerk

It is important that a book on adolescence should contain a chapter on slang and swearing because these are two features of adolescent linguistic behavior that attract more attention than they perhaps warrant, symbolizing as they do, the freedom that young people have at this stage of their lives to challenge linguistic norms, and at the same time to test interpersonal bonds and institutional constraints with their parents as they seek to establish new identities and relationships within their changing worlds. Children begin style-shifting in response to social context at a fairly early stage, and sociolinguists have long recognized that schoolchildren begin to speak more like their peers than like their elders as they emerge from childhood (Chambers, 2003:175). Thus the patterns of speech modeled on the speech of adults around them, as a result of intense and sustained contact, are slowly eroded by the patterns of speech used by their new peer groups, with whom they experience increased levels of contact. Changes creep in slowly, and when family and friends are at odds, the choice is invariably in favor of peers and their informal slang.

At this significant stage of their development, the 'subcultures' or peer-groups constituted by young people are typically confined to a segregated school environment, which, somewhat artificially, may bring together young people from a fairly wide range of social spheres. In cities, in small towns, and even in smaller rural areas, young people often find themselves meeting and interacting regularly, sharing the same classrooms, competing against each other on the sportsfield and relaxing and socializing together after organized school activities. In such a social 'hothouse,' fraught with competition, conflict and emotional changes, this heightened social and emotional activity is a prime breeding ground for intense preoccupation with clothing, other adornments, and general social behavior. In particular, there are huge influences on linguistic patterns and styles, as these young people seek to create their own social order and communities of practice (Eckert, 2000; also chapter 6, this volume). For this reason, a chapter on the slang and swearing and its use by young people offers particularly useful insights into the social meaning of variation more generally.

In addition, this topic is relevant to those (most commonly educators and adults more generally) who habitually criticize young people for their use of slang, and predict a general deterioration in language standards as a consequence of the indiscriminate use of such vague and informal language. It is important to understand the reasons for this linguistic behavior, reasons which relate to several different facets of the lives of young people: they need to be 'modern,' they need to establish themselves as different, and they need to belong, as members of a group whose habits and values are different from those of their parents, other adults, and other young people.

We live in an age in which patterns of communication are undergoing rapid change: reading (in the conventional sense) must increasingly compete with a range of other media, visual and auditory, which offer communication on a smorgasbord, including satellite TV, radio, cell phones, and the internet. Even our written messages to each other today are often shorter, terser and adapted to a faster-paced existence. Our oral communication is also becoming increasingly informal and the use of first names and acronyms is nowadays highly valued, especially, but not exclusively, among the younger generations. Using slang and swearing is one of the many ways in which members of groups can reflect their informality and modernity, ensuring that they are seen as 'cool,' fashionable, up-to-date and part of the speech community of young people, while at the same time distinguishing themselves as members of a distinctive peer group.

This chapter will start by providing a brief background description of the linguistic characteristics of slang and swearing before moving to a more focused discussion of why (although such language is also commonly used by many adult groups who find themselves living in close proximity in institutionalized contexts such as prisons or military camps), it may be particularly typical of adolescent speech. Subsequent sections of the chapter explore how the use of slang and expletives by young people can be viewed as a means of building cultural capital within their networks, while at the same time establishing boundaries between new adolescent in-groups ('us') and parents and nonmembers ('them'). A section on the use of pejorative terms further develops this theme of 'us' and 'them.' In addition, I also consider gender-based patterns of the ways young people use slang and expletives, and the subtle coercive effect such words have in regulating typical patterns of in-group behavior. Finally some suggestions are made regarding research questions that still require attention.

Slang and swearing: Some definitions

Slang comprises the vocabulary and idiom that is generally not appropriate to formal contexts of use or accepted as part of the standard by educated speakers of the language (Flexner & Wentworth, 1975). Because of their extremely informal effect, slang and expletives are most commonly associated with spoken rather than written language (indeed, deciding how to spell slang words is often problematic, since their brief, though often recycled, existence usually means that they do not get dictionary listings). Another commonly recognized feature of slang is that it typically evolves and develops in small, close-knit groups (e.g., army and school cohorts, sports teams) and tends to be somewhat short-lived. While the aura of freshness attached to slang may rather have something to do with the fact that it is constantly recycled in new groups, as well as with its rarity in formal discourse, there certainly is some truth in the claim that slang is evanescent and constantly changing, giving it a trendy or fashionable feel which makes those who use it feel 'cool.' In the words of a journalist who discusses the expressions *crashing* (staying over), and *hanging* (staying at home; doing nothing), 'It'd be risky to dwell on the words ... they may have undergone some permutations since I heard them a few hours ago' (Hall, 2002). This up-to-dateness of slang means that it is often very localized and topical, and may have a regionalized flavor. It certainly has an appeal for young people, who often aim to be fashionable and trendy in the way they use language just as much as the way they dress.

One of the most recognizable aspects of slang is the fact that these words are typically flippant and lightheartedly indecorous, and tend to reduce seriousness by being witty and clever. In essence, using slang and expletives is 'a style of language rather than a level of formality ... the distinguishing feature ... is the intention, however often unsuccessful, to produce rhetorical effect, such as incongruity, irreverence or exaggeration' (American Heritage Dictionary, 1969: xlvi). This humorous lack of sentimentality markedly lowers levels of formality, while at the same time revealing considerable delight in language as an expressive, almost poetic medium, evidenced by the rhyme, alliteration, metaphor, onomatopoeia and other linguistic forms it draws on.

In contrast, swearwords or expletives, including profanity, in which the name of a deity is used to express negative affect or disrespect, comprise a fairly limited set of words which seldom change. Swearwords are potentially far more offensive than slang, and their use can have a far more powerful emotive effect.

From the point of view of the majority of (at least Western) members of middle and upper classes, swearwords and slang form a continuum of nonstandard forms, with swearwords comprising the more shocking or taboo range of words and slang that which approaches acceptability. In testing whether most speakers could recognize which words were slang and expletives in their language, Dumas and Lighter (1978: 9) found that, when informants were presented with a list of sentences containing words of 'dubious virtue,' they showed a remarkable lack of consensus regarding which of them were slang. Distinguishing slang from expletives or swearwords also depends on the group which uses them: according to *Collins Dictionary* (Tweedie, 2003), only 16 of the 70 taboo words listed in the earlier edition remain taboo, and the rest (e.g., *bollocks*) have been downgraded to mere slang or informal expressions on the basis of frequency of use and of the 'majority' view of perceptions of the shock value of these words. Even strong expletives such as *fuck* may be so liberally used in some groups that they become largely unmarked and unnoticed.

Clear definitions of the meanings of commonly used slang terms and expletives are generally not available: the very essence of such words rests in their vagueness and adaptability. As Hall (2002) points out, *cool* can be used to describe a teacher (popular), a shirt (fashionable), a test (easy) or a potential problem (inconsequential). It generally connotes the fashionable or the approved, and includes an easygoing, laid-back attitude. Similarly, the exact meanings of verbs like *suck* (with negative connotations) and *rock* (with positive connotations), and adjectives like *hectic* (used to describe anything from a difficult lecture or a terrible car crash to an enjoyable meal), are all equally elusive. According to Sornig (1981:1) it is often difficult to explain the meanings of slang words because 'the reason for their very existence lies in the connotative part of the meaning.'

Not only are they semantically and etymologically elusive, but slang and expletives are typically also syntactically versatile, the words frequently acting on demand as adjectives, verbs or nouns: for example, the local South African slang word *arb* (possibly derived from *arbitrary*, although the original meaning has shifted) has several different meanings (unexciting, ordinary, not worthy of much comment, boring) and can act as a noun (*I saw this arb walking toward me*), an adjective (*this arb person suddenly came up*) or a verb (*we were just arbing around*), or an expletive (*arb man!*). Perhaps, more recognizably, the word *fuck* can serve as expletive (*oh fuck!*), verb (*fuck off*), adjective (*you fucking nerd*), adverb (*this is fucking impossible*) or noun (e.g., *Professor Smith, would you repeat those last two fuckers?*) (see Dumas & Lighter, 1978:14–15). The point about these words is that they refuse to obey the linguistic or grammatical rules to which other vocabulary is usually subject. At the same time that the use of these words also breaks grammatical taboos within the language, they also break certain social taboos.

Breaking the rules

A particular attraction that the use of slang and expletives may hold for young people is that they are a means to break the rules of convention and (adult) society. Linguistic taboos exist in most cultures, tabooed words generally being culture-specific and relating to bodily functions or aspects of a culture which are sacred. Such words are avoided, considered inappropriate, and loaded with affective meaning. It is interesting to consider which areas of life do *not* contain many slang terms or expletives, such as furniture, trees, writing materials or doors. These semantic fields are typically immune from the influence of slang because they refer to commonplace, unexciting areas of life which have very few emotive connotations. In contrast, slang and expletives augment the lexicon in certain areas to accommodate the needs of speakers (Bailey, 1985:12), areas in which existing words aren't enough and which interest particular subcultures. If this happens to be a group of motorbike enthusiasts, one expects many motorbike words, but in young people's peer groups, these words usually revolve around typical teenage interests, and most especially taboo and other liminal areas.

Thus one finds an abundance of slang terms and expletives in semantic areas relating to enjoyment and fun and pleasure: eating and drinking (often to excess), sleeping, money, cigarettes and drugs, and sexual activity (in the broadest senses). All of these are aspects of life which are interesting, enjoyable, exciting and often forbidden to the young. Then there are the embarrassing or sensitive aspects of life: parts of the body, scatological terms, mental and physical deficiencies, racist terms, conflict and death. Many of these are socially taboo, or frowned upon in some way by some or other group, and in slang we find a high proportion of terms for these aspects of humanity. In this sense, slang can be extremely hurtful and unsubtle, and crudely and harshly critical of any perceived imperfections. Used flippantly or lightheartedly among members of the ingroup, such words evoke humor and can, on occasion, serve as euphemisms, covering embarrassment about areas that worry, frighten or embarrass us.

Because slang and expletive usage is also associated with confidence and rebellion against adult norms, and growing sexual maturity is frequently accompanied by increased daring in the use of taboo items, these words are particularly strongly associated with males, and this is a strong cultural stereotype that has been expressed for years (e.g., Flexner & Wentworth, 1975; Jespersen, 1922; Milward, 1937; Pickford, 1956; Wilson, 1956). Such a view, although no longer necessarily accurate, is hardly surprising: male peer groups are typically larger and more hierarchical, close-knit and competitive than female groups (Cheshire 1984; Labov, 1966; Romaine 1984), which are smaller, more intimate, and do not value verbal posturing as much. Given the use of slang and expletives to defy linguistic or social convention and to lower the dignity of the occasion, this leads one to expect greater overall usage by males.

Using slang and expletives to build cultural capital

In terms of establishing different norms and values, especially as regards the linguistic behavior of young people, the concept of a linguistic market, derived from Bourdieu and Boltanski (1975) (see Eckert 2000:13), is particularly useful to describe what happens during the transitions of adolescence, and can explain to a large extent why young people may use more slang and expletives than do older people. In these terms, young people are driven to use language as a resource in order to earn dividends and to build up social and cultural capital, and the value of one's linguistic performance depends on issues such as variety and style. It is also worth remembering that it is possible to have more than one linguistic market operating in a broad linguistic community at the same time: the adult, global market, in which legitimate standard language holds the highest value, and will determine status and access to jobs, social privilege and power, and various submarkets, which operate in smaller, tightly knit networks. Among such networks (e.g., factory workers, members of sports teams, soldiers in training, criminal gangs) are groupings of young people who interact frequently, both formally and informally, and establish strong bonds with each other.

Within these multistranded high-density groupings, the value of adult modes of communication must now compete with new, informal styles, accents and vocabularies, which acquire a value of their own. Expletives and slang are prime symbolic assets in this marketplace, carrying markedly higher value during the adolescent years than in later years. In order for young people to make themselves marketable within their own sociocultural networks, they must recognize and use (and therefore attribute value to) the speech habits of the peer group. The teenager is therefore at one and the same time both the linguistic agent, which ultimately sets the values, as well as a commodity on the market.

The really valuable cultural 'capital' which young people need during this period is controlled by peers, and their success in achieving recognition and status in this adolescent world depends on their ability to command alliances with and get attention from valued members of the subculture (Eckert, 2000). Certain individuals can enter such a cultural system and influence its meanings and values more easily than others, depending on their status in similar communities. Thus young people with prior connections to older adolescents are likely to have greater value in their communities, known already to hang out with 'cool' people, and to be positively viewed as a reliable source of stylistic meaning and information (Eckert, 2000).

As a new understanding of the relation between power and ways of speaking emerges in such communities, each adolescent has to make choices, whether consciously or unconsciously, in adopting the mode of communication best suited to his or her needs. Although young people are no doubt aware— implicitly if not explicitly—of the social significance of standard speech, and the value it will play in the academic market and later in an employment market, they also intuitively understand that different values obtain in the adolescent linguistic market in which they are currently involved, and they may consider it worthwhile to 'invest' in it. In this sense, the use of new, stylish vocabulary which is either not understood by adults (such as a South African word like *lank* (which means 'a lot') or strongly disapproved by them (e.g., *fuck*) serves to distinguish its users from these more conservative members of the society, and challenge the value of their linguistic 'currency,' while at the same time setting up a different, competing set of linguistic values which bind its users together.

It is therefore in adolescence where linguists discover the highest levels of linguistic innovation. Such networks constantly renew and change old and familiar ways of doing things (including modes of expression, hairstyles and clothing), in order to maintain a sense of freshness and modernity, alongside a sense of being distinctive and different from established norms and values.

Thus the notions of prestige and stigma need to be viewed outside of traditional abstract socioeconomic hierarchies, because prestige is a matter of point of view and is differentially assigned by different speech communities (Milroy & Milroy, 1992; Romaine, 1981). Trudgill's notion of covert prestige (1972) goes some way toward recognizing that local market values can conflict with global ones. It is for this reason that 'most social dialectologists have found that young people use the highest frequencies of vernacular forms, especially if they are forms which people clearly recognize or identify as non-standard' (Holmes, 1992:184). Like slang, these forms act as markers of group membership. Such behavior peaks in adolescence, when peer group pressure not to conform to social pressure is arguably at its strongest, and then rises again in old age, when social pressures reduce and people move into a more 'relaxed' life stage. In other words, as people get older, their speech gets less dialectal and more standard (Holmes, 1992:184) and 'in their middle years, people are most likely to recognize the society's speech norms and use the fewest vernacular forms' (Holmes, 1992:185), with use of standard forms peaking at age 30–55. Those adults who are successful and who acquire social status along with the trappings of wealth are very likely ultimately to impose and uphold the very taboos against the use of slang and expletives which they flouted in their own youth; those with less social power or those who lack alternative means of displaying power are far more likely, as adults, to retain their covert status symbols and conform to the need to fit into local subcommunities by using the very words which those who have the power reject.

Thus, although many adults in tight-knit linguistic communities use slang and expletives themselves, most adults in middle-class conservative society commonly disapprove of their use, having allied themselves to a different linguistic market. In addition to the perceived lack of prestige of these words, the fact that they break social taboos and exclude nonusers by being part of a 'private' code, while increasing levels of informality, adds considerably to their negative effect on more conservative members of society.

Using slang in order to belong—and to exclude

Slang flourishes in groups which conflict in some way with the dominant culture (such as prison inmates), by emphasizing the values, attitudes and interests of the subculture, and thereby marking social or linguistic identity. As Crystal puts it, 'the chief use of slang is to show that you're one of the gang' (1987: 53). An important feature of slang is the fact that these words are part of a shared linguistic code, reinforcing group membership and indicating shared knowledge and interests. Because a sense of belonging is certainly important during the transitions of adolescence, one expects slang and expletives to abound among the young, who have a high degree of shared knowledge and interests (Matthews, 1997:343), because this shared code shows solidarity and reinforces group membership while simultaneously excluding others who do not use the code (such as parents and teachers). Indeed, there are many slang terms for those young people who fail to acquire insider membership of adolescent groups, such as *dweeb, geek, nerd* and *lame*.

A closer look at the nature and meaning of certain homophobic slang words (referring derogatorily to gay people, e.g., *homo, fag, queer* and *moffie*, an Afrikaans term for homosexual) reveals an interesting aspect of how slang usage may be used to include and to exclude [see O'Flynn—chapter 9, this volume]. Thurlow (2001) and Armstrong (1997) both write of the upturn in prejudice and hostility toward gays and lesbians (expressed both in terms of physical and verbal violence) and point out that derogatory language is especially common in the abuse of young gay males, serving to reinforce negative stereotypes against homosexuality and feminine gender attributes. In a study of my own with Antrobus (2004), we provide a similar case study which reveals high frequencies of such homophobic terms, especially from males, with females generally far less harsh in their judgments of males (see de Klerk & Antrobus, 2004).

Although it has often been pointed out that much of the slang used by males is derogatory of women and reinforces male dominance (Sutton, 1995), Armstrong (1997: 327) notes in addition that 'the language men sometimes direct towards one another also serves to maintain their hegemonic power over women' and to define what is regarded as normal masculine behavior. He examines homophobic slang terms and shows how they act coercively in signaling what is viewed as 'acceptable' behavior in contrast to effeminacy, which is seen as not conforming to the prevailing cultural code regarding 'normal' or acceptable sexual behavior. He shows that 'young people will refer to almost anything or anybody as "gay" if they disapprove of it or find it odd' (1997: 329) and the homophobic language occurs most frequently in multimale groups known to each other, to express disapproval of actions which are viewed as unmasculine (such as studying or not drinking). In so doing, the use of such terms affirms masculinity. With strong connotations of masculinity and toughness, abusive language is stereotypically used more by boys than by girls, and even boys tend to over-report their use of it in order to enhance this reputation (Sutton, 1995).

Cameron (1997) makes the same point in describing the social construction of male heterosexual identities: she shows how a group of college-age young men used homophobic terms to refer to people who were undoubtedly not gay but more broadly 'deviant' in terms of their gendered behavior, in relation to the in-group's norms for masculinity. These male speakers refer to 'four homos' hitting on 'the ugliest-ass-bitch in the history of the world,' whose homosexual behavior is judged as such not for sexual but for social reasons: 'proper masculinity requires that the object of … sexual interest be not just female but minimally attractive' (Cameron, 1997:53). Thurlow (2001) cites several other studies in this regard and points out that it is likely that the fear of being labeled by these names results in an effort by members of the ingroup to distance themselves from such ostracized groups, to the point where potential members of these very groups find themselves using these same pejorative terms in a chameleon-like effort to disguise themselves. In his own study of British highschoolers, Thurlow reports that the vast majority of homophobic terms reported referred to male homosexuality, with only 14 percent referring to female homosexuality. In much the same way, 'with apparently little concern for their antisocial ramifications, homophobic pejoratives, many of them vitriolic, constitute one of the most predominant categories of abusive language among adolescents' (Thurlow, 2001:32). 'Ugly names' for women reported by Sutton (1995) are similarly devoid of female homophobic terms. This is attributable either to a proportionate lack of available homophobic terms for females, or broader issues of inequality which disregard women in general. Taking this one step further, one even finds young females using words like *girls* or *ladies* as somewhat derogatory terms, or referring to themselves as *guys* or *chaps* in an effort to align themselves more closely to those who are socially powerful.

As Thurlow (2001) notes, abusive naming practices reveal the social attitudes of the community of users, distinguishing the outgroup from the insiders, and implicitly or explicitly declaring who one is and who one is not. He also points out that during adolescence, when belonging to the peer group is vital, language (and naming) is a primary resource to constitute the self, social categories and social relations. Part of this is 'the continual, vocal branding of Other' in order to identify 'Self' simultaneously. It is this combination of exclusion and bonding which makes slang and swearwords especially attractive to teenagers.

Thus, by labeling outsiders as 'faggots' one can simultaneously index their otherness while reaffirming one's own masculinity. For most users of these words, their actual meaning is overlooked, and the usage relates to belonging and reaffirming common values (and group boundaries) and reinforcing masculinity. In many cases, those who are labeled as 'gay' or 'queer' in all-male playful contexts often do not take offense, because their playful use indicates that the user actually does not assume the hearer to really be gay. If he were, the term would be avoided, in the same way that overtly racist terms are not normally used in the presence of members of the racial groups to which they refer. This maintains the invisibility of homosexuals, allowing adolescents (regardless of their sexual predisposition) to continue to use homophobic terms with scant regard for their effect.

This male hegemony is also reflected in the fact that most research on derogatory names for males and females (e.g., Sutton, 1995) reports more negative terms referring to women than to men, most of which carry sexual connotations. In our own case study, Antrobus and I (2004) have found interesting developments in the terms that young women are nowadays using to refer to themselves; female participants reported 14 percent more of these names than their male counterparts did. Words for physically unattractive or fat females outnumbered those for their male counterparts, and the terms were harshly critical (e.g., *swamp donkey, brak,* an Afrikaans term for an ill-bred dog, *cow, dog, gorilla, grunter, (g)rotweiler, mare, slut, steamroller, lorry, pie, pig* and *whale.* (Words referring to males included *elephant, whale, donkey, grunter, boulder* and *tuckshop.*) It is also interesting to note that among the words suggested by the girls were several with ironic or sarcastic overtones (e.g., *beaut, looker, pearl, special*) which were notably absent from the male examples. Among the derogatory terms referring to 'unpleasant' people, reference to females again outnumbered references to males, many of them explicitly sexual (e.g., *hoer* [Afrikaans for whore], *whore, slut, cunt, dickhead, pussy*). Many of the words suggested by males in this study were strongly sexual (e.g., *cunt, prick, dickhead, poes* [Afrikaans for cunt], *penis, arsehole*), in keeping with Sutton's (1995: 281) earlier claim that 'it is extremely rare to hear one woman refer to another as a cunt.' Contrary to expectations, when viewed proportionately, males in our study supplied only 3 percent more tokens than did females, and each group supplied an equivalent number of actual lexical items (types). Although this reinforces the view that females are no longer avoiding pejorative words (at least not in terms of numerical frequency), they do appear to opt for words which have a lower 'shock-value,' using milder and less offensive words.

It is also worth noting that there is some small irony in the reputation young people have for using refreshingly original and creative slang: a limited range of lexical items of slang and expletives are often used to such an extent within a small linguistic network of young people that these words have the potential to become boring and routine. It should be remembered that in many cases, when young people use in-group words in order to belong, some may be using these words as a 'front,' to pretend that they are 'normal,' heterosexual members of the group, whereas others may not actually know what the words they are using mean at all: using slang or expletives does not necessarily imply a full command of the meaning of these words. This is because such words are typically used on informal occasions among peers with a high degree of shared knowledge and common interests, forming part of a contextualized, restricted code, full of connotations, demanding extensive mutual understanding because of their implicit nature. Clear definitions are often not readily available, and such words are inherently vague. Speakers are therefore often unaware of the full import of the terms they use, or do not share the same understanding of their meanings, simply because they pick up the words through observation, and asking about the meaning of such words would be like admitting failure as a member of the group. In addition, habit and constant exposure can dull the power of words which are strongly taboo for non-group-members. Provocative slang may therefore not always be used with deliberate intent to exclude or criticize, although their careless use nonetheless has a negative effect (*cf* Thurlow, 2001).

Slang and swearwords as subtle forms of coercion

Although it is tempting in such articles as these to overgeneralize and give an impression that all young people behave in the same way, it is important to note the existence of many young people who do not fit the pattern described in this chapter, and who assert their identities in ways which are their own, and which obviously reflect their intelligence and personalities uniquely. In many ways young people find themselves constrained when it comes to slang and expletives. As was discussed earlier, many young people are very aware that slang and other vernacular forms are stigmatized in the global hierarchy, and although they may recognize that such words pay useful dividends in the local market-place, where they carry value, they might well prefer to avoid such words. How-ever, it is also true to say that most young people find themselves under consid-erable pressure, as they enter adolescence, to begin using these words even if they prefer not to, because, from an adolescent perspective, assimilation into the adult system potentially carries with it the ultimate stigma of failure to over-come childhood subordination to adults (Eckert, 2000:227).

As indicated, an important part of the coercion associated with slang and expletives relates to gender: being feminine or masculine is not so much about what we are but more about what we do (Cameron, 1997), and gender is con-stantly constructed and reaffirmed by publicly performing particular acts, in-cluding linguistic acts, in accordance with cultural norms. These norms are strongly coercive and regulatory, prescribing to people how to behave appropri-ately, depending on whether they are masculine or feminine. In this view, each human being is a conscious social agent who either follows or resists these strong norms, actively constructing their gendered selves in the process.

For example, according to Burgoon *et al.* (1983), use of expletives is closely related to socialization, with males in Western society learning habits of verbal aggression, thereby contributing to a perception that they are strong and power-ful, whereas females reportedly avoid their use (Crosby & Nyquist, 1977; Holmes, 1984; Key, 1975; McConnell-Ginet *et al.*, 1980; Spender, 1980). Thus, in a sense, males have a certain obligation to try them out and conform to the expectations of society in using expletives. It is also important to remember that although there is pressure on females not to use such words, there is obviously counterpressure on males to conform to masculine linguistic behavior, and al-though it takes considerable self-confidence to refuse to conform to the norms of the group, not all of them necessarily find the prospect of using slang and expletives equally tempting. Although young men might be expected to know and use far more of these words than young women, the fact is that most of them have very little choice. As Moreau (1984:60) puts it, the concrete and ver-bal practices of the dominant seem to induce the dominated to adopt specific language practices; the use of slang and expletives by adolescent males can be seen as a way of attempting to assert self, while at the same time it can be viewed as expected behavior which conforms to definition imposed by the dominant discourse more widely.

In addition, it has also been pointed out how the use of homophobic terms, which define what is regarded as 'normal' and valued in the subculture, also has a strongly coercive effect, by reinforcing conformity to the overriding masculine hegemony depicted by these terms. The consequence of the use of homophobic terms is that they signal inclusion and define what the group sees as 'normal,' while showing disapproval of inappropriate (feminine) behavior (Armstrong, 1997). Such 'normal' behavior is likely to result from efforts young people make to avoid being labeled as outsiders.

Even the slang used by females shows evidence of conformity to this pressure, with signs that they appear to be increasingly adopting and using the same sexist and homophobic terms used by males, and consequentially running the risk of being labeled butch (Armstrong, 1997:333). In addition, females are increasingly referring to themselves as *guys, chaps* or *chicks* (a term suggesting male possession) and using words like *girl* and *lady* as derogatory terms. Their use of female derogatory terms (e.g., *bitch, whore, slut*, as reported by Risch, 1987:357, in order to refer to males follows a similar subverted pattern). In a similar vein, I have previously found a very high number of such derogatory terms known by boys for ugly girls compared with the number of equivalent terms known by girls to refer to boys (de Klerk, 1990; 1992). Studies and lexical analyses by Miller and Swift (1978) and Schulz (1975) have also shown that there are many more unfavorable terms in English for females than for males, in conformity with the theory of semantic derogation of words which relate in any way to socially out of power groups (obviously females belong in this category).

Some directions for future research

It must be remembered that linguistic styles are options, only meaningful within and determined by current social circumstances. Instead of viewing verbal interaction as harmonious and cooperative, one needs to link linguistic choices to wider social processes, relationships and power. The potential for change comes when groups with different discourse norms or conventions find themselves interacting, and this is the case when males and females, or young people and adults, come together and use language in accordance with slightly different pre-established norms. Their linguistic preferences can provide a microcosmic study of the power relations that exist in that society and their discourse can be seen as representing a kind of delicate social power struggle which may often result in change, both in the mode of discourse and of wider social and cultural domains (Fairclough, 1992: 28–29).

Clearly, linguistic behavior in adolescence is not a simple matter of conformity to unambiguous role models, and there is plenty of evidence of deviance and opposition to the system of age-linked and gender-linked differences, suggesting that linguistic differentiation is neither smooth nor consensual. An assertion that young people typically use these words simply because they are adolescent is a risky one, to say the least. Being an 'authentic adolescent' has no fixed form. Each individual must go through the process of working out for him- or herself whether slang or expletives suit his or her image, and make him or her cool; for young females, using them breaks rules and thereby makes a clear statement; for young males, *not* using them makes a different kind of statement. The lack of conformity both within and across gender groups suggests that such words, instead of being regarded exclusively as signs of masculinity *per se*, are increasingly being regarded more as symbols of power more generally, equally available to both gender groups.

One area that calls for more detailed research is how female linguistic behavior appears to be changing. Young women face dual pressures from society as they enter adolescence: although they are expected to conform to social expectations and behave in traditional feminine ways, as early as 1943, Schlauch (1943: 287) noted tendencies for females to encroach on the all-male precinct of expletives, and Hertzler (1965) and Maurer (1976) make the same point. It would appear that with shifts in power, norms and habits of expletive usage are being challenged and signs of change are revealed in more recent studies by Oliver and Rubin (1975), Bailey and Timm (1976), Staley (1978), Risch (1987) and de Klerk (1990, 1991, 1992), all of whom indicate a growing resistance by females to conformity to stereotyped norms regarding the use of expletives as symbols of masculinity. In this regard, Waksler (1995) predicts a steady neutralization of gender, linguistically, in the future, with words which were previously the preserve of males and/or females being used more freely across categories (e.g., *guys* to refer to both males and females). This was only evident to a limited extent in the terms elicited in my research with Antrobus (de Klerk & Antrobus, 2004), several of which (e.g., *slob, ripper, porky, special, swamp donkey, troll*) referred equally to both gender groups. However, none of the terms with any sexual connotations had this versatility, and it will be interesting to monitor changes of this kind. Another interesting focus for future research is the extent to which females and males alike indulge in the use of harsh, abusive words in order to criticize and exclude those who are socially ostracized for one reason or another, all contributing to 'the reproduction of social inequalities and power relations' (Thurlow, 2001:35). Contrary to expectations, and claims that 'most studies in slang ... have seen women as linguistically conservative, adhering closely to the standard form of speech' (Sutton, 1995: 282), more recent studies (e.g., de Klerk & Antrobus, ibid.) reveal a fairly vigorous pejorative vocabulary used by females. Such trends could be seen as an attempt by females to parody or mimic male behavior and associate with the socially dominant group, or it is possible that an increasing number of women are trying to assert a new image of women which runs contrary to conventional stereotyped images of femininity. Whereas the terms used by males continue to devalue females and reinforce the hegemony of males, the terms used by females do the same in reverse, and appear to be taking control (albeit tentatively) of a semantic space in which they formerly had no place at all. Rather than trying to appear like men, they could be trying to construct a new identity which runs contrary to traditional definitions of femininity (*cf* Sutton, 1995: 290).

Notes

1. It is also important to point out that when one seeks to make generalizations about adolescent linguistic behavior, one faces the inevitable problem that such behavior is inherently colored by the social, cultural, geographical and temporal context of users. Although broad trends and truisms are evident, it must be clearly stated at the outset that the focus in this chapter is primarily on English-speaking, Western adolescent speech, with several examples drawn from South African English teenagers between 1990 and 2003.

References

Armstrong, J. D. (1997). Homophobic slang as coercive discourse among college students. In A. Livia & K. Hall (eds), *Queerly Phrased: Language, Gender and Sexuality* (pp. 326–334). New York: Oxford University Press.

Bailey, L. A. & Timm, L. A. (1976). More on women's and men's expletives. *Anthropological Linguistics*, 18, 438–449.

Bailey, R. (1985). South African English slang: Form, functions and origins. *South African Journal of Linguistics*, 3 (1), 1–42.

Bourdieu P. & Boltanski, L. (1975). Le Fetichisme de la langue. *Actes de la Recherche En Sciences Sociales*, 4 (2), 20–32.

Burgoon, M., Dillard, J. & Doran, N. (1983). Friendly or unfriendly persuasion. *Human Communication Research*, 10(2), 283–294.

Cameron, D. (1997). Performing gender identity: young men's talk and the construction of heterosexual masculinity. In S. Johnson & U. Meinhof (eds), *Language and Masculinity* (pp. 47–64). Oxford: Blackwell.

Chambers J. (2003). *Sociolinguistic Theory* (2nd ed.). Oxford: Blackwell.

Cheshire, J. (1984*).* Indigenous non-standard varieties and education. In P. Trudgill (ed.), *Applied Sociolinguistics* (pp. 564–588). London: Academic Press.

Crosby, F. & Nyquist, L. (1977). The female register: An empirical study of Lakoff's hypotheses. *Language in Society*, 6, 313–322.

Crystal, D. (1987). *The Cambridge Encyclopaedia of Language*. Cambridge: Cambridge University Press.

de Klerk, V. A. (1990). Slang: A male domain? *Sex Roles*, 22, 9(10), 589–606.

de Klerk, V. A. (1991). Expletives: Men only? *Communications Monographs*, 58, 156–169.

de Klerk, V. A. (1992). How taboo are taboo words for girls? *Language in Society*, 20 (2), 277–290.

de Klerk, V. & Antrobus, R. (2004). *Swamp-donkeys* and *rippers*: The use of slang and pejorative terms to name 'the other'. *Alternation*, 11(2), 264-284.

Dumas, B. K. & Lighter, J. (1978). Is slang a word for linguists? *American Speech*, 53, 5–17.

Eckert, P. (2000). *Linguistic Variation as Social Practice*. Oxford: Blackwell.

Fairclough, N. (1992). *Discourse and Social Change*. Cambridge: Polity Press.

Flexner, S. B. & Wentworth, H. (1975). *Dictionary of American Slang*. New York: Crowell.

Hall, L. (2002). Cool speak. *Hudson Review*. Autumn, 2002.

Hertzler, J. O. (1965). *A Sociology of Language*. New York: Random House.

Holmes, J. (1984). Women's language: A functional approach. *General Linguistics*, 24(3), 149–178.

Holmes, J. (1992). *An Introduction to Sociolinguistics*. London: Longman.

Hudson, K. (1983). *The Language of the Teenage Revolution*. London: Macmillan.

Jespersen, O. (1922). *Language: Its Nature, Development and Origin*. London: Allen & Unwin.

Key, M. R. (1975). *Male/Female Language*. Metuchen, NJ: Scarecrow Press.

Labov, W. (1966). *The Social Stratification of English in New York City*. Washington DC: Washington Centre for Applied Linguistics.

The Macmillan Dictionary of Contemporary Slang. (1995). London: Macmillan.

Matthews, P. (1997). *Oxford Concise Dictionary of Linguistics*. Oxford: Oxford University Press.

Maurer, D. W. (1976). Language and the sex revolution: World War 1 through World War 2. *American Speech*, 51 (2), 5–24.

McConnell-Ginet, S., Borker, R. & Furman, N. (eds). (1980). *Women and Language in Literature and Society*. New York: Praeger.

Miller, C. & Swift, K. (1978). *Words and Women: New Language in New Times*. New York: Anchor Doubleday.

Milroy, L. & Milroy, J. (1992). Social network and social class. *Language in Society*, 21(1), 1–26.

Milward, D. (1937). *The origin and development of the slang in use among the women students in the University of Cape Town in the year 1937*. Unpublished document, University of Cape Town, South Africa.

Moreau, N. B. (1984). Education, ideology and class/sex identity. In C. Kramerae, M. Schultz, and W. O' Barr (eds), *Language and Power* (pp. 43–61). London: Sage.

Oliver, M. & Rubin, J. (1975). The use of expletives by some American women. *Journal of Anthropological Linguistics*, 17, 191–197.

The Oxford Dictionary of Modern Slang. (1992). Oxford: Oxford University Press.

Pickford, G. R. (1956). American linguistic geography: A sociological appraisal. *Word*, 12, 211–233.

Risch, B. (1987). Women's derogatory terms for men: That's right, dirty words. *Language in Society*, 16, 353–358.

Romaine, S. (1984). *The Language of Children and Adolescents*. Oxford: Blackwell.

Schlauch, M. (1943). *The Gift of Tongues*. London: Allen and Unwin.

Schulz, M. (1975). The semantic derogation of women. In B. Thorne & N. Henley (eds), *Language and Sex: Difference and Dominance* (pp. 64–75). Rowley, MA: Newbury House.

Sornig, K. (1981). *Lexical Innovation: A Study of Slang, Colloquialisims and Casual Speech*. Amsterdam: John Benjamins.

Spender, D. (1980). *Man Made Language*. London: Routledge and Kegan Paul.

Staley, C. M. (1978). Male-female use of expletives: A heck of a difference in expectations. *Anthropological Linguistics*, 20 (8), 367–380.

Sutton, L. A. (1995). Bitches and skankly hobags: The place of women in contemporary language. In K. Hall and M. Bucholz (eds), *Gender Articulated: Language and the Socially Constructed Self* (pp. 279–296). New York: Routledge.

Thurlow, C. (2001). Naming the outsider within: Homophobic pejoratives and the verbal abuse of lesbian, gay and bisexual highschool pupils. *Journal of Adolescence*, 24, 25–38.

Trudgill, P. (1972). Sex, covert prestige and linguistic change in the urban British English of Norwich. *Language in Society*, 1, 179–196.

Tweedie, N. (2003). Bollocks and gangbang are now just slang. *Sunday Times* (South Africa) July 13.

Waksler, R. (1995). She's a mensch and he's a bitch: Neutralising gender in the nineties. *English Today*, 11(2), 3–6.

Wilson, J. (1956). *Language and the Pursuit of Truth*. Cambridge: Cambridge University Press.

8

The language of love: Romantic relationships in adolescence

Lauren Berger, Dana McMakin
and Wyndol Furman

Effective communication is often believed to be a hallmark of successful relationships. For example, married individuals in the United States maintain that communication is the single most important aspect of their relationship (Baucom *et al.*, 1990). Couples who communicate well also report higher satisfaction in their relationship, whereas distressed couples often lack good methods of communicating (Baucom *et al.*, 1990). In fact, communication is such a significant component of adult romantic relationships that researchers can accurately classify 80 percent of couples as being distressed or nondistressed by simply watching how they communicate about a conflict (Gottman *et al.*, 1977; Gottman, 1979; Weiss & Heyman, 1990). Additionally, couples' communication about positive events, such as each other's good news, is another important factor in determining long-term relationship satisfaction (Reiss & Gable, 2003). Taken together, these lines of research imply that relationship satisfaction is less determined by the sheer occurrence of conflict or positive events in the lives of couples, and more related to the ability of romantic partners to communicate successfully about important life issues.

Despite striking evidence for the importance of communication in adult couple relationships, scant research has examined communication in adolescent romantic relationships. Until recently, almost no work had been conducted on any aspect of adolescent romantic relationships. Researchers had shied away from studying romance in adolescence for several reasons: these relationships are often short-lived and difficult to study, some researchers questioned how important these early romantic experiences were, and few theories existed to guide the work (Brown *et al.*, 1999).

Today, however, we know that romantic relationships are central to young peoples' day-to-day lives. In the context of heterosexual socialization, fifteen- to eighteen-year-old U.S. high school girls interact or talk with boys almost ten hours a week, and boys interact or talk with girls about five hours a week (Richards *et al.*, 1998). In addition, girls think about boys another eight hours a week, and boys think about girls an additional five to six hours. Of course, these numbers are only self-reported approximations; some of these interactions with the other sex are with potential (vs. actual) romantic partners and some with other-sex friends. These estimates also do not include same-sex attractions or recently developed, popular methods of communication such as the internet. Furthermore, we suspect that the availability of cell phones is likely to have increased the amount of contact among young people in recent years [see McKay *et al.*—chapter 11, this volume].

Although it is difficult to get a *precise* estimate of how often young people are communicating with romantic partners, the point is clear. Young people spend a large amount of time focused on romantic relationships.[2] Dating and romantic relationships are principal topics of conversation among young people and their peers (Eder, 1993), and high school students interact more frequently with romantic partners than they do with parents, siblings or friends (Laursen & Williams, 1997). Moreover, emotional feelings about romantic relationships occupy the forefront of young people's minds. Young people actually have strong positive emotions and strong negative emotions about the other sex more often than they do about same-sex peers, family or school (Larson *et al.*, 1999).

Although we know that communication occurs frequently between young people and their romantic partners, we know very little about how communication is characterized in these emerging relationships. In this chapter, we discuss what is known and what we still think needs to be done to increase understanding of romantic relationships in adolescence. Although we believe that our remarks are for the most part applicable to both heterosexual and homosexual relationships, we point out instances when they seem applicable to only heterosexual attraction. We want to note at the outset that our comments are also limited to romantic relationships in industrialized Western societies, and may be even more constrained to specific countries or ethnic groups. Unfortunately, we know remarkably little about cultural differences in adolescent romantic relationships, but we expect that they are likely to be substantial.

Our chapter is guided by a *behavioral systems* approach to studying close relationships (see Furman & Wehner, 1994). Behavioral systems theory posits that relationships can serve four primary functions: (a) affiliation, (b) sexual/reproductive needs, (c) attachment and (d) caregiving. Each of these functions can be met by several relationships, yet certain relationships tend to fulfill a young person's primary affiliative, sexual, attachment, or caregiving needs. Which relationship—parent, friend or romantic partner—serves as primary in these domains changes over the course of the lifespan. For example, parents are primary attachment figures in childhood, but romantic partners are individuals' primary attachment figures in adulthood (Hazan & Zeifman, 1994). We find this approach valuable because it provides a framework for defining the principal functions of close relationships, and for comparing and contrasting different types of relationships at different times in life.

We propose that communication plays a central role in the functioning of the four behavioral systems in adolescent romantic relationships. The quality and characteristics of communication between young people and their romantic partners may facilitate or inhibit the functioning of each of these domains. For example, just as open, supportive communication between parents and young people is related to a more secure parent attachment relationship (Kobak *et al.* 1993; see also Noller—chapter 12, this volume), sensitive, empathic communication is essential if young people are to serve as caregivers or sources of support for their romantic partners (Reis & Patrick, 1996).

In the sections that follow we explore communication in each of these four domains. We discuss how existing research about these behavioral systems informs our understanding of communication in adolescent romantic relationships, and we also make suggestions for further studies to explore. In addition, we consider how communication in adolescent romantic relationships compares to communication in young people's relationships with parents and friends. Similarly, we describe developmental changes in behavioral systems and discuss how such developmental changes may be associated with changes in young people's communication with romantic partners.

In addition to examining communication in behavioral systems, we also discuss communication regarding two other domains: (a) conflict and (b) relationship status. Conflict and relationship status are essential issues to be negotiated in the course of young people's relationships with romantic partners. Importantly, young people's ability to communicate and resolve these issues has implications for the functioning of the behavioral systems.

Behavioral systems and romantic relationships

Affiliation

Affiliation refers to the companionship and stimulation components of a relationship (Furman, 1998; Weiss, 1998). Affiliative behaviors include spending time together, engaging in joint activities, and sharing interests. Most of the time, affiliation involves having fun and is characterized by positive affect. To be able to affiliate effectively with a boyfriend or girlfriend, communication skills such as conversational and narrative skills are important. Instrumental communication skills, such as being able to assert one's wishes and negotiating a mutually satisfactory activity, are also significant. Because affiliative behaviors mainly occur when individuals are in a positive or at least neutral mood, communication may be relatively easy as compared to communication in other contexts. Affiliative topics of communication are not likely to be highly emotionally laden or sensitive. A positive mood also increases creativity and mental flexibility (Isen, 1999), which may improve the ability of young people to engage each other in conversation and determine mutually satisfactory activities. Anyone who can remember the sounds and scenes in a school cafeteria knows that affiliative communication is certainly creative, boisterous and engaging to those involved.

In middle childhood and early adolescence, young people learn and practice these skills in the context of same-sex friend and peer relations, which are the most salient affiliative relationships during these developmental periods. As heterosexual young people approach adolescence, they become more interested in the other sex and begin to interact and communicate with them more often. We know less about the developmental course for young gay, lesbian or bisexual people, but many of them engage in similar activities with other-sex peers prior to or as part of the process of learning about their sexual identity (Diamond *et al.*, 1999; see also O'Flynn—chapter 9, this volume). The first conversations between other-sex peers are likely to be somewhat awkward as most young people are relatively inexperienced with interacting with the other sex in these terms. As these interchanges become more practiced, however, young people may begin to turn to their boyfriend or girlfriend for companionship and affiliation. Such affiliative interactions are believed to characterize romantic relationships throughout the rest of adolescence and adulthood. Adult romantic partners who serve as companions and participate in shared novel and arousing activities report more satisfying relationship quality (Aron *et al.*, 2000).

Although affiliative interactions are characteristic of romantic relationships throughout the lifespan, developmental changes in the nature of affiliation occur as well. Specifically, young people usually first interact with the opposite sex in a mixed group context, and then begin dating in a group context, before finally forming more exclusive, dyadic romantic relationships (Connolly *et al.*, forth.). Accordingly, we would expect early communication with the opposite sex not necessarily to have a romantic or sexual intent, or at least that such intent would not be acted upon. Similarly, early communication occurs in a group context, and may have some of the characteristics of group conversations, whereas subsequent communications patterns would be expected to have characteristics of interpersonal interaction.

A description of affiliative interactions also illustrates the likely differences between affiliative interactions with romantic partners and other close figures, such as parents or friends. By preadolescence, parents are less frequent sources of companionship than peers, and affiliation between parents and teens continues to decline throughout the course of adolescence (Furman & Buhrmester, 1992; Larson & Richards, 1994). Moreover, relationships with parents are hierarchical in nature, whereas those with peers are egalitarian; thus, it is less likely that interactions with parents will have the reciprocity that is intrinsic to affiliative interchanges (Hartup & Stevens, 1997). Accordingly, one would expect affiliative interactions and communication with romantic partners more closely to resemble communication with friends, as they are both peer relations. However, differences in young people's affiliative communication with friends and romantic partners may exist as well. For instance, same-sex peers are more likely to have similar interests and interactional styles in comparison to other-sex peers (Maccoby, 1990; 1998). Thus, young heterosexual people may face greater challenges in finding common interests and communicating with other-sex romantic partners than they would with same-sex friends. These issues may be less significant for young gay and lesbian people, although perhaps they are applicable to the degree that individuals of any sexual orientation are romantically attracted to the unknown or unfamiliar (Bem, 1996). Most adolescent romantic relationships are also shorter in length than friendships, and thus, the affiliative interactions may be somewhat different, at least in the early phases of the relationships.

Sexual behavior

Adolescence is of course marked by the onset of puberty and the emergence of more explicit sexual interest and sexual behavior. Adolescent romantic relationships are therefore a common context for erotic exploration and the activation of the sexual or reproductive behavioral system. The vast majority of research on adolescent sexuality has focused on sexual behavior itself. Numerous studies have provided descriptive information about the frequency of sexual behavior and the biological and social factors associated with sexual activity, especially heterosexual intercourse. Yet, very little work has examined how young people communicate about sexual behavior in romantic relationships. We know remarkably little about communication regarding sexual interest, sexual behavior and sexual safety. Given the high rates of risky sexual behavior, pressure to engage in sexual behaviors, and forced sexual activity among young people (Halpern *et al.*, 2001), we would think it important for research to begin to address how young people communicate in this domain.

Romantic partners may use a variety of verbal or nonverbal strategies to communicate about sexual interest and sexual behavior. Christopher and Frandsen (1990), for example, identified four general strategies of sexual communication: (a) *emotional and physical closeness*, where partners touch and seek close proximity to convey sexual wishes; (b) *logic and reason*, which is used to limit sexual intimacy through rational arguments, insistence on a particular level of involvement, and compromise with the partner; (c) *antisocial acts* that involve threats, force and guilt induction; and (d) *pressure and manipulation*, which involve pressure, deception or using drugs or alcohol. One would imagine that using logic and reason—communicating directly about sexual intimacy and sexual limits— would be the most sensible strategy for negotiating sexual behavior, especially because young people sometimes disagree about how sexually involved they should become with each other (Christopher, 1996). Unfortunately, partners often disclose very little about sexual topics (Byers & Demmons, 1999) and rarely discuss their sexual desires and behaviors directly with each other (Cupach & Metts, 1991). Given limited, indirect communication about sexual activity, misunderstanding seems inevitable.

Given their inexperience with sexuality and the newness of romantic relationships in general, communicating about 'how far to go' or 'what I'm comfortable with' may be particularly awkward and challenging topics for young people to talk about. Young lesbian and gay people face the additional challenge of determining whether a same-sex peer is sexually attracted to them and whether it is even safe to disclose their sexual orientation and sexual interest [see O'Flynn—chapter 9, this volume]. Developmentally, one could imagine that for all young people, experiences of communicating about sexual behavior in one relationship or sexual encounter might affect their communication strategies about these issues in later relationships. More research is needed to explore developmental changes in communication about sex, as well as what individual characteristics of the relationship might promote or inhibit partners' open and healthy communication about sexual behavior.

In spite of our limited knowledge about young people's communication about sex with romantic partners, some work has addressed teens' communication about sexual behavior with parents and friends. For example, although we suspect that young people infrequently discuss sexual behaviors with romantic partners, we know that they talk about these topics with mothers and friends. On this basis, we would speculate that parental conversations with teens about sexual behavior most likely focus on information about sexual safety or abstinence as well as on sexual values. Supportive communication with parents about these sexual issues leads to more responsible sexual behavior (Friedman, 1989). Discussions about sexual values with parents may socialize teens and provide a context for learning how to communicate comfortably about sex with future partners. Nonetheless, these topics are understandably not always comfortable for parents to address. Mothers become more didactic and dominant when discussing dating or sexuality (Lefkowitz *et al.*, 1996; Lefkowitz *et al.*, 2000). Mothers of younger adolescents also focus more on communicating about dating, and it is not until later in adolescence that the topic of sex becomes more frequent (Lefkowitz *et al.*, 2002). Throughout adolescence, however, the topic of sexuality remains a difficult one for most parents and young people alike. Not surprisingly, young people increasingly turn to peers instead of parents to discuss sexual behavior as they get older (Lefkowitz *et al.*, 2000). Whereas conversations with parents may address sexual values and safety, communication with friends may include a more candid exchange about actual sexual behaviors, social norms of sexual behavior, and personal sexual limits.

Attachment

The function of the attachment behavioral system is to maintain feelings of emotional and physical safety and security. Communication plays a central role in two primary components of the attachment system: (a) seeking out the partner as a safe haven in times of hurt or distress and (b) using the partner as a secure base from which to explore new activities or plans (Hazan & Zeifman, 1994). Communication is critical to signaling the need for support from a romantic partner. For example, support seeking can involve nonverbal communication, such as seeking physical proximity to an attachment figure or appearing distressed, as well as verbal communication, such as self-disclosing personal feelings of sadness or distress. Communication also plays an important role in the secure base phenomenon, such as when an adolescent explores a new interest or activity, a partner can serve as a secure base by communicating encouragement and confidence.

Young people use romantic relationships as safe havens, and to a lesser degree as secure bases. Rates of intimate disclosure and support seeking from romantic partners increase substantially from preadolescence to adolescence and throughout the course of adolescence (Buhrmester & Furman, 1987; Furman & Buhrmester, 1992). Similarly, the proportion of teens who use a romantic partner as a safe haven increases from middle childhood into early adolescence and increases further in middle adolescence (Hazan & Zeifmann, 1994). Thus, whereas romantic relationships in early adolescence are primarily affiliative in nature, the content of communication in romantic relationships in middle and late adolescence also contains emotional components, such as self-disclosure and support seeking. Young people in later adolescence are particularly likely to perceive romantic partners as individuals to turn to for support (Feiring, 1999).

One of the critical developmental tasks of adolescence entails gradually transferring attachment needs for emotional intimacy and support from parents to peer relationships (Buhrmester, 1996; Furman & Buhrmester, 1992; Hazan & Zeifman, 1994). During this transition, young people initially seek out same-sex close friends for support, but romantic partners increasingly begin to serve more of these functions as they get older (Furman & Buhrmester, 1992). It is also important to remember that parents nonetheless remain primary attachment figures in teens' lives throughout adolescence. It is not usually until early adulthood that romantic partners become primary attachment figures and provide the most support of all types of relationships (Furman & Buhrmester, 1992; Hazan & Zeifman, 1994).[3]

Although it is clear that communication with romantic partners increasingly serves attachment functions over time, we know less about how characteristics of young people's communication with romantic partners differ from those of communication with friends and parents. Because of the hierarchical nature of relationships with parents (Youniss & Smollar, 1985), intimate disclosures are more likely to be one-sided with parents, but reciprocal with romantic partners and other peers. Also, young people are likely to seek out different people, depending on the nature of the concern. For instance, peers are more influential on status norms and identity issues, whereas parents are more influential with regards to future aspirations or school achievement (Brittain, 1963). We know of no literature which addresses the nature of concerns that young people may communicate to romantic partners; nor do we know much about when young people tend to seek out friends and when they seek support from romantic partners.

Caregiving

Caregiving refers to an individual's behaviors aimed at providing support and protection for a partner. The caregiving system is parallel and complementary to the attachment system. In effect, caregiving can be thought of as an individual's attempt to serve as an attachment figure for a romantic partner—to be a safe haven or a secure base. Communication skills such as sensitivity and responsiveness are essential to providing competent support for a romantic partner (Reis & Patrick, 1996). Such skills are clearly important because good caregiving and high levels of emotional support are associated with relationship satisfaction (Carnelley *et al.*, 1996; Feeney, 1996) and well-being (Burleson, 2003). Our anecdotal impression is that most—though not all—young people enjoy being a caregiver to their boyfriend or girlfriend.

In romantic relationships, support seeking behaviors that characterize the attachment system frequently elicit supportive behaviors that also characterize the caregiving system, and vice versa, such that attachment and caregiving systems in healthy relationships interact harmoniously (Bowlby, 1982). Thus, most of the comments about the attachment system are equally applicable to the caregiving system; that is, caregiving is characteristic of and valued in these relationships (Feiring, 1996; Hand & Furman, forth.), and the frequency and amount of caregiving or providing support in romantic relationships increases with age (Furman & Buhrmester, 1992). Eventually, a romantic partner is likely to be perceived as the most supportive person in the social network, although typically not until early adulthood (Furman & Buhrmester, 1992).

Having said this, attachment and caregiving are not always reciprocal. Throughout childhood, the parent is expected to have the caregiving role, and the child is the one who seeks out the safe haven or uses the parent as a secure base. In most circumstances, especially in Western societies, the child or adolescent is not expected to be a major caregiving figure for the parent. It is not until adolescence that teens begin to serve as caregiving figures for friends and romantic partners. In these relationships, young people not only begin turning to peers for emotional support, but also reciprocally provide caregiving for the other. In fact, a close friendship is often the first time that an individual has the opportunity to develop and use caregiving skills. Being able to provide support is likely to require substantial development in communication. After these skills are learned and implemented with close friends, young people may begin to use these skills in their romantic relationships—particularly when these relationships move beyond affiliation, and caregiving and attachment become more prominent.

The negotiation of romantic relationships

We believe a behavioral systems approach to adolescent romantic relationships permits an examination of some of the major functions that communication serves in these relationships. We also have discussed how developmental changes in behavioral systems relate to changes in the characteristics of adolescent romantic relationships and in the functions of communication. A critical issue to address is how young people negotiate these changes in the context of relationships. Transitioning from a primarily affiliative relationship to a partnership that involves attachment, caregiving and sexual components requires interpersonal negotiation, because partners' desires and expectations do not always coincide. In fact, it is inherent in all romantic relationships that individuals' needs will differ at some points, and these differences call for them to negotiate conflict. In the following two sections, we discuss: (a) how young people communicate about the status of their romantic relationships and (b) how they manage conflict. These topics are important events in the course of relationships because they have the capacity to bring partners closer together or to push them apart. Conflict and relationship negotiation also have implications for the functioning of the behavioral systems. For instance, it is commonly understood that open and successful communication about relationship issues is central to maintaining a secure attachment, providing supportive caregiving, talking openly about sexual behavior, and enjoying each other's companionship.

Relationship status

We refer to communication about relationship status as discussions that directly or indirectly address the nature of the relationship with a romantic partner. Of course, in the earliest stages of sexual or romantic interest, these conversations involve communicating sexual or romantic interest in the other person. Among younger teenagers, this communication often takes place via a third party informant (Schofield, 1982). For example, a middle school student may ask a friend to ask someone if she likes him. Also, friends may pass notes in class about who has crushes on whom, or who is being dropped as a partner. For younger teenagers with little or no relationship experience, communicating romantic interest may be particularly awkward. This task is probably even more challenging for young lesbian and gay people, who face the additional difficulty of communicating romantic desires within an environment that still harbors discrimination against same-sex relationships [see O'Flynn—chapter 9, this volume].

After having some experience in interacting with romantic peers, young people may communicate sexual or romantic interest using a variety of other means, ranging from sexual advances to asking the person to go somewhere or do something. If two people are successful at communicating about a mutual romantic or sexual interest, often the next step is determining the extent of each partner's investment in the emerging relationship and their expectations about the relationship. When goals correspond between two persons in a romantic relationship, it is easier to achieve desirable outcomes such as fulfilling attachment and caregiving needs (Wieselquist *et al.*, 1999). A failure to communicate clearly may lead to misunderstandings that disrupt the relationship. For instance, one person might consider spending a lot of time with a third person to be acceptable, whereas the partner may label it as cheating.

In the middle or later stages of young people's relationships with romantic partners, communication about status might also involve discussing a number of issues pertaining to the ongoing relationship: feelings about each other (e.g., 'Are we in love?'), satisfaction with the current state of the relationship (e.g., 'I really enjoy being with you.'), the partners' level of commitment (e.g., 'It's important that we make time to see each other.'), or expectations about the future status of the relationship (e.g., 'I could see myself marrying you.'). Like adults, young people also need to communicate a sense of where the romantic relationship falls in their social network. Conflicts may occur around the amount of time spent with friends, rather than with a partner (Zani, 1993). For heterosexual young people, other-sex friends can sometimes trigger feelings of jealousy (Roth & Parker, 2001). Obviously, the process of trying to end any relationship is often very difficult, especially when the partner wants to continue the relationship.

Although young people's communication about relationship status shares some commonalities with adults' communication about these issues, significant differences exist as well. Compared to adult relationships, the romantic relationships of many young people are typically much shorter in duration and less committed. Thus, issues that arise in longer-term relationships in adulthood may not be as applicable to many adolescent romantic relationships. For example, communication in the process of relationship dissolution is likely to be quite different for a long-term adult commitment, such as a marriage, versus a shorter-term adolescent relationship.

Young people's communication about relationship status with romantic partners also differs from their negotiation of relationship status in other types of relationships. They may have multiple friendships, but romantic relationships are typically exclusive. As a consequence, it appears that there is more attention to and communication about the nature of a romantic relationship; friendships may wax and wane without explicit discussion or decisions being made. These ideas about communication regarding the status of the relationship are primarily speculative; as yet, we have little information about how often young people talk about relationship status with romantic partners, the strategies they use to communicate about these issues, or what types of strategies are related to more positive adolescent relationships.

Conflict resolution

Conflict is an issue that arises in all relationships, and adept communication plays a key role in its resolution. The capacity of young people to constructively resolve occasional conflicts and quarrels is linked to maintaining and solidifying friendships and romantic relationships (Laursen & Collins, 1994).

Not surprisingly, the specific communication skills involved in conflict negotiation in adolescent romantic relationships parallel those found in adult relationships. Young people report using compromise most often, distraction second most often, and avoidance third most often (Feldman & Gowen, 1998). Overt anger, violence, and social support are used less frequently. The use of compromise may be a particularly adaptive conflict negotiation strategy because it constructively addresses and resolves conflict, and serves the function of maintaining and perhaps even strengthening aspects of the relationship (Laursen & Collins, 1994).

The frequency of conflict in romantic relationships rises slightly over the course of adolescence (Furman & Buhrmester, 1992). During adolescence, conflict with romantic partners is less frequent than with parents, but similar in frequency to that with friends. In early adulthood, conflict with romantic partners is as common as with parents, and more frequent than with friends (Furman & Buhrmester, 1992). We know less about developmental changes in particular strategies of conflict resolution, although there is some suggestion that using compromise with romantic partners increases with age (Feldman & Gowen, 1998). This increase in compromise may occur because these relationships are likely to be longer in length and more intimate later on. Thus, young people in more serious relationships may rely on compromise more often because they have more at stake to lose.

The development of communication skills in conflict resolution may first begin to develop in the context of conflict negotiation with friends and parents; for instance, young adults' patterns of conflict resolution with parents and romantic partners are related to one another (Reese-Weber & Bertle-Haring, 1998). If anything, we might also expect the link between conflict resolution in friendships and romantic relationships to be stronger, as these are both voluntary, egalitarian relationships with peers. At the same time, conflict resolution in romantic relationships may be somewhat distinct, partly because romantic relationships carry an inherent risk of loss that seems greater than in other peer relationships or in parent-adolescent relationships. In support of this idea, young adults report using more constructive conflict negotiation tactics with romantic partners than with best friends (Creasey *et al.*, 1999). At the same time, young people also said that they engaged in more negative escalation and negativity, suggesting that these relationships are also more volatile.

Conclusion

In this chapter, we have presented a behavioral systems approach to examining the primary functions of adolescent romantic relationships. We believe that this is a promising and valuable framework because it anchors an exploration of communication to the underlying functions that it serves in these relationships. Considering communication in the context of behavioral systems also facilitates comparisons of communication with parents, friends, and romantic partners. Similarly, it moves beyond an effort merely to describe characteristics of adolescent romantic relationships and, instead, encourages us to think about adolescent romantic communication from a developmental perspective. Although we know that communication is perhaps the most critical component of adult romantic relationship satisfaction, we know almost nothing about how communication abilities and values develop from early adolescence to adulthood.

In this chapter, we have principally focused on the general characteristics of communication in adolescent romantic relationships. This approach is intended as a starting point, but is not meant to imply that individual differences aren't equally as important. Factors such as gender, culture, sexual orientation, and psychological characteristics also need to be considered to understand the characteristics and qualities of teens' communication with romantic figures. It is our intent that this chapter will serve as a springboard for further research on communication in adolescent relationships.

Notes

1. Preparation of this manuscript was supported by Grant 50106 from the National Institute of Mental Health (Wyndol Furman as principal investigator).
2. Editors: It is also true to say that young people (especially young women) are constantly positioned by frequent media depictions of 'teen love' and young (typically heterosexual) desire. In the year leading up to this book these were

just a few of the more popular titles: *Mean Girls, How to Deal, Chasing Liberty, Alex and Emma, 13 Going on 30, Jersey Girl, Sleepover,* and *A Cinderella Story.*

3. Editors: This extended transition from parental to romantic partner is often delayed these days by factors such as prolonged economic dependence (see Chisholm & Hurrelmann, 1995; Mortimer & Larson, 2002—cited in Thurlow & Williams—chapter 1, this volume).

References

Aron, A., Norman, C. C., Aron, E. N., McKenna, C. & Heyman, R. E. (2000). Couples' shared participation in novel and arousing activities and experienced relationship quality. *Journal of Personality and Social Psychology, 78,* 273–284.

Bem, D. J. (1996). Exotic becomes erotic: A developmental theory of sexual orientation. *Psychological Review, 103,* 320–335.

Baucom, D. H., Notarius, C. I., Burnett, C. K. & Haefner, P. (1990). In F. D. Fincham & T. N. Bradbury (eds), *The Psychology of Marriage: Basic Issues and Applications* (pp. 150–171). New York: Guilford.

Bowlby, J. (1982). *Attachment and Loss: Attachment.* New York: Basic Books.

Brittain, C. V. (1963). Adolescent choices and parent-peer cross pressures. *American Sociological Review, 28,* 385–391.

Brown, B. B., Feiring, C. & Furman, W. (1999). Missing the love boat: Why researchers have shied away from adolescent romance. In W. Furman, B. B. Brown & C. Feiring (eds), *The Development of Romantic Relationships in adolescence* (pp. 1–16). New York: Cambridge University Press.

Buhrmester, D. (1996). Need fulfillment, interpersonal competence, and the developmental contexts of early adolescent friendship. In W. M. Bukowski & A. F. Newcomb (eds), *The Company They Keep: Friendship in Childhood and Adolescence* (pp. 158–185). New York, NY: Cambridge University Press.

Buhrmester, D. & Furman, W. (1987). The development of companionship and intimacy. *Child Development, 58,* 1101–1113.

Burleson, B. R. (2003). The experience and effects of emotional support: What the study of cultural and gender differences can tell us about close relationships, emotion, and interpersonal communication. *Personal Relationships, 10,* 1–23.

Byers, E. S. & Demmons, S. (1999). Sexual satisfaction and sexual self-disclosure within dating relationships. *Journal of Sex Research, 36,* 180–189.

Carnelley, K. B., Pietromonaco, P. R. & Jaffe, K. (1996). Attachment, caregiving, and relationship functioning in couples: Effects of self and partner. *Personal Relationships, 3,* 257–277.

Christopher, F. S. (1996). Adolescent sexuality: Trying to explain the magic and the mystery. In N. Vanzetti & S. Duck (eds), *A Lifetime of Relationships* (pp. 213–242). Belmont, CA: Brooks/Cole Publishing Co.

Christopher, F. S. & Frandsen, M. M. (1990). Strategies of influence in sex and dating. *Journal of Social and Personal Relationships*, 7, 89–105.

Connolly, J., Goldberg, A. & Pepler, D. (forth.). *Romantic development in the peer group in early adolescence.* Manuscript under review.

Creasey, G., Kershaw, K. & Boston, A. (1999). Conflict management with friends and romantic partners: The role of attachment and negative mood regulation expectancies. *Journal of Youth and Adolescence*, 28, 523–543.

Cupach, W. R. & Metts, S. (1991). Sexuality and communication in close relationships. In K. McKinney & S. Sprecher (eds), *Sexuality in Close Relationships* (pp. 93–110). Hillsdale, NJ: Lawrence Erlbaum.

Diamond, L. M., Savin-Williams, R. C. & Dube, E. M. (1999). Sex, dating, passionate friendships, and romance: Intimate peer relations among lesbian, gay, and bisexual adolescents. In W. Furman, B. B. Brown & C. Feiring (eds), *The Development of Romantic Relationships in Adolescence* (pp. 175–210). New York: Cambridge University Press.

Eder, D. (1993). 'Go get ya a French!': Romantic and sexual teasing among adolescent girls. In D. Tanner (ed.), *Gender and Conversational Interaction* (pp. 17–31). London: Oxford University Press.

Feeney, J. A. (1996). Attachment, caregiving and marital satisfaction. *Personal Relationships*, 3, 401–416.

Feiring, C. (1996). Concepts of romance in 15-year-old adolescents. *Journal of Research on Adolescence*, 6, 181–200.

Feiring, C. (1999). Other-sex friendship networks and the development of romantic relationships in adolescence. *Journal of Youth and Adolescence*, 28, 495–512.

Feldman, S. S. & Gowen, L. K. (1998). Conflict negotiation tactics in romantic relationships in high school students. *Journal of Youth and Adolescence*, 27, 691–716.

Friedman, H. L. (1989). The health of adolescents: Beliefs and behavior. *Social Science Medicine*, 29, 309–315.

Furman, W. (1998). Friends and lovers: The role of peer relationships in adolescent romantic relationships. In W. A. Collins & B. Laursen (eds), *Relationships as Developmental Contexts: The 30th Minnesota Symposium on Child Development* (pp. 133–154). Hillsdale, NJ: Erlbaum.

Furman, W. & Buhrmester, D. (1992). Age and sex differences in perceptions of networks of personal relationships. *Child Development*, 63, 103–115.

Furman, W. & Wehner, E. A. (1994). Romantic views: Toward a theory of adolescent romantic relationships. In R. Montemayor, G. R. Adams & T. P. Gullota (eds), *Advances in Adolescent Development: Personal Relationships During Adolescence* (pp. 168–195). Thousand Oaks, CA: Sage.

Gottman, J. (1979). *Marital Interaction: Experimental Investigations.* New York: Academic Press.

Gottman, J., Markman, H. & Notarius, C. (1977). The topography of marital conflict: A sequential analysis of verbal and non-verbal behavior. *Journal of Marriage and the Family*, 39, 461–478.

Halpern, C. T., Oslak, S. G., Young, M. L., Martin, S. L. & Kupper, L. L. (2001). Partner violence among adolescents in opposite-sex romantic relationships: Findings from the National Longitudinal Study of Adolescent Health. *American Journal of Public Health*, 91, 1679–1685.

Hand, L. S. & Furman, W. (forth.). *Other-sex Friendships in Adolescence: Just Friends?* Manuscript submitted for publication.

Hartup, W. W. & Stevens, N. (1997). Friendships and adaptation in the life course. *Psychological Bulletin*, 121, 355–370.

Hazan, C. & Zeifman, D. (1994). Sex and the psychological tether. In K. Bartholomew & D. Perlman (eds), *Advances in Personal Relationships* (pp. 151–177). London: Jessica Kingsley.

Isen, A. M. (1999). Positive Affect. In T. Dalgleish & M. J. Power (eds), *Handbook of Cognition and Emotion* (pp. 521–539). New York: John Wiley and Sons Ltd.

Kobak, R. R., Cole, H. E., Ferenz-Gillies, R. & Fleming, W. S. (1993). Attachment and emotion regulation during mother-teen problem solving: A control theory analysis. *Child Development*, 64, 231–245.

Larson, R. W., Clore, G. L. & Wood, G. A. (1999). The emotions of romantic relationships: Do they wreak havoc on adolescents? In W. Furman, B. B. Brown & C. Feiring (eds), *The Development of Romantic Relationships in Adolescence* (pp. 19–49). New York: Cambridge University Press.

Larson, R. & Richards, M. (1994). Family emotions: Do young adolescents and their parents experience the same states? *Journal of Research on Adolescence*, 4, 567–583.

Laursen, B. & Collins, W. A. (1994). Interpersonal conflict during adolescence. *Psychological Bulletin*, 115, 197–209.

Laursen, B. & Williams, V. A. (1997). Perceptions of interdependence and closeness in family and peer relationships among adolescents with and without romantic partners. In S. Shulman & W. A. Collins (eds), *Romantic Relationships in Adolescence: Developmental Perspectives* (pp. 3–20). San Francisco: Jossey-Bass/Pfeiffer.

Lefkowitz, E. S., Boone, T. L., Sigman, M. & Kit-fong, T. (2002). He said, she said: Gender differences in mother-adolescent conversations about sexuality. *Journal of Research on Adolescence*, 12, 217–242.

Lefkowitz, E. S., Kahlbaugh, P. E. & Sigman, M. D. (1996). Turn-taking in mother-adolescent conversations about sexuality and conflict. *Journal of Youth and Adolescence*, 25, 307–321.

Lefkowitz, E. S., Romo, L. F., Corona, R., Au, T. K. & Sigman, M. (2000). How Latino American and European American adolescents discuss conflicts, sexuality, and AIDS with their mothers. *Developmental Psychology*, 36, 315–325.

Maccoby, E. (1990). Gender and relationships: A developmental account. *American Psychologist*, 45, 513–520.

Maccoby, E. (1998). *The Two Sexes: Growing up Apart, Coming Together.* Cambridge, MA: Belknap Press/Harvard University Press.

Reese-Weber, M. & Bertle-Haring, S. (1998). Conflict resolution styles in family subsystems and adolescent romantic relationships. *Journal of Youth & Adolescence*, 27, 735–752.

Reis, H. T. & Gable, S. L. (2003). Toward a positive psychology of relationships. In C. L. Keyes & J. Haidt (eds), *Flourishing: The Positive Person and the Good Life* (pp. 129–159). Washington DC: American Psychological Association.

Reis, H. T. & Patrick, B. C. (1996). Attachment and intimacy: Component processes. In E. T. Higgins & A. W. Kruglanski (eds), *Social Psychology: Handbook of Basic Principles* (pp. 523–563). New York: Guilford Press.

Richards, M. H., Crowe, P. A., Larson, R. & Swarr, A. (1998). Developmental patterns and gender differences in the experience of peer companionship during adolescence. *Child Development*, 69, 154–163.

Roth, M. A. & Parker, J. G. (2001). Affective and behavioral responses to friends who neglect their friends for dating partners: Influences of gender, jealousy, and perspective. *Journal of Adolescence*, 24(3), 281–296.

Schofield, J. W. (1982). *Black and White in School. Trust, Tension, or Tolerance?* New York: Praeger.

Wieselquist, J., Rusbult, C. E., Foster, C. A. & Agnew, C. R. (1999). Commitment, pro-relationship behavior, and trust in close relationships. *Journal of Personality and Social Psychology*, 77, 942–966.

Weiss, R. S. (1998). A taxonomy of relationships. *Journal of Social and Personal Relationships*, 15, 671–683.

Weiss, R. L. & Heyman, R. E. (1990). Observation of marital interaction. In F. D. Fincham & T. N. Bradbury (eds), *The Psychology of Marriage: Basic Issues and Applications* (pp. 87–117). New York: Guilford Press.

Youniss, J. & Smollar, J. (1985). *Adolescent Relations with Mothers, Fathers, and Friends*. Chicago: University of Chicago Press.

Zani, B. (1993). Dating and interpersonal relationships. In S. Jackson & H. Rodriguez-Tome (eds), *Adolescence and Its Social Worlds* (pp. 95–119). Hillsdale, NJ: Lawrence Erlbaum.

9

Ticket to a queer planet? Communication issues affecting young lesbian and gay people

Sarah O'Flynn

I work on an education project at a youth center in London. It is a popular center and lots of specialist youth groups meet there. One evening per week there is a lesbian, gay and bisexual youth group. The group has been set up by Connexions, the new National Careers and Advice Service for young people in England working with the Terence Higgins Trust.[1] It has been set up in response to Connexions workers becoming aware, through their casework, that the needs of lesbian, gay and bisexual youth were not being met (Connexions Service, 2003). In stark contrast to other groups which meet at the center, nothing advertises the day, time or location of the lesbian, gay and bisexual youth group. In order to join the group, you have to ring a help line at a designated time or text from a mobile. One of the youth workers will then arrange to meet you in a public location and will bring you to the youth group. The details of the group remain secret because of the homophobia among young people and in society at large.

Possibly because it is so difficult for young people to communicate with others about their (nonheterosexual) sexualities, there is very little research specifically about this. Scholars have found it almost impossible to research young Queer people, especially in schools and even post-secondary education institutions. Melinda Micelli (2002) observes that because of this young lesbian, gay and bisexual people are one of the most under-researched groups of adolescents. Furthermore, in their introduction to 'Young People's Views on Sex

Education,' Lynda Measor and her colleagues (2000) observe with frustration the impossibility of getting young people to make mention of homosexuality:

> We do not seek to exclude homosexuality, nor the concerns which face young people in early adolescence who feel they may have a same-sex sexual orientation. Our problem is that the young people we studied made little mention of it. In the schools we studied we did not find young people who were prepared to talk to us about their feelings and reactions in respect of homosexuality. (Measor *et al.*, 2000: 2)

That young people were not prepared to talk about same-sex sexual orientation to Measor and her colleagues is, as they say, totally unsurprising given the need for young people to keep themselves 'safe' through lack of communication (however unsafe such a strategy might have made them feel).

In preparation for this chapter, I have relied upon a combination of what literature there is within the field of communication studies, on social theorists of sexuality in other fields of study, on research with young people about sex and relationships more generally and on my own research to illustrate the (lack of) communication experienced by young lesbian and gay people. As such, this chapter seeks to map the context for their communication while indicating a series of key interactional issues and strategies.

For the young person who contemplates joining a youth group such as the one described above, there is clearly a set of quite formal and challenging social interactions with an adult or adults which need to be forced in order to access a lesbian or gay social world. This young person might have concerns about whether the group is genuine, or whether s/he looks 'queer' enough to be accepted, whether his/her attendance will be logged on an official record somewhere. S/he will almost certainly have concerns about meeting a stranger to discuss her/his sexuality. Safety campaigns in schools target children and young people to be aware of 'stranger-danger,' emphasizing the importance of not talking to strangers or accepting sweets from them or getting into their cars. To meet an unknown adult with the express purpose of disclosing and discussing one's sexuality would seem particularly risky within this discourse.[2]

In the United Kingdom, most young people under 16 do not have access to gay bars or clubs and in many US states the age at which young people can buy alcohol and frequent such bars is even higher—sometimes as high as 21. This means that an important part of gay culture is not ordinarily or legitimately available to young people, especially those under 16. The threat of homophobia also places a compulsion on young lesbian or gay people and those who provide services for them always to be careful, on the lookout for abuse, and to put in place safeguards against it. Even if, as a young person, one already has considerable experience of negotiating racism or discrimination on the grounds of one's religion, class or ability, homophobia is significantly different again; it is structured by the contrary demands for secrecy, on the one hand, and for telling all, on the other. In this way, tension is created between understanding that all sexuality is shifting and developing, while at the same time having, by necessity, to make a declaration of one's sexual identity in order to access the cultural worlds in which that identity might establish itself more securely.

My example therefore also draws attention to the difficulty of naming sexual identities and living within their definitions. At what point does one make a decision as a young person that one is lesbian or gay or bisexual? Or even transgender or transsexual? How meaningful and how useful are these terms? As Cameron and Kulick (2003) argue, sexual desires, practices and identities are not simply fixed realities which have always existed but rather categories produced by language and through which we attempt to organize our erotic impulses:

> the 'reality' of sex does not pre-exist the language in which it is expressed; rather, language *produces* the categories through which we organize our sexual desires, identities and practices (Cameron & Kulick, 2003: 19).

This point can sometimes be difficult to grasp as sexual desire is often considered an area of experience that 'exceeds the capacity of language to represent it' (p. 13). Yet as Cameron and Kulick go on to suggest, if this were indeed the case, then sex could not exist because it would be outside discourse. In this sense, the naming of oneself as lesbian, gay or bisexual is not merely a matter of coming to an understanding of an inner sexual essence or identity but rather a discursive constitution of that identity, through inscription of the individual into its meanings. Interestingly, the category of heterosexual operates rather differently, as Halley (1993: 83) observes: the category of heterosexual 'despite its representation as monolithic in its nonhomosexuality...is a highly unstable, default categorization for people who have not marked themselves or been marked by others as homosexual.' In this way, heterosexuality is an assumed category, from which one must actively opt out. Halley explores the interesting case of a high school teacher who, having counseled a student about his confusion over his sexual identity, felt obliged to tell the vice-principal of the school of her own bisexuality. She ended up losing her job, following a court case. The point Halley makes, however, is in relation to the student concerned:

> ...assuming the student heeds his lesson in silence, the class of heterosexuals, thus constituted will include him, despite his capacity for confusion about his sexual orientation. The resulting class of heterosexuals is a default class, home to those who have not fallen out of it. It openly expels but covertly incorporates the homosexual other...It can maintain its current boundaries and even its apparent legitimacy only if the student and others like him remain silent.

> And until they speak, it owes its glory days as a coherent social category to its members' own *failure to acknowledge* its discursive constitution, the coercive dynamics of its incoherence. (p. 85–86)

This means that the essentialism of sexual identity politics is actually of strategic importance to the continuing heterosexism of Western culture. It is therefore a highly problematic politics and we can see this clearly in the dilemma confronting any young person who, already uncertain about defining his/her sexuality, is thinking of attending a youth group which describes itself as 'lesbian, gay or bisexual'. The disowning of the label 'heterosexual' has real social costs and it is only the 'minority' categories of lesbian, gay, bisexual and transgender that draw the subject's attention to sexual identity as a discursive construct, rather than as an essence. Many groups use the terminology LGBT (lesbian, gay, bisexual or transgender) as a way of being inclusive and yet this always risks excluding other nonheterosexuals and even non-normative heterosexual practices. As a response to this, Sedgwick (1990) and many other scholars since use the term 'queer' to challenge what she has termed the 'minoritizing' view of sexual identity which sees 'homo/heterosexual definition as an issue of active importance primarily for a small distinct, relatively fixed homosexual minority' (Sedgwick, 1990: 1), rather than as something that is important in the lives of all people.[3] It is this minoritizing view of sexual identity which appears to be the dominant structuring process in youth groups aimed at young Queer people. However, homophobia ensures that these groups are often locked into this way of working in order to keep young people safe by keeping details of the group relatively secret but in the process keeping distinct the boundaries of heterosexuality.

The experience for a young person of joining a lesbian, gay, bisexual and/or transgender youth group is also a powerful introduction to the closet and the way in which it structures and constrains Queer lifestyles.[4] It announces to any young people struggling with issues around their sexuality that lesbian/gay/bisexual sexualities require a very different way of operating socially from the mainstream heterosexual society out of which they have just stepped. Most ironically, it is the closet, the homophobic societal demand that homosexuality remain a secret, that also means young people must make a public declaration of their sexuality to a stranger in order to access services. The experience of living with/in the closet is a structuring force in their lives, however 'out' of it they manage finally to become.

Epstein and Johnson (1998) have shown that even children are aware of the closet and work with it, in their encounters with Queer sexualities. Epstein and Johnson explored in some detail the reactions of a class of Year 5 pupils (aged about 10) from an inner London primary school to the announcement from their class teacher that he was gay. Given that so much school-based communication takes place in the form of gossip and, indeed, that gossip is a kind of 'social cement' for school communities, Epstein and Johnson expected the whole school to know of the teacher's sexuality within a very short time. Contrary to expectation, however, the children did not tell anybody outside the class but, in fact, closeted the information. When Epstein and Johnson asked the pupils why they had chosen to do this, one of the girls pointed out that 'people go a bit funny in this school' (p. 143) about lesbian and gay sexuality. Meanwhile her friend went even further to explain that parents would make the assumption that a gay teacher was a bad teacher, that a gay teacher might attempt to turn the pupils gay and that there were 'grown-ups' out there who were actually 'not very grown up' at all about homosexuality (ibid). The children were clearly very fond of their teacher but were also motivated by the fact that they did not want a susubtitute teacher to take his place and they feared this might happen if they chose to make more public his gay sexuality. Epstein and Johnson suggest, further, that constructing a closet around their class may also have been a mechanism of safety from perceived 'contamination' for themselves—if others knew they had a gay teacher, they too might be stigmatized. Thus we can see that even at an early age, the meaning of 'queer' (or lesbian, gay, bisexual and so on) as a stigmatized set of social identities has been communicated to children, who are apparently able to articulate clearly much of the dominant homophobic discourse.

The stigmatization of Queer: Keeping quiet

The exploration and negotiation of identity is much more complex for young Queer people but also in other ways more clumsy or awkward. This is because they are typically forced into an on-off position, or a kind of all-or-nothing identity; in other words, the labels available to them mean that they must decide: either I'm gay or I'm straight. For young people who believe they may not be heterosexual, the process of understanding and communicating about their sexualities subjectively is more of a matter of shadow and becoming, rather than a problem of clear communication about a once and for all given sexual identity. For a young person thinking about her/his sexuality, the secrecy one is forced into in order to join the group in my earlier example, makes it seem more like joining some clandestine criminal organization than a chance to meet other young people for a chat and a game of pool. One of the most noticeable themes in relation to the lives of young Queer people is that their lives are marked by the *absence* of communication. In relation to socio-political processes which are involved in the silencing of a subordinated group, Jaworski (1993: 125) has observed that

...the power group must alter the society's perception of the status of the opposition from clear to ambiguous. One effective way to do so is simply to question the opposition's right to exist, to ban or delegalize it, or to declare it subversive. Frequently, when the existence of a socio-political opposition or dominated group is acknowledged, this is accomplished by labeling and describing it in terms that completely alter its status.

The decision to join a social group under such conditions is, understandably, a very big decision in a young person's life. Ironically, it can be seen as part of the experience which, initially at least, confirms one's sense of delegitimization in the terms that Jaworski outlines. The young person is made to feel criminalized and pathological. His/her status is rendered ambiguous. By contrast, for young heterosexual people, even though the art of 'chatting up' someone may be complex, it retains a sense of informality, spontaneity, and ease.

Whatever point in adolescence a young person starts to think about her/his sexuality, most young people recognize, at a very early age, that same-sex desire is constituted by a stigmatized set of identifications. From his position as an American, Unks (1995) has suggested, for example, that 'homosexuals are arguably the most hated group of people in the United States.' Unks argues that although it is generally taboo for most Americans to use openly racist language, by contrast, anti-queer expletives are used almost routinely. Young people come to understand that it is acceptable, therefore, to express homophobic sentiments and that being Queer is not something that one would wish to be or admit to being. In his research about the use of homophobic abuse in schools, Thurlow (2001) similarly testifies to the fact that it is ubiquitous—even the UK government has at long last recognized that this is a problem which needs to be addressed (DfEE, 1999; DfEE, 2000). The word 'gay,' in particular, is used by young people and particularly by young men as a general term of abuse for anything of which they disapprove. What this means, in effect, is that the first communication that young people experience or participate in, in relation to Queer sexualities, is likely to be abusive and derogatory. The prolific nature of homophobia in schools in particular suggests that Queer sexualities are a significant source of tension and anxiety in adolescent worlds.

One of the key problems for young Queer people, then, is the fact that Queer identities are interpellated in public discourse through homophobia and, in schools, exclusively through homophobia (Gordon, 1999). The decision by young Queer people to recognize themselves in this discourse and to take up the term as a basis for opposition is highly complex. A point made by many writers on the subject is that adolescence is typically constructed as a time when young people struggle to come to terms with sexual identity. Gordon (1999: 10) observes that, for young people, 'heterosexuality will be constantly invoked, but its realization will be constantly delayed.' For young lesbian and gay people, this constant invocation of heterosexuality in adolescence means that this period of their lives is constituted as a time of great pressure and personal anxiety. It is also presented as a time of isolation. Plummer (1995) suggests that such isolation constitutes a key moment in the narrativization of the coming out experience for queer people and he identifies it as one of the 'key defining problems of stigmatized identities.'

In fact, isolation is a recurrent theme in research about Queer people or in stories and accounts by Queer people, usually identified retrospectively by those who are now 'out and proud' (Jennings, 1998). The stigma surrounding Queer identity means it is difficult, if not impossible, for any young GBLT person to have a sense of a collective identity, to feel part of a community in school or at home. In her case study of a young lesbian, Herr (1997), for example, identifies social isolation as the reason this young woman, previously identified by her primary school as 'gifted,' failed academically and dropped out of high school, choosing instead to immerse herself in a Queer community. In the same vein, Epstein and Johnson (1998: 159) explore the case of Lara, who, while at school, identifies as 'the only Asian lesbian in the world.' Given this, it is almost not surprising that Harbeck (1995) suggests that young Queer people are not only at greater risk of suicide than their peers but also at greater risk of becoming perfectionists, feeling that in order to compensate for their 'shameful' Queer identity only perfection in everything else will do. Social isolation may therefore lead to over-achievement, because immersion in study can be used by young Queer people to delay the onset of active sexuality and sexual relationships and thus avoid social interactions, which might expose their lack of competency in heterosexual dating and dumping.

Developing Queer identities in hostile settings: 'Speaking the language of the enemy'

Asserting one's Queer identity is also not easy, even if one has the confidence to make a declarative statement of it. Thurlow's study (2001) of the use of homophobic pejoratives in British schools by pupils is interesting because he found that even apparently neutral words to describe young Queer people, such as 'homosexual,' 'lesbian' and 'gay,' are used in schools as terms of abuse. The experience of language which so many young Queer people have is typically a negative one. Writing about the use of the word 'gay,' Thurlow (2001: 32) observes

> In spite of its being one of the playground weapons of preference, this is
> ironically the very word that many young homosexual people will more than

likely be choosing to describe themselves.

This blanket use in schools, of *all* the terms used to describe young Queer people as terms of abuse, means that the young Queer person is so completely interpellated through homophobia that it is very difficult, if not impossible, initially, to construct an identity that is positive, within that context. The language to do so does not exist. In fact, I would suggest that one of the only ways of making mention of homosexuality in schools is through homophobia. When Nayak and Kehily (1997) ask the question 'Why are young men so homophobic?' it may be, as they suggest, that homophobia is one of the strategies young men use to consolidate an uncertain masculinity and assert a coherent heterosexual identity [see also see chapter 7, this volume].

Cameron (1997: 61) has further explored how young men, in an all-male conversational context, use gossip about 'the repulsiveness of gay men' as the most appropriate way of displaying heterosexual masculinity. What Cameron points out is that acceptable talk for men is a complex matter in which contextual variables play a key part. In an all-male group, gay men provide an outgroup against which heterosexual masculinity can be defined. Cameron uses Butler's (1990) analysis of the performativity of gender to demonstrate that speech acts are also performative of gender. Thus the fact that the men in this study are gossiping—a speech style stereotypically associated with women's talk—does not change the fact that they are performing a gendered script, in which the most important point is 'being seen at all times as red-blooded heterosexual males: not women and not Queer people' (p. 62). Homophobic talk is a key strategy for achieving this (Cameron, 1997).

However, if we consider homophobia from the point of view of a young person who is Queer, it may be the safest way, sometimes even the only way, to begin to communicate a Queer identity. There are virtually no other ways to talk about Queer in school. Indeed, as research like Thurlow's indicates, all the vocabularies of Queer form part of the homophobic and heterosexist discourse in schools. Furthermore, some researchers, working with young Queer people (Friend, 1993), have identified the use of homophobia as one of the strategies they use for masking their sexuality in schools, or for passing as heterosexual, an important strategy in assimilating into heterosexual society. Active use of homophobia is one of the most aggressive assimilative strategies, because it involves or at least implies ridicule of the self. Yet the use of homophobia by young Queer people may not simply be a way of masking one's Queerness but perhaps is also the only language resource available through which to announce it. Such a process is beautifully described by Lorentz (2000), who explains how, at 12, he used to make his father laugh by doing impersonations of the gay weatherman on television. This allowed him to pass as straight, but also to enact his developing Queer identity. Although he felt complicit in his own oppression, he also takes account of the fact that it was a way of exploring and *communicating* a Queer identity.

> Passing was to be accomplished by excelling in athletics and through my flaming impersonation of the weatherman....and so I existed, as I believe many adolescents did, as queer Steppin Fetchit, trapped and speaking the language of the enemy in a twilight world somewhere between the homo and the hetero, uncomfortably complicit in my own oppression. (Lorentz 2000: 37)

Young Queer people are so stigmatized through homophobia that they are of necessity involved in contradictory, incoherent and often illogical ways of both announcing and closeting their Queerness, often simultaneously, as in the above example.

In the following extract, one of my current research participants (whom I have called Ann), in her final year of compulsory education, appears to use denial that she is Queer with a persistency and protestation that is excessive and which suggests that it is being used deliberately as a rhetorical device precisely to announce her Queer identity. Following a conversation about a very serious crush she has had on a female mathematics teacher, Ann's announcement of her Queer sexuality is done through the mobilization of homophobic discourse. As the listener, I am being invited to disagree with her homophobia. Ann holds the closet in place, announcing her Queer identity through loud silences and the use of the word 'it' (used ten times in this extract), which I, as the listener, am required to fill in or to substitute using the word 'lesbian' or 'Queer'. The burden of interpretation is thus passed to me as the listener, as a strategic ploy by Ann to get over the homophobia of the world that she inhabits. My task is to reinvest the words 'Queer' and 'lesbian' with positive meaning, to turn her world on its head. I would argue that in spite of the fact that she situates her Queer identity within a homophobic context, this announcement by Ann of her sexuality uses the only language she has available to do so and allows her the opportunity to communicate her Queerness and make possible its re-evaluation:

ANN: When I think of that and I think of how I feel for her then I really (pause) I ... it makes me hate myself. It makes me think, 'What the heck are you doing? Why are you doing this to yourself?' It's total rubbish. I just ...the main problem with the idea of it even being a possibility that I could be ...which I know I'm not. The whole possibility is mainly that I don't think that I'd accept it, whether or not anyone else would, so I don't really ... it's never really been something that's been discussed. It's nothing that's happened in our family, nothing of that sort. The friends that we all have, it's not the sort of thing that they'd do.

It's just the ... whole sort of circle of family and friends and ... just sort of outside of all of that.

SARAH: Um

ANN: I mean in that circle it's maybe only a joke, the whole idea ...

Ann can't use the word 'lesbian' positively, because that is not how it is ever used in school or in her home. She won't use 'lesbian' or 'Queer' negatively to describe herself, so she is reduced to referring to her lesbian sexuality as 'it.' Ann also raises the issue of how to communicate a Queer identity to a circle of significant people in one's life when it is outside their experience and at best seen as 'a joke.' For young Queer people the difficulty lies in investing the terms of abuse with positive meaning. To use them with reference to oneself while they are still negatively charged is evidence of internalized homophobia, and not to use them is evidence of denial of a stigmatized identity. Yet the cultural worlds of young people, at least at school and in daily communication with their peers, may allow them no positive context in which to reinvest those terms of abuse with positive meaning. The only cultural worlds in which Queer is sometimes invested with positive meaning are in the media and particularly on television and via the internet. Queer programming, however, often explores sexuality through comedic or hyperbolic performances.[5] This makes it difficult for someone like Ann to use it as a resource in her world. It is still 'maybe only a joke.' It is unreal and unlike her world. This begs the question to what extent young Queer people have difficulty imagining the gloss and shine of televisual reality in their own lives and in what ways they are able or not to incorporate these Queer images.

Ann did make use of the internet and popular culture to explore Queer sexualities. However, this is a process which is often fraught with problems for young people. In schools, for example, there are likely to be filters, or 'net-nannies,' which filter out words such as 'queer,' 'lesbian' or 'gay,' because these words are seen as homophobic, inappropriately adult, or likely to result in explicit sexual material, including pornography, on screen. Net nannies are also often used in family homes, to censure Queer content. Equally, watching television programs such as, for example, 'Queer as Folk,' or other overtly Queer material, in the context of a family setting in which one is not out, is likely to be fraught with anxieties—fear of exposure, stigma, becoming the source of worry for one's parents and so on.

Despite all these problems, some young people can and do come out while still at school. In this context, it is important to note that schools are not simply reactive to homophobia or heterosexism. Through institutionalized homophobia and heterosexism, schools contribute, albeit unwittingly, to the shaping of Queer identities themselves, in ways which impact on how young Queer people communicate intimately, even once they have established themselves firmly in

Queer social and cultural contexts. Schools continue to exert an influence on communication issues for young Queer people, long after they have left school. Quinlivan and Town (1999: 246–247), for example, found that sex education programs in New Zealand schools actually contributed to the way in which lesbian and gay male identities emerged and were responsible for exacerbating if not creating some of the specific communication issues that these young Queer people experienced:

> One of the effects …for the participants in general of their exposure to present practices of sexuality education within schools was the reinforcement of active/passive roles within male/female binaries. For the gay male participants this resulted in them perceiving that their sexuality was something to be acted upon but not talked about; as Andrew went on to state, the only image he had of gay adulthood was found in public sex venues:
>
> > When I was at school the gay community did not exist … I had no knowledge of it … the only knowledge I had was the toilets. (Andrew)

This research suggests that schools have a key role in shaping the ways in which young Queer people are able to communicate within Queer cultural worlds themselves rather than simply beyond them, in the ways in which they relate to a straight world beyond the closet.

Landing on the Queer planet: Beyond the closet?

Achieving a degree of happiness about one's Queer identity does not mean one escapes the closet. Negotiations about when and how and where and how much to be out continue to be a salient feature across the lifespan, as do the complicated social interactions which evolve through these negotiations. One perhaps becomes better at doing 'Queer' but developing and sustaining a Queer identity is not easy for adults either in heteronormative culture.

The personal testimonies of Queer adults lend some support to the idea that the discovery of Queer communities, the chance to participate in those communities and a sense of Queer history do help support and sustain Queer identities. It is this that has led to a dominant gay politics centered around representation. Lesbian and gay male role models in schools and representations of lesbians and gay men in the curriculum are seen as ways of supporting young Queer people to articulate their Queer identities. Although this may be the case, it is not often successful in lessening homophobia, because it tends to subscribe to the minoritizing view of homosexuality, as important only to those who are

Queer. Furthermore, it doesn't help young Queers expand the possible ways of being/doing Queer, which is important in ensuring that their identities have a sustainable future.

In their recent research, based on a longitudinal study of young people's transitions to adulthood, Thomson and Holland (2002) suggest that for all young people, imagined futures are constrained by the heteronormative goals of 'marriage and children by age 35.' Their interview with an eloquent 19-year-old self-identified gay man charts the difficulty he has in projecting future adulthood. In spite of his eloquence, the young gay man cannot find the language to articulate his future. He desperately wants children but cannot reconcile this with the type of gay male lifestyle upon which he has embarked and the definition of the gay identity through which he makes sense of his life. Thomson and Holland suggest that this forces their participant to live his life very much in the present. Alhtough they observe that Giddens (1992) and others have suggested that lesbian and gay relationships are in the vanguard in the transformation of intimacy, for the young gay man in their study, this appears not to be such an easy transformation, because he still cannot escape a heteronormative model of adulthood, which demands children. Thomson and Holland's analysis suggests that there is a pressure on gay and lesbian relationships and identities, because it is difficult for gay and lesbian young people to draw on normative cultural resources, especially their families, in the planning of their futures. In a sense, he is not trapped simply by the demands of heteronormativity but also by the demands of a statically conceived gay identity which doesn't allow him further reinventions of himself and his difference without the risk of exclusion from the gay community.

In much the same way, Pallotta-Chiarolli (1998; 2000) suggests that what is empowering for young people is the chance to express the complexity of their identities, across different social contexts. Pallotta-Chiarolli's work with young Australian women indicated their dissatisfaction with the binaries of the gay/straight divide, embracing a far more fluid conceptualization of sexuality and sexual practice. In fact, the anthology of young women's writing about sexuality and ethnicity edited by Pallotta-Chiarolli (1998) is one of the few texts which demonstrates a powerful and highly politicized understanding of issues of gender/race and sexuality by young women in their lives. It encourages in all young people a more sophisticated understanding of sexuality.

Conclusion

Communication issues for lesbian and gay people are complex, constrained through homophobia and the closet as an active and shaping presence in their lives. For many young Queer people this means being incommunicado about their sexuality, which in turn means that they have very restricted opportunities to imagine, explore and practice Queer sexual and romantic relationships. Some young people may develop performances of Queer identity that are uncertain, contradictory, or disguised by irony, in order to protect themselves. There is no positive mode of address to the young Queer in school and the homophobic address not only stigmatizes Queer identity but also conceptualizes gays, lezzies, poofs and Queers as static, deviant minority identities which are incapable of development within contexts of love or intimacy and which are certainly excluded from most conceptualizations of 'the family.' The necessity in our society of naming one's sexual identity and the constitution of adulthood through a developmental paradigm that demands heterosexuality make growing up Queer difficult. Young Queers are also trapped in adolescence through a dominant developmental psychology discourse, which insists on describing same-sex desire as 'a phase' of adolescence, such that it becomes difficult for young Queers to decide upon the moment when such a phase has gone on for so long that it can no longer be defined as such. This undermines Queer identities and makes intervention to support their development less likely. The relative lack of research in this area, as well as being evidence of how difficult it is to locate young Queer people, is also a real hindrance to evolving strategies that could offer support. More research is needed not simply on how young Queer people communicate with each other but also on how they communicate with their non-Queer peers or with Queer adults.

Notes

1. THT is the leading HIV and AIDS charity in the United Kingdom and the largest in Europe. It was one of the first charities to be set up in response to the HIV epidemic and has been at the forefront of the fight against HIV and AIDS ever since. The charity was established in 1982 as the Terrence Higgins Trust. Terry Higgins was one of the first people in the United Kingdom to die with AIDS. A group of his friends wanted to prevent more people having to face the same illness as Terry and named the trust after him, hoping to personalize and humanize AIDS in a very public way. For further information go to <www.tht.org.uk>.
2. For an interesting discussion about the production of lesbians and gay men within a regime of strangeness, as objects of fear, see Moran *et al.* (2003).
3. 'Queer' accepts that no sexual identity is a once and for all given, that people develop and change sexually in often unpredictable ways and that they do so throughout their lives, not merely in the period we choose to label adolescence. Nevertheless, it would be difficult to run a lesbian, gay and bisexual youth group using the word 'queer' in its title, because colloquially it is such a pejora-

tive word and any young 'queer' person may have had considerable experience of being taunted by the word. For further discussion of the use of the term Queer see pages 7–9 of Epstein, O'Flynn, *et al.* (2003).

4. The closet is used metaphorically by those who are queer, to denote the secrecy with which they are obliged often to lead their sexual lives. Hence, 'being in the closet' means not being open about one's queer sexuality and 'coming out of the closet' denotes the process of telling people about one's queer sexuality. For an interesting theoretical discussion of the importance of 'the closet' in queer as against mainstream culture, see Sedgwick (1990).

5. I am thinking here of US American comedy programs such as *Will and Grace*.

References

Butler, J. (1990). *Gender Trouble: Feminism and the Subversion of Identity*. New York: Routledge.

Cameron, D. (1997). Performing gender identity: young men's talk and the construction of heterosexual masculinity. In S. Johnson and U. Meinhof (eds), *Language and Masculinity*. Oxford: Blackwell.

Cameron, D. & Kulick, D. (2003). *Language and Sexuality*. Cambridge: Cambridge University Press.

Connexions Service, N. U. T. S. T. (2003). Information and Guidance on Engaging Young Lesbian, Gay and Bisexual People. 32.

DfEE. (1999). Circular 10/99: Social Inclusion: Pupil Support. HMSO, DfEE.

DfEE. (2000). Guidance on Sex and Relationship Education, DfEE.

Epstein, D. & Johnson, R. (1998). *Schooling Sexualities*. Buckingham: Open University Press.

Epstein, D., O'Flynn, S. & Telford, D. (2003). *Silenced Sexualities in Schools and Universities*. Stoke on Trent: Trentham Books.

Friend, R. (1993). Choices, not closets: Heterosexism and homophobia in schools. In L. Weis and M. Fine (eds), *Beyond Silenced Voices: Class, Race and Gender in United States Schools* (pp. 209–235). Albany: SUNY.

Giddens, A. (1992). *The Transformation of Intimacy: Sexuality, Love and Eroticism in Modern Societies*. Cambridge: Polity Press.

Gordon, A. (1999). Turning back: Adolescence, narrative and Queer theory. *GLQ: A Journal of Lesbian and Gay Studies*, 5 (1), 1–24.

Halley, J., E. (1993). The construction of heterosexuality. In M. Warner (ed.), *Fear of a Queer Planet: Queer Politics and Social Theory* (pp. 82–102). Minneapolis and London: University of Minnesota Press.

Harbeck, K. M. (1995). Invisible no more: Addressing the needs of lesbian, gay, and bisexual youth and their advocates. In G. Unks (ed.), *The Gay Teen: Educational Practice and Theory for Lesbian, Gay and Bisexual Adolescents* (pp. 125–133). New York and London: Routledge.

Herr, K. (1997). Learning lessons from school: Homophobia, heterosexism, and the construction of failure. *Journal of Gay and Lesbian Social Services*, 7 (4), 51–64.

Jaworski, A. (1993). *The Power of Silence: Social and Pragmatic Perspectives*. London and New Dehli: Sage.

Jennings, K. (1998). *Telling Tales Out of School: Gays, Lesbians, and Bisexuals Revisit Their School Days*. Los Angeles: Alyson Books.

Lorentz, J. K. (2000). Blame it on the weatherman: Popular culture and pedagogical praxis in the lesbian and gay studies classroom. In W. Spurlin (ed.), *Lesbian and Gay Studies and the Teaching of English: Positions, Pedagogies and Cultural Politics*. Illinois: National Council of Teachers of English.

Measor, L., Tiffin, C. & Miller, K. (2000). *Young People's Views on Sex Education: Education, Attitudes and Behavior*. Routledge: Falmer.

Micelli, M. S. (2002). Gay, lesbian and bisexual youth. In D. Richardson & S. Seidman (eds), *Handbook of Lesbian and Gay Studies* (pp. 199–204). London: Sage.

Moran, L., Skeggs, B., Tyrer, P. & Corteen, K. (2003). *Sexuality and the Politics of Violence and Safety*. London and New York: Routledge.

Nayak, A. & Kehily, M. J. (1997). Masculinities and schooling: why are young men so homophobic? In D. L. Steinberg, D. Epstein & R. Johnson. (eds), *Border Patrols: Policing the Boundaries of Heterosexuality* (pp. 138–161). London: Cassell.

Pallotta-Chiarolli, M. (1998). *Girls' Talk: Young Women Speak Their Hearts and Minds*. Sydney: Finch.

Pallotta-Chiarolli, M. (2000). 'Coming out/going home': Australian girls and young women interrogating racism and heterosexism. In J. McLeod & K. Malone (eds), *Researching Youth* (pp. 31–43). Sydney: Australian Clearinghouse for Youth Studies.

Plummer, K. (1995). *Telling Sexual Stories: Power, Change and Social Worlds*. London and New York: Routledge.

Quinlivan, K. & Town, S. (1999). Queer as fuck? Exploring the potential of queer pedagogies in researching school experiences of lesbian and gay youth. In D. Epstein & J. T. Sears (eds), *A Dangerous Knowing: Sexuality, Pedagogy and Popular Culture* (pp. 242–256). London and New York: Cassell.

Sedgwick, E. K. (1990). *The Epistemology of the Closet*. St Ives: Penguin.

Thomson, R. & Holland, J. (2002). Imagined adulthood: resources, plans and contradictions. *Gender and Education*, 14 (4), 337–350.

Thurlow, C. (2001). Naming the 'outsider within': homophobic pejoratives and the verbal abuse of lesbian, gay and bisexual high school pupils. *Journal of Adolescence*, 24, 25–38.

Unks, G. (ed.). (1995). *The Gay Teen: Educational Practice and Theory for Lesbian, Gay and Bisexual Adolescents*. New York and London: Routledge.

10

'Talkin', doin' and bein' with friends': Leisure and communication in adolescence

Leo Hendry and Marion Kloep

One of the misconceptions of modern times is that young people learn the really important preparatory life skills in school, although leisure is a time for relaxation, for recreation, and for fun. However, this point of view ignores the vast array of learning opportunities leisure can actually offer, not least the numerous occasions and various settings available for learning to communicate with others. Young people also use leisure to acquire many of their most valuable communication skills—because, in order to enjoy their leisure, they have to communicate with friends, peers, parents and other adults! As the quote in the title of our chapter shows, leisure and communication are intimately connected. Leisure plays an important part in human development, because, to a certain extent, it allows individuals to choose and pace the developmental tasks they encounter and the skills they learn. According to contemporary trends in developmental psychology theory, for example, development occurs every time an individual meets and overcomes a challenge that slightly exceeds their existing psychosocial resources (Hendry & Kloep, 2002). This adds new resources to their 'resource pool' and makes successful coping in the future more probable. Equally, if only a few new, challenging experiences are encountered, little (if any) new capabilities will be added, and a certain developmental stagnation occurs. Resources can also be lost when the individual is unable to cope with challenges, either because these challenges exceed existing resources or because there are too many challenges facing the individual simultaneously. Therefore, encountering challenges can be stimulating to the level of actually creating some anxiety in the individual, so that at times, if there is a choice, he/she avoids seeking challenges until feeling secure enough and believing that there are sufficient resources to cope. On the other hand, being underchallenged, though this provides security for the individual, can soon lead to feelings of boredom. Hence, people can stagnate and their development can be restricted and limited if their skills are not tested and their resource pool strengthened. Some of the most important sets of skills to master in the process of growing up are the skills of social relationships and interpersonal interactions, and some of the best opportunities for learning, practicing and trying out these skills are leisure settings of various kinds. Developmental resources can be of very different types: they may be a variety of skills, material advantages, enhanced self-esteem, biological advantages, social support, positive attitudes and so on—and what exactly makes them useful resources in a certain situation (and maybe not in another!) depends on the kind of challenge that individuals face. In other words, there is a dynamic interaction between challenges and resources, in which one defines the other. Hence, the same feature can be a resource in one situation and a challenge in another. If we consider, for example, communication skills and leisure, we can easily see that having a rich repertoire of leisure pursuits can provide excellent resources for making new friends. On the other hand, having friends and having good social and communication skills can serve as resources for coping with the challenges that leisure activities provide.

For many young people, adolescence is a time that offers many challenges. Apart from the onset of puberty and changes in body shape, schooling, examinations and career choices, and increasing adult rights and responsibilities, reconfigured social relationships with parents, peers and romantic partners all have to be negotiated. How do young people manage these challenges and maintain or even add to their 'resource pool' in the transition to adulthood?

Findings of one well-known study of adolescent relationships showed that attitudes to different relationships changed as a function of age, but more importantly the results also indicated that concerns about different issues reached a peak at different periods through adolescence (Coleman, 1978). This key finding led to the theoretical formulation of the 'focal model,' which provides one possible explanation for the successful adaptation of many young people to developmental demands. That is, they cope by dealing with one issue at a time, and spread the process of adaptation over a span of years, attempting to resolve first one issue and then the next. Different problems and different relationship issues come into focus and are tackled at different points in the adolescent developmental process, so that the stresses resulting from the need to adapt to new modes of behavior are rarely concentrated all at one time. The model suggests that at different phases, particular sorts of relationship patterns (relationships to peers, parents and romantic partners) come into focus, in the sense of being most prominent, though no pattern is specific to one phase only. Yet, even if a focal issue is not highly prominent at one specific point in the transition, it could still be critical for some individuals around that time. The focal model goes some way toward reconciling the apparent contradiction between the amount of adaptation required during the transitional process and the ability of most young people to cope successfully with the pressures inherent in that process. Results from studies in other countries (Kroger, 1985, in New Zealand and United States; Goossens & Marcoen, 1999, in Belgium) support this notion of different issues coming into focus at different times. As Goossens and Marcoen (1999: 65–80) state,

> The general pattern of peak ages for adolescents' interpersonal concerns provided support for the focal model. Negative feelings about being alone, relationships with parents, heterosexual relationships, small groups, and rejection from large groups do not all emerge all at once, but seem to be dealt with one issue at a time.

In a study of our own carried out in Sweden (see Kloep, 1999), we provided additional support for the notion that, where possible, adolescent developmental issues are dealt with one at a time, rather than all at once. In another series of studies (Hendry *et al.*, 1993; 1996; 2002), we and our colleagues used the focal model to provide a perspective on the way young peoples' leisure activities interact dynamically with their developmental needs in learning relational skills. These studies showed how young people move from one style of leisure involvement to another and one type of relationship to another as they progress through adolescence, demonstrating how there are a series of leisure transitions allied to these relational transitions. Young peoples' leisure patterns generally move through three transitional stages: 'organized leisure,' 'casual leisure' and 'commercial leisure.' These three transitions coincide with three relational 'shifts,' namely, developing a friendly/romantic interest toward the opposite sex, peer group acceptance, and gaining independence from parents. Such shifts and strategies ideally incorporate three phases of development, in each of which a consecutive set of new capabilities is learned, releasing young people step by step into the world of adult relationships.

Hence, this chapter looks at the dynamic interactions between leisure and communication in the psychosocial development of young people. We want to illustrate this association by presenting the voices of young people themselves, talking about their leisure pursuits and their leisure settings. When adults—be they academic theorists, researchers, youth professionals, policy makers or laypersons—consider young people's leisure, the adolescent's perspective is rarely included. Here we attempt to redress the balance by presenting what young people have said to us about various aspects of leisure in some of our recent research projects, and in particular what they have said about its role in creating and maintaining social relationships. We do this by extracting and interpreting what young people themselves have told us when we have talked with them about their lifestyles and leisure pursuits. The quotations we offer here are all taken from a number of fairly recent studies of young people that we have conducted in various regions of Sweden and Scotland. Our Scottish data comes from 20 focus group interviews (with 5–7 same age/sex young people in each group, N–80), and approximately 40 individual interviews with young people between 11 and 18 years of age from a study by Hendry *et al.* (1998). The Swedish data, on the other hand, is drawn from essays titled 'To be young in Jamtland,' written by 240 young people between 13 and 18 years of age (Kloep, 1998). This material—including that cited here—was translated by the second author, a bilingual speaker. (As you will see from the quotes, it is not unusual for many Swedish teenagers—and even a few Scots— to use the term 'one' instead of 'I' in their essays, as well as in their daily talk.) These qualitative studies were part of a larger research project investigating the lifestyles of young people in Scotland, Sweden and Norway, and some of the results are published in different journal articles (e.g., Hendry, Kloep & Wood, 2002; Hendry *et al.*, 2002; Kloep *et al.*, 2003).[1]

The stories young people have told us are presented in this chapter to show the complex process of developing communication and leisure skills throughout the teenage years. We start by looking at communication as a leisure activity, then go on to examine how leisure is used to learn relational skills, and conclude by giving examples of how leisure can be used more widely to communicate identity and 'style.'

Communication as leisure

Often, when asked what they do in their leisure time, young people will answer, 'Nothing—just hanging around with friends!' In fact, young people spend a great deal of their leisure time with friends (Flammer *et al*, 1999; Kloep, 1998), often 'not doing anything' but chatting, giggling and 'hanging out.' Indeed, many young people perceive 'fooling around' and laughter as among the most fulfilling of activities (e.g., Csikszentmihalyi & Larson, 1984). Being with others and being in communication is in itself a very important leisure activity for young people.[2] Through these interactions, they receive social support, offer feedback on new skills, give advice and comfort and provide security just by being 'there' for friends. Through such *apparently* meaningless conversations, social bonds are negotiated and strengthened.

The importance of 'special' friends is stressed again and again when young people discuss the role of friendship and support. Interpersonal communication seems vital in their leisure lives:

> I talk mostly with Anna, we can be talking more than an hour about nothing, really, and that is what makes it so enjoyable, I would think. (SWF 14)

> I should not forget my great friends. They make life worth living, and it is because of them that I have very few problems… (SCM 15)

> I am feeling very fine. What's really important is friends. And regarding friends, I am not in any need. I have not only a few of them… I have a best friend, but I cannot be so often with her, she lives 25 kilometres away… (SWF 13)

> I have quite a lot of friends and we can talk about everything and that makes me feel very secure… (SCF 15)

When friends cannot meet face-to-face the telephone is much in use to enable the talking to continue, particularly in rural areas (Hendry *et al.*, 1998). This means of communication is obviously not new; however, it has gained even greater importance more recently with the arrival of mobile phones, enabling young people to communicate at virtually every hour of the day, wherever they are. By being able to send text messages, young people can even communicate secretly in places otherwise not suitable for private communication, such as under the classroom desk, in toilet cubicles or at home under the duvet. Furthermore, the creation of new linguistic practices for technologies such as text messaging allow new ways of communicating to which adults are not always able to easily gain access.

Computer activities provide another relatively 'adult-free zone,' because often many parents are not as computer literate as their children, and so may not always be able to monitor a young person's communication in online environments such as chatrooms, email, instant messaging, online games and so on. To some extent, the use of computers and gaming technology has 'demoted' leisure reading, although computers still lag behind television, CDs and radio (see, for example, Beentjes *et al.*, 1999).

Concerned by this development, adults often speculate about possible dangers emerging from a device over which they have little control. A Canadian study (D'Amours & Robitaille, 2002) showed that nearly half the parents interviewed indicated that they did not feel sufficiently skilled to supervise their children's activities on the internet because they did not use it as actively as their children. Asked by these researchers what they primarily did on the internet, young people said they searched for information (78%), exchanged emails

(72%), listened to or downloaded music (70%), participated in chat rooms (66%) and played games online (56%). Compared to that, only 47 percent of the adults questioned used the internet for emails, and only 15 percent participated in chat rooms. Interestingly, in this Canadian study, young women used the net as much as boys, albeit for slightly different activities. Girls preferred email exchanges, whereas boys played online games (a gendered division that seems to mirror real-world differences). Arnett *et al.* (1995) view these cultural trends as new and important sources of socialization for young people, because to a large extent they select their own materials and programs.

Is extensive internet use preventing, substituting or complementing real life communication for teenagers? Research up to now has had few answers to that question. It seems that the lower young peoples' level of attachment to close friends is, and the fewer pro-social attitudes they express, the higher is their involvement with the internet (Mesch, 2001). However, that does not answer the question of whether the internet might be a convenient tool for shy people to try out social skills from a safe 'distance,' covered by anonymity and maybe an assumed identity, or if it prevents these individuals from going out into the real world and risking the challenges of face-to-face relationships. Nevertheless, some young people use the net to establish contacts initially: Wolak *et al.* (2002) showed that 14 percent of the teenagers they interviewed reported having formed close online relationships, often with same-aged peers and across gender lines. Most of these electronic links led to off-line contacts such as phone calls and meetings. Contrary to media stories, less than half a percent of these contacts were classified as being 'sexual in any way' [see chapter 11, this volume— for more discussion on these issues].

Quite often, computer activities are not only directed at communicating, but also engaged in as collaborative ventures. Young people meet together to play computer games, or to engage in online chats as a group:

> The main part of my leisure time I spend with X, one of my friends. We 'punish' his computer until the processor gets hot and the soundcard gives up. We also use X's house as a meeting place for me, X, Y and Zn, the famous PZ-gang. (SWM 15)

Since communication in many forms is an integral part of young people's leisure time activities, it offers both challenges and risks. Communication with friends is not unproblematic and involves many social skills that have to be acquired, practiced and tried out for effect. For this, leisure offers many opportunities to experiment, observe role models and rehearse skills, and to enact and try out future adult roles.

Leisure for communication

Personal choice, peer encounters, parental supervision, adult mentors, the commercial world and legal restrictions create the various leisure settings and contexts that young people seek out as they move from early adolescence toward adulthood. Yet these transitional patterns, following focal theory, are somewhat predictable.

Organized leisure

According to the leisure focal model described earlier, the first phase, running from childhood to the early adolescent years, involves young people associating with a range of adult-led organizations and activities and is concerned with conformity to adults and the observation and practice of 'appropriate' behavior in the presence of adults.

Adults play an important role in young people's leisure participation. Sports clubs, hobby groups, choirs and orchestras, youth clubs and uniformed organizations all tend to be arranged for young people by adults, and are often closely supervised by adults. Young people's involvement in such adult-sponsored situations, though nominally voluntary, may not be genuinely self-chosen, and may confront young people with the dilemma of choosing to participate in a setting which if anything perpetuates adult dominance in their lives, perhaps in exchange for the training of well-regarded skills and the advantages of acquired social status. Demonstrating the interests of early adolescence, one boy said,

> In winter one can go on slalom and cross country skis, skates, snowboard. During holidays and on weekends, there are always buses to the skiing area. I am interested in skating and hockey. We have a small sports hall. There we play indoor hockey, football, volleyball, basket, table tennis and so on… (SWM 14)

Many studies have shown a high involvement of school-age youngsters in fairly regular physical activity and sport. In Flammer *et al.*'s (1999) study, sport was the third most popular leisure activity during adolescence, after watching television/listening to music and meeting friends. However, there are age and sex/gender differences (Hendry *et al.* 1993; Kremer *et al.*, 1997). Put simply, younger male adolescents are the most likely group to be sports participants.

> Normally, when we come home from school, we'll be doing golfing, and straight after that we'll have a football tournament or something, football matches... We have training on Tuesdays, Thursdays and Sundays... (SCM 14)

Young women in all age groups are considerably less involved than young men (Hendry *et al.*, 2002; Mason, 1995). Future leisure participation patterns may, however, reveal fewer gender biases, and this is already emerging in countries where social equality between the sexes is more evident, such as Scandinavia (e.g., Wold & Hendry, 1998).

By what young people tell us themselves, it would seem that overall, in early adolescence many of them are not too dissatisfied with what is available for their leisure activities because the challenges they are offered in terms of activity skills, interactions with adult coaches and communication with peers in a secure environment more or less match their available psychosocial resources. But, with the onset of puberty, and as they move toward mid-adolescence, things seem to change.

As young people grow toward the mid-teens they become more critical, questioning and skeptical of adult-led organizations. They recognize that power and decision making in youth organizations lies with adults, though the adult leaders claim that they involve young people in decision making and offer truly collaborative participation (e.g., Love & Hendry, 1994). Furthermore, young people at this point feel more confident in communicating with peers in the organized and supervised setting of a leisure-time club.

When asked by Mahoney (1997) and by Hendry *et al.* (1993) the most important reason for dropping out, young people cited 'lack of interest' as the most important reason, together with the fact that other social activities had assumed more importance in their lives. This idea of conflicting social interests is mirrored in the comments of young people themselves. So what do mid-adolescents have to say about organized leisure, alternative leisure options, and their peer relationships? Now that they are more secure in their social skills, and would like to try them out in the peer group, an apparent rejection of adult organizations takes place, with social learning in the company of peers, 'hanging around' in the street, shopping malls or in the park, or at 'sleep-over' parties. In all cases, adults are not present except perhaps as peripheral, background figures.

> Well, just because I used to be quite athletic like I did a lot of running and stuff. I suppose it was when I started going out a lot I stopped. (SCM 17)

We found that views about youth clubs were particularly critical and negative, as the following quotations show:

> Youth club: Yeah there is but it's rubbish. They don't do anything. I used to go to it, it's all the popular ones and they're all in it and they just sit there and speak and it's just boring. You can play snooker but the boys always get there before you. There's a bit upstairs but you are not allowed to go up there anymore because they wrecked the joint. So it's just not worth it. (SWF 14)

> To be there is like being at home, constantly supervised by parents. (SCF 16)

Casual leisure

Having dropped out of organized leisure options, teenagers attempt to move into what they see as adult leisure settings, but they are seldom allowed to participate. Legal and practical restrictions such as pub and club laws, parental demands, prohibitive entry fees and the police all prevent young people from taking part in most aspects of adult leisure. Among the causes given for young people's frustration are lack of accessible contexts and the social sanctions prohibiting their use of such settings. There even exists a competition for 'space' (such as the local park, or shopping arcades) between young people and adults, which leads to entry restrictions and curfews (Hendry *et al.*, 2002). So, not quite voluntarily, young people move to the phase of 'casual leisure,' described in Hendry's leisure focal model.

During this phase, one of the most often stated complaints young people have is that there is 'absolutely nothing to do.' In a cross-cultural study of young rural people, we and our colleagues found that up to 60 percent of rural young people indicated that 'nothing to do' was a serious problem in the area where they live, young women being significantly more critical than young men (see Hendry *et al.*, 2002). 'Leisure boredom' seems to be a very prominent feature of teenagers' perceptions of rural living (e.g., Bone *et al.*, 1993, rural Queensland; Jones, 1992, rural Tasmania), though it emerges as an issue in urban areas too (Caldwell *et al.*, 1992; Shaw *et al.*, 1996, Canada):

> The one thing that is correct in the picture of society is the lack of something to do. I am not in the age yet to be worried about unemployment and hang around during the weeks, no it's weekends that are the problem. What should one do on free days, evenings, nights? One cannot go to sleep at eleven. ELEVEN on a Friday night! No, one has to go out, but where to? (SWF 16)

We have to continue to walk up and down the road. This society is not made for those of us between 14 and 18, sad but true. One looks into the youth club, circles the village, and if one is lucky, one is picked up by a car. Bloody shit is all I can say. If you want to have fun, you have to drink till you drop. But that's not good neither. (SWF 15)

I think about all these weekends that have been spent doing absolutely nothing. The only thing that can save me from fading away totally is sports… What is there to do? The weekends all have the same pattern. Go down to the youth club, talk some shit, go up and down the main road. Is it that what life is about? I understand exactly why more and more get drunk during weekends. (SWF 15)

Interestingly, this complaint did not necessarily correlate with the actual amount of time young people spent in pursuits nor with the number of different leisure activities young people were engaged in. Hendry *et al.* (2002) suggested that it might not be the quantity, but the quality, of the activities that create feelings of boredom. What is on offer is no longer a sufficient challenge:

When I was younger, I always knew what to do, and I could always be with my younger siblings. But when I grew older, all my interests vanished, and nowadays, there is nothing to do. (SWF 14)

If one looks for entertainment, one has to look for a long time. The only thing that catches my interest is the lure of fish… There is not a lot to do in winter, unless one is either snowboarding or horse-crazy of course. If anyone is like me, they have to sit at home and twiddle their thumbs. If it gets boring, one can change direction for a change! OK, I am exaggerating a bit, one can do a lot here if one has the right interests, whatever they might be. (SWM 14)

Shaw *et al.* (1996) concluded that frequent experiences of boredom were not simply a matter of too little to do, but were associated in a more complex way with a young person's relationship with the wider community. Naturally, young people want to have time on their own to experiment with new roles, want to be trusted to do things away from protective, controlling adults. This leads to a struggle with parents and teachers, who see unsupervised time as synonymous with unprotected time (e.g., Caldwell *et al.*,1999; Hendry & Kloep, 2002).

And there is a hotel-pub for those over 18. And a pizza-restaurant, there we can't even use the bathroom after 22.00 hours. (SWF 14)

It is awful to be young, because one doesn't have any money and one can't get into places, just because there is nothing for young people… (SWF 14)

The hypothesis presented here is that young people in many cases are not challenged enough. Overprotected by parents, teachers, youth leaders and the law, they are not given enough opportunity to try out their skills or to generate their own challenges; consequently they seize every opportunity to do so—only to find out that they often do not have the capabilities or resources to create meaningful leisure for themselves. Some retreat into passivity and boredom, whereas others overestimate their skills and engage in 'risky' behaviors as soon as they can escape from adult protection. Belonging to a generation that grew up being organized and entertained by adults since early childhood, young people might lack the skills necessary for organizing and entertaining themselves. As a consequence of earlier poor training in self-management, young people admit that they cannot organize their own leisure time, when they search for alternatives to adult-led offers.

In the meantime, many provisional locations serve as settings for the leisure pursuits of younger teenagers, such as supermarkets, urban shopping malls, amusement arcades, street corners, parks, bus stops or fast-food restaurants (Fisher, 1995; Giddens, 1991). Thus, young people are a common sight around many public places in the community. The possible effects of societal and cultural change in the last two decades may also impinge on patterns of leisure transition. It is possible to speculate, for instance, that involvement in casual leisure on the street corner has been replaced more and more by settings like cafés, pizzerias and fast-food restaurants as social meeting places.

Friends fill an obvious gap in providing guidelines for developing new social skills when organized leisure activities are abandoned. They provide young people with new sources of security in facing new challenges, such as romantic encounters [see chapter 8, this volume]. During mid-adolescence, dating, as an important leisure pursuit, begins to complement activities with friends, and romantic partners become a crucial source of social support at this time—and a source for acquiring new communication skills:

In leisure time, when we are with friends, we most often talk about boys… That is among the best things to do. Or else we go to a disco… preferably a disco down town, where one has a real chance to meet guys who are nice and sweet, and who do not sit in a corner with the gang, discussing how ugly and sexy the girls are and what big tits they have… (SWF 15)

But there are also peak moments in my life. The days I spend kissing and cuddling with my girl friend A. She is the best thing that's happened to me for a long time… and I have one of the world's nicest and sexiest birds. (SWM 15)

Unlike other aspects of social learning, young people receive very little help from family or school, and sometimes not even from peers, in the acquisition of romantic strategies and sexual techniques (e.g., Shucksmith & Hendry, 1998). As we ourselves have written (see Kloep & Hendry, 1999) such relational 'competencies' are seldom discussed, and only covered inappropriately in pornographic material accessed on the internet and in romanticized women's magazines, which offer a limited view of sexuality (Kaplan & Cole, 2003).

From their comments it becomes clear that both sexes in their teens start out with somewhat negative views of each other's romantic qualities:

> And all the boys of your age just sit in front of the TV and they're all boring and uninteresting. They're all sheep farmer's sons or football fanatics who don't care about girls. I think the ones you get on with are the ones that come up on holiday and stuff like that. They're nice. There are about 5 really nice good-looking ones but every single girl in the school is after them. It's a cat-fight who is going to get off with them at the next dance. And it turns out to be nobody. Because they are off with someone from the next village! (SCF 15)

> We played football and went to the dance. I pulled an ugly dog. I pulled a dog. I went to the dance and had a few drinks. I got off with her on the bus on the way home. I fell asleep on top of her and Tim stabbed me with a fag and Sally slapped me. I think that was what happened to me. I can't remember. Ugly girls. There's not that many tidy birds at all. There's only about 6 in the whole school, if that. Even if there are no good looking girls you still get off with them at dances... (SCM 15)

These quotes show how young heterosexual people hide their underlying anxieties and lack of romancing techniques behind a tough attitude and a 'sour grapes' reaction. Like other skills, the abilities needed to relate romantically to others have to be practiced. This is where the leisure sphere becomes highly significant and important. Many young people follow leisure activities not for the intrinsic value of the pursuits themselves but as contexts for making and meeting friends and beginning romantic attachments. Some commercial leisure venues are especially designed to enhance ambience, which enables romantic exploration (Alapack, 1991; 1999). However, any setting from pubs, clubs and cinema back rows to sports clubs, swimming pools and ski slopes will do:

> The best thing about snowboarding is that I can go with Jonas, Stefan and Andreas, who are the tastiest boys in school.... (SWF 14)

Commercial leisure

Once young people have learned some skills for relating to friends and romantic partners, and have reached an age when they are allowed to, they join the world of adult commercial leisure. Indeed, some teenagers simply and quickly skip casual activities and join commercial leisure contexts directly:

> I was friends with someone for a while and I think we went wandering around for one night and I got so bored. I thought 'No. It's so cold and rainy. It's cold'. And you see people sitting there all cold and wet but they still sit there. And you think why! It's the same, cruising round in cars. It's absolutely pointless. They go round the square, again and again. You might not be saying that when you've passed your test. Oh I hate it, I hate it. I think it is so boring. My sister does it and she goes round and round. It's all right a couple of times if you just want to see who is out and about, if you want to speak to someone. But there's folk that come onto the street 9 to 10 and they're still going round at 2 o'clock when the pubs close, and they've gone round and round. *We seem to have skipped the whole hanging around the streets bit and gone straight into pubs.* I just couldn't hang around. (SCF 17)

In the commercial leisure context, new challenges await them: communicating with adults, and being accepted and respected as adults themselves. Therein lies perhaps the main attraction of venues like pubs, restaurants and 'adult-only' activities: they are symbolic for showing the world that one has achieved the transition to adulthood. This leads to another function of leisure, its symbolic value to the world at large.[3]

Leisure as communication

Apart from being an opportunity to entertain oneself, to socialize with friends and to learn new skills, leisure pursuits are also aspects of self-image— expressing one's identity and lifestyle. By choosing certain activities, by wearing the 'right' gear and using the 'right' language, one can communicate to the world what kind of person one wants to be perceived as being. A mobile phone is not only a technology for interpersonal communication but it is also a fashion statement—its style, color, attached gadgets and price communicate quickly to the wider world what kind of person the owner is (or aspires to be). For that reason, many leisure activities are associated with a certain type of fashion, with distinctive behaviors and other symbols to mark the owner as a *skater*, a *surfer*, a *rebel*, a *fashion freak* or an *outsider*, to name but a few. We can all very quickly come up with our own stereotypic mental picture of a *punk*, a *goth*, a *soccer supporter* or a *lager lout*.

Further, when young people gather in public places, they invariably see other groups as somehow 'different' in style of dress and behavior, and, at times, perhaps threatening to give rise to 'trouble.' The attempt to establish and maintain a local 'identity' creates powerful rivalry among different adolescent crowds, and 'territory' is important to the creation of clear-cut—if varied—community 'identities.' Hendry, Kloep and Wood (2002) found that other groups were typically seen as either 'cool' or 'bad' or 'sad,' whereas friendship groups regarded themselves as 'normal' in their dress, interests and activities. This suggests that young people try to establish their identity through group belonging, thus compensating for the security lost when they left adult-led organizations. At the same time, this creates strong 'in-group/out-group' feelings and the creation of 'negative identities.'

> It's about the townies and the country boys. It's the ones from X and Y, and we don't want them. The boys from Z are supposed to be big and strong, and they always come and start fights, just because they're in the town. The boys from V normally get involved as well. It's a bit pointless, it just ends up happening. (SCM 15)

> There's an adventure playground in the park and everyone used to go there when it opened but it's all 18-year-olds and all that and they've graffitied all over it and all that and they just go and drink and smoke and all that. That's where they sit and all that, they don't let anybody else on it. The police are always doon ['down'] there and all that. It's not safe to go down there at night in case like they attack you or anything. They just sit on the swings and drink and all that. If you just look, glance at them they'll do you! (SCM 15)

The choice of leisure activity, and its accompanying symbols, is not only a signal to other peers about what kind of person one is. It is also a signal that the young person is ceasing to be a child and wants to be accepted in the adult world. This means abandoning 'childish' activities and distancing oneself from the past:

> I used to be a Brownie but I'm not in anything now. I played the clarinet until a little while ago but I got sick of it. (SCF 17)

In some cases, rebelling against adult-initiated leisure activities makes this point:

And the other half of my life is concentrated around slalom. Dad thinks it is really cool, but I don't. I have told him that I want to quit next year, but he seems not to understand. But next year I will quit forever… (SWF 15)

In their narratives, young people point out, that they now see through adult manipulation and vicarious achievement motivation, and distance themselves from it:

I learned a lot during these years. Amongst other things, that it is not always the children who compete. I saw many parents who were more engaged than their children. These are those who were not successful themselves in any sports, and who want success through their children. (SWF 16)

The void that is created by rejecting adult-led organized leisure creates certain problems for young people, who may lack the skills and the opportunities to organize their own leisure. Yet, this situation also provides them with an opportunity to communicate their resentment against being excluded from adult leisure venues, and puts responsibility for this situation onto adult society: 'Nothing to do' in leisure as an expression of rebellion:

A 'little' mistake that I cannot accept is that 99 percent of the youth fund's money goes to that fucking youth sport… OK, there is one percent left. That percentage goes in its totality to our YoUTh cLUb, which is as weird as I spell it. I am there myself now and then. That youth club has the motto: ' If you want to have fun, do it yourself'. That is nice, ok, if there were anything there to have fun with… (SWM 15)

In this context, young people like to put the blame for their own risk-taking on adults, because they do not provide them with appropriate leisure activities (seldom stating what exactly these activities could be):

I think that you adults and other persons should fix something for us youngsters to do at weekends. That would be better than us 'hanging around' in the streets and drinking ourselves 'senseless' and poisoned by alcohol as many of us do…But the community doesn't care a fig and invests in a lot of useless things. (SWF 14)

In later adolescence most of the social skills learned to date are carried out for their acceptance by grown-ups. Older adolescents want to try out adult behaviors, often within the commercial leisure sphere, as a way of testing whether they can be accepted as a 'real' adult, knowing only too well that adults would regard them as too young to do these things, and would prevent them if they could (e.g., the challenge of getting into a pub and to be served an alcoholic drink rather than to enjoy the actual drinking of it). In this way, young people observe, rehearse, and perform the skills and behaviors they perceive to be necessary for adult status. The need to feel both independent and secure may be the vital reason why older adolescents move toward commercial leisure provision. Because they suffer fewer legal and social restrictions, they can initiate their own developmental challenges. The factors leading young people toward an involvement in commercial leisure (pubs, clubs, discos, commercial squash or health clubs, window shopping, and even foreign travel) have to do with the desire to be seen as having an independent adult-like leisure role.

Hence, in the light of media advertising in Western societies, which are typically more affluent, the desire to access commercial contexts—in the company of peers—may have accelerated down the age-scale. Even in pre-adolescence, so-called 'tweenagers' want to be like teenagers, copy their behavior and attempt to be regarded as older than they actually are, with all the attendant social and psychological risks that may present themselves, and because older adolescents as 'emerging adults' want to protect their social domain, they don't want to be associated with younger teenagers. So they 'police the boundaries' in certain ways to make sure of exclusion from their territory by keeping the 'kids' out:

> Like discos. We'd love discos just for us, without like the druggies or the cruisers. Just like for us. But that's the problem ... there is not a lot of folk like us here. There's a lot that's younger, but we don't want them. (SCMs 15/16)

For example, Sharp and Lowe (1989) have suggested that young people's drinking is a part of the socialization process from child to adult and a symbolic practice related to their seeking social acceptance in adult society. Thus it is important to be sensitive to the subtext in what young people are trying to tell us about their drinking. In rural areas in Scotland, Sweden and Norway, for example, we found that young people reported that one of their main reasons for drinking was to be seen to be 'adult' and to be accepted into adult venues (Kloep *et al.*, 2001). Hence, there is supporting evidence for the finding that, among other reasons for drinking and smoking, it is the wish to gain adult status as soon as possible, at least symbolically, which leads many youngsters toward drink (e.g., Pavis *et al.*, 1997).

This desire for acceptance into adult society seems to lie behind much of young people's behavior that adults disapprove of, not fully realizing that it is actually imitative behavior, and, as young people perceive it, a wish to be socialized 'conventionally.' These are some of the symbols of adult society, well advertised through the mass media, which attract many young people to a process of emulating their older, adult role models and in meeting the challenge of the transitions to adult status.

Furthermore, even apparently risky activities such as underage drinking may contain elements of challenge, offering the potential of growth. Pape and Hammer (1996), for instance, suggest that young male abstainers, and men who were latecomers to drinking, show indications of a delayed entry into adult roles, and a reluctance to adopt adult role-behaviors. Thus, according to the authors, perhaps getting involved in drinking for the first time in mid-adolescence can be an ingredient within the normal developmental process of young people in Western societies.

Some concluding comments: Linking theoretical frameworks

In this chapter we have seen how important communication is to relationships throughout adolescence. Furthermore, we have argued that leisure activities and communication are intimately intertwined in the lives of young people as they progress through various relational transitions across adolescence. From the analyses of our qualitative data—from the ideas teenagers have given us—we have suggested three interrelated strands between leisure and communication.

Communication as leisure. Communicating can be a vital part of leisure time—just talking, relating, and being with each other are important relational aspects of leisure time. Yet, after a while, for a relationship to be sustained and strengthened, it needs the participants' engagement in activities that can be talked about, planned, participated in and reminisced about, together. Thus, communication and leisure become two sides of the same coin. Young people have told us how important these leisure times of apparently casual conversation are, when aspirations are shared, outings discussed, problems tackled, social skills and fashion styles rehearsed, sports events or tactics tried out, romantic strategies planned and so on.

Leisure for communication. This leads us to a second association between 'talkin', doin' and bein' with friends.' In leisure time and in leisure settings there are opportunities to actually acquire communication skills, negotiate social roles, and learn about rules, rule violation, time management, teamwork, leadership, conflict resolution and other interpersonal competencies. This is not unique to adolescence; for example, on becoming an adult, one has to learn new, additional communication skills—intergenerational communication with younger and older people at home, at work and in leisure, and interethnic communication in a multicultural society. However, adolescence is an important phase of the lifespan in which to begin learning and rehearsing these skills and competencies. The young people we have interviewed indicate that such an array of cultural and other communication abilities enable them to reflect on their identity development, acquire the ability to both 'fit in' with the crowd and yet retain a sense of self. Overall, they perceive such social and communicative 'navigations' as necessary to their mental health (e.g., Hendry & Reid, 2000).

Leisure as communication. Thirdly, we have outlined leisure as symbolic communication in social settings in which young persons can 'use' their appearance, hairstyle, makeup, clothes, language and fashion style to display a social identity, a subcultural allegiance or individualism. This can include identifying with a particular fashion style, 'being a sports fan,' demonstrating group membership of a local crowd such as being a 'goth' or a 'punk' and declaring 'separateness' from other groups (see Hendry, Kloep & Wood, 2002; Thurlow, 2001). Additionally, Maffesoli (1996) has stated that both adults and young people can 'dip into,' or sample, a range of varied groupings which meet regularly, even weekly, but all can possess different values and behaviors. Thus, contemporary (Western) society encourages individuals to display multiple identities and varied, if transient, allegiances to different social groups, which may cut across age, gender, class and ethnic boundaries [also see chapter 1, this volume]. For instance, we can imagine the varying 'identity displays' of dress and behaviors that a company director may provide at a formal dinner, at the tennis club, and with their partner on a casual outing to the pub: at all times the intention is to communicate to the world (and to the people with whom one is interacting) what leisure mode and context and what mood one is in. Thus, we should not be too surprised that teenagers use these symbolic and communicative identity displays of different kinds on different occasions as a means of trying out different identities. This phase Erikson (1968) described as being a psychosocial 'moratorium' in which the young person is given the opportunity by adult society to experiment with and rehearse social roles, develop a clear-cut identity and delay major life decisions.

These three leisure-communication styles we have described in this chapter are enacted in concert with the *focal* shifts in relationships (Coleman, 1978) and leisure types (Hendry *et al.*, 1996) apparent in young people's transitions to adulthood. We believe also that these focal transitions can be explained by what we have called a *Lifespan Model of Developmental Challenge* (Hendry & Kloep, 2002), which looks at developmental shifts from a challenge/risk perspective whereby people search for a balance between security, boredom and stagnation on the one hand, and challenge, anxiety and development on the other. Translated into the world of leisure, this means that young people try to find challenges in leisure contexts that match or just slightly exceed their leisure and communication skills. They choose leisure contexts that provide a 'goodness of fit' with their increasing communication resources and abandon those that do not offer any new challenges. They also choose friends and communication partners appropriate to their leisure interests. With increasing capabilities and experiences in communication and in the leisure 'sphere,' the nature of relationships and leisure interests will shift, as the leisure focal theory indicates: early adolescents engage in adult-led organized activities which provide them with developing 'status' skills and enough security to begin to try out the new skills of relating to peers. Once young people feel secure in mastering these relational skills, organized adult-dominated activities may become boring and adult-dominated from their perspective. Since peers now reaffirm identities, it is more challenging to 'try out' certain social roles and new skills informally in the peer group. Finally, these social skills are tested out for their acceptance in the adult world.

What the developmental challenges of adolescence are, and what resources are available to young people, of course, varies greatly with social class, gender/sexuality, ethnicity, nationality and so on. For instance, in the poorer countries young people face a completely different set of challenges and risks, and have to draw on different resources. Nevertheless, the mechanism of development—the interaction of challenges, resources and risks—are the same whatever the cultural context. Acquiring social skills in various contexts is a formidable developmental task, which may have to exist hand-in-hand with other cultural challenges such as exams or finding employment. We should not be surprised that some young people need help in acquiring such skills to progress successfully across the teenage years. In talking with young people, it seems that, consistent with our Lifespan Model of Developmental Challenge, they consider their leisure time in early adolescence to be a rich source of development and challenge. However, as they move into mid-adolescence young people often report that they are less satisfied with what is 'on offer.' There are insufficient challenges to test out their newly developing skills, and some young people slide into passivity and boredom. Others overreact and resort to risky acts and situations, where challenges exceed young people's resources, and into settings in which they take chances, do not reflect on goals and consequences, and do not assess risks effectively (see Parker *et al.*, 1998).

Leisure can act as a regulatory device in times of too many or too few challenges: if there are too few challenges in the young person's life, then leisure can be a 'life sphere' for the opportunity to face more challenges; and if there are too many tasks to meet in the young person's life, then leisure challenges can be reduced. Hence, leisure is a life sector for seeking out challenges and learning opportunities in times of little challenge from other sources—it is a self-administered antidote for boredom, and a context for fulfilling developmental tasks. It is important therefore for young people to acquire the ability to assess accurately the 'goodness of fit' between their resources and developmental leisure tasks, which varies not only between individuals, but also, depending on context, within the same individual. The array of interactive psychosocial factors involved suggests the importance of examining processes and mechanisms, as Rutter (1996) and we ourselves (Kloep & Hendry, 1999) among others have proposed. It is necessary for researchers to try to find out more about these interactive mechanisms in order to understand variations in leisure patterns and what they actually 'mean' for young people in acquiring the social and communicative skills for growing up in a rapidly changing and highly technological society. Such studies demand that the young person's perspective and the adolescent voice need to be given much more significance in future research.

Notes

1. In quoting our young participants' voices here, we have indicated a little biographical information in terms of nationality (SC = Scottish, SW = Swedish), sex (M = Male, F = Female) and age.
2. Editors: See also studies cited in chapter 1.
3. Editors: For more on the consumer lifestyles of young people we recommend Miles (2000) for a critical perspective.

References

Alapack, R. J. (1991). Adolescent first kiss. *The Humanistic Psychologist*, 19(1), 48–67.

Alapack, R. J. (1999). Jealousy in first love: Unwitting disclosure. In A. C. Richards & T. Schumrum (eds), *Invitations to Dialogue: The Legacy of Sidney M. Jourard* (pp. 91–106). New York: Kendall/Hunt.

Arnett, J. J., Larson, R. & Offer, D. (1995). Beyond effects: Adolescents as active media users. *Journal of Youth and Adolescence*, 25(5), 511–518.

Beentjes, H. J., d'Haenens, W. J., van der Voort, T. H. A. & Koolstra, C. M. (1999). Dutch and Flemish children and adolescents as users of interactive media. *Communications*, 24, 145–166.

Bone, R., Cheers, B. & Hil, R. (1993). Paradise lost—young people's experience of rural life in the Whitsunday Shire. *Rural Society*, 3, 1–7.

Caldwell, L. L., Darling, N., Payne, L. L. & Dowdy, B. (1999). 'Why are you bored?' An examination of psychological and social control causes of boredom among adolescents. *Journal of Leisure Research*, 31, 103–121.

Caldwell, L. L., Smith, E. A. & Weissinger, E. (1992). The relationship of leisure activities and perceived health of college students. *Leisure and Society*, 15, 545–556.

Coleman, J. C. (1978). Current contradictions in adolescent theory. *Journal of Youth and Adolescence*, 7, 1–11.

Csikszentmihalyi, M. & Larson, R. (1984). *Being Adolescent: Conflict and Growth in the Teenage Years*. New York: Basic Books.

D'Amours, L. & Robitaille, P-A. (2002). 99 % of Quebec teens use the internet! *CEFRIO*, Available (29 November 2004) online at: <http://www.cefrio.qc.ca/English/Communiques/commun_6.cfm>

Erikson, E. H. (1968). *Identity: Youth and Crisis*, London: Faber and Faber.

Fisher, S. (1995). The amusement arcade as a social space for adolescents. *Journal of Adolescence*, 18, 71–80.

Flammer, A., Alsaker, F. D. & Noack, P. (1999). Time use by adolescents in an international perspective. I: The case of leisure activities. In F. D. Alsaker & A. Flammer (eds), *The Adolescent Experience. European and American Adolescents in the 1990s* (pp. 33–60). Mahwah: Lawrence Erlbaum.

Giddens, A. (1991). *Modernity and Self identity: Self and Society in the Late Modern Age*. Oxford: Polity.

Goossens, L. & Marcoen, A. (1999). Relationships during adolescence: Constructive versus negative themes and relational dissatisfaction. *Journal of Adolescence*, 22, 49–64.

Hendry, L. B., Glendinning, A., Reid, M. & Wood, S. (1998). *Lifestyles, health and health concerns of rural youth: 1996–1998*. Edinburgh: Report to Department of Health, Scottish Office.

Hendry, L. B., Glendinning, A. & Shucksmith, J. (1996). Adolescent focal theories: age trends in developmental transitions. *Journal of Adolescence*, 19, 307–320

Hendry, L. B. & Kloep, M. (2002). *Life-span Development: Resources, Challenges and Risks*. London: Thomson Learning.

Hendry, L. B., Kloep, M., Glendinning, A., Ingebrigtsen, J. E., Espnes, G. A. & Wood, S. (2002). Leisure transitions: A rural perspective. *Journal of Leisure Studies*, 21, 1–14.

Hendry, L. B., Kloep, M. & Wood, S. (2002). Young people talking about adolescent rural crowds and social settings. *Journal of Youth Studies*, 5, 357–374.

Hendry, L. B. & Reid, M. (2000). Social relationships and health: The meaning of social 'connectedness' and how it relates to health concerns for rural Scottish adolescents. *Journal of Adolescence*, 23(6), 705–719.

Hendry, L. B., Shucksmith, J. S., Love, J. & Glendinning, A. (1993). *Young People's Leisure and Lifestyles*. London: Routledge.

Jones, G. W. (1992). Rural girls and cars: The phenomena of 'blockies'. *Rural Society*, 2, 4–7.

Kaplan, E. B. & Cole, L. (2003). 'I want to read stuff on boys': White, Latina and black girls reading *Seventeen* magazine and encountering adolescence. *Adolescence*, 38, 141–154.

Kloep, M. (1999). Love is all you need? Focusing on adolescents' life concerns from an ecological point of view. *Journal of Adolescence*, 22, 49–63.

Kloep, M. & Hendry, L (1999). Challenges, risks and coping. In D. Messer and S. Millar (eds), *Exploring Developmental Psychology* (pp. 400–416). London: Arnold.

Kloep, M. (1998). *Att vara ung i Jämtland: Tonåringar berättar om sitt liv*. Österåsen: Uddeholt.

Kloep, M., Hendry, L. B., Glendinning, A., Ingebrigtsen, J. E. & Espnes, G. A. (2003). Peripheral visions? A cross cultural study of rural youth's views on migration. *Children's Geographies*, 1, 105–123.

Kloep, M., Hendry, L. B., Ingebrigtsen, J. E., Glendinning, A. & Espnes, G. A. (2001). Young people in 'drinking societies': Norwegian, Scottish and Swedish adolescents' perceptions of alcohol use. *Health Education Research*, 16(3), 279–291.

Kremer, J., Trew, K. & Ogle, S. (1997). *Young Peoples' Involvement in Sport.* London: Routledge.

Kroger, J. (1985). Relationships during adolescence: A cross-national comparison of New Zealand and United States teenagers. *Journal of Youth and Adolescence*, 8, 47–56.

Love, J. & Hendry, L. B. (1994). Youth workers and youth participants: Two perspectives of youth work? *Youth and Policy*, 46, 43–55.

Maffesoli, M. (1996). *The Time of the Tribes.* London: Sage.

Mahoney, A. M. (1997). Age and sport participation. In J. Kremer, K. Trew & S. Ogle (eds). *Young People's Involvement in Sport* (pp. 98–113). London: Routledge

Mason, V. (1995). *Young People and Sport in England, 1994.* London: The Sports Council.

Mesch, G. S. (2001). Social relationships and internet use among adolescents in Israel. *Social Science Quarterly*, 82(2), 329.

Miles, S. (2000). *Youth Lifestyles in a Changing World.* Buckingham: Open University Press.

Pape, H. & Hammer, T. (1996). Sober adolescence—Predictor of psychosocial maladjustment in young adulthood? *Scandinavian Journal of Psychology*, 37(4), 362–377.

Parker, H., Aldridge, J. & Measham, F. (1998). *Illegal Leisure.* London: Routledge.

Pavis, S., Cunningham-Burley, S. & Amos, A. (1997). Alcohol consumption and young people. *Health Education Research*, 12, 311–322.

Rutter, M. (1996). Psychological adversity: Risk, resilience and recovery. In L. Verhofstadt-Deneve, I. Kienhorst & C. Braet (eds), *Conflict and Development in Adolescence* (pp. 21–34). Leiden: DSWO Press.

Sharp, D. & Lowe, G (1989). Adolescents and alcohol—a review of the recent British research. *Journal of Adolescence*, 12, 295–307.

Shaw, S. M., Caldwell, L. L. & Kleiber, D. A. (1996). Boredom, stress and social control in the daily activities of adolescents. *Journal of Leisure Research*, 28, 274–292.

Shucksmith, J. & Hendry, L. B. (1998). *Health Issues and Young People.* London: Routledge.

Thurlow, C. (2001). The usual suspects? A comparative investigation of crowds and social-type labelling among young British teenagers. *Journal of Youth Studies*, 4(3), 319–334.

Wolak, J., Mitchell, K. J. & Finkelhor, D. (2002). Close online relationships in a national sample of adolescents. *Adolescence*, 37, 441–456.

Wold, B. & Hendry, L. B. (1998). Social and environmental factors associated with physical activities in youth. In S. Biddle, J. Sallis & N. Cavill (eds), *Young People and Physical Activity* (pp. 119–132). London : Health Education Authority.

11

Wired whizzes or techno-slaves? Young people and their emergent communication technologies

Susan McKay, Crispin Thurlow
and Heather Toomey Zimmerman

> Today's youth are different from any generation before them. They are exposed to digital technology in virtually all facets of their day-to-day existence ... A communications revolution is shaping a generation and its world. (Tapscott, 1998a)

Although by no means in equal measure or with equal access, it is hard to imagine many young people experiencing life without computers, mobile telephones and the internet. Certainly in the world's richer countries, teens are all purported to be 'connected,' 'wired,' 'networked' or 'online.' Reflecting the common representation of teens as being somehow innately media-savvy and media-dependent, today's teens have been branded the 'net generation' or 'N-Gen,' and as 'cyberkids.'

In this chapter we want to examine the reality behind these labels by examining the place of emergent technologies in the lives of young people. In doing so, we review and synthesize some of the key research in this area, highlighting the principal topics and potential issues of interest for future study. Although much has been published in the popular media, until fairly recently relatively little had been written from a more scholarly perspective. The overview we offer here is based on a wide range of academic research dispersed through a variety of disciplines including geography, sociology, psychology, education, communication and media studies. Studies reviewed also include surveys and quantitative data analysis, ethnographies, interviews, observations, content analyses and focus groups. In addition, we have chosen to supplement this scholarly work by including background information from so-called 'webmetrics' (i.e., surveys of internet users and usership patterns) provided by independent research organizations or commercial analysts between 2000 and 2002.[2] Any webmetrics data needs to be contextualized within its for-profit, non-peer-reviewed status; nonetheless, given the ever-changing landscape of technology, these user surveys are useful in pointing to emergent conditions of use and other potential trends. (For the sake of clarity, we have listed these various citations as a series of 'weblinks' to be found on the following webpage: <http://faculty.washington.edu/thurlow/teen-webmetrics>.)

We focus our review specifically on digital communication technologies which allow for interpersonal interactions, rather than on those classified as mass media. This allows us to review some of the many ways that technologies such as the internet and mobile telephones are influencing and are influenced by teens' self-identity, relationships, social practices, family, schools, language and peer social groups. The first section of our chapter reviews the literature about the use patterns and demographics of young people who are using emergent technologies. This section also includes the reported effects of specific communication technologies, focusing on examples of computer mediated communication such as emailing, instant messaging, online gaming, and online chat. We then briefly consider the mediation of social interaction by mobile telephony (e.g., text messaging or SMS 'short messaging services'). In the final section of the chapter we take a broad look at some of the key issues related to young people and technology use, cutting thematically across all types of emergent media.

The demographic reality of the 'net generation'

> Can't understand what teenagers are talking about? You're not alone. …the Queen's English makes way for a new kind of slanguage… (Appleyard, 2001)

> Young and free but tied to the mobile. (Bryden-Brown, 2001)

As an example of a popular, nonacademic writer in this area, Tapscott (1998b) has suggested that the cultural life of the 'net generation' exhibits what he sees as certain key qualities, including:

- strong independence and autonomy;

- emotional and intellectual openness;
- greater social inclusion with technology;
- free expression and strong views;
- investigative interest in technology; and
- sensitivity to corporate interest.

Like much that is currently being written about the interplay between young people and new technologies of communication, however, Tapscott's observations are unfortunately somewhat impressionistic and oversimplistic—as such they are not unlike the kinds of media representations cited earlier. Not only do they present an overly homogenous, US-centric characterization of 'youth culture,' but they also fall into the trap of uncritical (or technologically deterministic) claims about the power of the internet to *necessarily* engender curiosity and an acceptance of diversity. Like a lot of writing about new media, this type of commentary also tends to avoid reflecting on the influence teens are having on technology. Additionally, although Tapscott's description may fit some young people, not all of them are eager users of technology nor do all teens have access to technology that the above description portrays. By contrast, research such as that by Livingstone (1998), Buckingham (1998, 2000), Holloway and Valentine (2001), and, in the United States, the Pew Research Foundation mark precisely the kind of ethnographically rich, demographically nuanced contributions which are now being made by scholars looking to understand where and how young people's communicative and other social practices are being reorganized by the emergence of technologies such as the internet.

The media rich and the media poor

The use of new technologies of communication such as the internet/web and mobile telephony continues to be the privilege of only a very small number of young people worldwide. Surveys by commercial internet providers find that as little as 10 percent of the world's population is actually online (Weblinks 1, 11 & 12). Although global patterns of technological inequalities are surely changing (Weblink 7), these newer technologies of communication principally remain the privilege of rich countries. Within these countries, it is also the wealthy and more educated who invariably continue to have greatest access to emergent technologies. So, although the popular image is one of all teens with cellular phones in their pockets, it is important to remember that the place of communication technologies in young people's lives is always relative. Notwithstanding this, and however polarized and unequal the distribution of internet and mobile phone technologies are, technologies such as the internet are unquestionably significant in the lives of those young people who do have access.

In the countries with strong online and computer infrastructure, teenagers are a significant force. In Europe, teenagers are believed to account for at least 12 percent of the total online population (Weblink 3). In the United Kingdom, for example, 75 percent of all 7- to 16-year-olds are internet users (Weblink 4). This number is similar to that in the United States, where teens also have a level of access to computer technologies which is higher than that of the average adult. Families with children are likely to be those with home computers, and teens increasingly have opportunities to access digital technologies at school and through community organizations. Figures supplied by commercial sources also show how rapidly young people's internet use is growing in many other countries around the world (e.g., Italy, Austria, Canada, Taiwan, South Korea).[3] In spite of increasing access, even in more 'internetted' countries like the United States, Canada and the Netherlands, not every adolescent can use or *wants* to use the technology available (Weblink 5). In their British ethnographic study, for example, Holloway and Valentine (2001) came across a number of teens who dis-identified with technology and were far less engaged than others in computer-related lessons. Not all young people are 'wired' nor are they necessarily attracted to technology just because it is 'new.'

Young people, then, can be divided into the 'ICT haves' and the 'ICT have-nots' (referring to 'information and communication technology')—or at least varying degrees of access and, thereby, varying technological literacies. Techno-logical literacies, or so-called new literacies, include not only the ability to produce and understand texts but also the ability to use technology for social inter-action, social practice, meaning negotiation, and the acquisition of skills and knowledge (Bruce, 2004). (The term 'technological fluency' is also used in a similar way, to include not only what people know about technology but what they can do with technologies so that they can adapt to change and organize their use of technology effectively.) Within countries where there is high inter-net penetration, technological access and literacies are again still influenced heavily by socioeconomic-related status; young people with parents who have professional, educated backgrounds are simply more likely to use the internet and therefore more likely to socialize their children into usage.

Ethnicity and race too play a factor in the access and use of technology. For example, surveys (e.g., Weblink 6) indicate that, within the United States, ethnic background is still a strong indicator of access, with 25 percent of young Latino people never having gone online, compared with 6 percent of young White and 13 percent of young Black people. Similarly, where 80 percent of White teens have internet access at home, the figures are noticeably smaller for young Black (66 percent) and Latino (55 percent) people. US internet users also show a marked difference between urban and rural internet use; whereas two-thirds of urban and suburban Americans are online, only half of rural Americans are online (Bell *et al.*, 2004). Certainly, more work is needed in this area to address the particular and persistent challenges faced by technologically marginalized young people such as these.

The digital sex divide in adolescence

Early research about gendered computer use presents a well-documented concern about unequal participation and interest in ICT by men/boys and women/girls—and especially with regard to computer technology (see, for example, Morahan-Martin, 1998). Most typically, writers were agreed on the existence of a digital sex divide by which males dominated internet use. For example, Chen's (1987) study of sex differences in the use and attitude toward computers demonstrated that at that time boys were more likely to have taken a computer programming course, even though there were no differences between male and female students who had taken courses for more general applications. Boys also held more favorable attitudes toward computers relating to general interest and perceived skill. More recently, however, Subrahmanyam *et al.* (2001) have shown that, although more boys than girls report using computers in school, no such gender differences appear outside of school.

In the same vein, a report by the organization Kids.net contradicts the assumption that the internet is the preserve of the adolescent boy; in Britain, at least, as many 7- to 16-year-old girls as boys in the same age range use the internet (Weblink 4). Figures for the US adult population likewise show that the traditional divide between male and female internet/web users has been closing (Weblinks 2 and 9). Indeed, some of the most dramatic growth in internet usage has been found among young girls between the ages of 12 and 17 (Weblink 2). With young people in the United Kingdom, this has apparently been the case for some time (Weblink 10). Patterns of use do of course vary, and although boys remain more likely to use the web for entertainment and downloading software, girls typically orient to interactive spaces on the internet such as online chat and instant messaging.

Despite this preliminary evidence of the closing gender divide, the Center for Women and Information Technology <http://www.umbc.edu/cwit/> warns that women 'are still seriously under-represented as developers of IT, and they are often not well served as IT users.' Girls are entering science, math, engineering and technology careers at a much lower rate than boys of their age. What is more, in countries beyond North America and Europe, men are still the dominant users of the internet (Weblink 2).

The internet and young people's cyberculture

Teenagers and children constitute one of the fastest growing internet popula-
tions, with 77 million under 18s expected online globally by 2005. They also
constitute the most important user population, with their adoption of the internet essential to ensuring its future (Weblink 13). As one of the most well-known
US-based surveys of its kind, a Pew report on the Internet and American Life
(2001) shows how the internet is increasingly important in children's lives, so
much so that time spent with television in young people's lives is increasingly
being replaced by time spent on the internet. By contrast, the telephone (terres-
trial and mobile) appears to be holding its own. The telephone continues to be
young Americans' main tool for communicating with friends. Research in the
United Kingdom which has centered on young people's communication experiences also shows how predominant the telephone is in the lives of young people—often more so for girls than for boys (Thurlow, 2001b). Likewise, Gross *et
al.* (2002) comment on the continued use of the telephone by young US people
as a means of sustaining friendships—perhaps augmented by more recent
trends toward mobile telephony (discussed below). Once again, age seems to
affect use patterns; for example, one large survey (Weblink 14) found that 56
percent of US 18- to 19-year-olds still prefer the telephone over the internet.
Interestingly, another commercial survey of five thousand US 6- to 11-year-olds
(Weblink 15) also indicates that children who use the internet are also more
likely to use other media such as television, magazines and movies. Possibly
confounding some adult expectations, these younger children were also found
to be more likely to read books for leisure and to play more sports. Whether
such patterns of consumption hold for teenagers is not clear; what these findings do reveal, however, is the extent and variability of young people's media
use more generally, and the complex interplay of existing and emergent technologies.

Emailing and instant messaging

Email and instant messaging are perhaps the most common forms of online
interpersonal communication. Surveys (e.g., Weblink 14) show not only that the
internet has become a key communication tool for young people in the US, but
how some 81 percent of 12- to 17-year-olds use it for emailing friends and rela-
tives, whereas 70 percent use it for instant messaging. These statistics are even
higher for older teenagers (18–19) at 91 percent and 83 percent respectively.

Just like adults, young people often use the internet to build meaningful new relationships, as well as to extend existing social networks (Parks & Floyd, 1996; see also Thurlow *et al.*, 2004 for a review of the literature). Young people use the internet most often for interpersonal communication and social contact, with some studies suggesting that girls in particular made strong use of this form of communication (Subrehmanyam *et al.*, 2001). In another study of teens and families online, teens identified possibilities for 'verbal intimacy and egalitarian relationships' through cyberdating, even though it is more often employed for "fleeting", "fun" relationships that hold little consequence in the "real" lives of the teens who engage in them' (Clark, 1998: 180). Gross *et al.* (2002) also talk about how the young people in their study were involved both in traditional means of social interaction and also spent time online; furthermore, time spent online was also often spent with offline friends. Emergent technologies such as instant-messaging are evidently not replacing but enhancing social interaction. (For a similar argument about mobile phones and text-messaging, see Thurlow, 2003.)

When young people do go online, their time is typically spent in social discourse rather than information research or 'surfing' (Weblink 16). Altough email remains popular (especially among girls and young women), more synchronous forms of chat and online discussion are usually preferred, in which group or personal interaction is possible in real time, with or without levels of anonymity. The widely cited study of young people's online activities by the Pew Internet and American Life project (2001) specifically examined the use of instant messaging by a representative sample of 754 young people in the United States between the ages of 12 and 17. What is striking about this study is just how essential this particular 'technology-within-a-technology' has become to young people's social lives. Only 10 percent of those surveyed reported feeling that their use of the internet had had a negative impact on their friendships.

Online chatrooms

Chatrooms, or chat forums, offer young people an additional online discussion space where group members exchange synchronous conversational messages. Unlike instant messaging, however, these social spaces are usually more public and therefore open to participants outside teens' usual or immediate friendship network. Most of the studies of internet-mediated language come from the study of more publicly available conversational environments such as these. One study of online chatroom discourse found that teens had altered the written text register to adapt to the visual aspects of computer-mediated communication by using numbers, color and text style (Greenfield & Subrahmanyam,

2003). By adapting language in this way, teens are able to keep conversational coherence with many chatters and maintain an ongoing text stream. Another study which focused on teenagers found that British girls were very competent at managing the technology and went on to comment on the ways in which these young people's linguistic innovation appear to be altering literacy as we know it (Merchant, 2001). (We return to this issue of language change and technology later in the chapter.)

Web publishing, websites and blogging

In other online contexts, teenagers can also be seen as coproducers of the web, creating and maintaining texts for their peers and others.[4] These texts can be included as part of a website established by a commercial or not-for-profit site (e.g., poetry and young people's 'zine' sites—i.e., electronic magazines). Again, sex differences do occur, and researchers have found that adolescent girls usually outnumber boys as producers of online 'zines' (Knobel & Lankshear, 2004).Teens can also produce unique, stand-alone content for the web—some of which, like blogs ('web logs'), allow for more dialogical, interactive opportunities. (As an example of a dedicated blog space for young people, see <http://teenblogs.studentcenter.org/>.) As with some of the newest aspects of online communication, research into web logs is still evolving. There is, as yet, little research which considers how young people are making use of blog technology. An exception here is Grimes' (2003) study, which revealed teens creating blogs as diary-style testimonials referring to the details of their everyday life, daily troubles, thoughts and emotions, even consumer talk, with listings of favorite brands, and television and movie critiques. As an extension of the kinds of autobiographical and cathartic storytelling of personal homepages (see, for example, Chandler, 1998), blogs are likely to be an increasingly popular interactional and identificational resource for teens.

Online gaming

Many teens (especially boys) communicate through, and about, networked games which allow for social interaction and communication with other players. Indeed, even non-networked games should not be overlooked as powerful influencers on young people's communication; these games might not always provide opportunities for synchronous interactivity, but they can provide a great deal of social capital (cf Putnam, 2000) for other conversations by young people.

Researchers have been examining how these games are influencing teens and what social influences derive from networked gaming platforms or computer games. For example, Gee (2003) lists more than 30 ideas of what he says can be gained through gaming, some of which are relevant to teens; for example, he considers how gamers develop a sense of identity, make meaning of their experiences, and how they select rolemodels. As something of a contrast, Ho and Lee (2001) found that boys who use computers mainly for playing games are less socially and physically active than those who use computers to do homework, 'surf' the internet, and communicate with others. The same study found patterns of computer usage were not as related to social and activity factors for girls. Research on the impact of these games on teens in both offline and online communication is rapidly growing as the popularity of video games also grows.

Other uses of internet technology by young people

In terms of chat, email and instant messaging, the internet is evidently an important interactional tool for young people. It should not be forgotten, however, that they are incorporating emergent technologies into their lives in other ways too. In particular, low-interactive uses (i.e., those which focus on information and documentation such as databases and encyclopedias) of the internet have also become a very attractive learning and lifestyle resource for young people (Weblink 3). Although the less communicative technologies of the internet are not the focus of this chapter, we do think it is worth making brief reference to them, because, like online gaming, these educational, entertainment and e-commerce sites can also become the content of teen's offline interactions.

Along with the Pew Report's (2001) earlier survey, figures elsewhere (Weblink 14) confirm that young people in the United States rely on the internet for educational purposes, often using the web to help them complete homework and access news and current events. According to Subrahmanyam *et al.* (2001), parents generally value computers as an educational resource. In fact, parents often consider the lack of computers an educational and vocational disadvantage (Holloway & Valentine, 2001). In fact, other studies suggest that the internet has become *the* medium of choice for young people in doing their research and homework (compared, say, to newspapers, magazines, television or radio), even though few use it for noninteractive entertainment, still preferring to watch television or listen to the radio (La Ferle *et al.*, 2000). However, this may be changing with the increasing popularity of personal portable digital audio products such as MP3 players, mini-disc devices, *iPods* and similar players which can be used to play downloaded music from internet sites. As well as using the internet to pursue topics directly relating to their school or college work, young people also use the internet to access health information, especially on sensitive topics. For example, a survey by the US-based Kaiser Family Foundation (Weblink 6) shows how young people are increasingly using the web for healthcare information. A similar, New York–based study has also found that half the young people sampled had used the internet to access information on topics such as sexually transmitted diseases, diet and fitness, and sexual behaviors (Borzekowski & Rickert, 2001). These authors suggest that easy access at home or at school, together with confidentiality and individualized advice, makes the internet a very suitable resource for young people seeking this type of information.

Although television continues to be very popular among teenagers, the increasing use of affiliated program websites also allows for online dialogue through fan websites and their related bulletin board or chat services. Again, these sites offer themselves as a powerful source of social capital for young people. In fact, as more use is made of the connection between different forms of technologies, increasing levels of convergence will continue to affect the way young people, like adults, use new technologies and interact online. A good example of this is the way that television networks are likely to continue producing more of their shows as convergent media productions (making use of other media to increase their appeal). Soap operas have made use of convergent technologies to involve the audience and offer them opportunities to interact more closely with the show. Viewers can go online to add their comments to message boards on the direction of the plot or on particular issues covered in the show. Global formats of reality television game shows also use these convergent technologies to maximize their audience participation and reach. Research by McKay and Rintel (2001) suggests that online forums offer a site for the creation of various forms of community through which viewers gain access not only to the shows' producers and to selected celebrities, but also to each other. In fact, McKay and Rintel found that many of these chat forums were still operating months after the actual program had finished.

In terms of use of other forms of computer-mediated communication (CMC), especially as it becomes more normalized (Wellman et al., 2001), researchers may want to look further at how these and other emergent forms of technology have become embedded in the cultural practices of everyday life. Questions arise around what teens now expect from the websites which advertise television, films, sports teams, and pop culture, as far as online interaction with the show content and other fans. Although academic research will inevitably take up some of the issues created by the wider discourses of hype and hysteria to which the popular media is so attached, a more fruitful line may well be to investigate young people's responses to the changing cultural realities and practices produced by new technologies with which they find themselves living.

Mobile phones and text-messaging

Hell is other people talking webspeak on mobile phones. (Humphrys, 2000)

No discussion about new communication technologies would be complete without some mention of mobile (or cellular) telephones. According to commercial figures (Weblink 17), as many as 50 percent of British 7- to 16-year-olds own a mobile phone—a figure which rises dramatically to 82 percent for 14- to 16-year-olds. It is clear that, for a range of economic and cultural reasons (e.g., relative costs of internet access), different technologies of communication compete for young people's attention. In the United States, for example, where instant messaging is so popular, only 25 percent of the 7,000 young people surveyed in one national survey reported using mobile phones (Weblink 14). (In 2004, cellular phone companies in the United States offered teens the opportunity to add instant messaging to their cellular phones, rather than text messages. It remains to be seen whether this will be popular as a mode of communication for young people.)

Although studies such as that of Leung and Wei (2000) report that mobility and immediate access are important factors in mobile phone use, it seems that young people use mobiles for more complex social reasons. The technology that provides mobility also provides a sense of independence, giving them a sense of control over their lives and independence from their families, while at the same time providing their parents with the assurance (albeit perhaps illusory) of contact and immediate access. Mobile phones can help (re-)organize adolescent social life to the extent that young consumers may even choose their provider on the basis of the choice of their social group on the understanding that calls among the group will be cheaper.

However practical a means of parents staying in touch with their children, and however integral a part of young people's social lives, mobile phones are unquestionably also a fashion accessory in themselves (see Kasesniemi & Rautianen, 2002). Owning a mobile phone can be something of a status symbol, not least thanks to careful marketing to this group. Options such as fancy covers, customized ring tones, downloadable text messages, and icons have become part of the appeal of mobile phone culture—and to younger consumers in particular (Leung & Wei, 2000). In the United Kingdom, practical evidence of this is to be found in another survey (Weblink 13) which reported that almost a quarter of all young British mobile phone users were on their third handset, whereas 46 percent had changed their handset cover and 45 percent had changed their ring tone.

As with the internet, adult concerns about young people's mobile telephone use range from anxieties about health risks, theft, bullying messages (e.g., Weblink 19) and uncontrollable costs, to the popular, but exaggerated, idea that young people are completely reinventing, and thereby destroying, standard (English) language use (Thurlow, 2003). To be fair, there is little doubt that text-messaging for many young people is very popular; toward the end of 2001, for example, it was reported in the press that the number of text messages sent in Britain each month reached 1 billion (Teather, 2001).[5] Text messaging via mobile phone provides an alternative method of communication which is often cheaper than a regular phone call. The brevity of these messages is part of their appeal as their seeming opacity to outsiders serves to reinforce the exclusiveness of shared social group membership. That the messages can be sent quietly and discretely is used to advantage especially by school and university students who want to stay in contact during classes or while in the library. Even the delay caused by the asynchronous nature of this type of messaging is not necessarily a disadvantage, with one young user commenting, 'If mum calls when I'm out drinking, I'll let it go and SMS her later' (Bryden-Brown, 2001).[7]

Teens and emergent communication technologies

In addition to discussing the types of technologies teens use, we have considered some of the potential impacts on social interaction through using emergent communication technologies, how these technologies are becoming important social and cultural capital in the lives of teenagers, and how communication technologies may be competing with, or even supplanting, other media-related activities (e.g., television use and landline telephony). In the light of this overview, several thematic points, which cut across different media, can also be made. On the one hand, adults seem to believe that young people nowadays are imbued with a 'natural' media literacy, which is not available to them as adults, and which provides young people with 'new opportunities for creativity, for community and for self-fulfillment' (Buckingham, 2000: 41). On the other hand, however, adults also tend to see young people as passive victims of new (and old) media, which exploit their vulnerability, undermine their individuality and destroy their innocence (p. 41). Similarly, adults are often concerned about the perceived antisocial and/or isolating impacts of young people's internet use (Turow, 1999; Pew Report, 2001). Such polarized, essentialist arguments are well known and widely used in mass market newspapers and magazines. Buckingham's (2000) critique of both the exaggerated optimism and the moral panic regarding new technology is therefore a relevant starting point.

As with so many debates about technological developments (see, for example, Standage, 1999; Kling, 1996), there are optimistic views and pessimistic views about the benefits of new ICTs; where the first tend to emphasize economic (e.g., employment) and educational possibilities through increased media literacy and awareness, the second are concerned that the same level of knowledge and use will result in dissolution of both intellect and social relations. It is interesting to note, for example, that poor school performance and increasing apathy in almost every successive generation of young people has been routinely blamed on their media consumption (Bonfadelli, 1993).

In terms of changing linguistic and communicative practices, our topic here brings together the two dominant 'hype and hysteria' myths in other ways too. As indicated by the newspaper article headlines included earlier, much popular attention is given to both 'teen-talk' and 'netlingo' (or 'webspeak') and both are all too often blamed for their supposedly negative impacts on standard or 'traditional' ways of communicating (Thurlow, 2001a). The same is also true of young people's use of mobile phones and text-messaging (or SMS), where they are understood to be—or rather *accused* of—reinventing the (English) language (Thurlow, 2003). Not only are such claims typically exaggerated and unfounded, but it is fair to say that new technologies of communication can also be empowering for young people as it becomes easier for them to communicate across traditional geographical and cultural boundaries, and as they explore and develop imaginative ways of making the technology work best for them.

Young people and notions of online risk

> Teenagers do their talking online: Today's teens communicate more using the internet than they do face-to-face, causing some parents to worry. (Palfini, 2001)

Reports (Weblinks 8 & 12) point to a number of common concerns about young people online, and surveys have shown how many girls and young women are harassed online and the kind of unwanted attention faced by young women in chatrooms. Although patterns of online-to-offline participation vary from country to country, adults are often concerned about the dangers of young people being persuaded into offline encounters, but there is at least some evidence to suggest that young people are becoming increasingly aware of some of these online risks (Weblink 11). There are ethical issues too associated with the possible exploitation of young people's blogs or websites being 'data-mined' for personal details by youth marketers (Grimes, 2003).

In the field of computer-mediated communication more generally (see Thurlow *et al.*, 2004), there has been some discussion about the possible negative impacts of internet use on individual well-being and existing social networks—especially among young people (e.g., Kraut *et al.*, 1998). Although CMC research has tended to treat with caution such simplistic generalizations—and especially any notion of 'internet addiction'—the idea that young people are somehow impoverished by their use of new technologies continues to hold popular sway.[6] The main attraction of the internet for many people is clearly not access to information but access to social environments (see Spears *et al.*, 2001; Walther & Parks, 2002); this is especially the case with younger users (Biocca, 2000). As a psychologist and internet researcher, Suler (1998) offers a list of what he sees as some of the potentials of cyberspace for young people: identity (and sexual) exploration and experimentation, intimacy and belonging, separation from parents and family, venting frustrations, and learning about the world. In the same vein, a survey of college students' email use by Kelly *et al.* (2001) is just one example of a growing body of research concerned also with pedagogical applications of communication technologies. In this instance, however, Kelly and her colleagues also discovered how beneficial email was for 'reticent' young people in communicating with their teachers. This finding ties in well with other CMC research which in fact points to some of the obvious advantages in certain modes of communication technology for ameliorating *offline* risk factors such as people who feel intimated by conventional face-to-face interaction (see, for example, Utz, 2000).

New media are of course also having an impact on families, with the emergence of cellular phones and computer technologies in particular. Not only are parents now choosing to stay in touch with their children by mobile phone, but they are also reshaping spaces in their homes in significant ways to include computer and other types of emergent media (Facer & Furlong, 2001; Holloway & Valentine, 2001). Computer and internet access are increasingly to be found in young people's own bedrooms. Based on interviews with 245 US participants aged 8 to 17, for example, figures suggest that 61 percent of young people have a television, 17 percent have a computer and 9 percent have internet access in their bedrooms (Weblink 20). The organization Knowledge Networks also found that nearly half (46 percent) of the young people with a TV in their rooms do all their watching on that set. The study also found that 35 percent have a video game system in their room, and 14 percent have their own DVD player.

This chapter has outlined some of what is already known about young people's ongoing relationship with emergent communication technologies; to a large extent, however, it remains unclear how they will continue to shape and be shaped by these technologies. Not only are the social demographics of users of new technologies constantly changing and evolving, but so too are the technologies themselves. A more recent trend, for example, reveals the effect that broadband (i.e., high speed) internet access is having on usership patterns, whereby young people are able to spend much more time online, using streaming video and playing internet games (Weblink 14). Another popular scenario is to be found in the way young women especially are turning to webcams as a source/resource for entertainment, identification and, indeed, commercial gain. (Emmett, 2001, offers a nonacademic account of this trend.) Although the technical affordances of any media will necessarily have an impact on how they are used, young people inevitably bring to technology their usual needs for information, entertainment and socializing. Notwithstanding the unpredictability of the uses and impacts of emerging technologies, the issues that arise in the research we identify here are likely to be key frameworks for understanding the interplay of interactional and technological changes in young people's lives.

Notes

1. This paper is based in part on a colloquy report for the *Journal of Language and Social Psychology* on language and communication in adolescence—see Thurlow & McKay (2003).
2. Examples of the kind of commercial data sources we have used are *Cyberatlas* and *Nua Internet Surveys*, which merged in 2003 to form *ClickZ Stats*. In too much writing about the internet, little explicit distinction is drawn between academic, research-based writing and journalistic commentary, making it hard sometimes to separate empirical evidence from opinion. It is also always important to recognize both the methodological variability underpinning indicative internet statistics, and also the difficulty in attaining reliable figures—not least because users and usership patterns are constantly and rapidly shifting.
3. Helpfully, the 'webmetric' organization *Nua* <www.nua.com/surveys/> has previously offered a separate section relating specifically to teenagers.
4. For information on online content creation (using interview data from over 18s) see <http://www.pewinternet.org/pdfs/PIP_Content_Creation_ Report.pdf>.
5. Anecdotally, online reports indicate how this is true also of Australia (e.g., <http://www.itouch.com.au/news/news5.html>) and Singapore (e.g., <http://www.inq7.net/inf/2002/jan/27/inf_10-1.htm>), amongst others.
6. For a discussion of what is now sometimes termed *Pathological Internet Use*, see Griffiths (2000).
7. Adults too recognize the potential of text-messaging. British examples of this include the Department of Health, which launched a 2001 antismoking cam-

paign directed at young people using SMS (see <www.mobileyouth.org/view_item.php/188>), and the University of Bradford, which has used SMS to promote itself to prospective students (see <www.brad.ac.uk/admin/pr/September/text.htm>).

References

Appleyard, B. (2001). It's so unfair. *The Sunday Times*, 05 August.

Bell, P., Reddy, P. & Rainie, L. (2004). *Rural Americans' Internet Use Have Grown but They Continue to Lag Behind Others*. Washington, DC: Pew Internet & American Life Project. Available (12 December 2004) online at: <http://www.pewinternet.org>.

Biocca, F. (2000). New media technology and youth: Trends in the evolution of new media. *Journal of Adolescent Health*, 27, 22–29.

Bonfadelli, H. (1993). Adolescent media use in a changing media environment. *European Journal of Communication*, 8, 225–256.

Borzekowski, D. & Rickert, V. (2001). Adolescent cybersurfing for health information: A new resource that crosses barriers. *Archives of Pediatrics and Adolescent Medicine*, 155(7), 813–817.

Bruce, B. (2004). Diversity and critical social engagement: How changing technologies enable new modes of literacy in changing circumstances. In D. Alvermann (ed.), *Adolescents and Literacies in a Digital World* (pp. 1–18). New York: Peter Lang.

Bryden-Brown, S. (2001). Young and free but tied to the mobile phone. *The Australian*, 10 August.

Buckingham, D. (1998). Review essay: Children of the electronic age? Digital media and the new generational rhetoric. *European Journal of Communication*, 13(4), 557–565.

Buckingham, D. (2000). *After the Death of Childhood: Growing up in the Age of Electronic Media*. Cambridge: Polity Press.

Chandler, D. (1998). *Personal Home Pages and the Construction of Identities on the Web*. Available (12 March 2003) online at <http://www.aber.ac.uk/media/Documents/short/ webident.html>.

Chen, M. (1987). Gender differences in adolescents' uses of and attitudes toward computers. In M. McLaughlin (ed.), *Communication Yearbook 10* (pp. 200–216). Newbury Park: Sage.

Clark, L. S. (1998). Dating on the net: Teens and the rise of 'pure' relationships. In S. Jones (ed.), *Cybersociety 2.0: Revisiting Computer-Mediated Community and Technology* (pp. 159–183). London: Sage.

Emmett, S. (2001). The cam girls. *The Guardian Newspaper*, 28 August.

Facer, K. & Furlong, R. (2001). Beyond the myth of the 'cyberkid': Young people at the margins of the information revolution. *Journal of Youth Studies*, 4(4), 451–469.

Gee, J. P. (2003). *What Video Games Have to Teach Us About Learning and Literacy*. New York: Palgrave Macmillan.

Greenfield, P. M. & Subrahmanyam, K. (2003). Online discourse in a teen chatroom: New codes and new modes of coherence in a visual medium. *Journal of Applied Developmental Psychology*, 24(6), 713–738.

Griffiths, M. (2000). Internet addiction: Does it really exist? In J. Gackenbach (ed.), *Psychology and the Internet* (pp. 61–75). San Diego, CA: Academic Press.

Grimes, S. (2003). All about the blog: young people's adoption of internet technologies and the marketers who love them. *Computers and Society,* 33(1).

Gross, E. F., Juvonen, J. & Gable, S. L. (2002). Internet use and well-being in adolescence. *Journal of Social Issues*, 58, 75–90.

Ho, S. & Lee T. (2001). Computer usage and its relationship with adolescent lifestyle in Hong Kong. *Journal of Adolescent Health*, 29(4), 258–266.

Holloway, S. & Valentine, G. (2001). *Cyberkids: Youth Identities and Communities in an Online World.* London: Routledge.

Humphrys, J. (2000). Hell is other people talking webspeak on mobile phones. *Sunday Times Newspaper*, August 27.

Kasesniemi, E. & Rautiainen, P. (2002). Mobile culture of children and teenagers in Findland. In J. E Katz & M. A. Aakhus (eds), *Perpetual Contact: Mobile Communication, Private Talk, Public Performance* (pp. 170–192). Cambridge: Cambridge University Press.

Kelly, L., Duran, R. L. & Zolten, J. J. (2001). The effect of reticence on college students' use of electronic mail to communicate with faculty. *Communication Education*, 50(2), 170–176.

Kling, R. (1996). Hopes and horrors: Technological utopianism and anti-utopianism in narratives of computerization. *CMC Magazine*. Available (15 May 1999) online at: <http://www.december.com/cmc/mag/1996/feb/kling.html>.

Knobel, M. & Lankshear, C. (2004). Cut, paste, publish: The production and consumption of zines. In D. Alvermann (ed.), *Adolescents and Literacies in a Digital World* (pp. 164–185). New York: Peter Lang.

Kraut, R., Lundmark, V., Patterson, M., Kiesler, S., Mukopadhyay, T. & Scherlis, W. (1998). Internet paradox: A social technology that reduces social involvement and psychological well-being. *American Psychologist*, 53(9), 1017–1031.

La Ferle, C., Edwards, S. M. & Lee, W. N. (2000). Teens' use of traditional media and the internet. *Journal of Advertising Research*, 40(3), 55–65.

Leung, L. & Wei, R. (2000). More than just talk on the move: Uses and gratifications of the cellular phone. *Journalism and Mass Communication Quarterly*, 77(2), 308–320.

Livingstone, S. (1998). Mediated childhood: A comparative approach to young people's changing media environment in Europe. *European Journal of Communication*, 13(4), 435–456.

McKay, S. & Rintel, E. S. (2001) Online television forums: Interactivity, access, and transactional space. *Electronic Journal of Communication/ La Revue Electronique de Communication*, 11(2). Available (11 December 2003) online at <http://www.cios.org/ getfile%5Cmckayrin_v11n201>.

Merchant, G. (2001). Teenagers in cyberspace: An investigation of language use and language change in internet chatrooms. *Journal of Research in Reading*, 24(3), 293–306.

Morahan-Martin, J. (1998). Males, females and the internet. In J. Gackenbach (ed.), *Psychology and the Internet: Intrapersonal, interpersonal, and transpersonal implications* (pp. 169–197). San Diego, CA: Academic Press.

Palfini, J. (2001). Teenagers do their talking online. *PC World*, 21 June. Available (31 August 2001) online at: <http://www.pcworld.com/resource/printable/article/0,aid,53444,00.asp>.

Parks, M. R. & Floyd, K. (1996). Making friends in cyberspace. *Journal of Computer Mediated Communication*, 1(4). Available (5 February 2000) online at: <http://www.ascusc.org/jcmc/vol1/issue4/parks.html>.

Pew Internet and American Life Project. (2001). *Teenage Life Online: The Rise of the Instant-Message Generation and the Internet's Impact on Friendships and Family Relationships*. Available (21 June 2001) online at: <http://www.pewinternet.org/reports/toc.asp?Report=36>.

Putnam, R. (2000). *Bowling Alone: The Collapse and Revival of American Community*. New York: Simon and Schuster.

Spears, R., Lea, M. & Postmes, T. (2001). Social psychological theories of computer-mediated communication: Social pain or social gain. In W. P. Robinson and H. Giles (eds), *The New Handbook of Language and Social Psychology* (pp. 601–623). Chichester: John Wiley and Sons.

Standage, T. (1999). *The Victorian Internet: The Remarkable Story of the Telegraph and the Nineteenth Century's On-Line Pioneers*. New York: Walker and Company.

Subrahmanyam, K., Greenfield, P., Kraut, R. & Gross, E. (2001). The impact of computer use on children's and adolescents' development. *Applied Developmental Psychology*, 22, 7–30.

Suler, J. (1998). *Adolescents in Cyberspace: The Good, the Bad, and the Ugly*. Available (31 July 2001) online at: <http://www.rider.edu/users/suler/psycyber/adoles.html>.

Tapscott, D. (1998a). *The Net-Generation and the School*. Milken Family Foundation. Available (8 May 2003) online at: <http://www.mff.org/edtech/article.taf?_function=detail&Content_uid1=109>

Tapscott, D. (1998b). *Growing Up Digital: The Rise of the Net Generation*. New York: McGraw-Hill.

Teather, D. (2001). Text-messaging breaks 1bn-a-month barrier. *Guardian newspaper*, 23 August.

Thurlow, C. (2001a) Language and the internet. In R. Mesthrie & R. Asher (eds), *The Concise Encyclopedia of Sociolinguistics* (pp. 287–289). London: Pergamon.

Thurlow, C. (2001b) Talkin' 'bout my communication: Communication awareness in early adolescence, *Language Awareness*, 10(2&3): 1–19.

Thurlow, C. (2003). Generation Txt? The sociolinguistics of young people's text-messaging. *Discourse Analysis Online*. Available online (31 January 2005) at: <http://www.shu.ac.uk/daol/>.

Thurlow, C., Lengel, L. & Tomic, A. (2004). *Computer Mediated Communication: Social Interaction and the Internet*. London: Sage.

Thurlow, C. & McKay, S. (2003). Profiling 'new' communication technologies in adolescence. *Journal of Language & Social Psychology*, 22(1), 94–103.

Turow, J. (1999). *The Internet and the Family: The View From the Family, the View From the Press.* Available (5 November 2001) online at: <http://www.appcpenn.org/internet/family/rep27.pdf>.

Utz, S. (2000). Social information processing in MUDs: The development of friendships in virtual worlds. *Journal of Online Behavior,* 1(1). Available (25 March 2002) online at: <http://www.behavior.net/JOB/v1n1/utz.html>.

Walther, J. B. & Parks, M. (2002). Cues filtered out, cues filtered in: Computer mediated communication and relationships. In M. L. Knapp & J. A. Daly (eds), *The Handbook of Interpersonal Communication* (pp. 529–563). Thousand Oaks, CA: Sage.

Wellman, B., Quan Haase, A., Witte, J. & Hampton, K. (2001). Does the internet increase, decrease, or supplement social capital? Social networks, participation, and community commitment. *American Behavioral Scientist,* 45(3), 437–456.

Part III

**Young people in
communication with adults**

12

Communication with parents and other family members: The implications of family process for young people's well-being

Patricia Noller

> When adolescents are satisfied with their family's way of seeing the world and structuring interpersonal interactions, optimal individual functioning results. (White, 1996: 142)

Although theorists have generally moved away from the old psychodynamic view of adolescence as 'Sturm und Drang' (or storm and stress), there is no doubt that adolescence is a critical time when decisions that adolescents make and the behaviors in which they become involved can have serious implications for the rest of their lives. This issue stands out most starkly when we think about the adolescent who becomes a heroin addict, has a baby before even finishing school or commits suicide. Of course, such issues arise for only a small proportion of adolescents, with the great majority moving through adolescence and into adulthood relatively unscathed. It may be because of such risks, however, that the literature on families with adolescents tends to focus on the family factors that predict the psychological adjustment of adolescents and some young people's involvement in problem behaviors such as drug abuse, binge drinking, self-harming and premature sexual activity, as well as delinquent or 'acting-out' behaviors such as joyriding or shoplifting.

These studies of adjustment and problem behaviors in adolescence tend to be based on a model involving four factors: family stress, adolescent adjustment and/or problem behaviors, protective factors and risk factors. The idea is that adolescents most at-risk of developing adjustment or behavioral problems are those whose families have experienced severe stress. These family stress factors would include parental mental health problems, family breakdown and economic hardship. The fact that many adolescents will experience these family stress factors without developing adjustment or behavioral problems is accounted for by the presence of protective, or buffering, factors that protect the adolescent from negative outcomes. Protective factors include high family cohesion, high family support, a positive parent-child relationship and positive communication with parents. Risk factors, on the other hand, include weak family bonds, poor family functioning and a hostile and coercive relationship with parents. Risk factors increase the likelihood that a young person will have negative outcomes in response to family stressors.

I should comment here that it is not always easy to decide whether particular factors are family stressors or risk factors, as both family stressors and risk factors increase the likelihood of negative outcomes for the adolescent. It could be argued, for example, that parental mental health is a stressor at the time of onset but a risk factor if it persists. Because researchers do not always make such distinctions, I have included parental mental health as a family stressor.

Stress factors

There is some evidence for universality of reactions to stress in adolescents in terms of emotional and psychosomatic disorder, conduct disorder, hyperactivity and impaired self-esteem. Bagley, Mallick *et al.* (1999) studied adjustment, stress and family life in families with adolescents in six countries (Canada, Britain, Pakistan, India, Hong Kong and the Philippines). In terms of levels of stress, the greatest similarities were among students in Canada, Britain, Hong Kong and the Philippines, whereas students in India seemed to be particularly well-adjusted and those in Pakistan had the most problems.

However, it seems likely that the number of stressors is more important than the type of stressor (Forehand *et al.*, 1998). These researchers explored a range of stressors such as parental divorce, inter-parental conflict, parental depressive mood, parental physical health problems and conflictual parent-child relationships. Cumulative stressors resulted in longitudinal, but not concurrent, difficulties in adjustment. Coping with an accumulation of stressors decreased academic achievement both concurrently and long-term. These researchers also found that an increase from three to four risk factors was associated with a marked increase in internalizing and externalizing behavior in young adulthood and a marked decrease in academic achievement in adolescents. Internalizing behaviors are those associated with anxiety and depression (feeling anxious or sad, having little energy) and externalizing behaviors include acting-out behaviors such as binge drinking, joyriding and other behaviors associated with delinquency.

A range of stressors have been studied in terms of their impact on adolescents, including fathers' problem drinking (Farrell *et al.*, 1995), divorce and family breakdown (Rubenstein *et al.*, 1998; Amato, 2001; Antognoli-Toland, 2001), economic hardship (Barrera *et al.*, 2002), witnessing family and community violence (Muller *et al.*, 2000; Kliewer *et al.*, 2001), and parental mental health problems (Shiner & Marmorstein, 1998). These family stressors tend to increase the risk of adjustment difficulties and problem behaviors in adolescents. I will report some of these studies below to provide examples of the ways that family stressors can have an impact on adolescents.

Parental mental health

Several studies point to a link between parent mental health, and the mental health of adolescents. Shiner and Marmorstein (1998), for example, found that a greater proportion of depressed adolescents had depressed mothers, and these adolescents reported poorer family functioning than did the adolescents whose mothers had not experienced depressive episodes. Both maternal depression and poor family functioning were associated with adolescent depression, and adolescents were most at risk when both of these factors were present, although some genetic predisposition to depression is also likely.

Maternal depression would seem to affect family functioning because of its impact on family cohesion and the positive behaviors associated with cohesion such as expressing appreciation and spending time together. In addition, maternal depression seems to have an impact by increasing parent-adolescent conflict, decreasing mother-adolescent involvement and diminishing adolescent regard for parents. In the Shiner and Marmorstein (1998) study, the relational problems also extended to the father-adolescent relationship, and may have left the adolescent without a single adult who was really supportive of their development.

Adolescents whose mothers have a history of depression tend to be at elevated risk of suicidal behavior (Garber *et al.*, 1998). In Garber *et al.*'s study, the association between a mother's history of depression and her adolescent's self-harming behavior was mediated by family functioning. In other words, the mother's parenting style tended to be dysfunctional due to depression, which in turn led to poor family functioning, which increased the likelihood of suicide attempts or self-harming in the adolescent.

Family breakdown

Family structure can also affect adolescent adjustment, and there is evidence that children from divorced families tend to be lower in achievement, and have poorer adjustment, lower levels of well-being, more negative self-concepts, more conduct problems and more long-term health problems than children from intact families (Amato, 2001). In addition, children from divorced families tend to be less socially competent and report higher levels of loneliness than other adolescents, because they see their parents as less supportive, and report having fewer opportunities to be with their parents and to engage in activities with them (Antognoli-Toland, 2001). From a study of adolescents who had engaged in self-harming behavior, Rubenstein *et al.* (1998) found that intact families were the least likely to include a suicidal adolescent, whereas separated or divorced families were at intermediate risk, and remarried families were at the highest risk. In addition, children from intact families reported less stress overall.

Amato (2001) argues that divorce is less disruptive for children if both parents maintain positive relationships with the child, parental conflict subsides after the separation or divorce, and the child is not seriously deprived of economic resources. Unfortunately, for many separated and divorced families with children, the conflict between the parents continues long after the separation. In a study of separated and divorcing families with adolescents, my colleagues and I found that these families reported more parent-parent conflict, more parent-adolescent conflict and more sibling conflict than a comparison sample of intact families (Noller *et al.*, 2004).

Economic hardship

Economic hardship is another family stressor likely to have an impact on the well-being of adolescents. Moreover this problem could lead to the development of internalizing and externalizing symptoms in adolescents (Barrera *et al.*, 2002). Internalizing disorders include depression and anxiety, whereas externalizing disorders involve the acting-out behaviors discussed earlier, such as various types of delinquent behavior. In addition, parents struggling with economic hardship were more likely to be depressed and to find it difficult to provide the kind of supportive parenting for their children that would buffer them from becoming depressed and anxious themselves. It is important to note that family breakdown is also likely to lead to economic hardship.

Protective factors

A number of protective factors have been shown to buffer adolescents from the negative impact of family stressors on their psychological adjustment and involvement in problem behaviors. These factors include being in a strong family, having a cohesive family and having a supportive family.

Being in a strong family

Being in a strong family would seem to be particularly important for adolescents in terms of protecting them from the negative effects of family-related stressors on their psychological adjustment and their involvement in problem behaviors. Greeff and Le Roux (1999) directly explored adolescents' and parents' perceptions of what makes a family strong in a sample of South African families with adolescents who had been identified specifically as well-functioning families. Family members were asked to rate their family on six characteristics previously identified by researchers as characteristic of strong families (Brigman *et al.*, 1986; Trivette *et al.*, 1990). These characteristics are appreciation, spending time together, commitment, good communication patterns, high religious orientation and ability to deal positively with crises. All of these variables correlated significantly with perceptions of family strength, with the strongest correlations being for time spent together and appreciation of each other. These findings suggest the importance of families with adolescents spending time together for meals and other activities, and expressing their appreciation for one another, either verbally or nonverbally. These findings also point to the need for good communication among family members, which I will define more specifically a little later.

A widely used model of family functioning is that proposed by Olson and his colleagues (Olson *et al.*, 1979; Olson *et al.*, 1983), and known as the Circumplex Model. According to this model, three dimensions are essential to understanding family functioning: cohesion, adaptability/flexibility and communication, where cohesion is defined as the emotional bonding between family members, and adaptability/flexibility is defined as the ability of a family system to change in response to stress arising from particular situations or developmental stages. An adaptable family is able to change roles and rules as children age and as circumstances change. Communication is seen as the means by which cohesion and adaptability are expressed and modified. Cohesion is expressed both verbally and nonverbally through statements of caring and concern and such nonverbal behaviors as smiling and touching. Adaptability is likely to be expressed through assertion, and through processes of conflict management such as negotiation and problem solving. Families with adolescents tend to function best if they are moderate in both cohesion and adaptability (Olson *et al.*, 1983). In very rigid families (low on adaptability), negotiation between parents and adolescents will not be allowed because adolescents are expected to obey the rules and do as they are told, and in very disengaged families (very low on cohesion), family members will spend little time together and hence show little care and concern for one another.

Positive communication in the Circumplex Model involves being able to keep to the point and stay on track with other family members, and to show respect and regard for other family members, even during disagreements, so that family members can share their ideas without fear of being put down or belittled. Communication should also be clear, rather than vague or ambiguous, and family members should feel free to express their true feelings and attitudes and to talk about the relationships between family members. Being able to deal with conflict and to solve problems by negotiation are also considered important. Solutions that will suit all family members are most likely to be found where family members are encouraged to express their true feelings and opinions in ways that respect the feelings and opinions of other family members.

In support of the Circumplex Model, there is evidence that conduct-disordered adolescents (those engaging in delinquent behavior) see their families as low in both cohesion and adaptability (that is, rigidly disengaged), and are less satisfied with their family's functioning (Pillay, 1998). Rigidly disengaged families are less likely to engage in the positive behaviors associated with cohesion and more likely to find the resolution of conflict difficult or even impossible because of their inability to negotiate change. Pillay cautions that the effect may be due to the negative blaming behavior characteristic of conduct-disordered individuals, and not necessarily a reflection of the true state of the family. Of course, it is also important to remember that adolescents' perceptions of their families are likely to affect their behavior more than the actual state of those families.

Kashani *et al.* (1998) found several distinctive characteristics in the families of suicidal adolescents. Adolescents with a high risk of suicide had significantly lower pride in their families, and rated them as less adaptable than did adolescents with no suicide risk. These findings suggest that the rigid controls characteristic of families low in adaptability, and the difficulties these adolescents are likely to have in negotiating a more appropriate balance of autonomy and control as they get older, put them at greater risk for suicide attempts.

Strong family bonds also have an important role in reducing alcohol abuse (Bahr *et al.*, 1995). Adolescents from families with strong family bonds are less likely to be involved in problem drinking, at least in part because of their high educational commitment. In another study involving a large sample of Colombian youth, weak parent-child attachment, parents providing little structure for the adolescents and sibling drug use were all associated with the adolescents' marijuana use (Brook *et al.*, 1998).

Family cohesion

Family cohesion seems to be a particularly powerful protective factor for adolescents, decreasing the probability of such problems as depression and suicide. Adolescents who perceive less cohesion in their families tend to have higher levels of depression (Stewart *et al.*, 1994), and depression is also associated with poorer communication with parents, where good communication was assessed as spending time together, being open to the expression of feelings and opinions, and having trust and honesty in the relationship. Even after family structure and parent education are controlled for, adolescents in more cohesive families seem to have fewer depressive symptoms (McKeown *et al.*, 1997). In addition, when perceptions of family cohesion increased over time for these adolescents, depressive symptoms decreased. Further, adolescents in more cohesive families have fewer negative thoughts and less depression (Aydin & Oeztuetuencue, 2001).

Family cohesion was found to buffer the effects of fathers' problem drinking on adolescent distress, problem behaviors and heavy drinking in a longitudinal study (Farrell *et al.*, 1995). As expected, the effects of fathers' problem drinking on adolescent distress and deviance were most pronounced when family cohesion was low, and decreased as family cohesion increased. Thus when family communication is warm and open, adolescents are less likely to be affected by the problem drinking of their fathers. This finding fits with Wolin and Bennett's (1984) theory suggesting that families that are able to maintain rituals consistent with high cohesion, such as engaging in family activities and experiencing warm and open communication, will be better able to cope with serious stressors such as a father's heavy drinking.

Family cohesion can also buffer adolescents from the negative effects of family breakdown. According to a study by Rubenstein *et al.* (1998), although parental separation, divorce and remarriage predicted self-harming behavior, family cohesiveness was a protective factor against suicide attempts for those in nonintact families. In other words, those in cohesive families did not react to family breakdown by engaging in self-harming behavior. These researchers also

214 214 | TALKING ADOLESCENCE

found that closeness in the family had a protective effect that closeness in the peer group did not, perhaps because adolescents in this situation are looking for assurance that, despite the breakdown, they will still have a family that cares about them. It has been suggested that it may be more difficult for adolescents in nonintact families to focus on the normative developmental tasks of adolescence such as negotiating increased autonomy (Hetherington *et al.*, 1992).

Family support

Family support, a variable similar to cohesion, has also been found to protect adolescents from emotional and behavioral problems in the face of family stressors. Supportive family relationships tend to involve having positive relationships with parents, strong family bonds, affection and involvement. As we will see from the examples provided here, family support seems to be critical to adolescent well-being across a range of cultures.

Adolescents in a Dutch sample who reported low levels of family support were more likely than adolescents with no such problems to be experiencing behavioral or emotional problems (Garnefski & Diekstra, 1996). Behavioral problems would include various kinds of drug abuse as well as acting-out or delinquent behaviors. Emotional problems would generally involve anxiety or depression. Family support in this study included being comfortable at home and getting on well with mothers and fathers. It is likely, of course, that these relationships are reciprocal, with low family support leading to higher levels of emotional and behavioral problems, and high levels of emotional and behavioral problems leading to poor family support.

In the study reported earlier of the effects of economic hardship on adolescents (Barrera *et al.*, 2002), family support was found to have a strong association with adolescent mental health. In this study, supportive parenting included affection, involvement and monitoring, and these behaviors were seen as helping adolescents form strong bonds with their parents. Supportive parenting was negatively associated with internalizing problems, but was not related to externalizing problems or to association with deviant peer groups.

In a longitudinal study, adolescents who reported more family support also reported more positive mood two years later, particularly if they perceived family support to increase over the two years of the study (Rathunde, 2001). In addition, Sheeber and Sorensen (1998) found that depressed adolescents described their families as being less supportive and more conflicted than those described by other adolescents. This study is one of the few studies in which the actual behavior of mothers and their adolescents was observed during a problem-solving interaction. Depressed adolescents engaged in less problem-solving behavior, and their mothers were less facilitative in their interactions. In this study, problem-solving included statements with positive or neutral affect that identified problems or proposed solutions. Facilitative behavior included 'statements made with happy or caring affect as well as approving or affirming statements that serve to maintain the conversation' (1998: 271).

In a South American sample, family support was shown to buffer the effects of exposure to serious violence both in the wider community and against family members, particularly for girls and younger adolescents (Kliewer et al., 2001). The protective aspects of family support in this study included a high-quality parent-adolescent relationship, family cohesion and open communication that allowed the adolescents to talk about the violence and their fears. In addition, in a sample of high-risk adolescents admitted to a psychiatric institution, family support provided a buffer against the maladaptive effects of experiencing domestic violence (Muller et al., 2000). It is interesting to note that for these adolescents, a similar buffer was not provided by social support outside the family. Again, it seems that family support is a critical protective effect for adolescents, and that support provided by those outside the family cannot replace support provided inside the family, especially when the problem is family related.

In a study of Hawaiian families, family support reduced the risk of internalizing symptoms such as anxiety and depression in adolescents who had suffered family adversity, but the findings were less clear for externalizing symptoms such as delinquent behavior (Goebert et al., 2000). On the other hand, for adolescents in Hong Kong and mainland China, family support did not moderate the relationship between family stress and adolescents' psychological distress (Ngai & Cheung, 2000), suggesting that this effect, at least, does not apply in all cultures.

Lau and Kwok (2000) examined the relationships among family environment, depression and self-concept of adolescents in Hong Kong. They found that the quality of family relationships is predictive of both depression and self-concept, and concluded that the type of family environment that is conducive to the most positive development in adolescents in that culture is one that is cohesive, orderly, and encouraging of achievement. In an Australian study, however, Hurd (2005) showed that a strong family emphasis on achievement was related to self-harming behavior in adolescents, suggesting that too much encouragement of achievement can also put intolerable pressure on adolescents.

Family communication

Family communication has an important role to play in determining the levels of adolescent sexual activity of adolescents (Pick & Palos, 1995). Young girls in the Pick and Palos (1995) Mexico City sample who spoke frequently to their mothers about sex were less likely to have begun sexual relations or to be pregnant, and those who were sexually active were more likely to use contraceptives. Furthermore, young men who had good communication with their parents were less likely to get their partner pregnant.

Family communication also has an important role to play in knowledge and attitudes about sexuality, contraception and sexually transmitted diseases (Huerta-Franco *et al.*, 1996). These researchers explored the relations between family functioning and sexual knowledge and attitudes, using the seven factors of the McMaster Model of Family Functioning (Epstein et al., 1978). Compromise between parents, responding positively, communication and problem solving within the family and behavior control were all important for attitude transmission from the parents to the adolescents.

Family differentiation

A third factor that seems to be important to adolescent well-being in the family is differentiation, or the family's tolerance for individuality and intimacy. This concept is related to Olson's concept of adaptability. Rigid families, for example, have little tolerance for individuality and uniqueness. Gavazzi (1993: 463) describes differentiation as 'patterns of family interaction that to a greater or lesser extent encourage an age-appropriate balance of individuality and intimacy.' He argues that high differentiation levels in the family allow the adolescent to leave the family to test his or her identity and uniqueness, and also to return home from time to time to experience belonging within that family. He argues that high levels of differentiation help the adolescent by promoting identity development, and also help parents to view the adolescent's development positively, even when it is not what they as parents would have chosen for their child. Gavazzi also assessed the ability of differentiation in the family to predict a number of presenting problems in adolescents. Higher levels of differentiation in the family were negatively related to a range of problem behaviors such as illegal activities, difficulties with peer relationships, school-related difficulties and individual factors such as depression, low self-esteem, and suicide ideation.

Adolescent responsibility taking in the family

Allowing adolescents to take responsibility in the family may also be beneficial to familial and adolescent well-being. In one study (Taylor *et al.*, 1997), those adolescents who believed that they had assumed more responsibility in their families reported less depression, more intimate relationships with their parents and higher self-esteem. Adolescents also viewed responsibility taking as a positive experience. Allowing adolescents to take responsibility in the family requires that parents trust their adolescents to be faithful in performing the tasks entrusted to them. It is possible, of course, that responsibility is most likely to be given to adolescents who are well adjusted and have positive relationships with their parents. In addition, there are almost certainly adolescents who have to take on too much responsibility in the family, and who could be described as taking on roles that really should be the responsibility of parents.

Risk factors

Risk factors are generally considered to be those factors that increase the likelihood of family stressors having a negative impact on an adolescent in terms of their psychological adjustment, their involvement in problem behaviors, or both. Tamplin and Goodyer (2001) considered four particular risk factors when they categorized German adolescents as being at high or low risk of developing a major depressive disorder. Adolescents who fulfilled at least two of the following criteria were considered at high risk: (1) they had experienced two or more highly undesirable events in the previous year (these could be family or external stressors), (2) they scored above the 80th percentile in emotionality (in other words, they were highly emotional and became upset relatively easily), (3) they had experienced two or more significant losses during their lives, or (4) there were problems in the parents' marriage. The two groups differed in terms of their scores on the Family Assessment Device (Epstein *et al.*, 1983), with high-risk families reporting lower levels of role-effectiveness than low-risk families. In addition, both mothers and fathers of adolescents considered at high risk for depression reported poorer mental health than did the parents of low risk adolescents.

Of course, given the importance of families providing a supportive and cohesive environment for adolescents, it would seem obvious that adolescents in families that are low in support and cohesion are likely to be at higher risk, particularly if they experience the kinds of family stressors mentioned earlier, or if they could be categorized as high risk in terms of the criteria suggested by Tamplin and Goodyer above.

Impaired relationships with parents

Both depressed and externalizing adolescents report more impaired relationships with their parents than do nonclinic adolescents (Pavlidis & McCauley, 2001). A study by Kim *et al.* (1999) showed that adolescents' externalizing behaviors were significantly related to parental hostility or coercion, especially when mothers were the parent engaging in coercive, blaming and/or threatening behaviors. Stewart *et al.* (1994) also found, in a sample of rural adolescents, that those whose families had experienced stressful events because of rural crisis tended to have higher levels of depression and to report poorer communication with their parents, particularly their mothers. Of course, it is important to recognize the problems of trying to specify cause and effect with correlational data. Although it is possible that poor parent-adolescent relationships are causal for depression, it is important to remember that parents are likely to find relating to depressed adolescents difficult.

Family conflict

Family conflict has been shown to predict depression and distress in adolescents, particularly when there is a history of sexual and/or physical abuse (Meyerson *et al.*, 2002). Both physically abused and sexually abused females reported that high levels of conflict and low levels of cohesion characterized their family environments. Physically abused males reported more conflict in their families than did other males. I will discuss the issue of familial abuse in more detail later.

In a sample of European, African and Chinese Americans, family conflict seemed to moderate the association between aspects of the home environment (such as responsivity, learning materials, and variety of experiences) and adolescent well-being (Bradley & Corwyn, 2000). These associations were stronger in high-conflict families, leading the researchers to conclude that there was a heightened sensitivity to social exchanges and family events in these high-conflict families. On the basis of their comparison of the family environments of depressed and healthy adolescents, Sheeber and Sorensen (1988) showed that both the depressed adolescents and their mothers described their families as less supportive and more conflicted than did nondepressed adolescents and their mothers. In addition, both the depressed adolescents and their mothers demonstrated more depressive behaviors and fewer facilitative behaviors during a problem-solving interaction. Behaviors coded as depressive included anxious whining or pain affect, complaints and negative comments about themselves. Facilitative behaviors included statements that were made with happy or caring emotional tone, approving or affirming statements and statements that served to keep the conversation going and allowed family members to express their points of view.

As would be expected, given the findings with regard to the positive effects of family cohesion and support, low parental warmth and high levels of family conflict seem to be associated with depressive symptomatology in both Chinese and US samples of adolescents (Greenberger *et al.*, 2000). Interestingly, grades in school had a stronger effect on depressive symptoms in Chinese than in American young people, perhaps because of high pressures for achievement in these families. Gender differences in depressive symptoms were greater in the American than in the Chinese sample, with American males reporting the lowest levels of depressive symptoms of the four groups of teenagers. Of course, this difference could be one of willingness to report, rather than a real difference between males and females in American culture.

Parental conflict seems to have a strong association with suicide. More than three-quarters of a South African sample of adolescent suicide survivors indicated they had had conflict with their parents a few hours before their suicide attempt (Pillay & Wassenaar, 1997). More suicide attempters reported family conflict, problems at school or problems with their partner over the preceding six months than did those in the control group. The suicide attempters also reported lower levels of family satisfaction. Pillay and Wassenaar suggest that suicide attempts (or self-harming) may be used by some adolescents as a means of expressing their distress. Engagement in self-harming behaviors could also be a means of distracting the parents from their own conflicts, and providing them with a new focus—the troubled adolescent. The idea that adolescents engage in self-harming behavior to express their distress is supported by Rubenstein *et al.* (1998), who found that about a third of the suicide attempts made by the participants in their study were to 'let someone know' that they were having problems.

The level of treatment follow-through for hospitalized suicidal adolescents is also dependent on several family factors. King *et al.* (1997) assessed a wide range of treatment programs, and found that treatments tended to be less effective when families were more dysfunctional, mothers were depressed and father-adolescent communication was unsatisfactory. In other words, positive family communication and support are necessary before suicidal adolescents can even benefit from treatment.

Abuse and violence

Abuse and violence in the families of adolescents tend to have negative consequences for them, with abused adolescents at higher risk for drug abuse, suicide and homelessness (Acierno *et al.*, 2000; Martin, 1996; McLean *et al.*, 1999; Ryan *et al.*, 2000; Whitbeck *et al.*, 1997a; Wolfe *et al.*, 1999). Sexual or physical assault, witnessing violence as well as a family history of drug or alcohol abuse increased the probability that an adolescent would be currently smoking cigarettes in a sample of American youth that included Caucasians, African Americans and Hispanics, with the Caucasians more likely to smoke than adolescents from the other two groups (Acierno *et al.*, 2000). Sexual abuse is also a major risk factor for suicide or self-harming behavior. Martin (1996) found that sexual abuse was associated with depression, substance abuse and multiple attempts at suicide. Abused adolescents had six times the suicide risk of nonabused adolescents from dysfunctional families, suggesting that abuse is a stronger risk factor than family dysfunction.

There is also evidence that the type of abuse endured by adolescents results in different mental disorders (Ryan *et al.*, 2000). Homeless adolescents who had experienced both physical and sexual abuse were more likely to be depressed than others. Suicide attempts were common among youths who had been abused sexually, or both physically and sexually. In addition, these adolescents were more likely to be victimized on the streets. Those youths with previous sexual abuse reported a higher incidence of rape, whereas those with previous physical abuse were more likely to be physically assaulted.

Whitbeck *et al.* (1997a) found that a background in an abusive family provided 'basic training' in antisocial behaviors that increased the likelihood of homeless youths' involvement with deviant peers. Early family abuse has a direct and persistent effect on subsequent physical and emotional victimization, with girls more at risk from sexual victimization than boys. Wolfe *et al.* (1999) focused on the family background of homeless adolescents, comparing them to an equivalent group who were living with their families. They found that the families of homeless adolescents featured significantly more parental maltreatment, conflict, and verbal and physical aggression between parents and children. There was also significantly less family cohesion and less frequency of contact with family among the homeless youths. Comparing the perspectives of runaway and home-based adolescents with those of their parents or caretakers, Whitbeck *et al.* (1997b) found that parents and adolescents tended to see the problems in the family similarly, with less monitoring, less warmth and more rejection in the families of the runaways than in the families of home-based adolescents. The runaway families also reported higher levels of family violence. Parents and adolescents reported essentially the same levels of externalizing behavior, well above that of non-runaway groups. Overall, the study found that adolescents and their parents tell essentially the same story, and that households producing runaways are often marked by serious and often dangerous family problems.

Peer group versus family

As noted previously, some researchers have found evidence that family factors are more important than peer group factors in protecting adolescents from becoming involved in problematic behaviors (Muller *et al.*, 2000; Rubenstein *et al.*, 1998). Bahr *et al.* (1995) showed the positive effects of strong family bonds on adolescent problem behavior. In this study of drug use in a large random sample of students in grades 7 to 12, family bonds affected the abuse of drugs indirectly through the peer group, with those adolescents who came from cohesive families being less likely to have friends who used drugs.

The results of a study by Frauenglass *et al.* (1997) also support the role of the family in reducing adolescent substance abuse and peer pressure. In their sample of adolescents in an impoverished and crime-ridden part of Miami, it was found that increasing family support reduced the likelihood of the adolescent being involved in substance abuse or gang-related activities, and the likelihood that their peer group would be involved in such activities.

On the other hand, becoming involved in a deviant peer group increases the likelihood of an adolescent abusing drugs. Adolescents from families that have a member with a drug or alcohol problem are more likely to have contact with a peer group that also uses drugs or alcohol, and contact with such a peer group is strongly related to the adolescent's own substance abuse (Bahr *et al.*, 1995; Brook *et al.*, 1998). It is likely, of course, that there are lower levels of support in families in which a member is involved in drug abuse, so these young people would tend to lack that protective factor.

In a study of African-American adolescents, Farrell and White (1998) found similar peer influences on drug use. The influence of peers on involvement in drug abuse was greatest among girls, and in homes without fathers or stepfathers. The link between peer pressure and drug use tended to increase with increases in the level of conflict and distress in the mother-adolescent relationship, particularly for those adolescents who were not living with fathers or stepfathers.

It also seems clear that family factors are more influential than peer group factors in preventing psychopathology (Bachar *et al.*, 1997). In a path model, neither social support from friends nor having a preadolescent chum had as strong an influence on adolescent mental health as family factors such as bonding and family support. In addition, having a preadolescent chum only buffered adolescents against psychopathology, when bonds with parents were weak. In a study of predominantly Hispanic families in an impoverished environment in Miami, Frauenglass *et al.* (1997) showed that although involvement with deviant peers was strongly associated with drug use, family support actually reduced that influence in terms of tobacco and marijuana use.

These findings provide support for the contention by Sheppard *et al.* (1985) that even though the peer group assumes new importance in the lives of adolescents, family relationships are still central to their well-being. They claim that,

> The peer group, contrary to what is commonly believed, has little or no influence as long as the family remains strong. Peers take over only when the family abdicates. (p. 951)

General conclusions

In trying to make sense of the large amount of research presented here, I have grouped the many factors mentioned under three basic headings—family stress factors, protective factors and risk factors—and explored the impact of each of these factors on adolescent psychological adjustment and problem behaviors. In general, there is a strong link between family stress factors and adolescent adjustment problems and problem behaviors, but buffering and risk factors are also important. Buffering factors tend to decrease the probability of family stresses leading to problems in adolescent adjustment and behavior. Risk factors, on the other hand, tend to increase the likelihood that family stresses will have a negative impact on adolescent adjustment and behavior.

As an example, we saw that high family cohesion and support tend to buffer the effects of fathers' problem drinking on adolescents' distress, problem behaviors and heavy drinking. We also saw that high family cohesion following divorce or separation can buffer adolescents from the negative effects of family breakdown, decreasing the likelihood that adolescents in separated and divorcing families will engage in self-harming behavior. In addition, family support has been shown to buffer adolescents against the negative effects of exposure to serious family violence, in a way that nonfamily support could not.

In families struggling with economic hardship, on the other hand, parental depression increased the probability that adolescents would report internalizing symptoms, because the depressed parents were unable to provide the kind of support needed to buffer the adolescents against the effect of economic hardship. In addition, poor family functioning seems to increase the likelihood that an adolescent with a depressed parent will also become depressed, with adolescents experiencing both a depressed parent and poor family functioning most at risk.

Clearly, family factors play a crucial role in the lives of adolescents. It is important, however, to recognize that the links between family stress and adolescent problems is not straightforward. Family factors can serve either to increase an adolescent's risk of adjustment and behavior problems in the face of family stresses, or to lessen that risk. In therapeutic work with families with adolescents, it seems important to try to increase the buffering factors such as family cohesion and family support, and to decrease or neutralize the risk factors such as weak family bonds, parental hostility and coercion, and involvement with a deviant peer group. It is interesting to note that the number of studies from non-Western cultures reported here suggest that these patterns generally apply to families across the world.

References

Acierno, R., Kilpatrick, D. G., Resnick, H., Saunders, B., De Arellano, M. & Best, C. (2000). Assault, PTSD, family substance use, and depression as risk factors for cigarette use in youth. *National Survey of Adolescents. Journal of Traumatic Stress,* 13, 381–396.

Amato, P. (2001). Children of divorce in the 1990s: An update of the Amato and Keith (1991) meta-analysis. *Journal of Family Psychology,* 15, 355–370.

Antognoli-Toland, P. L. (2001). Parent-child relationship, family structure and loneliness among adolescents. *Adolescent and Family Health,* 2, 20–26.

Aydin, B. & Oeztuetuencue, F. (2001). Examination of adolescents' negative thoughts, depressive mood and family environment. *Adolescence,* 36, 77–83.

Bachar, E., Canetti, L., Bonne, O., Kaplan de Nour, A. & Shalev, A. Y. (1997). Pre-adolescent chumship as a buffer against psychopathology in adolescents with weak family support and weak parental bonding. *Child Psychiatry and Human Development,* 27, 209–219.

Bagley, C., Mallick, K., Verma, G., Bolitho, F., Bertrand, L., Madrid, S. & Tse, J. (1999). Adjustment, stress and family life in adolescents in Canada, Britain, Hong Kong, India, Pakistan and the Philippines. *International Journal of Adolescence and Youth,* 7, 263–278.

Bahr, S. J., Marcos, A. & Maughan, S. L. (1995). Family, educational and peer influences of the alcohol use of female and male adolescents. *Journal of Studies on Alcohol,* 56, 457–469.

Barrera, M. Jr., Prelow, H. M., Dumka, L. E., Gonzales, N. A., Knight, G. P., Michaels, M. L., Roosa, M. W. & Tein, J. Y. (2002). Pathways from family economic conditions to adolescents' distress: Supportive parenting. *Journal of Community Psychology,* 30, 135–152.

Bradley, R. H. & Corwyn, R. F. (2000). Moderating effect of perceived amount of family conflict on the relation between home environmental processes and well-being of adolescents. *Journal of Family Psychology*, 14, 349–364.

Brigman, K. M. L., Schons, J. & Stinnett, N. (1986). Strength of families in a society under stress: A study of families in Iraq. *Family Perspective*, 20, 61–73.

Brook, J. S., Brook, D. W., de la Rosa, M., Duque, L. F., Rodriguez, E., Montoya, I. D. & Whiteman, M. (1998). Pathways to marijuana use among adolescents: Cultural/ecological, family, peer and personality influences. *Journal of the American Academy of Child and Adolescent Psychiatry*, 37, 759–766.

Epstein, N., Baldwin, L. M. & Bishop, D. S. (1983). The McMaster Family Assessment Device. *Journal of Marital and Family Therapy*, 9, 171–180.

Epstein, N. B., Bishop, D. S. & Levin, S. (1978). McMaster Model of Family Functioning. *Journal of Marriage and Family Counseling*, 4, 19–31.

Farrell, A. D. & White, K. S. (1998). Peer influences and drug use among urban adolescents: Family structure and parent-adolescent relationship as protective factors. *Journal of Consulting and Clinical Psychology*, 66, 248–258.

Farrell, M. P., Barnes, G. M. & Banerjee, S. (1995). Family cohesion as a buffer against the effects of problem-drinking fathers on psychological distress, deviant behavior and heavy drinking in adolescents. *Journal of Health and Social Behavior*, 36, 377–385.

Forehand, R., Biggar, H. & Kotchik, B. A. (1998). Cumulative risk across family stressors: Short and long-term effects for adolescents. *Journal of Abnormal Child Psychology*, 26, 119–128.

Frauenglass, S., Routh, D. K., Pantin, H. & Mason, C. A. (1997). Family support decreases influence of deviant peers on Hispanic adolescents' substance use. *Journal of Clinical Child Psychology*, 26, 15–23.

Garber, J., Little, S., Hilsman, R. & Weaver, K. R. (1998). Family predictors of suicidal symptoms in young adolescents. *Journal of Adolescence*, 21, 445–457.

Garnefski, N. & Diekstra, R. F. W. (1996). Perceived social support from family, school and peers: Relationship with emotional and behavioral problems among adolescents. *Journal of the American Academy of Child and Adolescent Psychiatry*, 35, 1657–1664.

Gavazzi, S. M. (1993). The relation between family differentiation levels in families with adolescents and the severity of presenting problems. *Family Relations*, 42, 463–468.

Goebert, D., Nahalu, L., Hishinuma, E., Bell, C., Yuen, N., Carlton, B., Andrade, N. N., Miyamato, R. & Johnson, R. (2000). Cumulative effect of family environment on psychiatric symptomatology among multiethnic adolescents. *Journal of Adolescent Health*, 27, 34–42.

Greeff, A. P. & Le Roux, M. C. (1999). Parents' and adolescents' perceptions of a strong family. *Psychological Reports*, 84, 1219–1224.

Greenberger, E., Chen, C., Tally, S. R. & Dong, Q. (2000). Family, peer and individual correlates of depressive symptomatology among U.S. and Chinese adolescents. *Journal of Consulting and Clinical Psychology*, 68, 209–219.

Hetherington, E. M., Clingempeel, W. G., Anderson, E. R., Deal, J. E., Hagan, M. S., Hollier, E. A. & Lindner, M. S. (1992). Coping with marital transitions: A family systems perspective. *Monographs of the Society for Research in Child Development*, 57, 1–240.

Huerta-Franco, R., Diaz de Leon, G. & Malacara, J. M. (1996). Knowledge and attitudes towards sexuality in adolescents and their associations with the family and other factors. *Adolescence*, 31, 179–192.

Hurd, K. P. (2005). *Family factors in adolescent depression and self-harming*. Ph.D thesis, University of Queensland, Australia.

Kashani, J. H., Suarez, L., Luchene, L. & Reid, J. C. (1998). Family characteristics and behavior problems of suicidal and nonsuicidal children and adolescents. *Child Psychiatry and Human Development*, 29, 157–168.

Kim, J. E., Hetherington, E. M. & Reiss, D. (1999). Associations among family relationships, antisocial peers, and adolescents' externalising behaviors: Gender and family type differences. *Child Development*, 70, 1209–1230.

King, C. A., Hovey, J. D., Brand, E. & Wilson, R. (1997). Suicidal adolescents after hospitalisation: Parent and family impacts on treatment follow-through. *Journal of the American Academy of Child and Adolescent Psychiatry*, 36, 85–93.

Kliewer, W., Murrelle, L., Mejia, R., de-G, Y. T. & Angold, A. (2001). Exposure to violence against a family member and internalising symptoms in Colombian adolescents: The protective effects of family support. *Journal of Consulting and Clinical Psychology*, 69, 971–982.

Lau, S. & Kwok, L. K. (2000). Relationship of family environment to adolescents' depression and self-concept. *Social Behavior and Personality*, 28, 41–50.

Martin, G. (1996). Reported family dynamics, sexual abuse, and suicidal behavior in community adolescents. *Archives of Suicide Research*, 2, 183–195.

McKeown, R. E., Garrison, C. Z., Jackson, K. L., Cuffe, S. P., Addy, C. L. & Waller, J. L. (1997). Family structure and cohesion, and depressive symptoms in adolescents. *Journal of Research on Adolescence*, 7, 267–281.

McLean, M. G., Emby, L. E. & Cauce, A. M. (1999). Homeless adolescents' paths to separation from family: Comparison of family characteristics, psychological adjustment and victimization. *Journal of Community Psychology*, 27, 179–187.

Meyerson, L. A., Long, P. L., Miranda, R. J. & Marx, B. P. (2002). The influence of childhood sexual abuse, physical abuse, family environment and gender on the psychological adjustment of adolescents. *Child Abuse and Neglect*, 26, 387–405.

Muller, R. T., Goebel-Fabbri, A. E., Diamond, T. & Dinklage, D. (2000). Social support and the relationship between family and community violence exposure and psychopathology among high risk adolescents. *Child Abuse and Neglect*, 24, 449–464.

Ngai, N. P. & Cheung, C. K. (2000). Family stress on adolescents in Hong Kong and the mainland of China. *International Journal of Adolescence and Youth*, 8, 183–206.

Noller, P., Feeney, J. A., Sheehan, G. & Darlington, Y. (2004, July). *Conflict in divorcing and two-parent families*. Paper presented at the Biennial Conference of the International Association For Relationship Research, Madison, WI.

Olson, D. H., Russell, C. S. & Sprenkle, D. H. (1983). Circumplex model of marital and family systems, VI: Theoretical update. *Family Process*, 22, 69–83.

Olson, D. H., Sprenkle, D. H. & Russell, C. S. (1979). Circumplex model of marital and family systems, 1: Cohesion and adaptability dimensions, family types and clinical applications. *Family Process*, 18, 3–27.

Pavlidis, K. & McCauley, E. (2001). Autonomy and relatedness in family interactions with depressed adolescents. *Journal of Abnormal Child Psychology*, 29, 11–21.

Pick, S. & Palos, P. A. (1995). Impact of the family on the sex lives of adolescents. *Adolescence*, 30, 667–675.

Pillay, A. L. (1998). Perceptions of family functioning in conduct-disordered adolescents. *South African Journal of Psychology*, 28, 191–195.

Pillay, A. L. & Wassenaar, D. R. (1997). Recent stressors and family satisfaction in suicidal adolescents in South Africa. *Journal of Adolescence*, 20, 155–162.

Rathunde, K. (2001). Family context and the development of undivided interest: A longitudinal study of family support and challenge and adolescents' quality of experience. *Applied Developmental Science*, 5, 158–171.

Rubenstein, J. L., Halton, A., Kasten, L., Rubin, C. & Stechler, G. (1998). Suicidal behavior in adolescents: Stress and protection in different family contexts. *American Journal of Orthopsychiatry*, 68, 274–284.

Ryan, K., Kilmer, R. P., Cauce, A. M., Watanabe, H. & Hoyt, D. R. (2000). Psychological consequences of child maltreatment in homeless adolescents: Untangling the unique effects of maltreatment and family environment. *Child Abuse and Neglect*, 24, 333–352.

Sheeber, L. & Sorensen, E. (1998). Family relationships of depressed adolescents: A multimethod assessment. *Journal of Clinical Child Psychology*, 27, 268–277.

Sheppard, M. A., Wright, D. & Goodstadt, M. S. (1985). Peer pressure and drug use: Exploding the myth. *Adolescence*, 20, 949–958.

Shiner, R. L. & Marmorstein, B. A. (1998). Family environments of adolescents with lifetime depression: Associations with maternal depression history. *Journal of the American Academy of Child and Adolescent Psychiatry*, 37, 1152–1160.

Stewart, E. R., McKenry, P. C., Rudd, N. M. & Gavazzi, S. M. (1994). Family processes and mediators of depressive symptomatology among rural adolescents. *Family Relations*, 43, 38–45.

Tamplin, A. & Goodyer, I. M. (2001). Family functioning in adolescents at high and low risk for major depressive disorder. *European Child and Adolescent Psychiatry*, 10, 170–179.

Taylor, S., Field, T., Yando, R., Gonzales, K. P., Lasko, D., Mueller, C. & Bendell, D. (1997). Adolescents' perceptions of family responsibility–taking. *Adolescence*, 32, 969–976.

Trivette, C. M., Dunst, C. J., Deal, A. G., Wilson-Hamer, A. & Propst, S. (1990). Assessing family strengths and family functioning style. *Home Economics Research Journal*, 14, 112–122.

Whitbeck, L. B., Hoyt, D. R. & Ackley, K. A. (1997a). Abusive family backgrounds and later victimization among runaway and homeless adolescents. *Journal of Research on Adolescence*, 7, 375–392.

Whitbeck, L. B., Hoyt, D. R. & Ackley, K. A. (1997b). Families of homeless and run-away adolescents: A comparison of parent/caretaker and adolescent perspectives on parenting, family violence and adolescent conduct. *Child Abuse and Neglect*, 21, 517–528.

White, F. (1996). Family processes as predictors of adolescents' preferences for ascribed sources of moral authority. *Adolescence*, 31, 133–144.

Wolfe, P. A., Toro, P. A., & McCaskill, P. A. (1999). A comparison of homeless and matched housed adolescents on family environment variables. *Journal of Research on Adolescence*, 9, 53–66.

Wolin, S. J. & Bennett, L. A. (1984). Family rituals. *Family Process*, 23, 401–420.

13

Young people's communication with adults in the institutional order

John Drury

Relations, and hence communications, with authority and the institutional order take on new dimensions in adolescence. As they move from childhood to adolescence, more young people get involved in both full- and part-time work (McKechnie *et al.*, 1996; Coleman, 1999). Young people who have left school are treated more like adults, whether they are in work, in further education or claiming benefits. Further, in comparison to other age groups, young people are particularly likely to be in contact with the police. This is not only because participation in criminal activities is relatively high among young people relative to adults (Emler & Reicher, 1995; Furlong & Cartmel, 1997; Graham & Bowling, 1995) but also because many young people are themselves the victims of crime (Loader, 1996; Rutter *et al.*, 1998), particularly young males (Coleman, 1999). In general, compared to children, young people are expected to exercise more control over their own behavior and are held more legally responsible for their actions (Coleman & Hendry, 1999).

However, although young people have greater abilities and responsibilities than children, they are still subject to the authority (parental, legal, educational, political, economic) of adults *qua* adults. Their changing relations with the institutional order, alongside the development of adolescent 'autonomy' (Silverberg & Gondoli, 1996), means that young people are inevitably conscious of the *power differential* between themselves and adults (Entwhistle, 1990; Emler, 1993; Emler & Reicher, 1995). Given this power differential, adults in authority may be able to define the context, form and meaning of communication between themselves and young people. Interaction between such adults and young people may therefore serve to instantiate or reinforce particular adolescent identities with their associated understandings and behavioral repertoires.

This chapter focuses on communication and interaction between young people and those adults in the institutional order with whom young people may be in contact for the first time: police officers, employers, benefits officers, social workers and so on. The chapter begins by considering how such adults perceive and construct their communication with young people, before describing the research on young people's own perspectives. Taken together, the research points to sharp contrasts between young people and adults in authority in their perceptions of communication with each other. However, although institutional support means that adults generally have greater power, there is also evidence that their ability to impose their perceptions and definitions in communication with young people is sometimes effectively resisted by those adolescents.

The adult perspective

An overwhelming impression from the research is that adults in the institutional order, and indeed nonfamily adults generally, perceive young people as having 'problems' with communication. In particular, young people are said to be uncommunicative and even hostile [see also Garrett & Williams, chapter 3, this volume]. Thus, according to UK sources, professionals report a growth in recent years of antiauthority attitudes and 'barbarity' among young people (Guardian, 2001; MacDonald, 1998). The implication is that many young people—and, in particular, young men (Frosh *et al.*, 2003)—lack the social skills, and indeed even the desire, to be polite, cooperative etc.; they are therefore not able to communicate as well as they 'should.' Thus a study comparing the perceptions of a number of different professional groups including police officers and benefit officers found that most participants had something to say about what they saw as young people's communication problems (Dennison & Drury, 1998). Indeed, among the professional groups studied, police officers and benefits officers were those most likely to say that young people lack adults' communication 'skills.'

This raises the question of what these adults count as communication 'skills.' Police officers have been found typically to conceptualize young people's communication skills in terms of motivation; young people are said not to *want* to communicate with them (Drury & Dennison, 2000). Similarly, benefits officers referred not only to a lack of knowledge and experience, but also to young people's 'attitude' and lack of motivation (Drury & Dennison, 1999).

In contrast, '*good* communication' between themselves and young people is often defined by professional groups generally in terms of disclosure from the adolescent (*cf* McKay, 2003; and also chapter 15, this volume). When interviewed, police officers and benefits officers have stressed their own willingness and ability to listen to the adolescent as an essential ingredient of good communication (Dennison & Drury, 1998). However, an ethnographic study by Loader (1996) led him to conclude that police officers understand effective communication simply as a one-way process: of them getting a message across to young people.

There is some ambiguity in adults' accounts of the extent to which their own power plays a role in their communication with young people. For example, most benefit officers interviewed in the study by Drury and Dennison (1999) acknowledged that their own power was an issue, but at the same time some also denied the importance of power. Among all the professional adults interviewed in the study by Dennison and Drury (1998), police officers were the group most likely to attribute communication problems to power difference (paralleling young people's own perceptions: see below). However, they explained the problem in terms of young people's *perceptions* of them (the police) as authority figures rather than their own (use of) power itself being a problem. Moreover, although police officers recognized that they were powerful and that young people did not have the same communication 'skills' as adults, they also sometimes referred to treating teenagers as adults. Like most of the other professional adults interviewed by Dennison and Drury (1998), police officers stated that they aimed to be honest and open and not talk down to young people: in effect, to gloss over the power difference by treating the adolescent as an equal (Drury & Dennison, 2000).

The discursive turn in psychology (e.g., Edley, 2001; Edwards & Potter, 1992; Parker, 1992) suggests that language does not simply represent but also constructs social relations. Recent research has therefore examined the role of language not simply as a tool of communication but as discourse which positions speakers and hearers in various ways. This research has been particularly useful in demonstrating the (often detrimental) consequences of particular discourses operating as part of the interaction between young people and adults in authority. In particular, Griffin (1993, 1997) has detailed the development and ideological consequences of the 'representations of youth' that have shaped theory and policy on adolescence. Thus the dominant biologistic 'storm and stress' model of adolescence as a sudden period of endogenous turbulence has rationalized institutional policies in which 'youth is trouble,' and therefore needs to be controlled by professional adults. The related discourses of 'youth-at-risk' have similarly been shown to be mobilized in the service of increased surveillance of, and intervention into, young people's lives by schools, police, health services and juvenile justice systems (Kelly, 2000) [see Thurlow—chapter 1; Wyn—chapter 2, this volume].

These and other discourses therefore feature—as rationalizations and explanations—in adults' accounts of their communication with young people. Thus the police officers interviewed by Drury and Dennison (2000) explained young people's unwillingness to communicate with them in terms of the latter's antiauthority attitudes, which in turn they typically attributed either to the inherent 'storm and stress' of adolescence or to irrational peer group pressure. Whether adolescent behavior is constructed as a function of biologically fixed repertoire or of supposed indiscriminate malleability (Griffin, 1993), the social function is the same. It is to absolve the adults themselves of responsibility for poor communication; they are rendered as merely the passive recipients of unreasonable hostility from young people. Use of these kinds of representations of young people thereby operates as a self-serving attribution at the intergroup level (cf Hewstone, 1989).

Drury and Dennison's (1999) interview study with benefit officers suggested that on the one hand—and consistent with an 'underclass' representation (Bagguley & Mann, 1992; MacDonald, 1998)—benefit officers stated that young people as a group lack communication skills and motivation. On the other hand—and consistent with contemporary discourses of individualization (Furlong & Cartmel, 1997) and political correctness—benefit officers typically denied that generalizations about young people were possible and instead stressed individual responsibility.

The adolescent perspective

A recent survey of more than 4000 young people examined good and satisfactory communication between young people and adults outside the family (Catan et al., 1996). This good communication is typically explained by young people in terms of the communicator's personal abilities and skills, and their own achievement of practical aims. However, much of the research on communication between young people and adult authority figures has examined dissatisfaction and conflict. Adults' perceptions that their communication with young people is often problematic is reciprocated. Catan et al.'s (1996) survey included free-choice items in which respondents were able to describe communication experiences in their own words. Analysis showed that the number of young people describing experiences of bad communication with adults outside the family outweighed the number describing good experiences, whereas the reverse was true for experiences of communication with adults within the family (Drury *et al.*, 1998). Moreover, whereas adults outside the family commonly attribute communication problems to the young people (Dennison & Drury, 1998), young people themselves tend to attribute problems in communication to the adult (Catan *et al.*, 1996). Among the different professional groups with which young people have communications, the survey suggested that young people rate communication with benefits officers less positively than with most others. Forty-one percent of the 90 who reported contact with officers from the Department of Social Security rated it as 'bad,' and only 11 percent were 'pleased' with such contact (Catan *et al.*, 1996).

Consistent with the suggestion that young people are acutely aware of the power imbalance inherent in their relationships with adults in the institutional order (Emler, 1993; Emler & Reicher, 1995), power has been found to be one of the explanations offered by young people for their dissatisfactory communication with these adults. For example, young people often see the power of police officers as a problematic issue in their communication with them (Drury *et al.*, 1998). Similarly, in the case of communication with benefits officers, young people with some income have been found to feel more positive about communicating with benefits officers than do those with no income; the latter may be more likely to feel that they are at the mercy of the benefits system (Drury & Dennison, 1999).

In explaining communication problems with employers, young people typically refer to their own lack of courage, the very nature of the relationship and their own lack of skill (Drury *et al.*, 1998). The reference to courage and the nature of the relationship is again consistent with awareness of power differentials. Thus, in describing how they resolved communication problems with their employers, a common explanation offered by adolescent survey respondents was that of finding courage (whereas young people explaining resolutions with family adults were more likely to refer to establishing favorable conditions).

The other main explanations young people give for the communication problems they experience with adults in authority include one-sidedness and what they perceive as a lack of respect for the adolescent's point of view. In the case of police officers, it is often the style and demeanor of police officers (brusque, aggressive, impolite) rather than specific outcomes of contact (such as being arrested, charged or helped) that is the focus of young people's complaints about the police (Hopkins, 1994b; *cf* Fielding, 1984). Whereas, as discussed above, police officers find young people hostile and uncommunicative, from the adolescent's point of view one of the reasons for not wanting to communicate with the police—even when the adolescent is the victim rather than the alleged perpetrator of an offence—is that complaints will not be listened to let alone taken seriously (Loader, 1996). Although young people feel that greater dialogue with those in authority is desirable, they feel they cannot have the same kind of influence possessed by those in authority and hence any dialogue cannot be mutual; the police, for example, 'are able to bring into existence that which they utter' (Loader, 1996: 152; *cf* Stott & Reicher, 1998).

In contrast to negative stereotypes and the suggestions from some professionals that young people lack skills, are inarticulate and are uncommunicative, research on adolescent communication abilities and resources indicates a great deal of knowledge and awareness of the nature of communication, and of what constitutes effective communication in different contexts, on the part of young people. For example, Burleson (1982) found that comforting communication strategies increased in number, variety and sensitivity with age from child to adolescent, and that such strategies were relatively consistent across different social locations. Moreover young people appear quite aware that communication may take various forms and may therefore be nonlinguistic. For example, confrontation, avoidance and even violence can be understood as strategies of communication rather than functions of any supposed limited capacities (e.g., Brody & Catan, 1999; McLachlan, 1981;).

Moreover, although dominant discourses and institutions position young people as the objects of adult surveillance and control, young people have been found to use language to construct alternative identities and relations between themselves and powerful adults. Thus Rymes (1995) shows how high school dropouts use grammatical limiters to mitigate their agency in explaining violence with authority figures. Such discursive work serves to construct these adolescent speakers as ordinary people trying to be good, rather than as heroes or villains. Rymes suggests that these young people's accounts are a progressive alternative to the dominant discourse of youth-at-risk. She argues that their attempt to develop accounts of themselves within moral frameworks needs to be encouraged—for example by providing the necessary space for such talk.

Using a conversation-analytic framework, Kerby and Rae (1998) similarly suggest that the discursive and indeed empathic and moral capabilities of young people have been overlooked (*cf* Elkind, 1967, 1981; Kohlberg, 1981). In their study, young offenders' talk of encounters with the police contained reflexive analyses of how their moral position is visible to the police, which in turn served as a resource to analyze the moral position of the police themselves. In other words, these young people were able to use references to the normative role of the police in order to characterize their own identities in a way which indicated their own awareness of others' perspectives. McDonald (1999) suggests there are gender differences in the way young people define themselves through their construction of their relationship with the institutional order. In his study, both young men and young women were verbally hostile to a police officer. For the women this was a way of affirming a positive identity based around community, which police power was said to undermine. But for the men the identity reinforced in such encounters was one of competition and risk—as expressed, for example, in graffiti as an act of resistance against the police.

Young people's subcultures, which have been defined as '[m]eaning systems, modes of expression or life styles developed by groups in subordinate structural positions in response to dominant meaning systems' (Brake, 1985: 8–9), can provide an 'argot' for young people which marks out the boundaries of an identity distinct from that of rival (sub)cultures and the adult world (e.g., James, 1995). In psychology and sociology, accounts of adolescent 'subculture' as powerful forces of resistance and counterhegemony (e.g., Hall & Jefferson, 1975) have become less fashionable in the last 15 to 20 years, perhaps reflecting the current relative weakness of working class resistance more generally (Griffin, 1993). Recent research has analyzed adolescent subcultural identities not as social forces but as discursive resources used strategically (and variably) by young people in conversation and argument (e.g., Widdicombe & Wooffitt, 1995), reflecting the recent discursive and even postmodern turn in the social sciences and humanities.

However, recent studies also suggest how the peer group can be a source of solidarity and liberating constructions for young people—important issues when considering their interaction with powerful adults. Thus, in an innovative study of girls' expressions of anger, Brown (1998) shows how, in the peer group setting, adolescent girls are able to appropriate (and subvert) the language of others in line with their own needs. For example, linguistic creativity was used by the girls to collectively problematize their middle class teachers' use of dominant definitions of femininity to interpret their experiences and behaviors.

Theorizing adolescent communication with adults in the institutional order

What is the theoretical significance of communication between young people and adults in authority? More specifically, and first of all, how might good communication—defined by participants in terms of disclosure, listening, personal communication skills and achieving practical aims—affect sociocognitive development in adolescence? One suggestion, based on Vygotskyian developmental research and theory on children (e.g., Vygotsky, 1978), is that adult completions of the young person's communicative actions serve to produce in the young person new social understandings (Drury et al., 1998). The complementarity of the adult to the young person might provide a 'scaffolding' for the child's action and cognition. The following types of adult communicative actions are suggested as constituting such 'scaffolding': prompting questions, provision of sub-goals, rephrasing of issues, and verbal and nonverbal encouragement (Rogoff, 1990).

Could unsatisfactory and conflictual communication between young people and adults in the institutional order also contribute to sociocognitive developmental processes in adolescence? The research on conflictual communication between young people and adults in the institutional order suggests a series of oppositions. First, whereas the adults describe young people as poor communicators who lack communication skills, young people's own accounts suggest that they are capable of employing, articulating and reflecting upon a range of communicative strategies and empathic abilities. Second, adults in the institutional order see their power as a given, as necessary, and as a problem only insofar as the adolescent reacts badly to it—as evidenced by young people's perceived unwillingness to speak and their hostility to authority. But young people themselves perceive the adult's power as a problem in itself, and complain of a lack of respect being shown to them by adults in their communication. Third, whereas adults may understand young people's antiauthority responses as a function of endogenous 'storm and stress' or other fixed individual features, young people's own accounts suggest that their actions are contextually dependent on and sensitive to those of the adult. It is unclear whether this discrepancy is a function of the biologistic discourse of adolescent development or is simply a case of the more general fundamental attribution error, whereby perceivers overestimate the role of dispositional factors and underestimate situational influences on others' behavior (Ross, 1977). Finally, whereas adults in the institutional order see the peer group as a source of uncritical social influence, young people experience their peer groups as a source of social support for their linguistic and other strategic resistance.

One way of understanding the relation between these oppositions is as a dynamic struggle over identities. Moreover, because conflictual communication is often social-categorical rather than personal—between young people and police officers, benefits officers, employers etc. *as* police officers, benefits officers, employers etc.—the identities being struggled over are collective (i.e., group) as well as personal. The contribution of such conflictual communication to the developmental and sociocognitive processes of adolescence may therefore be to transform or to reinforce particular adolescent social identities, depending in large part on the outcomes of the communication.

Conflictual communication between young people and police officers can serve as an illustration (Drury & Dennison, 2000). Police officers' representations of young people as hostile to authority may not simply reflect the given reality of tension and conflict in their relationship (Fielding, 1995; Reiner, 1992; Southgate, 1986), but may also serve to *contribute* to this relationship. In terms of this representation, it is rational for police officers encountering young people to expect uncooperativeness or even outright aggression. Police officers' possibly defensive initial reactions (e.g., firmness, formality) might be read by young people as an attempt to use institutional power to threaten their freedom (for example, to 'hang about' in the street; Girling *et al.*, 2000; Loader, 1996). The young people's response to this perceived threat—particularly if supported by the peer group—could serve to confirm police officers' initial expectations. Hence conflict escalates, and the most readily available and apparently effective form of communication open to young people would seem to be defiance (Loader, 1996). By the same token, where young people themselves bring to an interaction the expectation that police behavior will be illegitimately and indiscriminately hostile and disrespectful, this too can serve to produce the very antagonistic interaction expected, almost as a self-fulfilling prophecy. In either case, oppositional identities and reputations develop *(cf* Emler & Reicher, 1995): police generally come to be defined as 'pigs' (Hopkins, 1994b) and the young people themselves as generally antiauthority.

This account of communication conflict as a struggle over identity between groups across time, and thus including the role of their intergroup relationship history, derives from research on intergroup dynamics in collective action (e.g., Drury & Reicher, 2000; Reicher, 1996; Stott & Reicher, 1998; *cf* Waddington, 1992, 2001). As such, it is consistent with current research and theory in social psychology more broadly, according to which different social relations form the basis of different identities; because individuals have many different social relations so each individual is the locus of multiple social identities (Ellemers *et al.*, 1999; Turner *et al.*, 1987; Turner *et al.*, 1994).

Although recent sociologically oriented work on adolescence has embraced the notion of multiple (and conflicting) identities (e.g., Rattansi & Phoenix, 1997), psychological work on adolescence continues to be dominated by a 'personality' approach to identity inherited from Erikson (1963) and Marcia (1966), according to which self or identity is unitary, with a single core (e.g., Coleman & Hendry, 1999; Kroger, 1996) [see Thurlow—chapter 1, this volume]. Thus the social identity approach in social psychology has so far been applied in only limited areas of research on adolescence—notably to issues of delinquency (Emler & Reicher, 1995) and peer group influence (Hopkins, 1994a).

Some implications for practice

It has been argued by some that a developed communicative ability may enable young people to be more equal partners in interactions with the adults around them, allowing them to negotiate their own place, whether at school, at work or at home in the family (Lerner & Busch-Rossnagel, 1981). On the other side of the communicative relationship, research has suggested how those in authority might be better able to communicate with young people. For example, Aye Maung's (1995) survey concludes that explaining to young people why they have been approached is an important way that the police could improve young people's satisfaction with their encounters with them (cf Wiley & Hudik, 1974).

However, although situations of mutual willingness will allow these suggestions to be successfully implemented, there are also structural, historical and ideological factors which operate against satisfactory communication taking place between young people and adult authority figures (Loader, 1996). Indeed, unless such structural, historical and ideological impediments are taken into consideration, advice on improving communication may actually serve to reproduce these impediments.

Thus, a focus on improving the communication and other skills of the adolescent has historically been part of an ideological agenda which has worked against disadvantaged young people. As Griffin (1993) argues, the concern among researchers and employers alike with young people's 'employability' can serve to focus attention on qualities (and deficits) of the individual and hence away from the structure of labor markets which may operate to discriminate against young people (Pollock, 1996). The individualizing discourse of 'personal qualities' and 'skills' may therefore lead to self-blame for the young person unable to find a decent job (Furlong & Cartmel, 1997). Put differently, the structural determinants in the transition from school to work (Roberts, 1993) means that the possession of a range of communication strategies may not be enough.

Moreover, what are experienced by young people as problems in communication may arise not because professional adults are communicating ineffectively, but because these adults have aims which conflict with the need for good communication—without denying, of course, that teenagers themselves may have aims which conflict with the need for good communication with adults. For example, Fielding (1995) notes that, though explanations from police officers might serve to allay distrust, giving such explanations to young people could easily be interpreted as a sign of weakness. Similarly, the concern with maintaining authority in relation to young people means that it may be difficult for police officers to apologize for mistakes. Apology is very difficult for those in positions of authority whose job is, in a sense, to be right, and who are very concerned not to lose face with people they deal with in case they no longer respect that authority (Southgate, 1986).

Conclusions and implications for further research

Research on adolescent communication with adults in the institutional order has been given relatively little attention relative to that between young people and family members. However, some clear themes emerge from what little research has been carried out. First, there is an issue of power which appears to affect the nature of communication (and the perception of that communication) between young people and adults in authority. Second, the availability of certain discourses of adolescence feed into the communication process, and operate to justify adult practices toward young people. Third, and as a consequence, how young people define themselves and understand their social world is a function at least in part of their interaction with adults in the institutional order. Put differently, the power of adults, and young people's cooperation with or resistance to the discourses that they employ, serves to construct forms of identity for young people.

However, theorizing in this field is limited by reliance on studies which have analyzed adolescent and adult *accounts* of their communication rather than that communication itself. If communication between young people and adults has consequences for sociocognitive development and identity, research is needed which can detail the actual processes involved rather than merely infer them. The methods used in social psychology by social identity researchers and discursive psychologists, whereby interaction itself is recorded and analyzed, could usefully be applied to the study of adolescent communication with adults in authority.

What is necessary, therefore, is some kind of interactive study, able to take measures of adolescent and adult communication and perceptions across time *in situ*. Ethnography (e.g., Hammersley & Atkinson, 1995) would be ideally suited for research on young people's communication with nonfamily adults, but has tended to be used more in sociology than in psychology. A study using ethnographic researchers, perhaps even in two teams, would be able to gather fine-grained contemporaneous data on the actual interaction between young people and adults in authority, tracing possible processes of 'scaffolding' or identity struggle *in vivo*.

References

Aye Maung, N. (1995). Young People, Victimization and The Police: British Crime Survey Findings on Experiences and Attitudes of 12–15 Year Olds. *Home Office Research Study 140*. London: HMSO.

Bagguley, P. & Mann, K. (1992). Idle thieving bastards? Scholarly representations of the underclass. *Work, Employment & Society*, 6, 113–126.

Brake, M. (1985). *Comparative Youth Cultures: the Sociology of Youth Culture and Youth Subcultures in America, Britain and Canada*. London: Routledge.

Brody, R. & Catan, L. (1999). Young people's understanding of communication: Implications for educational initiatives. *Youth & Policy*, 63, 1–12.

Brown, L. M. (1998). *Raising their Voices: The Politics of Girls' Anger*. Cambridge, MA: Harvard University Press.

Burleson, B. R. (1982). The development of comforting communication skills in childhood and adolescence. *Child Development*, 53, 1578–1588.

Catan, L., Dennison, C. & Coleman, J. (1996). *Getting through: Effective Communication in the Teenage Years*. London: BT Forum/Trust for the Study of Adolescence.

Coleman, J. (1999). *Key Data on Adolescence 1999*. Brighton: Trust for the Study of Adolescence.

Coleman, J. C. & Hendry, L. (1999). *The Nature of Adolescence*. Routledge: London.

Dennison, C. & Drury, J. (1998). *Professionals' Perceptions of Communication with Teenagers*. Unpublished Manuscript: Trust for the Study of Adolescence.

Drury, J. & Dennison, C. (1999). Individual responsibility versus social category problems: Benefit officers' perceptions of communication with teenagers. *Journal of Youth Studies*, 2, 171–192.

Drury, J. & Dennison, C. (2000). Representations of teenagers among police officers: Some implications for their communication with young people. *Youth & Policy*, 66, 62–87.

Drury, J. & Reicher, S. (2000). Collective action and psychological change: The emergence of new social identities. *British Journal of Social Psychology*, 39, 579–604.

Drury, J., Catan, L., Dennison, C. & Brody, R. (1998). Exploring teenagers' accounts of bad communication: A new basis for intervention. *Journal of Adolescence*, 21, 177–196.

Edley, N. (2001). Analysing masculinity: Interpretative repertoires, ideological dilemmas and subject positions. In M. Wetherell, S. Taylor & S. J. Yates (eds), *Discourse as Data: A Guide for Analysis* (pp. 189–228). London: Sage/Open University.

Edwards, D. & Potter, J. (1992). *Discursive Psychology*. London: Sage.

Elkind, D. (1967). Egocentrism in adolescence. *Child Development*, 38, 1025–1034.

Elkind, D. (1981). *Children and Adolescents: Interpretive Essays on Jean Piaget*. (3rd edition). Oxford: Oxford University Press.

Ellemers, N., Spears, R. & Doosje, B. (eds). (1999). *Social Identity: Context, Commitment, Content*. Oxford: Blackwell.

Emler, N. (1993). The young person's relationship to the institutional order. In S. Jackson & H. Rodriguez-Tomé (eds), *Adolescence and its Social Worlds* (pp. 229–250). Hove: Lawrence Erlbaum.

Emler, N. & Reicher, S. (1995). *Adolescence and Delinquency: The Collective Management of Reputation.* Oxford: Blackwell.

Entwhistle, D. R. (1990). Schools and the adolescent. In S.S. Feldman & G.R. Elliott (eds), *At the Threshold: The Developing Adolescent* (pp. 197–224). Cambridge, MA: Harvard University Press.

Erikson, E. H. (1963). *Childhood and Society.* Harmondsworth: Penguin.

Fielding, N. (1984). Police socialization and police competence. *British Journal of Sociology,* 35, 568–590.

Fielding, N. (1995). *Community Policing.* Oxford: Clarendon Press.

Frosh, S., Phoenix, A. & Pattman, R. (2003). The trouble with boys. *The Psychologist,* 16, 84–87.

Furlong, A. & Cartmel, F. (1997). *Young People and Social Change: Individualization and Risk in Late Modernity.* Buckingham: Open University Press.

Girling, E., Loader, I. & Sparks, R. (2000). *Crime and Social Change in Middle England: Questions of Order in an English Town.* London: Routledge.

Graham, J. & Bowling, B. (1995). *Young People and Crime.* Home Office Research Study 145. London: HMSO.

Griffin, C. (1993). *Representations of Youth: The Study of Adolescence in Britain and America.* Cambridge: Polity.

Griffin, C. (1997). Representations of the young. In J. Roche & S. Tucker (eds), *Youth in Society: Contemporary Theory, Policy and Practice* (pp. 17–25). London: Sage/Open University.

Guardian (2001). The panel. *Guardian Newspaper,* 26 September.

Hall, S. & Jefferson, T. (eds). (1975). *Resistance Through Rituals.* London: Hutchinson.

Hammersley, M. & Atkinson, P. (1995). *Ethnography: Principles in Practice.* London: Routledge.

Hewstone, M. (1989). *Causal Attribution: From Cognitive Processes to Collective Beliefs.* Oxford: Blackwell.

Hopkins, N. (1994a). Peer group processes and adolescent health-related behaviour: More than 'peer group pressure'? *Journal of Community and Applied Social Psychology,* 4, 329–345.

Hopkins, N. (1994b). School pupils' perceptions of the police that visit schools: Not all police are 'pigs'. *Journal of Community and Applied Social Psychology,* 4, 189–207.

James, A. (1995). Talking of children and youth: Language, socialization and culture. In V. Amit-Talai & H. Wulff (eds), *Youth Cultures: A Cross-Cultural Perspective* (pp. 43–62). London: Routledge.

Kelly, P. (2000). The dangerousness of youth-at-risk: The possibilities of surveillance and intervention in uncertain times. *Journal of Adolescence,* 23, 463–476.

Kerby, J. & Rae, J. (1998). Moral identity in action: Young offenders' reports of encounters with the police. *British Journal of Social Psychology,* 37, 439–456.

Kohlberg, L. (1981). *The Philosophy of Moral Development: Moral Stages and the Idea of Justice.* San Francisco: Harper & Row.

Kroger, J. (1996). *Identity in Adolescence: The Balance between Self and Other.* London: Routledge.

Lerner, R. & Busch-Rossnagel, N. (1981). *Individuals as Producers of their Own Development.* London: Academic Press.

Loader, I. (1996). *Youth, Policing and Democracy.* Basingstoke: Macmillan.

MacDonald, R. (1998). Youth, transition and social exclusion: Some issues for youth research in the UK. *Journal of Youth Studies*, 1, 163–176.

Marcia, J. E. (1966). Development and validation of ego identity status. *Journal of Personality & Social Psychology*, 3, 551–558.

McDonald, K. (1999). *Struggles for Subjectivity: Identity, Action and Youth Experience.* Cambridge: Cambridge University Press.

McKay, S. (2003). Adolescent risk behaviours and communication research: Current directions. *Journal of Language and Social Psychology*, 22, 74–82.

McKechnie, J., Lindsay, S. & Hobbs, S. (1996). Child employment: A neglected topic? *The Psychologist*, 9, 219–222.

McLachlan, P. (1981). Teenage experiences in a violent society. *Journal of Adolescence*, 4, 285–294.

Parker, I. (1992). *Discourse Dynamics: Critical Analysis for Social and Individual Psychology.* London: Routledge.

Pollock, G. (1996). Unemployed and under 18: Struggling between subsistence and destitution. *Youth & Policy*, 54, 38–53.

Rattansi, A. & Phoenix, A. (1997). Rethinking youth identities: Modernist and postmodernist frameworks. In J. Bynner, L. Chisholm & A. Furlong (eds), *Youth, Citizenship and Social Change in a European Context* (pp. 121–150). Aldershot: Ashgate.

Reicher, S. (1996). 'The Battle of Westminster': Developing the social identity model of crowd behaviour in order to explain the initiation and development of collective conflict. *European Journal of Social Psychology*, 26, 115–134.

Reiner, R. (1992). *The Politics of the Police.* New York: Harvester Wheatsheaf.

Roberts, K. (1993). Career trajectories and the mirage of increased social mobility. In I. Bates & G. Riseborough (eds), *Youth and Inequality* (pp. 229–245). Buckingham: Open University Press.

Rogoff, B. (1990). *Apprenticeship in Thinking: Cognitive Development in Social Context.* New York: Oxford University Press.

Ross, L. (1977). The intuitive psychologist and his shortcomings: Distortions in the attribution process. In L. Berkowitz (ed.), *Advances in Experimental Social Psychology* (pp. 174–220). New York: Academic Press.

Rutter, M., Giller, H. & Hagell, A. (1998). *Antisocial Behavior by Young People.* Cambridge: Cambridge University Press.

Rymes, B. (1995). The construction of moral agency in the narratives of high-school drop-outs. *Discourse & Society*, 6, 495–516.

Silverberg, S. B. & Gondoli, D. M. (1996). Autonomy in adolescence: A contextualized perspective. In G. R. Adams, R. Montemayor & T. P. Gullotta (eds), *Psychosocial Development during Adolescence: Progress in Developmental Contextualism* (pp. 12–61). Thousand Oaks: Sage.

Southgate, P. (1986). Police-Public Encounters. *Home Office Research Study 90*. London: HMSO.

Stott, C.J. & Reicher, S. (1998) Crowd action as intergroup process: Introducing the police perspective. *European Journal of Social Psychology*, 26, 509–29.

Turner, J. C., Hogg, M. A., Oakes, P. J., Reicher, S. D. & Wetherell, M. S. (1987). *Rediscovering the Social Group: A Self-Categorization Theory*. Oxford: Blackwell.

Turner, J. C., Oakes, P. J., Haslam, S. J. & McGarty, C. (1994). Self and collective: Cognition and social context. *Personality and Social Psychology Bulletin*, 20, 454–63.

Vygotsky, L.S. (1978). *Mind in Society*. Cambridge, MA: Harvard University Press.

Waddington, D. (1992). *Contemporary Issues in Public Disorder: A Comparative and Historical Approach*. London: Routledge.

Waddington, D. (2001). Trouble at mill towns. *The Psychologist*, 14, 454–455.

Widdicombe, S. & Wooffitt, R. (1995). *The Language of Youth Subcultures: Social Identity in Action*. New York: Harvester Wheatsheaf.

Wiley, M. G. & Hudik, T. (1974). Police-citizen encounters: A field test of exchange theory. *Social Problems*, 22, 119–27.

14

In the classroom: Instructional communication with young people

Joseph Chesebro

How does a teacher take his or her knowledge and convey that knowledge to students effectively? This question crystallizes the challenge for teachers at all levels, including those who teach adolescents. The answer to this question necessarily involves a considerable focus on the teacher's communication behavior, as the difference between knowing and teaching is communication in the classroom (Hurt *et al.*, 1978). Over the past three decades a number of researchers in the communication discipline have been studying this very process, which is referred to as Instructional Communication.

Instructional Communication is concerned with the role of communication in teaching and learning processes (as opposed to Communication Education, which focuses on the teaching of communication as a specific subject). Instructional communication researchers examine the role that a number of teacher and student behaviors play in the classroom. These behaviors have included nonverbal aspects of teachers' delivery, the organization of teachers' messages, and verbal aspects of teachers' messages. The impact of these behaviors has been examined in terms of students' affect for course material and instructors, motivation to learn from a teacher, perceptions of teachers' credibility, perceptions of how much cognitive learning has occurred, and actual cognitive learning. Almost all of the research conducted in this area has investigated communication between college teachers and college students. Therefore, the purpose of this chapter is to extend the scope of instructional communication research and consider the ways in which it can contribute to the successful teaching of adolescents. However, this task is filled with the challenge of applying research findings from one context to a context which has similarities but also is different in a variety of ways.

Instructional communication in adolescent classrooms

This concern with the applicability of instructional communication research to classrooms with students of different ages and at various stages of development is not new. Nussbaum and Prusank (1989) identified a bias in instructional communication literature toward studying college classrooms and identified a number of ways in which the context of K–12 classrooms (kindergarten through 12th grade, encompassing students approximately 5–18 years of age) is different than that of college classrooms.

First, Nussbaum and Prusank argue that discipline is a more prevalent concern in primary and secondary classrooms than it is in college classrooms. Furthermore, even if discipline is an equal concern among all of these levels, events that prompt the need for discipline may vary across the different levels of education. In addition, strategies of disciplining students are likely to be different across these different levels of education. As a result, discipline research conducted on college students may not be applicable entirely to other educational contexts.

Second, Nussbaum and Prusank argue that students' knowledge of their instructors is likely to be far greater at the primary and secondary levels than it is at the college level. This is likely because K–12 students are likely to spend more than three days each week with their teachers, may interact with teachers longer than a typical college semester permits, and may have greater interaction with teachers outside of the classroom. Thus the quality and nature of teacher-student relationships may differ across educational levels. This difference that might appear across education levels also is likely to apply to student-student relationships, as K–12 students are likely to have student-teacher relationships that differ from those of college students.

A third area identified by Nussbaum and Prusank recognizes the greater involvement of primary and secondary teachers with their students' extracurricular activities. Below the college level, these activities would include involvement in student clubs and organizations. Although Nussbaum and Prusank recognize these interactions as 'fundamentally important to students who must learn how to interact with their teachers outside of the classroom' (p. 341), instructional communication research, with its focus on college students, has not investigated this particular kind of communication interaction with teachers and students. In fairness, instructional communication has begun to examine out-of-class communication between teachers and students, and this research might help provide a better understanding of teacher-student relationships and their communication during extracurricular activities. However, so far this research has studied college students and teachers. Given the ways in which out-of-class communication might differ at the secondary and college levels, it is reasonable to suspect that this research might yield different results if it studied secondary teachers and students.

In addition to the differences between contexts outlined by Nussbaum and Prusank, a number of other key differences may exist. First, inclusive classrooms (which are comprised of some students who have special developmental needs or disabilities and some students who do not) are a characteristic of K–12 classrooms, but are less likely to be a salient characteristic at the college level. This difference is quite important, as it is a very new challenge that teachers face, and much remains to be learned about effective communication in these inclusive classrooms.

Second, literature is increasingly investigating the concept of student bullying at the K–12 level. Again, this is a concept that is largely a nonconcern in the college classroom. Still, the role that communication plays with respect to bullying probably is quite important. First, teachers need communication skill to recognize bullying. Second, they need a diverse array of skills to navigate a situation in which one or more students is being bullied. Skills related to control, assertiveness and influence likely are needed to take charge of any situation and at least temporarily stop the problem. Then skills related to empathy and responsiveness are needed to effectively communicate with the person being bullied. Even though the situation outlined here is oversimplified, the need for considerable communication skill is evident.

Finally, one very key difference between K–12 and college classrooms is the extent to which teachers are likely to find themselves communicating with their students' parents or guardians. In fact, the teacher-parent relationship, and the communication that creates it, may be a key factor in student success at the K–12 level. For example, teachers rate parent support and interest as the change most needed to improve student success (Langdon & Vesper, 2000). Furthermore, research has identified a relationship between parents' lack of cooperation with schools and rises in classroom misbehavior (National Center for Education Statistics, 2001). This issue is a great concern and source of controversy, as the aspects of students' education for which schools/parents should or should not be responsible continually are a source of potentially problematic negotiation. All one has to do is ask a teacher about communicating with parents, watch the teacher's expression, and listen to gain a full sense of both the importance of parent-teacher communication as well as the ways in which it is problematic.

As the above review demonstrates, the task of applying college teacher–college student communication to adolescent teacher–adolescent student communication can be problematic. It is likely that many research results can apply to both levels. However, the presence of additional variables, such as those outlined above, suggests that the application of these results may need to be qualified in any number of ways. The following review of key instructional communication research is offered with this caveat in mind. After each concept is reviewed and existing conclusions are offered, I will discuss how the concept might apply to adolescent classrooms. This is more likely to generate hypotheses than to supply definitive conclusions. However, this is entirely acceptable, as it can stimulate discussion among those using this text in the classroom, and stimulate research ideas for those interested in adolescents. At the very least, it is hoped that this can be a springboard for instructional communication researchers to broaden their focus to the adolescent context, a goal that is very much in line with the philosophy of this entire volume on adolescent communication.

First, a number of important instructional communication variables are reviewed, including nonverbal immediacy, content relevance, teacher clarity, teacher confirmation, and teacher-student out-of-class communication. Then two recently developed theories are outlined to integrate all of the variables into a framework that can enable a meaningful examination of teacher-student communication in adolescent classrooms.

Instructional communication skills

Nonverbal immediacy

Over the past 20-plus years, more instructional communication research has been published on nonverbal immediacy than on almost any other variable related to teacher behavior. Mehrabian (1971) identified immediacy to capture the ways people approach things they like and avoid things they dislike. Nonverbal immediacy has been applied in instructional communication research as a cluster of behaviors which increases others' perceptions of being physically or psychologically close to us (McCroskey & Richmond, 1992). So in a teaching context, students would consider themselves to be closer to teachers who exhibit at least some of these behaviors than they would to nonimmediate teachers. Immediacy behaviors include the following, preferably in moderation: smiling, having a relaxed body posture, speaking with vocal variety (not monotone), maintaining eye contact, and gesturing.

Research on nonverbal immediacy has consistently demonstrated its positive role in the classroom. First, students of immediate teachers report having more positive affect both for their teachers and for the course material taught by those teachers. This result has been identified using both survey research (Chesebro & McCroskey, 2001; Frymier, 1994; Richmond, 1990) and experimental research (Chesebro, 2003; Titsworth, 2001b). Students of immediate teachers also report that they are more motivated to learn from those teachers (Chesebro & McCroskey, 2001; Christophel, 1990; Richmond, 1990) and rate those teachers as being more credible (Thweatt & McCroskey, 1998). The link between immediacy and student learning is less clear. Students of immediate teachers perceive that they learn more from those teachers (Chesebro & McCroskey, 2001; Christophel, 1990; Richmond, 1990), and research has demonstrated that students' perceptions do correlate highly with their actual performance on a recall test (Chesebro & McCroskey, 2000). However, the majority of experimental research on the actual effect of immediacy on learning has tended to yield nonsignificant or weak results (Chesebro, 2003; Kelley & Gorham, 1988; Messman & Jones-Corely, 2001; Perry & Penner, 1990; Witt & Wheeless, 1999). Given these results, the link between nonverbal immediacy and cognitive learning warrants further study. However, other outcomes, particularly those which establish the positive relationship between immediacy and student affect, suggest the highly important role that immediacy plays in the classroom.

Furthermore, the immediacy of teachers of adolescents and its relationship with the perceptions of adolescent students actually has been studied. In a sample that involved both senior high and college students, immediacy emerged as an important predictor of students' affect (Plax et al., 1986). This finding is important because it demonstrates that students at various levels respond positively to immediate teachers. Even when considering the potential caveats I outlined earlier, it is still quite plausible that teacher immediacy would have a widespread and positive effect with adolescent students (both in and out of the classroom) and their parents. Richmond and McCroskey (2000b) proposed the following principle of immediacy:

> The more communicators employ immediate behaviors, the more others will like, evaluate highly, and prefer such communicators, and the less communicators employ immediacy behaviors, the more others will dislike, evaluate negatively, and reject such communicators [see also chapter 11, this volume].

This assertion is supported by research which has revealed the benefits of immediacy in a number of contexts, including physician/patient (Richmond et al., 2001) and in organizational relationships (Richmond & McCroskey, 2000a). Although immediacy is an important teacher behavior, it alone cannot account for all positive instructional outcomes. Teachers need to complement immediacy with other skills, including the ability to make their content relevant to their students.

Content relevance

Although a teacher may be able to get positive student attention by being non-verbally immediate, he or she must complement that immediacy with effective verbal communication. Much of this involves making content relevant to students' past, present or future experiences, interests and goals. More specifically, content relevance refers to a student perception of the extent to which course content satisfies personal needs, personal goals and/or career goals (Keller, 1983). Keller (1987) identified a number of ways to make content relevant. First, teachers can identify the future usefulness of course material, in terms of how it relates to learners' future activities or goals. Second, teachers can discuss the present worth of the material, in terms of how the material will benefit students immediately. Third, students' needs can be matched to the material when teachers provide students with the opportunity to exercise influence. Fourth, teachers can relate material to students' experiences, in terms of how the material builds on existing skills or is familiar to learners in some other way. Fifth, teachers can model enthusiasm for the subject (not entirely unlike being immediate). Finally, students may be provided with choices, such as alternative methods on an assignment, or even alternative assignments. Although there is room for future research to develop this framework more completely, it exists as a good starting place for teachers wishing to make their content more relevant.

Although relevance has not been researched extensively, the research that does exist speaks to its important role in the classroom. For example, in a study on strategies used by teachers, only relevance was related to students' on-task behavior (Newby, 1991). Students who perceive their teachers to be relevant are more likely to be motivated to learn from those teachers than they are from less relevant teachers (Frymier & Shulman, 1995). Students of relevant teachers also report greater positive affect for those teachers and the course material they teach, as well as a greater sense of empowerment within their classrooms (Frymier et al., 1996). Furthermore, students of teachers who make content relevant are more likely to engage in effective learning behaviors (Frymier et al., 1996). Although these findings have failed to be replicated experimentally, this may be because there was a problem with the manipulation of relevance in the study (Frymier & Houser, 1998). Additional support for relevance comes from research in which students offered written responses about motivational teacher behaviors. This research revealed that the 'perceived relevance of and interest in the subject area' was the most important factor which influenced motivation to learn in a specific class (Millette & Gorham, 2002: 144). This finding echoes similar results observed by other researchers (Cruickshank & Kennedy, 1986; Newby, 1991). Given all of this evidence, it is clear that relevance is an important teaching strategy in the college classroom.

When considering the ways in which the relevance research might apply to adolescent classrooms, it is important to keep a key point in mind regarding the issue of choice. Unlike college students, adolescent students are required to be in school. As a result, though relevance is important at the college level, it likely is considerably more important in adolescent classrooms, as adolescents probably are less likely to be taking courses based on their interests or future goals. Therefore, adolescent students may be less likely to see the relevance of content they are learning. This suggests that being relevant may be a key factor in successful teaching in adolescent classrooms.

However, because of a different kind of issue involving choice, it may be even harder for teachers of adolescents to make their content relevant to their students. Whereas many college teachers have flexibility in choosing the content they teach and how they assess their students' learning, teachers of adolescents may be much more bound to follow state regulations of what content must be covered. Furthermore, their students may be assessed by some form of statewide or nationwide standardized test. So although relevance is likely to be very important in adolescent classrooms, it is important to note the additional challenges teachers in these contexts may face when it comes to making material relevant to students.

Teacher clarity

Although nonverbal immediacy and content relevance can function to gain students' attention and make material more interesting to them, teachers still must take advantage of that attention and deliver their content effectively. The clarity of a teacher's message is an important part of this effective delivery. Clarity is defined as a 'cluster of teacher behaviors that contributes to the fidelity of instructional messages' (Chesebro & Wanzer, 2005 in press; see also chapter 5, this volume).

Research on teacher clarity has led to the identification of a number of teacher behaviors which enhance the clarity of instructional messages. Most recently, these behaviors have been classified into two dimensions: structural clarity and verbal clarity (Chesebro, 2003). Structural clarity includes a number of teaching strategies, including using visual aids, previewing and reviewing course content, providing clear transitions from one topic to the next, and providing skeletal outlines of lesson content. Verbal clarity involves fluent speaking, effective explanations, and the appropriate pacing of instruction. Space precludes a thorough discussion of this topic but more complete overviews of clear teaching behaviors are available in the communication literature (Chesebro, 2002; Chesebro, 2003; Chesebro & Wanzer, 2005 in press; Civikly, 1992; Cruickshank & Kennedy, 1986; Daly & Vangelisti, 2003).

Research on clarity has consistently supported the conclusion that clarity is a key teacher behavior, regardless of the level of education or even the geographical location. Bush, Kennedy, and Cruickshank (1977) generated their list of clarity behaviors by surveying approximately 1500 ninth-grade students, and the list they generated was replicated when students in Australia, Tennessee, and Ohio were studied (Kennedy *et al.*, 1978). Hines (1981) then replicated these findings with college students. Positive outcomes of the use of clear teaching behaviors have been observed in research that has used a variety of methods. Instructional communication research has revealed that, as opposed to unclear teachers, clear teachers are perceived by students to be more credible (Sidelinger & McCroskey, 1997). Furthermore, students of clear teachers have less receiver apprehension (Chesebro & McCroskey, 1998), and more positive affect for both the teacher and the course material (Chesebro, 2003; Chesebro & McCroskey, 2001; Titsworth, 2001b). Students of clear teachers also report that they learn more from their teachers (Chesebro & McCroskey, 2001). Most important, the effect of clarity on actual cognitive learning has been demonstrated in experimental research (Chesebro, 2003; Titsworth, 2001a). Given the consistently positive findings for clarity that exist across various levels of education, it is evident that clear teaching likely is as key in adolescent classrooms as it is in college classrooms.

Teacher confirmation

Rather than being concerned with the delivery or relevance of content, the idea of confirmation is focused more on the quality of interaction between teachers and students on a more relational level. Although confirmation has barely been researched in the instructional context, it is included in this review based on the important role it likely plays in the classroom and the need to research confirmation in the classroom more extensively. Confirming behaviors are those that communicate recognition and acknowledgment of others and therefore offer a validation of others' self-images (Cissna & Sieburg, 1981). Disconfirming responses are those that do not recognize or endorse others as unique or valuable human beings (Ellis, 2000). In the classroom context, an example of confirmation would be listening to and responding thoughtfully to a student question or comment, whereas in the same example, a disconfirming response might include ignoring the comment, ridiculing it, or neglecting to attempt to provide a relevant response.

Cissna and Sieburg (1981) provided a model in which they identified four general types of confirming responses: recognizing the other's existence, acknowledging the presence of a relationship with the other, recognizing the other person's worth, and validating the other person's experiences. Cissna and Sieburg also identified three general types of disconfirming responses: indifference, imperviousness, and disqualification. Indifference involves the variety of ways an individual could ignore someone, ranging from refusing to respond and avoiding eye contact, to interrupting the person or interjecting with irrelevant comments. Imperviousness involves denying the other person's feeling, responding only to comments that meet with our approval, misrepresenting the other person's statement, and denying the importance of the experience being communicated by the other person. Finally, disqualifying responses involve insults of the other person, nonverbal indicators of disapproval or disgust, or providing an equivocal response.

As mentioned, little research has examined confirmation in the classroom. Leth (1977, cited in Ellis, 2000) found that confirming teachers were more likely to have positive relationships with their students and that female instructors were perceived as more confirming than male instructors. More recently, Ellis (2000) more formally and completely introduced the construct to the instructional context. In creating a measure to assess students' perceptions of teacher confirmation, she identified and validated a measure which comprises three factors of confirmation that are relevant to the instructional context: response to questions, demonstrated interest, and teaching style. The 'response to questions' factor involves behaviors such as taking time to answer students' questions, listening attentively to students' questions or comments, and being available for questions before or after class. The 'demonstrated interest' factor includes communicating interest in students' learning, making an effort to get to know students, and asking students informally for feedback on how things with class are going. The 'teaching style' factor involves using an interactive teaching style, checking for student understanding before moving on to new points, and using a variety of teaching techniques. In this study students who perceived their teachers to be more confirming reported greater positive affect for their instructors and the course material and perceived that they learned more than did students from teachers who were perceived to be disconfirming.

Although the literature review of teacher confirmation begins and ends with this single study, the results of this study might stimulate future research, and research in this area could help teachers identify important teaching practices. It is reasonable to expect that teacher confirmation would be just as important, if not more important, with adolescent students. Adolescent students are likely to need even greater validation of their self-concepts and of the comments they make than are college students.

Out-of-class communication

This represents one area identified by Nussbaum and Prusank (1989) that has received some subsequent research attention. This research has shed light on the importance of positive teacher-student out-of-class interactions. For example, informal teacher-student interaction is positively related to student persistence (Pascarella & Terenzini, 1991). Furthermore, research indicates that out-of-class communication is related to increased student feelings of confidence and self-worth (Kuh, 1995), higher educational goals (Pascarella & Terenzini, 1991) and greater academic and cognitive development (Terenzini et al., 1996). Also, the frequency of visits, amount of communication, and communication of informal topics during out-of-class contact are positively related to student perceptions of immediacy and student motivation to learn from a particular instructor (Jaasma & Koper, 1999).

Interestingly, although out-of-class communication between teachers and students appears to be a very important part of education, these interactions are relatively infrequent, at least at the college level (Fusani, 1994; Jaasma & Koper, 1999). When applying these findings to middle- and high-school students, it is worth revisiting Nussbaum and Prusank's (1989) identification of out-of-class communication as likely being a more salient feature of secondary education than of postsecondary education. Therefore, research on out-of-class communication in middle and high schools may reveal that it is more common than it is at the college level. Furthermore, it would be interesting to study the nature and benefits of out-of-class communication at this level. As Nussbaum and Prusank argued, it might be a much more important aspect of education at this level than it is at the college level.

Additional instructional communication variables

A number of additional important behaviors not covered in detail by this chapter also are likely to contribute to the development of strong relationships between teachers and their adolescent students. Some of these behaviors include a teacher's humor (Chesebro & Wanzer, 2005 in press; Wanzer, 2002), a teacher's level of assertiveness and responsiveness (Richmond, 1990), and a teacher's communicator style (Nussbaum, 1992). A study by Downs, Javidi, and Nussbaum (1988) offers some understanding of how some of these behaviors function at various levels of education. The presentation styles of award-winning teachers from college, high school, and middle school were examined in terms of humor, self-disclosure, and the use of narratives. The results indicate that award winning college teachers use humor more than teachers at lower levels and that award-winning middle school teachers use self-disclosure and narratives less than teachers at higher levels. Award-winning teachers at all levels were more verbally active than non-award-winning teachers. This study provides a good synopsis of how instructional communication research is likely to extend beyond the college level, but that some findings might be different due to the different education level.

Additionally, research is beginning to examine the role that student behaviors play in the teacher-student relationship (Mottet, Beebe & Fleuriet, 2005 in press; Mottet & Richmond, 2002). This research has examined student nonverbal immediacy (Baringer & McCroskey, 2000) and students' motives for communicating with their teachers (Martin, Myers & Mottet, 2002).

A framework for all of these skills: Instructional communication theory

For some time, the variables discussed in the previous section have been studied in relative isolation from each other, or at least have not generated a great deal of theory. Addressing this void, Mottet, Frymier, and Beebe (2005 in press) have synthesized much of the instructional communication research and posited three theories to explain communication in instructional contexts. Two of these theories, Rhetorical/Relational Goal Theory, and Relational Power and Instructional Influence Theory, are outlined here. The ways in which these theories might inform teaching in adolescent classrooms also are discussed. Although some of the propositions in these theories are yet to be tested, each theory provides a useful framework through which we can view communication with adolescent students.

Rhetorical/Relational Goal Theory

Rather than focusing on teacher and student behaviors, Rhetorical/Relational Goal Theory focuses on the goals that both students and instructors have for classroom interactions and outcomes. These goals are placed in two general categories: rhetorical goals and relational goals. Rhetorical goals can be thought of as instrumental goals which may involve, for teachers, influencing students, enhancing student learning, or accomplishing other instructional objectives. Relational goals are more concerned with developing good working relationships with students. Students also approach instruction differently, and their goals likely are based on the needs they bring to the classroom. For example, one category of student needs would involve the need for knowledge and achievement. In addition, students also may look to teachers to satisfy relational needs. Based on these distinctions, three propositions of this theory have been extended:

1. Students have both relational and knowledge needs; however, not all students are equally driven by each need. For some students, knowledge needs will dominate, for others relationship needs will dominate, and some students will be equally driven by the two needs.
2. Teachers have both rhetorical and relational goals; however, teachers differ in regard to the emphasis they put on each goal.
3. Teachers at all levels have relational and rhetorical goals; however, the exact nature of those goals and how those goals are accomplished differ with different grade levels and different contexts. Students at all levels have relational and knowledge needs; however, those needs differ in intensity at different ages of development and how those needs are satisfied differs across contexts and stages of development (Mottet, Frymier & Beebe, 2005 in press; see also chapter 13, this volume).

This theory suggests that, to better reach all students in a classroom, teachers should be sensitive both to students' knowledge needs and relational needs, as students are likely to vary in the needs that shape their goals in the classroom. This theory also offers a framework to better understand how instruction in adolescent classrooms may differ from that in college classrooms. Research on differences between the needs of adolescents and young adults can help those who teach adolescents have greater empathy for their students' perspectives. Although the propositions need to be tested in classrooms at different developmental levels, this framework is a step in a promising direction because it signals a greater sensitivity to the differences in classroom communication at various developmental levels.

Relational Power and Instructional Influence Theory

This theory examines the crossroads between two areas of research and the ways in which they intersect with instructional communication research. It examines the relationships between the levels of influence (Kelman, 1958) and bases of power (French & Raven, 1959) others may grant us. According to the theory, the extent to which power is granted to us depends on the verbal and nonverbal messages we use in the classroom to create good working relationships with our students. In outlining this theory, Mottet, Frymier and Beebe (2005 in press) advance three propositions:

1. the teacher-student relationship is similar to other types of interpersonal relationships in that the relationship involves influence;
2. teachers and students influence each other by yielding each other power, which is a by-product of the teacher-student relationship;
3. the quality of the teacher-student relationship is dependent on the types of verbal and nonverbal messages that are exchanged and created between teachers and students.

The levels of influence referenced above can range from being relatively weak and short-lived to strong and longer lasting (Kelman, 1958; McCroskey, 1998). Compliance, a short-lived level of influence, is when an individual is willing to be influenced solely because he or she will be rewarded for complying or punished for not complying. Individuals influenced at the identification level are influenced because they want to establish or maintain a relationship with the person who is influencing them. The longest-term level of influence is internalization, which is when one accepts influence because whatever is being requested is intrinsically rewarding and consistent with her or his value system. Applied to the classroom, a student who will comply with a teacher only if promised a reward or threatened with punishment is being influenced at the compliance level (doing the basic minimum to avoid a bad grade, or caring only about a good grade). A student who complies because he or she likes the teacher and values the teacher-student relationship is under the identification level of influence (the student will purposefully work harder for those teachers with whom he or she can identify). A student who complies because he or she enjoys whatever is being asked and needs little prodding from the teacher is influenced at the internalization level (the student works hard because she or he values the work or achievement involved). From a teacher's perspective, it is clear that there are some advantages when students grant us influence beyond the compliance level.

This theory also considers the various bases of power identified by French and Raven (1959). These five bases represent the kind of power others grant us. When students grant us *legitimate power*, they do so only because we have the title of "teacher" and therefore they know that we have the right to expect certain things of them. Students grant us *coercive power* when they perceive us to be in a position to punish them and *reward power* when they perceive us to be in a position to reward them. Students grant us *expert power* when they perceive us to be competent and knowledgeable when it comes to our course material and teaching. Finally, students grant us *referent power* when the student identifies with and wants to please the teacher.

In their theory, Mottet, Frymier and Beebe (2005, in press) connect bases of power with the levels of influence, arguing that the more pro-social expert and referent bases of power are likely to result in longer lasting influence (identification and internalization). Although this specific relationship has not been tested by researchers, research does indicate that students whose teachers earn expert and referent power bases are at an advantage in terms of desirable instructional outcomes. In a research program known as the 'Power Studies,' McCroskey, Richmond, Kearney and Plax conducted a number of studies to examine the relationships between perceptions of teachers' power and instructional outcomes. Using a sample of 2,600 students ranging from seventh grade through college, Richmond and McCroskey (1984) found that students' perceptions of teachers' referent and expert power were positively related to cognitive and affective learning wheras coercive and legitimate power were negatively related. Subsequent research in this series revealed that the use of pro-social behavior alteration techniques to gain students' compliance was related to students' affective and cognitive learning (Plax & Kearney, 1992). This research provides strong support for Relational Power and Instructional Influence Theory and suggests that this theory applies well both in college and in adolescent classrooms.

By now one may notice that power is being discussed as something that is very relational, as opposed to being a property of one person. This perspective on power has been offered by a number of researchers (Barraclough & Stewart, 1992; Hartnett, 1971). An understanding of this perspective is crucial to truly understanding influence in the classroom, as the level of power our students grant us is likely to increase in proportion to the quality of our relationships with our students (Mottet, Frymier & Beebe, 2005 in press). In other words, the establishment of positive relationships with students is a key to influencing them in any sort of long-term manner.

This emphasis on the importance of the student-teacher relationship is supported by research by Frymier and Houser (2000) and Nussbaum and Scott (1980) that examines student-teacher relationships more specifically. Nussbaum and Scott found that a closer student-teacher relationship (discussed in terms of solidarity) is positively related to affective learning and that a moderately close student-teacher relationship is related to cognitive learning. This study is important because it establishes the links between teacher communication behaviors, the establishment of relationships with students, and important instructional outcomes such as positive affect and cognitive learning. This connection also points to the final aspect of Relational Power and Instructional Influence Theory. The establishment of student-teacher relationships, and therefore bases of power, depends on the verbal and nonverbal messages teachers use in the classroom.

These behaviors are likely to include the ones that have been reviewed in this chapter: teacher immediacy, the relevance and clarity of messages, confirming behavior, and quality of out-of-class communication with students. Interestingly, when examining these behaviors in the context of Rhetorical/Relational Goal Theory (Mottet, Frymier & Beebe, 2005 in press), one can see that some of the above teacher behaviors are devoted to rhetorical goals (relevance, clarity, and any out-of-class communication focused on students' knowledge needs) whereas some behaviors are more oriented toward relational goals (immediacy, confirmation, and some aspects of out-of-class communication).

Still, even the more rhetorical or instrumental behaviors can contribute to a strong student-teacher relationship because most are likely to be related to increased student perceptions of instructor credibility (Sidelinger & McCroskey, 1997; Thweatt & McCroskey, 1998). The student-teacher relationship can be thought of as a professional relationship, comprised both personal and professional concerns. Because credibility involves perceptions of a teacher's competence, character, and good will toward her or his students, it represents the balance of task and personal elements in professional relationships. This helps explain how all of the teacher behaviors reviewed in this chapter can enhance students' perceptions of their instructor's credibility, and therefore contribute to positive professional student-teacher relationships.

Conclusion

This chapter has demonstrated the ways in which instructional communication research has contributed to a greater understanding between teachers and their adolescent students. In the process, it also has identified several areas in which further research is needed to enable us to better understand how teaching at this level is different from teaching at the college level. Still, the benefits of key behaviors such as immediacy, relevance, and clarity are well established, as are the benefits of developing positive working relationships with students. So regardless of the level at which one teaches, we should expect to find the needs to balance instrumental and relational goals and to develop good relationships with students at the heart of effective teaching.

References

Bariger, D. K., & McCroskey, J. C. (2000) Immediacy in the classroom: Student immediacy. *Communication Education*, 48, 178–186.

Barraclough, R. A. & Stewart, R. A. (1992). Power and control: Social science perspectives. In V. P. Richmond & J. C. McCroskey (eds), *Power in the Classroom: Communication, Control, and Concern* (pp. 1–18). Hillsdale, NJ: Lawrence Erlbaum Associates..

Bush, A. J., Kennedy, J. J. & Cruickshank, D. R. (1977). An empirical investigation of teacher clarity. *Journal of Teacher Education*, 28(2), 53–58.

Chesebro, J. L. (2002). Teaching clearly. In J. L. Chesebro & J.C. McCroskey (eds), *Communication for Teachers* (pp. 93–103). Boston, MA: Allyn & Bacon.

Chesebro, J. L. (2003). Effects of teacher clarity and nonverbal immediacy on student learning, receiver apprehension, and affect. *Communication Education, 52*, 135–147.

Chesebro, J. L. & McCroskey, J. C. (1998). The relationship between teacher clarity and immediacy and students' experiences of state receiver apprehension when listening to teachers. *Communication Quarterly*, 46, 446–455.

Chesebro, J. L. & McCroskey, J. C. (2000). The relationship between students' reports of learning and their actual recall of lecture material. *Communication Education*, 49, 297–301.

Chesebro, J. L. & McCroskey, J. C. (2001). The relationship of teacher clarity and immediacy with student state receiver apprehension, affect, and cognitive learning. *Communication Education*, 50, 59–68.

Chesebro, J. L. & Wanzer, M. (2005 in press). Instructional message variables. In T. P. Mottet, V. P. Richmond & J. C. McCroskey (eds), *Handbook of Instructional Communication: Rhetorical and Relational Perspectives*. Boston: Allyn & Bacon.

Christophel, D. (1990). The relationships among teacher immediacy behaviors, student motivation, and learning. *Communication Education*, 39, 323–340.

Cissna, K. N. & Sieberg, E. (1981). Patterns of interactional confirmation and disconfirmation. In C. Wilder-Mott and J. H. Weakland (eds), *Rigor and Imagination: Essays from the Legacy of Gregory Bateson* (pp. 253–282). New York: Praeger.

Civikly, J. M. (1992). Clarity: Teachers and students making sense of instruction. *Communication Education*, 41, 138–152.

Cruickshank, D. R. & Kennedy, J. J. (1986). Teacher clarity. *Teaching & Teacher Education*, 2(1), 43–67.

Daly, J. A. & Vangelisti, A. L. (2003). Skillfully instructing learners: How communicators effectively convey messages. In J. O. Green & B. R. Burelson (eds) *Handbook of Communication and Social Interaction Skills* (pp. 871–908). Mahwah, NJ: Lawrence Erlbaum.

Downs, V. C., Javidi, M. & Nussbaum, J. F. (1988). An analysis of teachers' verbal communication within the college classroom: Use of humor, self-disclosure, and narratives. *Communication Education*, 37, 127–141.

Ellis, K. (2000). Perceived teacher confirmation: The development and validation of an instrument and two studies of the relationship to cognitive and affective learning. *Human Communication Research, 26,* 264–291.

French, J. R. P., Jr. & Raven, B. (1959). The bases of social power. In D. Cartwright (ed.), *Studies in social power* (pp. 150–167). Ann Arbor, MI: University of Michigan Press.

Frymier, A. B. (1994). A model of immediacy in the classroom. *Communication Quarterly, 42,* 133–144.

Frymier, A. B. & Houser, M. L. (1998). Does making content relevant make a difference in learning? *Communication Research Reports, 15,* 121–129.

Frymier, A. B. & Houser, M. L. (2000). The teacher-student relationship as an interpersonal relationship. *Communication Education, 49,* 207–219.

Frymier, A. B. & Shulman, G. M. (1995). 'What's in it for me?': Increasing content relevance to enhance students' motivation. *Communication Education, 44,* 40–50.

Frymier, A. B., Shulman, G. M. & Houser, M. (1996). The development of a learner empowerment measure. *Communication Education, 45,* 181–199.

Fusani, D. S. (1994). "Extra-class" communication: Frequency, immediacy, self-disclosure, and satisfaction in student–faculty interaction outside the classroom. *Journal of Applied Communication Research, 22,* 232–255.

Hartnett, R. T. (1971). Trustee power in America. In H. L. Hodgkinson & L. R. Meeth (eds), *Power and Authority* (pp. 25–28). San Francisco: Jossey Bass.

Hines, C. (1981). *A further investigation of teacher clarity. The observation of teacher clarity and the relationship between clarity and student achievement and satisfaction.* Unpublished doctoral dissertation, Ohio State University.

Hurt, H. T., Scott, M. D. & McCroskey, J. C. (1978). *Communication in the Classroom.* Reading, MA: Addison-Wesley.

Jaasma, M. A. & Koper, R. J. (1999). The relationship of student-faculty out-of-class communication to instructor immediacy and trust and to student motivation. *Communication Education, 48,* 41–47.

Keller, J. M. (1983). Motivational design of instruction. In C. M. Reigeluth (ed.), *Instructional Design Theories: An Overview of Their Current Status* (pp. 383–434). Hillsdale, NJ: Lawrence Erlbaum.

Keller, J. M. (1987). Strategies for stimulating the motivation to learn. *Performance and Instruction, 26* (8), 1–7.

Kelley, D. H. & Gorham, J. (1988). Effects of immediacy on recall of information. *Communication Education, 37,* 198–207.

Kelman, H. C. (1958). Compliance, identification, and internalization: Three processes of attitude change. *Journal of Conflict Resolution, 2,* 51–60.

Kennedy, J., Cruickshank, D., Bush, A. & Myers, B. (1978). Additional investigations into the nature of teacher clarity. *Journal of Educational Research, 72,* 3–10.

Kuh, G. D. (1995). The other curriculum: Out-of-class experiences associated with student learning and personal development. *The Journal of Higher Education, 66,* 123–155.

Langdon, C. & Vesper, N. (2000). Teachers' attitudes toward the public schools. *Phi Delta Kappan*, 81, 607–611.

Leth, P. (1977). *Self-concept and interpersonal response in the classroom: An exploratory study.* Doctoral dissertation, Purdue University.

Martin, M. M., Myers, S. A. & Mottet, T. P. (2002). Students' motives for communicating with their instructors. In J. L. Chesebro & J. C. McCroskey (eds), *Communication for Teachers* (pp. 35–46). Boston: Allyn & Bacon.

McCroskey, J. C. (1998). *An Introduction to Communication in the Classroom.* Acton, MA: Tapestry Press.

McCroskey, J. C. & Richmond, V. P. (1992). Increasing teacher influence through immediacy. In V. P. Richmond and J. C. McCroskey (eds), *Power in the Classroom: Communication, Control, and Concern* (pp. 101–120). Hillsdale, NJ: Lawrence Erlbaum.

Mehrabian, A. (1971). *Silent Messages.* Belmont, CA: Wadsworth.

Messman, S. J. & Jones-Corley, J. (2001). Effects of communication environment, immediacy, and communication apprehension on cognitive and affective learning. *Communication Monographs*, 68, 184–200.

Millette, D. & Gorham, J. (2002). Teacher behavior and student motivation. In J. L. Chesebro & J. C. McCroskey (eds), *Communication for Teachers* (pp. 141–154). Boston: Allyn & Bacon.

Mottet, T. M., Beebe, S. A. & Fleuriet, C. (2005 in press). Students' influence messages. In T. P. Mottet, V. P. Richmond & J. C. McCroskey (eds), *Handbook of Instructional Communication: Rhetorical and Relational Perspectives.* Boston: Allyn & Bacon.

Mottet, T. M., Frymier, A. B. & Beebe, S. A. (2005 in press). Theorizing about instructional communication. In T. P. Mottet, V. P. Richmond & J. C. McCroskey (eds), *Handbook of Instructional Communication: Rhetorical and Relational Perspectives.* Boston, MA: Allyn & Bacon.

Mottet, T. P. & Richmond, V. P. (2002). Student nonverbal communication and its influence on teachers and teaching. In J. L. Chesebro & J. C. McCroskey (eds), *Communication for Teachers* (pp. 47–64). Boston: Allyn & Bacon.

National Center for Education Statistics (2001). *Statistics on School Safety.* Washington, DC: Government Printing Office.

Newby, T. J. (1991). Classroom motivation: Strategies of first-year teachers. *Journal of Educational Psychology*, 83, 195–200.

Nussbaum, J. F. (1992). Communicator style and teacher influence. In V. P. Richmond & J. C. McCroskey (eds), *Power in the Classroom: Communication, Control, and Concern* (pp. 145–158). Hillside, NJ: Erlbaum.

Nussbaum J. F. & Prusank, D. T. (1989). The interface between human development and instructional communication. *Communication Education*, 38, 334–344.

Nussbaum, J. F. & Scott, M. (1980). Student learning as a relational outcome of teacher-student interaction. In D. Nimmo (ed.) *Communication Yearbook 4* (pp. 533–552). New Brunswick, NJ: Transaction.

Pascarella, E. T. & Terenzini, P. T. (1991). *How College Affects Students: Findings and Insights From Twenty Years of Research.* San Francisco, CA: Jossey-Bass.

Perry, R. P. & Penner, K. S. (1990). Enhancing academic achievement in college students through attributional retraining and instruction. *Journal of Educational Psychology*, 82, 262–271.

Plax, T. G. & Kearney, P. (1992). Teacher power in the classroom: Defining and advancing a program of research. In V. P. Richmond & J. C. McCroskey (eds), *Power in the classroom: Communication, control, and concern* (pp. 67–84). Hillsdale, NJ: Lawrence Erlbaum Associates.

Plax, T. G., Kearney, P., McCroskey, J. C. & Richmond, V. P. (1986). Power in the classroom VI: Verbal control strategies, nonverbal immediacy and affective learning. *Communication Education*, 35, 43–55.

Richmond, V. P. (1990). Communication in the classroom: Power and motivation. *Communication Education*, 39, 181–195.

Richmond, V. P. & McCroskey, J. C. (1984). Power in the classroom II: Power and learning. *Communication Education*, 33, 125–136.

Richmond, V. P. & McCroskey, J. C. (2000a). The impact of supervisor and subordinate immediacy on relational and organizational outcomes. *Communication Monographs*, 67, 85–95.

Richmond, V. P. & McCroskey, J. C. (2000b). *Nonverbal Behavior in Interpersonal Relations* (4th edition). Needham Heights, MA: Allyn & Bacon.

Richmond, V. P., Smith, R. S., Jr., Heisel, A. D. & McCroskey, J. C. (2001). Immediacy in the physician/patient relationship. *Communication Research Reports*, 18, 211–216.

Sidelinger, R. J. & McCroskey, J. C. (1997). Communication correlates of teacher clarity in the college classroom. *Communication Research Reports*, 14, 1–10.

Terenzini, P. T., Pascarella, E. T. & Blimling, G. S. (1996). Students' out-of-class experiences and their influence on learning and cognitive development: A literature review. *Journal of College Student Development*, 37, 149–162.

Thweatt, K. S. & McCroskey, J. C. (1998). The impact of teacher immediacy and misbehaviors on teacher credibility. *Communication Education*, 47, 348–358.

Titsworth, B. (2001a). The effects of teacher immediacy, use of organizational lecture cues, and students' notetaking on cognitive learning. *Communication Education*, 50, 283–298.

Titsworth, B. (2001b). Immediate and delayed effects of interest cues and engagement cues on students' affective learning. *Communication Studies*, 52, 169–179.

Wanzer, M. B. (2002). Use of humor in the classroom: The good, the bad, and the not-so-funny things that teachers say and do. In J. L. Chesebro & J. C. McCroskey (eds), *Communication for Teachers* (pp. 116–125). Boston: Allyn & Bacon.

Witt, P. L. & Wheeless, L. R. (1999). Nonverbal communication expectancies about teachers and enrollment behavior in distance learning. *Communication Education*, 48, 149–154.

15

Communication and 'risky' behavior in adolescence

Susan McKay

As is apparent throughout this book, the social construction of adolescence as a period of adjustment in the transition between childhood and adulthood has important consequences for the ways in which young people are viewed by others and how young people think about themselves. This is particularly the case in matters related to personal health. The teenage years are a healthy time for most, with a relatively low incidence of chronic disease, in contrast with other periods such as infancy and old age. According to the 'storm and stress' approach to understanding adolescence, it is also a time of uncertainty, even volatility, when young people experiment, rebel and take risks through potentially health-damaging activities such as violent behavior, consumption of alcohol and drugs, smoking, risky driving and unprotected sexual activity. As a result, many of the major threats to young people's health and well-being, especially those adolescent activities which concern adult society, are social, environmental and behavioral in origin, rather than disease-based, and as such are considered preventable (Millstein & Litt, 1990: 433).

The literature certainly supports the prevalence of 'risky' behaviors in this age group, listing not wearing seat belts, driving too fast without due attention, taking drugs, smoking, drinking to excess, and having unprotected sex as important factors which impinge on the health status of young people. Many of these, of course, represent the inconsistencies in expectations that adults have for health behavior for young people as opposed to those that have more social acceptance in older groups. A range of models have been used to explain these risky behaviors, which are said to characterize adolescence along with a similarly broad range of risk reduction or intervention strategies (see for example, Jessor, 1998; Romer, 2003; Coleman & Hendry, 1999; Feldman & Elliott, 1990; DiClemente *et al.*, 1996). However, as Kelly (2000) warns, we need to be careful about the ways in which expert knowledge itself can produce discourses that in turn construct a category of 'youth-at-risk' as a normative truth. For Kelly, the identification of adolescence in terms of 'deviancy, delinquency and deficit' (2000: 466) and its accompanying youth-at-risk discourse provide governments and other regulators with the opportunity to regulate young people's behavior, and to structure preferred outcomes through direct policing policies such as increased surveillance of public spaces, or by provoking new interventions based on professional concerns about youth welfare. Although the popular labeling of this group has profound implications for the regulatory authorities referred to by Kelly, there are considerations for researchers here too. Kelly sees a danger in the microanalysis of adolescent behaviors and young people's activities, especially those categorized as risky, because they problematize, even catastrophize, adolescent behaviors and dispositions, preempting increasingly sophisticated regulation and intervention strategies. Although it would be drawing a rather long bow to say that studies like those reported in this chapter could lead to an increasing mesh of social control, Kelly's argument serves to warn of the dangers of isolating a group as diverse as young people and then categorizing them as 'at risk.'

The concept of risk does not belong only within the sphere of young people. At a more general level, expectations of experiencing good health over a lengthening lifespan have resulted in the identification of a huge raft of potential 'harms' as a variety of environmental and individual factors threaten our existence. We have become preoccupied with risk to the extent that we live in what Giddens (1991: 115) has termed a 'climate of risk' or in what Beck has described as 'risk society' (1992: 19) so that risks seem to be everywhere; they pervade everything we do or everything we might think we want to do. This is not to say that we are living in time more dangerous than other periods of human history, but rather that we have a concept of risk that was unknown in the past, when dangers were a given and could be traced back to acts of God or to fate itself (Giddens, 1998). Modern ideologies of prevention have become associated with the absolute eradication of risk, and in the process a range of new risks are constructed as targets for intervention (Castel, 1991). Risk and the discussion of how risk is communicated and how it might be reduced is an important part of any reflection on communication and health, but is especially so where young people are concerned, given the degree to which as a group they are deemed to be 'at risk.'

With that in mind, this chapter now turns to the traditional adolescent risk domains which reinforce the notion of adolescence as a period of volatility and vulnerability before discussing some of the ways in which communication issues fit into these risk patterns from the perspective of both how communication factors might predict risky behaviors, and how communication might mitigate their effects. It will discuss the influence of families and peers, and the effectiveness of intervention campaigns. Before this, I need to outline briefly the customary categories of young people's behavior to demonstrate the extent to which they have been constructed as an 'at-risk' group.

Risky behavior among young people: Traditional risk domains

The major causes of death among this age group are usually attributed to social, environmental or behavioral factors (or even a mix of these) rather than to disease. Indeed, accidents, suicide and homicide account for 75 percent of adolescent deaths in the United States (Millstein & Litt, 1990, Kann *et al.*, 2000). In addition, behaviors such as violence, substance use and abuse, unprotected sex, poor diet and physical inactivity rate strongly as causes of morbidity among young people and can have considerable impact on the life course not only of the young people themselves, but of their families and friends, as well as a wider financial and social cost.

In 1990, the Centers for Disease Control and Prevention (CDC)[2] in the United States implemented an ongoing risk behavior survey (the High School Youth Risk Behavior Survey) to collect national data on specific health-related behaviors among young people which were seen to be contributing to the main causes of death, disease, disability, and social problems in that age group. The survey identifies and monitors six categories of health risk behaviors among young people/young adults using national, state and local samples:

- behaviors that contribute to intentional or unintentional injuries;
- tobacco use;
- alcohol and other drug use;
- sexual behavior that leads to unintended pregnancy and sexually transmitted diseases;
- unhealthy dietary behaviors; and
- physical inactivity.

The importance of recognizing these behaviors is emphasized in much of the research into adolescent health, an important assumption being that some of these risk behaviors may continue into adult life and become established as part of adult lifestyle. These behaviors, established during adolescence, are interrelated and often preventable (Kann *et al.*, 2000). These categories form the routine domains for research into adolescent health risk behaviors and are of most concern to government and community as presented in the recent literature (far less attention has been paid to more structural forms of risk related to the effects of war, political oppression, hunger and poverty, all of which can also affect health in this group). They reinforce the notion of adolescence as a 'vulnerable' time. More than that, research into these behaviors underpins many stereotypical understandings of young people as 'at-risk.' Although problems associated with adolescence dominate this research, I do not want to overemphasize the incidence of risk-taking behaviors. In spite of media coverage to the contrary, many, if not most, young people do not use drugs, fall pregnant, or fail at school (Scales, 2001). Many adolescent risk-taking behaviors are occasional rather than regular, and their outcomes are transitory rather than permanent (Steinberg & Morris, 2001).

Communication influences on risk behaviors

Having established the main adolescent risk-taking categories related to adolescent health, this section now turns to the findings of research more directly related to communication and language, and where communicative strategies fit into adolescent risk patterns especially through the influence of families and peer pressure. Apart from research into the immediate social realm of families and friends, the influence of media messages and the design of health intervention campaigns have come under scrutiny as the adolescent health care field has shifted its emphasis on detection, diagnosis and treatment to take more account of educating young people about their health and preventing illness and injury. Sources of reliable health information need to be available and must be sensitively supplied, taking account of age gradations, gender, ethnicity and subcultural differences. Media campaigns and health interventions relating to risk, and targeting health messages at young people, need to be carefully designed if they are not to alienate at-risk groups.

The role of the health care provider shifts during adolescence in two different ways. Because the causes of morbidity and mortality are regarded as primarily social (rather than organic or infectious) in this age group, the emphasis moves away from clinicians to initiatives that are school- or community-focused. When young people do consult a health professional, the context they find themselves in has shifted from a pediatric model, which is centered on the parent toward a more autonomous adult model. Young people may see their doctors and other health professionals with or without their parents. It is a time of transition in which disclosure, consent, and confidentiality issues suddenly become more salient, especially for sensitive health issues or those with special needs (Blum *et al.*, 1993; Geenen *et al.*, 2003).

Research into adolescent health and health risk, therefore, covers a broad field including aspects of interpersonal communication skills, assessment of communication effectiveness and evaluation of information sources and although these underpin health communication research across the lifespan, they are especially evident in research into adolescent risk behavior. Not surprisingly, underlying much of this research is an assumption that improved communication may result in improved health outcomes (and less risky behavior) for this group. Few of the studies claim to find a single variable explanation of adolescent risk behavior and many studies go even further and show that adolescent risk behaviors often cluster together. They emphasize the complexity of the influences on adolescent risk behavior and offer insights into how communication might mitigate the consequences of young people's risk behaviors.

However, this work comes with its own difficulties. As discussed in an earlier chapter [see Thurlow & Marwick—chapter 4, this volume] and indeed as has been apparent throughout this edited collection, 'communication' as a term, together with what it covers, can be contested at best and is vaguely indeterminate at worst. This is particularly the case when trying to unpack notions of communication related to risk issues when communication is measured by self-reported perceptions. The literature is full of problematic references to 'good' and 'bad' communication, or to 'good' relationships and 'openness'; to references to 'support' on one hand (usually in relation to families), or to 'pressure' on the other (usually in the context of peer groups), where notions of communication are implied rather than made explicit; and to intervention campaigns or educational programs where 'communication' is not mentioned at all.

On a different level, research into young people's health issues and especially into communication and risk-taking behaviors poses other problems. Although many researchers will experience difficulty in obtaining personal disclosures, there is evidence to suggest that sensitive topics, such as those laid out above, may be especially difficult for young people to discuss frankly, not only among their peers but with their families, medical personnel and even with researchers (Hern *et al.*, 1998). Self-reporting of sexual behavior in particular has been criticized, with sexual experiences in this age group over-reported by males and under-reported by females (Karofsky *et al.*, 2001), making it even harder to draw connections between what young people do and what they report they do.

Rather than being focused on a checklist of the six risk behavior categories listed earlier, this section is organized around some examples of recent research that link issues of communication to adolescent risk behaviors. The scope of this chapter does not permit more than a superficial glance at this body of work. The studies included here cover a variety of disciplines and methodologies, denoting the range of researchers interested in this area and exemplifying some of the directions in current research. What is apparent is the strong theme of the influence of families and peers as predictors of risky behavior.

Communication in families

The role of the family is central in much of the work on communication and young people [see Noller—chapter 12, this volume]. Research has used various constructs of family environment including family conflict, role models, parental monitoring, and family cohesion or attachment to investigate the effect of the family on adolescent behavior. In spite of media messages to the contrary, there is little evidence to support the existence of serious intergenerational conflicts within families, with researchers reporting mainly good relationships between parents and teenagers (Coleman & Hendry, 1999: 78–81), but there is evidence to suggest that the quality of communication between young people and their parents varies across social background, age and religious beliefs (Noller & Callan, 1991). However, not surprisingly perhaps, the literature on parenting across a range of variables including time, ethnic groups and socioeconomic status suggests that parental communication which clearly articulates parental expectations and values has a strong preventive influence on risk behavior (Stanton & Burns, 2003; Romer, 2003).

Some families, of course, do have serious difficulties in parent-teen relationships. Hurd *et al.* (1999), reporting on parent relationships with young people who were depressed or who self-harmed, found that self-harmers had the least satisfactory relationship with their parents and had more conflict with their mothers. The same study showed that nonclinical controls reported better relationships with their parents with more communication and less conflict than was reported by the clinical subjects. Groholt *et al.* (2000) studied young people who had either attempted suicide and had been hospitalized, or who had reported suicide attempts. Their work recommended that prevention of adolescent suicide needed to center on dealing with depression and with feelings of low self-worth along with improving family communication. Although the risk factors associated with drug abuse are also many and varied, many studies list poor communication with parents as an indicator of risk (for example, see

Lloyd, 1998). In a study of drug use, Spooner (1999), in her review of a range of studies, reported family communication, especially blaming and criticism, as among a wide range of factors contributing to drug abuse by young people.

Just as parental communication has been studied as a predictor of risky behaviors such as self-harming or taking drugs, adolescent-parent relationships and communication are much studied aspects of sexual risk-taking behavior too. Rosenthal and Feldman (1999) found that the young people in their Australian study held little regard for their parents' advice on private sexual matters but that parents had a much more important role in communicating about sexual safety.

Young people who perceive they have strong levels of communication with their parents are less likely to engage in sexual intercourse (Karofsky et al., 2001), and more likely to use effective contraception (Crosby et al., 2001). Empirical research on the role of families (including communication about sexuality and safe sex behavior) in the prevention of HIV risk behaviors has been recently reviewed by Perrino et al. (2000). Their review found that positive and open parent-adolescent communication about sex and condom use protected young people from sexual risk taking, but that the timing of the communication was important. Not only do discussions about sexual behavior need to be developmentally appropriate, but they need to precede first sexual experience (Perrino et al., 2000).

Research into diet behaviors and disorders also uses measures of communication. Moreno et al. (2000) found that females with disordered eating behavior had poorer communication with their mothers, although young women with anorexia had better communication with their mothers than those with bulimia or those who were obese. There were no differences reported in communication with fathers. However, another study into family communication, family support and obesity in adolescence (Valtolina & Marta, 1998) found no differences between obese and nonobese young people with respect to levels of communication with their mothers and fathers and to support given and received from them, nor was there any difference between parents of obese young people and parents of normal-weight young people regarding openness and problems in communication. In terms of risk, the relationship with mothers was important for both obese and nonobese young people, but for the latter group, both support and communication were important, whereas for the obese young people only support appeared to be really important.

Communication between young people and their parents appears to be an important factor in adolescent risk research, but as these examples demonstrate, the story is not clear-cut and it may be only one factor among many.

Communication with peers

Although the relationship young people have with their peers is usually constructive as they move away from relying on their families to developing a more autonomous identity, the notion of peer pressure has become an expedient (if overly simplistic) explanation for some adolescent behaviors (Coleman & Hendry, 1999). It is reported as a significant factor in both smoking (Pearson & Michell, 2000) and alcohol consumption (Coffey *et al.*, 2000). Caprara *et al.* (1998), for example, tested young people's perceptions of ability to resist peer pressure for high-risk activities. Their study found that young people reporting a strong sense of resisting negative peer influences and a low engagement in substance abuse or delinquent conduct, also reported open communication with parents about activities outside the home. Being able to say 'no' is a skill that young people learn, but it seems that there are gender effects. Charlton *et al.* (1999) examined the refusal skills of English secondary school students and reported that although girls were at greater risk of being offered a cigarette repeatedly, they were more likely than boys to accept it after more than two offers. Using a self-perception profile, their study showed that girls with high self-perception scores for all domains except social competence were at lowest risk of being offered a cigarette, whereas for boys this was only applicable in behavioral conduct. Incidentally, the factor most strongly related to multiple offers of cigarettes was having a best friend who smoked. Young people who had never smoked were most likely to have simply said 'No, thank you' to proffered cigarettes but most had used several responses, with boys tending to use more refusal mechanisms.

Cotterell (1996) demonstrates the cultural importance given to drinking and drinking contexts in Western societies as a means to acquire adult status. According to Cotterell, drinking, like smoking, is viewed by young people as socially sophisticated. Adolescent drinking, especially binge drinking, can be linked to particular contexts such as parties and social gatherings where peer pressure seems to be particularly influential. The main motives promoting excessive consumption revolve around benefits such as overcoming shyness or improving social relationships with the opposite sex. Cotterell describes contexts for Australian students at the end-of-school celebration and at Orientation Week prior to commencing university, where drinking is an end in itself and where peer pressure to 'have a couple' and not to be 'wowsers' is quite strong. Many of these activities may be symbolic as young people try to model what they perceive to be adult patterns of behavior or they may be a way of gaining acceptance in a peer group (Coleman & Hendry, 1999).

Investigations into peer influence and peer norms sometimes produce unusual results. Although peer influence has been widely accepted as a strong predictor of adolescent drug use, peer behavior and not verbal persuasion, is more influential in some situations. In a study of injection practices of active adolescent drug users, Hawkins *et al.* (1999) found that those who had observed their peers engaging in safer injection practices were more likely to report lower incidences of sharing unclean needles and more likely to always clean needles. On the other hand, verbal persuasion about reducing HIV risk was not associated with reduced risk behavior and, indeed, peer encouragement to clean needles was likely to increase the risk of sharing unclean needles.

A different aspect of peer communication relates to research into safe sex practices. For example, high risk male young people do not necessarily discuss their concerns about sexually transmitted diseases with their partners. Roberts *et al.* (2000) report that although most subjects in their study were concerned about acquiring an STD from their partner, and most knew where to obtain treatment, less than half had discussed contraception or HIV. Lock *et al.* (1998) also looked at how young people discussed sexual risk behavior with partners. Their study found that women usually initiated safe sex discussions, but that men were willing to talk about it once the topic was started. Cobb (1997) too reports research in this area. Her study showed that young women who asked their new sexual partner about their disease risk status were more likely to practise safer sexual practices.

Although parent or peer communication was seen as a vital element in many of the studies and as a prerequisite for limiting risky behavior, other work has highlighted the importance of effective communication between young people and those who work as health-related external service providers. Hern *et al.* (1998) reported a small study on young people who had been admitted to hospital as a result of trauma injuries and who then had difficulty talking about sensitive topics such as their substance use. They noted differences in the young people's self-reports of substance use and the reports from their parents. They recommended several strategies for conducting research on sensitive topics, including the need to modify the approaches used for adults and the need to design what they term more 'adolescent-friendly instruments,' such as asking nonthreatening questions, protecting confidentiality and using an empathic interviewing style.

Peer influence, like the influence of families, is taken as an important factor in predicting and/or preventing risky behaviors. Educative programs and intervention campaigns play a role as well.

Communication through intervention campaigns

The results of prevention efforts to decrease risk taking among young people are often disappointing (Spooner & Hall, 2002; D'Amico & Fromme, 2002). Although young people themselves are often quite well informed about risk prevention, many of them fail to act accordingly (Greene *et al.*, 2000). As with other health promotion initiatives, health campaigns directed at young people need to appeal to their target groups and not just be based on improving information and knowledge about risk taking. Steinberg (2003) argues that adolescent risk taking is not necessarily due to a lack of perception and knowledge about risks but to immature judgment. By the age of 16, young people perceive and appraise risks as well as adults do, at least as reported in decision-making studies and risk-taking questionnaires. Yet, out of the controlled environment of research studies, they still take risks because, he says, they are less emotionally mature, more susceptible to peer pressure, less future-oriented and less able to control their impulses.

'Just say no' campaigns aimed at young people may have limited success for risk behaviors, such as drinking, that are normative for adults. Aspects of social or cultural identity including age, class, gender and ethnicity need to be considered along with other more personal determinants. HIV awareness campaigns need to take account of gender and culture, especially for adolescent mothers. Lourie *et al.* (1998) found that although the inner-city adolescent mothers in their study had basic knowledge about HIV, they also held common misconceptions. The study concludes that culturally relevant, gender-specific interventions and the promotion of assertive condom use need to be part of HIV prevention communication. Antismoking advertisements and campaigns also have difficulty on occasion conveying their message to young people. Shevalier (2000) suggests that using stereotypes of age, class and gender in tobacco education literature needs to be carefully considered to take account of subcultural contexts, especially for at-risk young people. This is particularly apparent in work such as that of Chapel *et al.* (1999) on antigang television advertising. They used the opinion of young people living in a gang environment to come up with advertising strategies with anti-gang messages to appeal to this subgroup.

Other studies indicate that interventions should target groups from specific sociodemographic backgrounds identified as those at risk: for example, occasional smokers as the group of young people more likely to succeed in smoking cessation programs (Holmen *et al.*, 2000); or early maturing girls as the at-risk group for developing bulimia (Kaltiala-Heino *et al.*, 2001). Peer support too may be an important factor in health promotion (Turner, 1999). Carroll, Hebbert and Roy (1999) report a youth-driven violence prevention project in several Canadian schools which used midday discussion and the production of an interactive television talk show to increase awareness of violence and violence prevention. However, the influence of peers in relation to health campaigns needs to be treated carefully. Cotterell (1996) recognizes the value of peer relationships but warns against attempts which center on teaching young people to resist peer pressure. Such programs, he argues, may have only limited success, and rather than try to engender self-control and resistance skills, they need to recognize the social awareness and social skills that young people already have.

Demonstrable behavioral change is very difficult to achieve using media messages in health campaigns. Shanahan *et al.* (2000) reviewed Australian mass media campaigns which addressed young people's risk taking and judged campaigns to be effective if they increased levels of awareness rather than behavioral change. They found that effective campaigns paid a great deal of attention to their target audience, clearly identifying who they were, their attitudes and motivations and what they perceived to be risk taking and not risk taking, They note that some young people will not respond to media campaigns at all and that other means, such as comics or community-based activities, might be needed.

Other studies have suggested more unusual factors in designing and evaluating health promotion messages. Greene *et al.* (1996) make a predictive link between measures of egocentrism and adolescent risk behavior that can be utilized in health promotion messages. The results from their study demonstrate that egocentrism can predict intentions to avoid risk behaviors. As young people learn to understand more about their peers and understand that others are not always thinking about them, they can develop the confidence to behave in ways that differ from peer expectations. Greene and her colleagues suggest that health promotion interventions that promote thinking and generate alternatives to risk-taking behaviors may be more useful than messages which give answers and knowledge or merely scare young people. Language may also predict those at risk. Krizek *et al.* (1993) have suggested that the language young people use may indicate potential risky behavior such as drinking or taking drugs. Their study showed that patterns of language such as themes and metaphors elicited in interviews with high school students about expectations and attitudes to drugs and alcohol could be used to predict those at risk. They suggest that the language of those at low to medium risk of taking drugs or alcohol be used in prevention messages aimed at younger children to prevent the onset of drug involvement.

Young people's propensity for excitement and sensation can also be used in media messages and health promotion. Donohew *et al.* (1998) noted a strong connection between sensation-seeking behavior and risk taking in this group. Using this connection, their work on televised antidrug campaigns suggests that those with a high need for sensation and novelty require unusual messages or novel formats to hold their attention, such as those which are exciting or stimulating, graphic or explicit, ambiguous, unconventional, fast paced or suspenseful (1998: 459). However, there is also evidence to suggest that young people value realism in health messages targeted at them. Andsager *et al.* (2001) surveyed American college students for their responses to alcohol advertisements and antidrinking public service announcements, finding that the public service announcements seemed too negative to be realistic and were not particularly relevant to them.

Whether new health promotion initiatives and more closely targeted intervention strategies will be effective in reducing risk behaviors remains to be seen. Many of the programs reported to date relate to isolated measures, associated with specific adolescent risk behaviors. It would seem that more work remains to be done on integrating the findings with a view to a more systematic approach to addressing the whole network of adolescent risk behaviors and their consequences.

The role of communication in health and risk for young people

So, what is the role of communication in the study of adolescence, health and risk? The research outline above suggests that communication within families (in all its guises as good, bad, strong, weak, supportive, high levels, low levels, relevant, well-timed etc.) has been used as a predictor of risk, although what is meant by 'communication' is not always made explicit. The influence of peers is used extensively as well, with peer pressure as a predictor of negative outcomes associated with risk, and peer support as an indicator of positive outcomes associated with resistance and prevention. The design and evaluation of health promotion campaigns and media messages are also important in developing health awareness and risk reduction in young people.

Moore and Parsons (2000) outline some of the work still to be done and note the need to encourage more use of qualitative methodologies to generate new quantitative studies. Silbereisen (1998) sets out an agenda for future research based on the following: a new emphasis on the person rather than on the behavior; a distinction between development trajectories as precursors of risk behaviors; an increasing awareness of biological determinants; and a new emphasis on the importance of contexts. Communication and language research can take on some of these dimensions too. In particular, there is a need for more qualitative work to inform and expand the quantitative studies, and the existing work on the importance of contexts needs to be encouraged. In addition, more work needs to be done on how risky behavior is promoted, reinforced and sustained especially through in-groups and subcultures with the view to designing appropriate and effective intervention strategies. Interventions through health promotion and other education campaigns continue to need to be evaluated for their effectiveness at either the individual or the community level (or both). The new research starting to appear on young people's use of the Internet to access health information (e.g., Borzekowski & Rickert, 2001) may lead to other fruitful lines of inquiry. Research too is still needed into health care delivery systems and the degree to which they satisfy the needs of young people.

However, Kelly's (2000) argument as outlined at the beginning of this chapter is a timely one. We do need to be careful in undertaking this work that we do not contribute further to the construction of the category of youth-at-risk as an uncritical norm for understanding young people's health issues and its accompanying youth-at-risk discourse. The media are accused of marginalizing this group and framing it in negative terms [e.g., see Wyn—chapter 2, this volume]. There is danger in close scrutiny of young people's activities, especially those categorized as risky, because it may pathologize adolescent behaviors as different from those of other social groups. One alternative, which does not completely solve the dilemma but certainly gives a wider perspective, is to endeavor to move away from the risk behavior research paradigm and to put communication research into adolescent health into a more natural context, by integrating it with similar research into other groups so that adolescence becomes seen as just another transitional life stage and adolescent risk behavior as just one element of the more general risk culture which characterizes the societies in which we live.

Notes

1.   This work was originally undertaken for the International Association of Language and Social Psychology's *Task Force on Adolescence Report* (2001–2002), and an earlier, abbreviated version was published in *JLSP Special Edition on Adolescence* (2003) as 'Adolescent Risk Behaviors and Communication Research: Current Directions.'

2.   Details about the US surveys and archives of the results can be accessed online via the CDC website at <http://www.cdc.gov/nccdphp/dash/yrbs/index.htm>.

References

Andsager, J., Weintraub Austin, E. & Pinkleton, B. (2001). Questioning the value of realism: Young adults' processing of messages in alcohol-related public service announcements and advertising. *Journal of Communication* 5, 121–142.

Beck, U. (1992). *Risk Society: Towards a New Modernity*. Trans. Mark Ritter. London: Sage.

Blum, R., Garell, D., Hodgman, C., Jorrisen, T. W., Okinow, N. A., Orr, D. P. & Slap, G. B. (1993). Transition from child-centered to adult health care systems for adolescents with chronic conditions. *Journal of Adolescent Health*, 14, 570–576.

Borzekowski, D. & Rickert, V. (2001). Adolescent cybersurfing for health information: A new resource that crosses barriers. *Archives of Pediatrics & Adolescent Medicine*, 155, 813–817.

Caprara, G., Scabini, E., Barbaranelli, C., Pastorelli, C., Regalia, C. & Bandura, A. (1998). Impact of adolescents' perceived self-regulatory efficacy on familial communication and antisocial conduct. *European Psychologist*, 3, 125–132.

Carroll, G. B., Hebbert, D. M. C. & Roy, J. M. (1999). Youth action strategies in violence prevention. *Journal of Adolescent Health*, 25, 7–13.

Castel, R. (1991). From dangerousness to risk. In G. Burchell, C. Gordon & P. Miller (eds), *The Foucault Effect: Studies in Governmentality* (pp. 281–298). Chicago: University of Chicago Press.

Chapel, G., Peterson, K. M. & Joseph, R. (1999). Exploring anti-gang advertisements: Focus group discussions with gang members and at-risk youth. *Journal of Applied Communication Research*, 27, 237–257.

Charlton, A., Minagawa, K. & While, D. (1999). Saying 'no' to cigarettes: A reappraisal of adolescent refusal skills. *Journal of Adolescence*, 22, 695–707.

Cobb, B. K. (1997). Communication types and sexual protective practices of college women. *Public Health Nursing*, 14, 293–301.

Coffey, C., Lynskey, M., Wolfe, R. & Patton, G. C. (2000). Initiation and progression of cannabis use in a population-based Australian adolescent longitudinal study. *Addiction*, 95, 1679–1690.

Coleman, J. & Hendry, L. (1999). *The Nature of Adolescence*. London: Routledge.

Cotterell. J. (1996). *Social Networks and Social Influences in Adolescence*. London: Routledge.

Crosby, R. A., DiClemente, R. J., Wingood, G. M., Sionean, C., Cobb, B. K., Harrington, K., Davies S. L., Hook, E. W III. & Oh, M. K. (2001). Correlates of using dual methods for sexually transmitted diseases and pregnancy prevention among high-risk African-American female teens. *Journal of Adolescent Health*, 28, 410–414.

D'Amico, E. & Fromme, K. (2002). Brief prevention for adolescent risk-taking behavior. *Addiction*, 97, 563–574.

DiClemente, R., Hansen, W. & Ponton, L. (eds). (1996). *Handbook of Adolescent Health Risk Behavior*. New York: Plenum Press.

Donohew, L., Lorch, E. P. & Palmgreen, P. (1998). Applications of a theoretic model of information exposure to health interventions. *Human Communication Research*, 24, 454–468.

Feldman, S. & Elliott, G. (eds). (1990). *At the Threshold: The Developing Adolescent.* Cambridge, MA: Harvard University Press.

Geenen, S. J, Powers L. E., & Sells, W. (2003). Understanding the role of health care providers during the transition of adolescents with disabilities and special health care needs. *Journal of Adolescent Health*, 32, 225–233.

Giddens, A. (1991). *Modernity and Self-identity: Self and Society in the Late Modern Age.* Palo Alto, CA: Stanford University Press.

Giddens, A. (1998). Risk society: The context of British politics. In J. Franklin (ed.), *The Politics of Risk Society* (pp. 23–34). Cambridge: Polity Press.

Greene, K., Krcmar, M., Walters, L. H., Rubin, D. L., Hale, J. & Hale, L. (2000). Targeting adolescent risk-taking behaviors: The contributions of egocentrism and sensation-seeking. *Journal of Adolescence*, 23, 439–461.

Greene, K., Rubin, D. L., Hale, J. L. & Walters, L. H. (1996). The utility of understanding adolescent egocentrism in designing health promotion messages. *Health Communication*, 8, 131–152.

Groholt, B., Ekeberg, O., Wichstrom, L. & Haldorsen, T. (2000). Young suicide attempters: A comparison between a clinical and an epidemiological sample. *Journal of the American Academy of Child and Adolescent Psychiatry*, 39, 868–875.

Hawkins, W. E., Latkin, C., Mandel, W. & Oziemkowska, M. (1999). Do actions speak louder than words? Perceived peer influences on needle sharing and cleaning in a sample of injection drug users. *AIDS Education and Prevention*, 11, 122–131.

Hern, M., Miller, M., Sommers, M. & Dyehouse, J. (1998). Sensitive topics and adolescents: Making research about risk behaviors happen. *Issues in Comprehensive Pediatric Nursing*, 21, 173–186.

Holmen, T. L., Barrett-Connor, E., Holmen, J. & Bjermer, L. (2000). Adolescent occasional smokers, a target group for smoking cessation? The Nord-Trondelag Health Study, Norway, 1995–1997. *Preventive Medicine*, 31, 682–690.

Hummert, M. L. & Nussbaum, J. (eds). (2001). *Aging, Communication, and Health: Linking Research and Practice for Successful Aging.* Mahwah, NJ : Lawrence Erlbaum Associates.

Hurd, K. P., Wooding, S. & Noller, P. (1999). Parent-adolescent relationships in families with depressed and self-harming adolescents. *Journal of Family Studies*, 5, 47–68.

Jessor, R. (1998). New perspectives on adolescent risk behavior. In R. Jessor (ed.), *New Perspectives on Adolescent Risk Behavior* (pp. 1–10). Cambridge: Cambridge University Press.

Kaltiala-Heino, R., Rimpela, M., Rissanen, A. & Rantanen, P. (2001). Early puberty and early sexual activity are associated with bulimic-type eating pathology in middle adolescence. *Journal of Adolescent Health*, 28, 346–352.

Kann, L., Kinchen, S. A., Williams, B. I., Ross, J. G., Lowry, R., Grunbaum, J. A. & Kolbe, L. J. (2000). Youth risk behavior surveillance—United States, 1999. *Journal of School Health*, 70, 271–285.

Karofsky, P. S., Zeng, L. & Kosorok, M. R. (2001). Relationship between adolescent-parental communication and initiation of first intercourse by adolescents. *Journal of Adolescent Health*, 28, 41–45.

Kelly, P. (2000). The dangerousness of youth-at-risk: The possibilities of surveillance and intervention in uncertain times. *Journal of Adolescence, 23,* 463–476.

Krizek, R., Hecht, M. & Miller, M. (1993). Language as an indicator of risk in the prevention of drug use. *Journal of Applied Communication* 21, 245–262.

Lloyd, C. (1998). Risk factors for problem drug use: Identifying vulnerable groups. *Drugs: Education, Prevention and Policy,* 5, 217–232.

Lock, S. E., Ferguson, S. L. & Wise, C. (1998). Communication of sexual risk behavior among late adolescents. *Western Journal of Nursing Research,* 20, 273–294.

Lourie, K. J., Brown, L. K., Flanagan, P., High, P., Kumar, P. & Davis, S. (1998). Teens, tots and condoms: HIV prevention and cultural identity among young adolescent mothers. *International Journal of Adolescent Medicine and Health,* 10, 119–128.

Millstein, S. & Litt, I. (1990). Adolescent health. In S. Feldman & G. Elliott (eds) *At the Threshold: The Developing Adolescent* (pp. 431–456). Cambridge, MA: Harvard University Press.

Moore, S. & Parsons, J. (2000). A research agenda for adolescent risk-taking: Where do we go from here? *Journal of Adolescence,* 23, 371–376.

Moreno, J.K., Selby, M.J., Aved, K. & Besse, C. (2000). Differences in family dynamics among anorexic, bulimic, obese and normal women. *Journal of Psychotherapy in Independent Practice,* 1, 75–87.

Noller, P. & Callan, V. (1991). *The Adolescent in the Family.* London: Routledge.

Pearson, M. & Michell, L. (2000). Smoke rings: Social network analysis of friendship groups, smoking and drug-taking. *Drugs:Education Prevention and Policy,* 7, 21–37.

Perrino, T., Gonzalez, S. A., Pantin, H. & Szapocznik, J. (2000). The role of families in adolescent HIV prevention: A review. *Clinical Child and Family Psychology Review,* 3, 81–96.

Roberts, J., Boker, J. R., Oh, M. K. & DiClemente, R. J. (2000). Health care service use and sexual communication: Past experience and future intention of high-risk male adolescents. *Journal of Adolescent Health,* 27, 298–301.

Romer, D. (ed). 2003. *Reducing Adolescent Risk: Toward an Integrated Approach.* Thousand Oaks: Sage.

Rosenthal, D. & Feldman, S. (1999). The importance of importance: Adolescents' perceptions of parental communication about sexuality. *Journal of Adolescence,* 22(6), 835–851.

Scales, P. (2001). The public image of adolescents. *Society,* 38, 64–70.

Shanahan, P., Elliott, B. & Dahlgren, N. (2000). Review of public information campaigns addressing youth risk-taking: A report to the National Youth Affairs Research Scheme. Australian Clearinghouse for Youth Studies.

Shevalier, R. (2000). Context dissonance in tobacco education literature. *Journal of Drug Issues,* 30, 407–434.

Silbereisen, R. K. (1998). Lessons we learned: Problems still to be solved. In R. Jessor (ed.), *New Perspectives on Adolescent Risk Behavior* (pp. 518–543). Cambridge: Cambridge University Press.

Spooner, C. (1999). Causes and correlates of adolescent drug abuse and implications for treatment. *Drug and Alcohol Review,* 18, 453–475.

Spooner, C. & Hall, W. (2002). Preventing drug use by young people: we need to do more than 'just say no.' *Addiction* 97, 478–481.

Stanton, B. & Burns, J. (2003). Sustaining and broadening intervention effect: social norms, core values and parents. In D. Romer (ed), *Reducing Adolescent Risk: Toward an Integrated Approach* (pp. 193–200). Thousand Oaks, CA: Sage.

Steinberg, L. & Morris, A. (2001). Adolescent development. *Annual Review of Psychology*, 52, 83–110.

Steinberg, L. (2003). Is decision making the right framework for research on adolescent risk taking. In D. Romer (Ed). *Reducing adolescent risk: toward an integrated approach*, (18–24). Thousand Oaks: Sage..

Tam, T. W., Weisner, C. & Mertens, J. (2000). Demographic characteristics, life context, and patterns of substance use among alcohol-dependent treatment clients in a health maintenance organization. *Alcoholism-Clinical and Experimental Research*, 24, 1803–1810.

Turner, G. (1999). Peer support and young people's health. *Journal of Adolescence*, 22, 567–572.

Valtolina, G. G. & Marta, E. (1998). Family relations and psychosocial risk in families with an obese adolescent. *Psychological Reports*, 83, 251–260.

Wagner, B. M. (1997). Family risk factors for child and adolescent suicidal behavior. *Psychological Bulletin*, 121, 246–259.

Contributors

The editors

Angie Williams [williamsa@cardiff.ac.uk] is Senior Lecturer (Associate Professor) in Communication at the Centre for Language and Communication Research, Cardiff University, Wales (UK). Broadly speaking, Angie's research focuses on intergroup communication, particularly as it relates to culture, age, lifespan and health issues. She has published numerous book chapters and journal articles on these topics in outlets such as the *Journal of Language and Social Psychology*, *Human Communication Research*, and *Communication Research*. Her recently published coauthored books are *Intergenerational Communication Across the Lifespan* (2001, with Jon Nussbaum) and *Investigating Language Attitudes: Social Meanings of Dialect, Ethnicity and Performance* (2003, with Peter Garrett and Nik Coupland).

Crispin Thurlow [thurlow@u.washington.edu] is Assistant Professor in Social Interaction with the Department of Communication, University of Washington (USA); he also holds the honorary position of Associate Research Fellow in the Centre for Language and Communication Research at Cardiff University (Wales, UK). Crispin's research focuses on *discourse and difference*: critical intercultural studies of interpersonal and mediatized communication in various contexts of inequality. His work concerning young people has been published in journals such as the *Journal of Adolescence*, the *Journal of Youth Studies* and the *Journal of Language and Social Psychology*. Crispin is coauthor (with Laura Lengel and Alice Tomic) of *Computer Mediated Communication: Social Interaction and the Internet* (2004) and his coauthored books (with Adam Jaworski and colleagues) *Tourism Discourse* and *Language, Tourism and Globalization* are due in 2006 and 2007 respectively.

The contributors

Stuart Allan [s.allan@uwe.ac.uk] is Reader in the School of Cultural Studies at the University of the West of England (England). He is the author of *News Culture* (1999; 2nd ed., 2004) and *Media, Risk and Science* (2002). Recent edited collections include *Journalism After September 11* (2002), *Reporting War: Journalism in Wartime* (2004) and *Journalism: Critical Issues* (2005). He is the editor of the 'Issues in Cultural and Media Studies' book series published by the Open University Press, and he serves on the editorial boards of several journals.

Lauren Berger [lberger@du.edu] is a doctoral candidate in child clinical psychology at the University of Denver. She received her BA in psychology from the University of Virginia. Her research primarily focuses on the role of relationships in the development of adolescent and young adult psychopathology and adjustment. She is currently conducting a series of studies examining close relationship influences on body image, depression, and eating pathology in emerging adulthood.

Cynthia Carter [cartercl@cardiff.ac.uk] is a Lecturer in the School of Journalism, Media and Cultural Studies at Cardiff University (Wales). She is coauthor of *Violence and the Media* (2003), and coeditor of *News, Gender and Power* (1998), *Environmental Risks and the Media* (2000) and *Critical Readings: Media and Gender* (2004). She is coeditor of the journal *Feminist Media Studies*.

Joseph Chesebro [jchesebr@brockport.edu] is an Assistant Professor in the Department of Communication at The State University of New York at Brockport (USA). He teaches graduate seminars in interpersonal and organizational communication and communication training and development, and undergraduate courses in interpersonal and organizational communication and communication theory. Joe's research has appeared in journals such as *Communication Education, Communication Quarterly,* and *Communication Research Reports.* He also is coeditor (with James McCroskey) of *Communication for Teachers* (2002).

Vivian de Klerk has been Professor and Head of the Department of English Language and Linguistics at Rhodes University (South Africa) since 1991. She was President of the Linguistics Society of Southern Africa from 1995 to 2002, and is the ministerial appointee on the South African Geographical Names Council. She also serves on the boards of the South African Academy of Science and the English National Language Body. Her research interests over the years have included issues in language and gender, personal naming practices, and language shift. Currently she is working on a spoken corpus of Black South African English, specifically Xhosa English, aiming to explore the linguistic characteristics of this emergent variety of English.

John Drury [j.drury@sussex.ac.uk] is a Lecturer in Social Psychology in the Department of Psychology, University of Sussex (England). Before taking up his current post, he worked at the Trust for the Study of Adolescence, researching adolescent communication. His current research interests include crowd behavior and psychological change, mass emergency evacuation, and critical discourse analysis.

Penelope Eckert [eckert@stanford.edu] is Professor of Linguistics at Stanford University (USA). Her research examines the role of phonological variation in the construction of styles and identities, combining ethnographic methods for data collection with quantitative analyses of social and linguistic constraints on variation. Her work focuses on adolescents and preadolescents, and she has done extensive ethnographic sociolinguistic work in and around schools. She is author of the high school ethnography *Jocks and Burnouts* (1989), as well as *Linguistic Variation as Social Practice* (2000), a sociolinguistic study of the relation between language and participation in high school social categories, and coauthor (with Sally McConnell-Ginet) of *Language and Gender* (2003).

Wyndol Furman [wfurman@nova.psy.du.edu] is Professor and Director of Clinical Training in the Department of Psychology at the University of Denver. He is primarily interested in studying adolescents' and young adults' close, especially romantic, relationships, and is coeditor (with Bradford Brown and Candice Feiring) of *The Development of Romantic Relationships in Adolescence* (2000). He is currently conducting a longitudinal study examining the links among different close relationships and adjustment in adolescence and young adulthood.

Peter Garrett [garrettp@cardiff.ac.uk] is a Senior Lecturer at the Centre for Language and Communication Research, Cardiff University (Wales). His primary research is on subjective factors in language and communication, such as awareness, attitudes, evaluations, ideology and values. His current focus is on issues of globalization, attitudes to language and use, social identity, and evaluations of intergenerational communication. Most recently, he coauthored (with Angie Williams and Nikolas Coupland) the book *Investigating Language Attitudes: Social Meanings of Dialect, Ethnicity and Performance* (2003). He is editor of the journal *Language Awareness*.

Leo Hendry [lhendry@glam.ac.uk] is Professor of Psychology, University of Glamorgan (Wales) and Emeritus Professor of Education, University of Aberdeen (Scotland). During his career he has written many books, book chapters and journal articles on various aspects of adolescence, and has been awarded over $2.5 million in research grants from national and international funding agencies. Among his better-known texts are the coauthored *Young People's Leisure and Lifestyles* (1993), with Janet Shucksmith, *Health Issues and Adolescents* (1998), and his well-known coauthored (with John Coleman) book *The Nature of Adolescence* (3rd ed., 1999).

Marion Kloep [mkloep@glam.ac.uk] is a Reader in the Department of Psychology at the University of Glamorgan (Wales). She has been researching children and adolescents in Albania, Sweden, Norway and Scotland, and has published several articles and books on the topic; more recently, this includes her coauthored (with Leo Hendry) book *Lifespan Development: Resources, Challenges and Risks* (2002), which has also been translated into Italian. Currently, she is researching the development of national identity among young people in Wales.

Alice Marwick [amarwick@u.washington.edu] is a graduate student in the Department of Communication at the University of Washington (USA). She holds a degree in Women's Studies and Political Science from Wellesley College in Massachusetts. Her interests include cyberculture studies, identity and authenticity online, concepts of the body in entertainment media and queer theory. She is a fellow at the Center for Internet Studies and a former project manager in the web, software, wireless and video game industries.

Susan McKay [s.mckay@uq.edu.au] is a Senior Lecturer in Communication, Cultural Studies and Media Studies at the University of Queensland (Australia). Her research centers on language and the media, and representations of health issues. In 2001–2002, she was part of the international task force formed by the International Association of Language and Social Psychology to review aspects of research into language and communication in adolescence. She has coauthored (with Lloyd Davis) a book on academic writing, *Structures and Strategies: An Introduction to Academic Writing* (1996).

Dana McMakin [dmcmakin@du.edu] is a doctoral student in child clinical psychology at the University of Denver. Her research focuses on the development and treatment of adolescent psychopathology, with a specific emphasis on cognitive and interpersonal processes of emotion regulation.

Patricia Noller [pn@psy.uq.edu.au] is Emeritus Professor in the School of Psychology at the University of Queensland (Australia). She has published extensively in the areas of marital communication, parent-adolescent relationships and attachment theory. She was founding editor of *Personal Relationships: Journal of the International Society for the Study of Personal Relationships* (now the *International Association for Relationship Research*) and president of that society from 1998–2000. She is a fellow of the Academy of the Social Sciences in Australia and of the National Council on Family Relations (USA).

Sarah O'Flynn [sarah.oflynn@merton.gov.uk] is a doctoral student in education at Cardiff University (Wales). Her interests are in sexuality and education, particularly in relation to inequality. She is currently writing her thesis exploring the links between young women's sexualities and academic achievement. Sarah has worked for fifteen years in secondary schools in London, teaching English and drama; she currently works with young people who have been excluded from school.

Heather Toomey Zimmerman [htoomey@u.washington.edu] is a doctoral candidate in Education and Cognitive Studies at the University of Washington (USA). In her research, she analyzes how people think, know, and interact across social settings. By observing and interviewing children, young people, and adults about their science and technology activities, she documents social interaction and thinking processes as they are situated and distributed within specific contexts. Heather's research focuses on the role of language and semiotic systems associated with learning science and using technology as well as gender issues around children's participation and identification with scientific and technological disciplines and activities.

Johanna Wyn [johanna@unimelb.edu.au] is Professor in Education and Director of the Youth Research Centre at the University of Melbourne (Australia). She publishes widely in the field of youth transitions, health and education and leads the Youth Research Centre's longitudinal research program (Life-Patterns) as well as being involved in a range of other youth research projects. She is well known for her book (with Rob White) *Rethinking Youth* (1997). Her most recent book (with Rob White) is *Youth and Society: The Social Dynamics of Youth* (2004).

Index

A

abuse
  homophobic, 146, 152–156
  physical/sexual, 218, 211–220
  substance, 15, 41, 207, 213–214,
    220–222, 267, 270–272
  verbal, 118
adaptability, 114, 211–212, 216
adjustment (psychosocial), 14, 41, 207–211,
    217, 222, 265
advocacy, 9
African
  American, 220–221, 103–140
  North, 98, 105–106
  South, 114, 212, 219
age groups, 35, 37, 42–44, 48, 94, 229
age segregation, 96
ageism, 5, 41–42
antisocial
  behavior, 134, 220
  internet use, 196
attachment, 13, 40, 131, 135–139, 168, 174,
    213, 270
authority, 10, 14, 96, 103, 229–239
autonomy, 25, 27–29, 36, 40, 46–47, 105,
    186, 212, 229

B

'bad' communication, 233
behavioural systems, 13, 131–132, 138, 141
benefit officers, 230–232
bisexual, 13, 133, 147–159
boredom, 62, 164, 171–173, 180–181
buffering, 208, 222–223
bullying, 196, 247

C

care giving, 13, 131, 137–138
categorization, 36, 97–98, 100, 149
cell phones (*see* mobile phones)
chatrooms, 167, 192–193, 197
Cicumplex Model, 211–212
citizenship, 12, 73–75, 81–83, 87

cognitive learning, 245, 249, 252, 258
collaborative talk, 99–100
comforting communication, 234
communication
  accommodation (CAT), 35, 38–39, 42–45
  apprehension, 12, 54–58, 60–63, 69
  awareness, 63
  boundaries, 46–47
  breakdown, 7
  capital, 6–7, 63
  education, 55, 65, 245
  evaluations, 11, 38, 42–44
  'ignorant', 10, 57
  satisfaction, 44–45, 129
  skills, 132, 137, 140, 163–164, 173,
    179–180, 235, 248, 269
    (critique of), 45, 48, 54–56, 58–59,
    61, 63, 231, 236
communities of practice, 12, 96–99, 103,
    112
companionship, 132–133, 138, 142
compliments, 39, 101
computer, 38, 79, 167–168, 185–194, 198
  mediated communication, 194, 198
  literacy, 192, 188
confirming (behaviors), 252–253, 259
conflict, 13, 46–47, 61–62, 111, 115,
    129–131, 138–141, 179, 208–210,
    212, 218–219, 232, 236–237, 270
content relevance, 14, 24–28, 250–251
crime, 30, 105, 212, 229
critical media analysis, 80
crowds, 40, 95, 176
Cultivation Hypothesis, 28
cyberculture, 79, 190

D

dating, 130–133, 135, 153, 173
  cyberdating, 191
depression, 41, 209–210, 213–214,
    216–218, 220, 222, 270
digital sex divide, 189
disclosure (self-), 136, 213, 235, 255, 269

discourse, 2, 7–8, 10–12, 15, 28–30, 37, 47, 54, 59, 61, 80, 84, 87, 93, 100, 102, 106, 113, 122–123, 148, 151–155, 194, 231–232, 234, 236–237, 266, 277
Discourse of Hope, 30
divorce, 208–210, 213, 222
drinking, 115, 119, 177–179, 207, 209, 213, 222, 265, 272–276

E
economic hardship, 6–7, 11, 27–28, 208–210, 214, 222
embarrassment, 47, 58, 115
emerging adulthood, 4, 37, 48
emotion/s, 36, 39, 41, 44, 86, 107, 112, 130–132, 134–137, 192, 208, 211, 214, 217–218, 220, 274
emotional autonomy, 39
empathic communication, 131, 234, 236, 273
empowerment, 14, 62, 64, 66, 75, 86, 158, 197, 250
English (language), 93, 104–106, 123, 196–197
erotic, 133, 149
ethnicity, 15, 30, 35–36, 96–97, 101, 106, 130, 158, 179–181, 188, 268–270, 274
expletives, 64, 112–118, 121–124
externalizing, 208, 210, 214–215, 217–218, 220

F
family
    breakdown, 61–62, 208–210, 213, 222
    cohesion, 208–209, 213–215, 219–220, 222–223, 270
    conflict, 218–219, 270
    stress, 14, 207, 210, 214–215, 217, 222–223
    support, 37, 208, 214–215, 221–222
femininity, 124, 235
Focal Theory, 169, 182
friends, 42–43, 81–82, 95, 100, 111, 130–133, 135–141, 164–182, 190–191, 221, 267–8, 272

G
gaming (online), 167, 186, 192–193

gangs, 96, 116
gay/s, 14, 119, 119, 134–145, 159
gender, 13, 15, 25, 31, 97, 100–107, 119–125, 141, 149–150, 154, 158, 168–170, 181, 189, 219, 234, 268, 272, 274–275
generation gap, 8
Generations X and Y, 23, 26, 30, 32, 37, 41
generational change, 11, 24–25, 27, 30–32
globalization, 7, 30, 78, 83, 116, 187, 194
'good' communication, 12, 35, 44–45, 48, 54, 60, 211–213, 216, 231–235
grammar (grammatical rules), 97, 114
group boundaries, 13, 38, 112, 120, 150, 178, 180, 197, 235

H
health care, 268, 277
health
    campaigns, 274–275
    information, 268, 277
        (online), 194
    outcomes, 269
    promotion, 274–277
heterosexual, 13, 119, 130, 132–134, 139, 147–154, 159, 174
Hispanic, 220, 222
HIV, 159, 271, 273–274
homophobia, 147–161

I
iconization, 93
identity, 4–5, 10, 95, 101, 104–106, 125, 132, 136, 149–151, 166, 175–176, 180, 198, 216, 234–235, 237, 274
    construction, 12, 14, 62, 107
    development, 41, 180, 216
    politics, 150, 157
immigrant, 96, 105–106
ingroup/outgroup, 11–13, 36–37, 119
inoculation (media effects), 77
institutional, 1, 9, 11, 13–15, 45, 53, 55, 60–64, 94–96, 102–105, 111–113, 156, 230–240
instructional communication, 12, 14, 246–259
Instructional Influence Theory, 255, 257–259
insults, 100–102, 253

intensifiers, 97
intergenerational, 11, 16, 35–39, 41–42,
    45–46, 48, 189, 270
intergroup communication (theory), 4, 7,
    11, 35–39, 44–45, 47, 237
internalizing, 208–210, 214–215, 222
internet, 83, 112, 130, 156, 167–168, 174,
    186–200, 277
interpersonal communication, 13, 45, 167,
    175, 190–191, 269

L
labels (group/social), 37, 39, 62, 97–98,
    102, 119–120, 150–152, 187, 266
language, 7, 9, 12–13, 38, 54, 63–64, 93–97,
    101–102, 104–107, 116–119,
    120–122, 148, 152–155, 180, 186,
    191–192, 195–196, 231, 233, 236, 275
Latino, 101, 104, 106, 188
leisure, 13, 25, 93, 164–182, 190
lesbians, 14, 119, 119, 134–145, 159
lexical innovation, 94, 98–99
lifespan (communication/research), 4–6,
    10–11, 16, 39, 42, 45, 48, 65,
    131–133, 157, 189–190, 266, 269
Lifespan Model of Developmental Change,
    13, 180–181
lifestyles, 12, 23, 27, 53, 150, 166, 175, 182,
    193
literacy (see also computer, media), 12, 77

M
Mallspeak, 93
masculinity, 103–104, 119–120, 124, 154
media
    education, 12, 75–77
    literacy, 75, 77-79, 196-197
    representations, 7, 24–31, 41, 77, 187
miscommunication, 48
misunderstanding, 134, 139
mobile phones, 113, 130, 167, 192,
    196–197
morality, 32, 76, 74, 84, 234
moral panic, 23, 25, 27, 32, 197

N
narrative, 11, 23, 28, 99–100, 132, 177, 255
Net Generation, 14. 185–187
networks (social), 37, 39, 96–97, 112,
    116–117, 191, 198

noncommunication, 42, 45
nonverbal communication, 10, 59,
    134–135, 211–212, 236, 245, 253,
    258–259
nonverbal immediacy, 15, 248, 251, 255
norms (social), 2, 56, 62, 95–97, 99–102,
    104, 111, 115–117, 119, 122–124,
    135–136, 273

O
outgroup (see ingroup)

P
parental mental health, 209
patronization, 82, 85
peer groups, 12, 42, 95–96, 111, 115–116,
    214, 236, 269
peer pressure, 42, 107, 221, 268, 272,
    274–275, 277
police, 44, 98, 171, 229–237
politics, 3, 73–74, 79–80, 87
    of culture, 1
poor diet, 267
power, 2, 6, 14, 31, 42, 64, 95, 103–104,
    117–119, 121, 123–124, 152, 170,
    187, 230–237, 239, 256–259
prevention (ideologies of), 266, 270–271,
    274–276
privacy, 46–47

Q
Queer (see gay, lesbian)

R
race, 7, 31, 35, 96, 101, 105–106, 158, 188
reciprocity, 134
relational power, 255, 257–259
relationship status, 131, 138–140
Rhetorical Relational Goal Theory,
    255–260
risk ('at risk'), 15, 23, 27, 30, 40, 61, 209,
    220, 222–223, 266–267, 274–275
risky behavior, 15, 267–270
role models, 270
romantic relationships, 13, 29, 129–141,
    159

S
self-harm, 207, 209–210, 213, 219–220,
    222

sex (sexual behavior), 135, 147–148, 149, 216, 265, 271, 273
sex education, 157
shyness, 56–58, 60, 62, 67, 272
slang, 12–13, 98–99, 105
smoking, 15, 178, 220, 265, 272
antismoking, 199, 274
social capital, 192, 164
social change, 3, 24, 26–28, 30–32, 94, 97, 106
social distance, 4, 29, 40
social identity (theory), 4, 35–36, 38, 98, 180, 237, 239
social isolation, 153
social learning, 170, 174
social values, 97
solidarity, 99–100, 118, 235, 258
standard language, 102, 116
stereotyping, 8, 10, 11, 23–24, 27–29, 32, 36–39, 41–42, 58, 64, 93, 100, 115, 118, 125, 234, 274
stigmatization, 41, 104, 117, 122, 151–153, 155–156
Storm and Stress, 2, 5, 8, 41, 207, 231–232, 236, 265
stressors, 14, 208–209, 211–214, 217
style (stylistic practice), 12, 43, 94, 101–104, 106–107, 117

suicide, 153, 207, 209, 212–213, 216, 219–220, 267, 270
supportive communication, 131, 135
swearing, 12, 111–113
symbolic capital, 7, 12, 61, 62, 63, 112, 116, 196

T
taboo, 103, 114–118, 152
television, 23, 28–29, 31, 80, 86, 154, 156, 167–169, 190, 192–194, 196, 198, 274–275
text-messages, 191, 195–196
transition (to adulthood), 23, 27, 30, 40, 103, 116, 118, 158, 165, 180, 189

U
uncommunicative, 42, 67, 230, 233–234

V
vernacular, 102–104, 117, 122
violence, 23, 25, 84, 118, 140, 209, 215, 219–220, 222, 234, 267, 274–275

W
willingness to communicate, 59–60, 71, 243

Howard Giles
GENERAL EDITOR

This series explores new and exciting advances in the ways in which language both reflects and fashions social reality—and thereby constitutes critical means of social action. As well as these being central foci in face-to-face interactions across different cultures, they also assume significance in the ways that language functions in the mass media, new technologies, organizations, and social institutions. Language as Social Action does not uphold apartheid against any particular methodological and/or ideological position, but, rather, promotes (wherever possible) cross-fertilization of ideas and empirical data across the many, all-too-contrastive, social scientific approaches to language and communication. Contributors to the series will also accord due attention to the historical, political, and economic forces that contextually bound the ways in which language patterns are analyzed, produced, and received. The series will also provide an important platform for theory-driven works that have profound, and often times provocative, implications for social policy.

For further information about the series and submitting manuscripts, please contact:

Howard Giles
Department of Communication
University of California at Santa Barbara
Santa Barbara, CA 93106-4020
HowieGiles@cox.net

To order other books in this series, please contact our Customer Service Department at:

(800) 770-LANG (within the U.S.)
(212) 647-7706 (outside the U.S.)
(212) 647-7707 FAX

Or browse online by series at:

www.peterlang.com